W9-DJN-935

343.730409
R27c

143156

DATE DUE			

CONSTITUTIONAL HISTORY OF THE AMERICAN REVOLUTION

CONSTITUTIONAL HISTORY OF THE AMERICAN REVOLUTION

THE AUTHORITY TO TAX

JOHN PHILLIP REID

CARL A. RUDISILL LIBRARY
LENOIR RHYNE COLLEGE

THE UNIVERSITY OF WISCONSIN PRESS

343.730409
R27c
143156
Feb, 1988

Published 1987

The University of Wisconsin Press
114 North Murray Street
Madison, Wisconsin 53715

The University of Wisconsin Press, Ltd.
1 Gower Street
London WC1E 6HA, England

Copyright © 1987
The Board of Regents of the University of Wisconsin System
All rights reserved

First printing

Printed in the United States of America

For LC CIP information see the colophon

ISBN 0-299-11290-X

For
Martin and Marcella "Sally" Ridge
of the Huntington Library

CONTENTS

CONSTITUTIONAL
HISTORY OF THE
AMERICAN REVOLUTION

INTRODUCTION

Scholars who would explore eighteenth-century British constitutionalism must steer an uncharted course. The problem is not that the headlands and channels are unmarked; it is that they are not identified with the certainty of precise definition. Even the shores that confine the limits of the word "constitution" were not accurately surveyed in the eighteenth century. The fact may not be easily credited, but even eighteenth-century lawyers were not always certain what the word "constitution" meant. True, that century is remembered as "the classic age of the English constitution," a time about which it recently has been said that "[p]erhaps never before and surely never since has any single nation's constitution so dominated Western man's theorizing about politics." Indeed, it did more, dominating theorizing not only about politics but also about the force of law and nature of government. A 1757 writer was not exaggerating when he claimed that there was "no other Name more powerful or more solemn" than constitution; "it includes our dearest most valuable Possessions, Liberty and Religion." Even so, experts on that constitution, including the renowned jurist Sir William Blackstone, have been perceived by later scholars to have been so confused about its function and form that their

3

writings have been dismissed as products of "a prolific school of constitutional mythologists." "[M]ore powerful" and "more solemn" than any other word, "constitution" in the eighteenth century was "a sort of usable tautology."[1]

It is not enough to assert that the American Revolution resulted from a dispute about the meaning of the British constitution; we should also ask whether participants appreciated what was being disputed. "There is scarce a word in the English language so frequently used, and so little understood as the word Constitution," a magazine writer observed the year the Stamp Act passed and the revolutionary controversy commenced. "There is nothing so much talked of, and yet nothing so little understood, as the *English Constitution*," the earl of Abingdon agreed. "Every man quotes it, and upon every occasion too: but few know where to find it." "What is the constitution of England?," a political *Catechism* asked the year that the Stamp Act was repealed. "It is not like wit, 'a thing much talked of, not to be defined;' but it is like many other matters, a thing much talked of, and little understood." It was so little understood that one commentator thought it futile even to debate constitutional questions. "It may appear, at first sight, unaccountable," he mused, "that men should agree in the principle upon which they argue, and yet differ so widely in their conclusions. This difficulty will soon vanish, when we reflect that nothing is more common than for men to agree in the words they make use of, when the ideas they annex to them are as opposite as light to darkness." A book reviewer summed it up: "This poor word *Constitution* has been more abused than any in the English language. Many have attempted to explain it; few have been satisfactory on the subject."[2]

Recent scholars, when writing of eighteenth-century constitutional events, have not used the word "constitution" with more precision. Many treat the concept with remarkable looseness, using the word "political" when "constitutional" might be more graphic, and often not differentiating between "constitutional" and "legal." Drawing distinctions between "constitutional" and "political" or between "constitution" and "law" is not always necessary, as meaning is generally clear, but if we seek the precision of pellucid usage, the distinction can be valuable. To leave lines unclear runs the risk that concepts may become blurred. It is through words that we convey meaning, and the words "constitutional" and "political" do not always conjure up the same concepts. Nor do the words "constitution" and "law."[3]

When one looks backward 200 years, there is a tendency to compound what was then "law" with what is now "constitution," or, too often, project the preciseness of today's terms back on the infinity of eighteenth-century constitutionality, and thus conjoin what was legal in eighteenth-century Great Britain with what is constitutional in twentieth-century United States. It is a tendency that must be guarded against: what was "constitutional" in the eighteenth century may be "legal" today, falling most likely still in the category of "public" rather than "private" law, but no longer thought of as "constitutional"; by the same token, certain actions, such as the arrest of citizens charged with crimes, may now lead to intricate constitutional litigation turning on facts and occurrences that no one in the eighteenth century could have been persuaded involved a legal issue. During the 1770s, virtually everything pertaining to law and the legal system was embraced in varying degrees by the word "constitutional"; by 1900, the academic teaching of law, at least in the United States, had spun a more narrow usage in which "constitutional" came to pertain more to the rights of citizens and the limits of government power.

For an eighteenth-century legal theorist to argue that standing armies were unconstitutional in Great Britain was not to argue that they were illegal. That is an error peculiar to Americans, that British or Canadians would be less likely to make. What the judiciary in twentieth-century United States rules to be unconstitutional is, *ipso facto*, illegal. The meaning of law and constitution in the eighteenth century was markedly different. When eighteenth-century British or Americans made the claim that standing armies were unconstitutional, they did not mean that the existing British army was an unlawful force. Of course it was legal; it had been sanctioned by Parliament. But Parliament's promulgation only made law, it did not settle arguments about constitutionality. The relativeness of the term "constitutional" in the eighteenth century may be difficult for Americans to comprehend today, but then it made legal sense to say that the militia was "a more frugal and constitutional measure, than a Standing Army," but that the navy was "the most constitutional force" of all. The army, militia, and navy were equally legal, but not equally constitutional.[4]

Along with "legal," a second conceptual arrangement of historical material that should be distinguished from "constitutional" is "political." To compound "political" with "constitutional" is not necessarily error. It may, however, be a matter of changing the emphasis of the revolutionary debate from an eighteenth-century to a twentieth-century context. The "striking similarities" between the North Carolina lawyers, Martin Howard and Maurice Moore, one imperialist and the other colonial whig, have been explained in terms of their "broad reading in the classics and history" and of the "fundamental conservatism" that they shared. "Both men were trained as lawyers, practiced for a time, and served as judges," we are told. "Each man approached the issue of parliamentary taxation from his basic conservatism." In truth, they approached the issue in terms of what it was, a constitutional problem, and the "striking similarities" came not from political conservatism, but from the fact they both argued the same constitution and sought their authorities from the same maxims of law.[5]

In the eighteenth century the word "constitutional" was much broader in meaning than it is in today's United States, but quite narrower than the word "political." Then to describe as "constitutional" a course of action was to say that to take that action would be to act in conformity to law, in conformity to custom, and in conformity to the current arrangement of governmental conventions. Also understood was an implication that departure from that course of action would be legally inadvisable, contrary to established custom, and not in conformity to the current arrangement of governmental conventions. For a person to assert that an action was "constitutional" was to associate that action with accepted legal practice, at least to the extent that it was in accord with the operational tradition of certain official institutions and could be justified as consistent with that tradition.

These distinctions—"constitutional," "legal," and "political"—should be kept in mind when considering the scope of this study. It is concerned only with the *constitutional* aspects of the American Revolution, not with its *social* causes, *political* origins, *economic* history, or *nationalistic* motivations. Another topic that is not covered is the *legal* history of the Revolution, thus eliminating large areas of historical discussion about eighteenth-century law— questions, issues, and disputes more properly belonging to legal than to constitutional history, among the more obvious of which are the controversies, regulations, and subterfuges associated with the Navigation Act and other laws of trade. Also not covered in this constitutional history are chapters and volumes belonging to the legal history of the American Revolution, including the difficulties created by colonial whigs for British efforts to enforce the Mutiny Act, the purposeful behavior of the whig crowd by which its "lawfulness" may be measured, the Boston Massacre trials, the implementation of the nonimportation associations, the role played by colonial juries applying a criminal-law-type sanction against imperial officials for enforcing "unconstitutional" statutes of Parliament, the powers exercised by the British army as a police force in the North American colonies, and the manner in which local whigs and imperial officials created, manipulated, and argued facts to support the respective constitutional doctrines they wished to establish. There are, of course, topics containing aspects of both "legal" and "constitutional" history. An example is the tax on tea which was resisted as an "unconstitutional" imposition by methods the whigs thought "legal." There are, however, very few in which the "constitutional" considerations cannot be separated from the legal. The most notable — the doctrine that standing armies during peacetime were contrary to the British constitution, and the legal rules that were a consequence of that doctrine — have been treated in a separate study.[6]

A final introductory caution is to remind the reader of the title of this book which states that the topic is the authority to tax. It does not deal with other aspects of the constitutional history of the American Revolution, a vast and as yet largely unexplored task. Some, thinking they know the answer, may dismiss constitutional history by asking of the American Revolution, "Why concern ourselves with constitutional and legal ideology?" Although Charles Howard McIlwain has written an invaluable preliminary study, the truth is that we have only begun to investigate the question. The often-cited works of George Burton Adams and Charles F. Mullett expounded a nineteenth-, not an eighteenth-century definition of law, and the book by Robert Livingston Schuyler was based on a constitutional theory that would have been nonsuited in any court of law. It is simply not correct to say that the entire constitutional argument of the American Revolution was contained in the denial "that Parliament could not legislate for Americans because they were not represented at Westminster," or by saying "that only local legislatures in which the Americans were represented could make laws for the colonies."[7] As this book seeks to show, there were many other constitutional doctrines that commanded the serious attention and respect of people in the 1760s and 1770s, including the trade-regulation criterion, the commerical contract, the imperial contract, and the taxation-legislation dichotomy. These doctrines are discussed below. Not discussed are constitutional issues unrelated to the authority to tax but of vital importance to the history of the revolutionary constitutional debate, pertaining to such matters as the authority to legislate, the concept of representation, the authority to govern, the concept of liberty, the rights of British citizens, and the constitutional principle of the rule of law. Under these general topics are most of the constitutional issues that American whigs debated with imperialists during the revolutionary era: the right to common law, the right to jury trial, the right to property, the binding force of custom, the tension between two constitutional theories, the distinction between right and power limiting sovereign command, the original contract, the emigration contract, the legislative nature of ministerial instructions to colonial governors, the concept of arbitrariness, the doctrine of consent, the corporation theory, and several other issues about which participants in the revolutionary controversy argued. Until these matters are made the subject of study, the constitutional history of the American Revolution will remain unknown.

CHAPTER ONE

THE CONSTITUTIONAL IMPERATIVE

There is a preliminary consideration so often overlooked that it must be noted here: to write the constitutional history of the American Revolution is to write the history of more than one constitution. The point is so elementary that once stated it becomes obvious, yet it has generally been misunderstood, ignored, or left unmentioned. Close attention should be paid to words, keeping in mind, however, that scrutiny is something eighteenth-century words often cannot sustain. The term "constitutional" was one of several words used in what are today unfamiliar ways and unexpected purposes. Another was "liberty" and a third, which did not appear as frequently, was "independence." "The words Liberty, Constitution and Independence," a member of Parliament remarked in 1770, "are indeed words that convey ideas of the utmost importance; but I am sorry to say, that it is of late become a custom to use them, not as conveying ideas, but as forming a spell."[1]

There was perhaps no orator of the revolutionary era more talented at casting spells with words than Edmund Burke, yet he was one of a very few to keep a relatively tight rein on the meaning of "constitutional." From beginning to end of the revolutionary era, Burke concentrated attention on the constitutional nature of the controversy between Great Britain and its colonies. It was possibly Burke, writing the *Annual Reg-*

ister for the last time in 1766, who summed up the first public parliamentary debate on colonial taxation by pointing out that "arguments of *natural* lawyers, as Locke, Selden, Pufendorf, and others, are little to the purpose in a question of constitutional law." A decade after the Revolutionary War had ended and American independence was established, Burke still was saying that the conflict between Great Britain and its colonies had something to do with constitutional law. "He believed," Burke wrote of himself in the third person, "that they [the colonists] had taken up arms from one motive only: that is, our attempting to tax them without their consent,— to tax them for the purposes of maintaining civil and military establishments." Recently, a writer commenting on this argument said that Burke was reiterating "his original belief that the Americans 'were purely on the defensive in that rebellion,' and that their original aim was not to secure independence from Britain, but to secure the legal rights of subjects under the English constitution." It is possible that Burke would have made this argument, but not likely; in contrast to many twentieth-century American historians, he knew that, although in most contexts the term "English constitution" could be interchanged with "British constitution," the colonies sought to secure rights *under* the British, not *under* the English constitution. Indeed, Burke appreciated the fact that the constitutional debate swirled around more constitutions than a mere two. "[T]he Constitution of the British Empire," he once reminded the House of Commons, had to be "distinguished from the Constitution of Britain." He might have added that both should be distinguished from what no less a lawyer than Alexander Wedderburn, destined to be England's solicitor general, attorney general, lord chief justice of the Court of Common Pleas, and lord chancellor, referred to as "the British American constitution."[2] And even beyond that, on the other side of the Atlantic, lay "the Constitutions of the colonies."[3]

The general assumption of British parliamentarians like Burke was that the revolutionary controversy turned on various interpretations of either the British or the English constitution. In fact, the colonial constitutions were as much involved, as many British and American lawyers well understood. Consider, for example, Richard Jackson, who was a barrister of Lincoln's Inn, future bencher of the Inner Temple, and who served as secretary to George Grenville at the time the Stamp Act was being planned. "A Revenue to be raised in America for the Support of British Troops is not now to [be] argued against," he wrote Benjamin Franklin the year before any of the new taxes were enacted. "I only contend that it should be built on a foundation consistent with the Constitutions of the Colonies." Six days before the Stamp Act became a reality, the freeholders of Marblehead, Massachusetts, applying Jackson's test, concluded that the tax was not "consistent" with their colony's constitution, and instructed their delegate to the House of Representatives not to vote for any bill "that will imply the Willingness of your Constituents, to submit to any internal Taxes, that are imposed otherwise than by the Great and General Court of the Province, according to the Constitution of this Government."[4]

The voters of Marblehead were saying that the Massachusetts constitution was a shield protecting them from parliamentary taxation. The Connecticut House of Representatives converted the argument from the negative to the positive, and extended it just about as far as it could be taken. The Connecticut constitution, it resolved, was more than the arrangement of local government. It was the band of union cementing the colony to Great Britain.

> That wee look upon the well being and greatest Security of this Colony to depend (under God) on our Connections with Great Britain, which wee ardently wish, may continue to the latest Posterity, And that it is the humble Opinion of this House That the Constitution of this Colony being understood and practiced upon, as it has been ever since it existed, is the surest Band of Union, Confidence, and mutual Prosperity of our Mother-Country, and Us, and the best Foundation, on which to build the good of the whole, whether considered in a civil, military or mercantile light.[5]

The potential conclusions from this constitutional theory may be lost in speculation. Did it mean that, when asking whether an imperial action or edict was constitutional, the local provincial constitution took precedence over the British constitution or the constitution of the British Empire? Perhaps so, if the Connecticut House meant what it said. There is no answer, not because the question was not recognized in the eighteenth century, but because there was no need to answer it: with only a few exceptions, every constitutional right the Americans put forward could be as readily defended on the basis of the British constitution as on the colonial constitutions. Principles were so interchangeable that even the long-defunct English constitution could be argued as soundly as the British, imperial, or local provincial constitutions. "It is well known," Virginia's Richard Henry Lee would contend after the fighting had commenced at Lexington, "that the original cause of our present unhappy difference is the lately assumed right and practise of Parliament, to raise revenue on the subject in America, contrary to the clearest principles of justice and the English constitution, which exempt from payment of Tax, Tallage, Aid or other like charge not set by common consent."[6]

THE GENESIS OF TAXATION

The question of whether Parliament possessed constitutional authority to tax the American colonies was one that most British government officials thought easily answered when the possibility was first discussed in 1764. Americans were informed by their newspapers that the House of Commons "determined in the Affirmative" that "they had power to lay such a Tax, on the Colonies" even though the people of North America "had no Representative in parliament."[7] This statement from the *Boston News-Letter* is quoted to establish at the outset a central point to be made in this chapter, a point that may easily be misunderstood: it is not that the leaders of Great Britain rejected the main constitutional issue that would be raised by American whigs, but rather that they acknowledged the issue as constitutional and relevant even before American whigs stated their objections to parliamentary taxation.

George Grenville, as first lord of the treasury and chancellor of the exchequer, led the Commons debates on the budget resolutions for 1764. After preliminary remarks on accounts and potential sources of taxation, he introduced "the resolution to raise the revenue in America for defending itself." It would, Grenville assured the House, be fair and equitable to impose upon the colonies a tax for the purpose of raising a revenue. According to Virginia's agent, the first lord "put the House in mind that the national debt amounted to [£] 146,000,000" and "that America gave birth to the last war, which cost us [£] 74,000,000." "We have expended much in America," he argued. "Let us now avail ourselves of the fruits of that expense." Having established the political justification for departing from precedent and for introducing a new system of taxation, Grenville took up the constitutional issue, asserting that he was "convinced this country have the right to impose an inland tax" on the North American colonies. If any member doubted the constitutionality of American taxes imposed by Parliament, he suggested taking "the opinion of a committee [of the whole House] immediately." The very fact that the leader of the administration made this proposal indicates some uncertainty. Grenville "hoped that the power and sovereignty of Parliament, over every part of the British dominions, for the purpose of raising or collecting any tax, would never be disputed." He had, however, heard "hints of this nature dropped" by persons not in Parliament and that was why he asked if any member "doubted." If one did, "he would take the sense of the House." Grenville not only hoped to stop any talk of unconstitutionality, but perhaps even set a precedent so that the question would not again be raised in the Commons. "He then called for the sense of Parliament, and that the House might not suffer objections of that nature at a future day." Virginia's agent reported that the "Members interested in the plantations expressed great surprise that a doubt of that nature could ever exist."[8]

There is no record indicating who the "Members interested in the plantations" were that conceded so important a constitutional right. Only one account of the debate is extant, and it indicates that, besides George Grenville, four speakers addressed the Commons, one of whom did not mention the constitutional question. None of them expressed any doubt about Parliament's authority to tax the colonies. The second speaker, a man regarded in London as an expert on American trade, agreed "perfectly to our right to tax the colonies" but questioned the authority of the executive branch of the imperial government. "[T]he power of the crown," he claimed, "extends no further over the colonies than it does in England. And yet this power has been exerted as by orders passed here by the King in Council which have gone to the plantations as kind of laws." Here, at the very commencement of the revolutionary controversy, is an indication of how complicated the constitutional issues would become. Old whigs and commonwealthmen, fearful of resurging Crown power in Great Britain, were concerned about recent trends in the governance of the colonies. Since the end of the war with France, the ministry, exercising and expanding traditional imperial authority, had been instructing colonial governors, promulgating proclamations, and issuing Privy Council rulings to America that had the appearance of legislative fiat. Although the words are not as clearly reported as we could wish, it appears that the second speaker was saying that Parliament should tax the colonies in order to assert itself against the Crown at home. The constitutional struggle of Parliament against prerogative rule in Great Britain, then, provided an impetus for extending parliamentary governance over North America.[9]

The third speaker — a lawyer and a joint secretary in the treasury under Grenville — reinforced what had previously been said. "He could easily confirm the right of England to impose taxes upon North America from Acts of Parliament and resolutions of the House of Commons." Put another way, Parliament's authority to tax the colonies could be established by Parliament's own acts and resolutions. In time American whigs would regard this as the ultimate argument of British supremacy: no matter what their case against Parliament, the final judge of its validity was Parliament itself.[10]

The last recorded speaker was a native of New Hampshire, who had also lived in Massachusetts. He too thought the issue was Crown, not parliamentary power. "No doubt can exist of the right to tax North America in England," he believed. "We know we are subject to the legislature of this country but not to the King's instructions to his Governors."[11]

These speeches constitute the first discussion held by Parliament on the topic of taxing Americans for the purpose of raising a revenue. They are significant not merely for the obvious reason that no one spoke against Grenville's resolutions, but more because, even though everyone was in agreement, the constitutional issue was nevertheless raised — and dismissed.

The First American Reaction

By early May of 1764 it was known in America that Parliament was contemplating internal taxation of the colonies. Eight days after the news was printed in the local newspapers, Boston's voters instructed their representatives to the lower house of the Massachusetts General Court that it would strike "at our Brittish Privileges" if "Taxes are laid upon us in any shape without our having a legal Representation where they are laid." When the legislature convened, the representatives reiterated the same constitutional principle, expressing it in the absolute terms of exclusive right: "That the sole right of giving and granting the money of the people of that province, was vested in them, or their representatives; and that the imposition of duties and taxes by the parliament of Great Britain upon a people not represented in the house of commons, is absolutely irreconcileable with their rights. That no man can justly take the property of another, without his consent; upon which original principles, the power of making laws for levying taxes, one of the main pillars of the British constitution is, evidently founded."[12]

In a petition to George III, voted in October, the New York House of General Assembly elaborated on the point made by the Massachusetts House that taxation by a Parliament in which they were not represented was as unconstitutional as were prerogative taxes imposed by the Crown without the concurrence of any legislative body. The constitution, the New Yorkers asserted, "forbids, that any Part of a Community shall, as individuals, claim the Right of taxing the whole." It would, they said, "be the basest Vassalage, to be taxed at the Pleasure of a Fellow Subject." And to those fellow subjects, the Commons of Great Britain, the New York House expressed "Concern and Surprize" at having "received Intimations of certain Designs lately formed, if possible, to induce the Parliament of *Great Britain*, to impose Taxes upon the Subjects *here*, by Laws to be passed *there*." It was, therefore, their duty "to trouble" the Commons "with a seasonable Representation of the Claim of our Constituents, to an Exemption from the Burthen of all Taxes not granted by themselves."[13]

Of the other colonial assemblies it is useful to consider only those of the two Carolinas as they, in contrast to Massachusetts and New York, are generally not thought to have been contributors as early as 1764 to the revolutionary debate. Legislators in those provinces were as aware of the constitutional implications of parliamentary taxation as were their northern colleagues, but were less overt in the manner in which they voiced their concern. North Carolina's lower house avoided a challenge to Parliament's right to tax by emphasizing their own right, complaining of "new Taxes and Impositions laid on us without our Privity and Consent, and against what we esteem our Inherent right, and Exclusive privilege of Imposing our own Taxes." South Carolina's Commons House of Assembly buried its complaints against the Stamp Act in a long list of nonconstitutional grievances sent to the colony's agent. Yet there is no doubt that the legislators of South Carolina understood the constitutional issue posed by Parliament's threat to levy internal taxation. "The first, and in our opinion the principal reason, against such a measure," the Commons House explained, "is its inconsistency with that inherent right of every British subject, not to be taxed but by his own consent, or that of his representative."[14]

The statements of the Boston town meeting and of the lower houses of Massachusetts, New York, and the Carolinas do not exhaust the protests of Americans prior to passage of the Stamp Act, but they are sufficiently representative to summarize what most colonies were telling London. "[I]nstead of sending over to their agents discretionary instructions," William Knox complained, some colonial assemblies "framed petitions themselves, positively and directly questioning the authority and jurisdiction of parliament over the properties of the people in the colonies." Knox's words, published in 1765, provide evidence that at least one imperial official, a subminister respected as an expert on colonial affairs, understood that American whigs had formulated a constitutional argument in opposition to parliamentary internal taxes during the very first year of the controversy. As the historian Jack P. Greene observed of the North Carolina and South Carolina protests, "[h]ere, in essence, before the debate had really begun was the whole American case against taxation by Parliament."[15]

Officials in the highest levels of British government also understood what the colonies were saying. After reading the petitions and addresses of Massachusetts Bay and New York, the Board of Trade resolved "that in the said votes and addresses, the Acts and resolutions of the British Parliament were treated with indecent disrespect, and principles of a dangerous nature and tendency adopted and avowed." The Board voted to refer the documents to the Privy Council which, after determining them to be "of the highest consequence to the Kingdom, and the Legislature of Great Britain," ordered them laid before the two houses of Parliament. The British reaction to American constitutional protests was as strong as that of the Americans to the Stamp Act itself. The colonial resolutions "against the right of Parliament to tax them," Edward Sedgwick, an undersecretary of state, told a friend, was one reason that the government decided it must "establish that Right . . . and in the strongest instance, an internal Tax, that of the Stamp Duty." Jared Ingersoll, in London on private business, was asked by the Connecticut Assembly to assist its agents in defeating the Stamp Act. He discovered almost immediately that official reaction to the tone and substance of the American protests had rendered the task impossible to achieve; no member of the House of Commons would sponsor a petition questioning Parliament's authority to tax the colonies. "I own I advised the Agents if possible to get that point Canvassed that so the Americans might at least have the Satisfaction of having the point Decided upon a full Debate, but I found it could not be done."[16]

DEBATE IN THE HOUSE OF COMMONS

On the sixth of February 1765, the House of Commons resolved itself into a committee of ways and means, and George Grenville moved consideration of the stamp tax. "[I]f the right of taxing was disputed," he had said the previous year, he "would not delay the question a moment." He "[w]ished now to avoid that question if possible, because he thinks no person can doubt it." Grenville was referring to the votes and petitions sent to London by the colonial assemblies, for he "expressed much Concern at the undue Spirit of the Addresses, but forbore to be particular, lest it should exasperate the House, and requested they would proceed with Coolness and Moderation."

The chancellor of the exchequer turned next to the American arguments against parliamentary taxation, and in rejecting them he misstated them. "The objection of the colonies," Grenville assured the Commons, "is from the general right of mankind not to be taxed but by their representatives. This goes to all laws in general. The Parliament of Great Britain virtually represents the whole Kingdom, not actually great trading towns. The merchants of London and the East India Company are not represented. Not a twentieth part of the people are actually represented."

Grenville touched on three issues that in time would prove central to the controversy. First, he was agreeing with the American "addresses" that the dispute was constitutional. Second, he asserted the supremacy of Parliament over the colonies, insisting that the authority to legislate included the authority to tax. Third, although he acknowledged the constitutional validity of the American whig argument that all British subjects had the constitutional right not to be taxed except by a legislature in which they are represented, Grenville insisted that there was a distinction between actual and virtual representation, and that the American colonists were virtually represented in Parliament. From that argument Grenville went on to raise other considerations, most of which were also constitutional. It was, as Jared Ingersoll reported, "a pretty lengthy Speech," yet it is of vital importance and, at the risk of presenting principles and doctrines that will have to be repeated later, should now be summarized. What Grenville said must be weighed against the charge made in more recent times that American constitutional arguments were mere rhetoric designed to disguise what were the real motivations for the Revolution: motivations originating in economic causes such as a desire to be free of British trade regulations, social causes arising from class conflict, or just plain nationalism. That Grenville and other parliamentary defenders of the Stamp Act anticipated the American constitutional case is not proof that that case had legal validity. It is, however, impressive evidence that that case, being known in London before it was even stated, would be based on familiar principles. And the reason that those principles were familiar to Grenville and his colleagues in the House of Commons was that the American constitutional claims were all derived from the former English constitution, the current British constitution, or the British imperial constitution.[17]

Grenville began by considering the colonial charters, and, as if to show how well he had been briefed, discussed the four — Maryland, Pennsylvania, Connecticut, and Rhode Island — that would figure most prominently in the debate that was to ensue for the next decade. He then took up precedents for parliamentary taxation of the colonies, again demonstrating his preparation by discussing most of the relevant statutes. The argument was that a series of imperial taxes, imposed by Parliament since the twenty-fifth year of Charles II, established the precedent of taxation and therefore "the right" to tax, a point Grenville stressed "in consequence of the strange language he has met with in conversation and public writings upon this subject."[18]

Other constitutional considerations raised by the chancellor in his opening speech were the contract, especially the third or "imperial contract," the theory of precedent, the imperial perspective, the doctrine of constitutional reciprocity,[19] and the ultimate argument: parliamentary supremacy. He also took up nonconstitutional considerations such as the need to maintain military forces in North America and the ability of the colonies to contribute to their own defense, but concluded by defending the Stamp Act on the grounds of the second or constitutional contract. "This law is founded on the great maxim that protection is due from the Governor, and support and obedience on the part of the governed."

Grenville was followed by William Beckford, who had been born in Jamaica, and who, despite the fact he lived most of his life in England, was the island's largest landowner. Due to the nature of eighteenth-century parliamentary reporting the argument of this former mayor and present alderman of London is not clear, but it appears that he took the American side by drawing a distinction between internal and external taxation, mistakenly telling the Commons that colonial whigs acknowledged Parliament's authority to impose external taxes but not internal. Beckford admitted the "right of taxing the imports and exports of the colonies," and said that "the colonies all admit this principle." "The North Americans," he claimed, "do not think an internal and external duty the same."[20]

The third speaker, Isaac Barré, was the only one besides Beckford to question the constitutionality of the Stamp Act, an entirely different matter than saying that there was a constitutional issue. Most members of Parliament seem to have acknowledged the legitimacy of the issue but assumed the tax was constitutional and a great deal of time and debate occurred before a substantial number had doubts. It is interesting to speculate how many would have opposed the Stamp Act had they understood the Americans' constitutional objections as well as they would be understood a year later. One man who claimed he would have was William Pitt. "When the resolution was taken in the house to tax America," he later told the Commons, "I was ill in bed. If I could have endured to have been carried in my bed, so great was the agitation of my mind for the consequences! I would have solicited some kind hand to have laid me down on this floor, to have borne my testimony against it." Charles Pratt, a justice on the Court of Common Pleas, was not as politically influential as Pitt but more respected as a student of the constitution. He was not a member of the Commons and could not join the debate, but he made his opinion known. Later, as Lord Camden and a member of the upper house, he would make perhaps the strongest argument by a British official denying the Stamp Act's constitutionality. "As the affair is of the utmost importance," he told the Lords, "and in its consequences may involve the fate of kingdoms, I took the strictest review of my arguments; I re-examined all my authorities; fully determined, if I found myself mistaken, publickly to own my mistake, and give up my opinion. But my searches have more and more convinced me, that the B[ritish] P[arliament] have no right to tax the A[merican]s."[21]

When the Stamp Act was being considered in 1765 Colonel Barré was less bold than either Pitt or Camden would be in 1766 when the tax would be repealed. He did not challenge the law's constitutionality directly, but reminded his listeners of the legal distinction between "power" and "right." "We are working in the dark," he warned, "and the less we do the better." The reason was because the ministry, anxious to justify its American tax, had neglected or ignored the need to separate power from right. Caution, Barré argued, had "to be exercised lest the power be abused, the right subverted, and 2 million of unrepresented people mistreated and in their own opinion [made] slaves."[22]

The next speaker, Richard Jackson, a barrister and future reader in the Inner Temple, was the London agent for both Massachusetts Bay and Connecticut and so might have been expected to support Beckford. There was, however, what today we might call a conflict of interest. Jackson was also secretary to George Grenville and had to proceed with some care. He demonstrated his caution by persuading Massachusetts' second agent that the Commons would not hear counsel retained to argued the colony's right to tax itself exclusively. Not only did he correctly sense the mood of the House, but Jackson believed that "No Sober wise man can doubt the constitutional Authority of the Parl[iamen]t to impose Taxes of every sort on every part of the British Dominions." He was therefore "[n]ot inclined to dispute whether the Americans ought to bear a share of the burden they occasion or to dispute the power of Parliament." However, Jackson did want the Commons to consider the constitutional issue of representation. True, "the Commons in Parliament assembled represent all the subjects of Great Britain whether represented [i.e., electors] or not, and that all are bound by the acts of the legislature." Still, there was a precedent from the time of Henry VIII for not taxing persons who were not represented: the county of Chester had not been represented, and when it was taxed for the first time by Parliament, the "right was given to Chester in consequence to be represented."[23]

Jackson's argument, like most others made in the Commons that day, gains significance if placed in the context of the subsequent constitutional debate. It contains even more interest if Jared Ingersoll's account of what Jackson said is also taken into consideration. He reported that Jackson cited the precedent of Durham as well as Chester; that "Mr. Jackson produced Copies of two Acts of Parliament granting the priviledge of having Members to the County Palitine [sic] of Chester & the Bishoprick of Durham . . . being Subject to the general Authority of Parliament, were taxed in Common with the rest of the Kingdom, which taxes by reason of their having no Members in Parliament to represent their Affairs, often proved hard and injurious &c and upon that ground they had the priviledge of sending Members granted them — & if this, say they, could be a reason in the case of Chester and Durham, how much more so in the case of America."[24] It appears that Jackson had copies of the two acts with him, indicative of the extent to which the constitution was on everyone's mind, and how well the participants understood the issues before the American side of the debate has been fully aired. Even an ambivalent speaker like Jackson, who did not have the least doubt of Parliament's authority to tax the colonists, but had reason to wish the Stamp Act would not be enacted, was as well briefed as Grenville and the spokesmen for the ministry.

Lord North, speaking next, apparently attempted to answer Jackson. He referred to "[t]he representation from the colonies," and pointed out that "none of them that he has seen complained particularly of this tax of stamps." Colonel Barré again got up to challenge North. He did not know "what representation[s] have come from the colonies," Barré said, for the "words" of the assemblies' resolutions "were rather doubtful." It was, however, the member from Liverpool, Sir William Meredith, a man destined to support Lord North against the Americans in 1776, who went to the heart of the representation issue, and raised some of the most penetrating objections against the Stamp Act that were mentioned that day. "The safety of this country," he contended, "consists in this with respect that we cannot lay a tax upon others without taxing ourselves. This is not the case in America. We shall tax them in order to ease ourselves. We ought therefore to be extremely delicate in imposing a burden upon others which we not only share ourselves but which is to take it far from us."[25]

Rose Fuller, a West Indian planter and once chief justice of Jamaica, was the only speaker on record to raise the issue of expediency. He admitted "the right" of Parliament to tax the colonies, but doubted "the propriety of laying this tax." He was also the only one to predict colonial reaction to the Stamp Act, saying he was "afraid of the discord and confusion with it may produce." Fuller was so certain of the right, however, he would not have permitted lawyers for the colonies to argue the question of constitutionality at the bar of the House.[26]

The debate makes clear that the constitutional issue was on the mind of almost every speaker, just as it had been considered by almost every government official who, in former years, had proposed taxing the colonies. True, a correspondent writing to South Carolina could complain that the Stamp Act had passed the first reading "without a syllable being said. . . . There has not been so much opposition as to a common Turnpike-bill." The lack of opposition, however, derived not from unawareness that an important change in the imperial constitution was being introduced, but from general agreement about the value of imposing the Stamp Act on the American colonies and the constitutional *right* to do so. After all, as reported in Boston newspapers, "not a Man spoke who did not declare his Opinion that America ought to be taxed: Nor would any one introduce a Petition which should impeach the Parliament's Right." "[E]ven Co[lone]l Barry [sic] who spoke so warmly in our favour," Jared Ingersoll told the Connecticut General Assembly, "said . . . that he believed no man in that house would Deny the Authority of Parliament to tax America, & he was pleased to add, that he did not think the more sensible people in America would deny it. In short, altho there was about forty Members in the Negative . . . yet their Op[p]osition to it was not on account of its being Unconstitutional, but because they th[ough]t the measure imprudent & perhaps burdensome."27

Isaac Barré's belief that most sensible Americans would not deny the authority of Parliament to tax the colonies would not be verified. Americans did deny it, and within a year many members of the Commons who had voted for the Stamp Act believing they understood the constitutional issues would have a different appreciation of what those issues involved. The debate had just begun. By 1775, Arthur Lee of Virginia could truly remark of parliamentary colonial taxation that "so much has been said on the right to do this, that nothing but inspiration can throw new light upon the subject." There would eventually be a broad base of constitutional agreement, but first there was a startling contrast to perceptions on the two sides of the issue. The contrast may be summarized by comparing the words of two men, one a subordinate and the other a critic of George Grenville, the first an Englishman with many American friends, the second an American living in London. "The great measure of the session is the American Stamp Act," Thomas Whately wrote John Temple in Boston. "I give it the appellation of a great measure on account of the important point it establishes, the right of Parliament to lay an internal tax on the colonies. We wonder here that it was ever doubted. There is not a single Member of Parliament that will dispute it." Stephen Sayre from Long Island thought the Stamp Act not a great measure, but an unconstitutional catastrophe. "[T]his obstinate blunderer," he wrote of Grenville, "in defiance of equity, honour, policy[,] freedom, persuasion, or humanity, ventured to set the example, and tried the dreadful experiment, which no minister ever attempted before; and at a single stroke enslaved every Englishman in America."28

THE ENGLISH CONNECTION

Participants in the revolutionary debate well understood that the American whig case against parliamentary taxation was connected not only

with current British constitutional principles, but also with English constitutional tradition. "It happened you know," Edmund Burke told the
House of Commons in 1775, "that the great contests for freedom in this
country were from the earliest times chiefly upon the question of taxing.
. . . [T]he people must in effect themselves, mediately or immediately,
possess the power of granting their own money, or no shadow of liberty
could subsist." More than a decade earlier, before the Stamp Act was
enacted, an American saw exactly the same connection between English
constitutional history and the threat by Parliament to impose an internal
tax upon the colonies. An anonymous correspondent writing to the *Providence Gazette* pointed out that John Hampden's opposition to Charles
I's attempt to impose ship money by prerogative right

> was many years before 1641, and at a time when a civil war was
> no more foreseen or expected than in 1764. When *Hambden* [Hamp-
> den] made this noble appeal, taxes were laid on the people of *England*,
> otherwise than by their own representatives. Then it was that the
> people began to whisper that such taxes were illegal, and to *mur-
> mur* at their imposition. In the year 1764, it was proposed to tax the
> *Americans* without the consent of their own representatives: This
> occasioned whispers and *murmurs* amongst them. Now whether there
> be any resemblance between these cases and times, let every man
> judge.

Edmund Burke also thought of Hampden's opposition to ship money when
he drew a connection between the American present and the English past.
"The feelings of the colonies were formerly the feelings of Great Britain,"
Burke said when arguing for the repeal of Parliament's tax on colonial
tea imports. "Theirs were formerly the feelings of Mr. Hampden, when
called upon for the payment of twenty shillings. Would twenty shillings
have ruined Mr. Hampden's fortune? No! but the payment of half twenty
shillings, on the principle it was demanded, would have made him a slave.
It is the weight of that preamble, of which you are so fond, and not the
weight of the duty, that the Americans are unable and unwilling to bear."[29]
    Burke, intending to explain why American whigs looked at English
history to find arguments against parliamentary taxation, was also explaining America's English connection. Two men, one British and the other
American, each took one sentence to sum up that connection. "I take
it," a future chief Baron of the Exchequer said when arguing a case at
King's Bench in 1774, "that laying on imposts without consent of parliament was one of the great points on which the Revolution turned; and
another revolution much earlier; and Magna Charta, and almost innumerable statutes." "[T]he raising money upon *British* subjects, without

their consent," Stephen Hopkins, governor of Rhode Island, explained, "is the first step that those Kings who aimed to change the *British* constitution into a tyranny, have ever taken in order to effect it." Burke knew what Hopkins intended. "Formerly . . . the kings of England were in the practice of levying taxes by their own authority upon the people of England," he reminded the House of Commons. "[I]n general they made use of the very arguments in favour of the king's indefeasible right to tax the people of England that are now used by the parliament of England to tax the people of America."[30]

Burke said "England" in the last sentence when he meant "Great Britain," just as in the previous quotation he said "Great Britain" when he meant "England." The interchanging of these words was acceptable usage in the eighteenth century, just as it is now among historians and journalists, so Burke cannot be accused of error. The words are noted, however, because the distinction is important in constitutional history and must be kept in mind. Great Britain was a union of the former kingdoms of Scotland and England. The kingdom of England and the English constitution no longer existed, but English law and Scots law survived as two independent jurisdictions administering two separate legal systems. Of even greater important to the revolutionary constitutional controversy was another survival: the former English constitution may no longer have had existence, but in both theory and practice its doctrines, maxims, and precedents remained valid. They were the primary source, almost the exclusive source, of the British constitution. "The principles of the British Constitution," Sir Edward Creasy, a lawyer turned historian, explained in 1872, "are substantially the same that grew up in England as the principles of the English Constitution." There were even occasions when writers might mix the words "English" and "British" in the same thought; to say, for example, that "mutual Security, is the Basis of *British* Freedom: — The great Art and peculiar Design of the *English* Constitution, is seen in it's constantly separating the legislative and executive Powers; in uniting in it's Administration the three different Ranks of King, Nobility, and People, so that each Order is a Check and Barrier to the Encroachments of the other." These words, published in 1776, were correct even though both "British" and "English" appear in the same sentence because the "mutual Security" to which they referred, and which was one of the foundations of current *British* freedom, was based on the *English* doctrine of the balanced constitution under which the antagonism between the estates of king, lords, and commons served to restrain power and prevented the growth of arbitrary government. It was an English constitutional principle embodied in the current British constitution.[31]

The distinction becomes more significant when it is appreciated that

American whigs, in their quarrel with London, almost always sought recognition of English rights, or, put more correctly, British rights of English origins. They certainly did not seek or want Irish rights. It is also likely that at least until the Declaration of Independence, if then, they never officially asked for or referred to a natural right. And as far as is known, Arthur Lee of Virginia is the only American to cite a Scots right. Most colonials, like most Englishmen, would have rejected a Scottish standard. In 1765, Virginia petitioned against the proposed Mutiny Act, which would have permitted the billeting of soldiers in private houses in the colonies. The practice was contrary to the English Petition of Right and hence incorporated into the British constitution, Americans contended; it was therefore, a right to which they were entitled.[32] When George Grenville reminded the House of Commons that the practice was still constitutional in Scots law, "Thomas Townshend spoke well and warmly against making the Scotch law our precedent." Largely due to English constitutional principles that were part of the British constitution, Parliament never seriously considered billeting troops in American homes.[33]

An institutional consideration strengthening the English connection was that, because there was no British law, there was no British attorney general. The Crown law officers to whom the ministry and Parliament turned for rulings and advice on American questions were the attorney and solicitor generals of England. The lord advocate and the solicitor general of Scotland were not consulted. It was English law and only English law that was in contention during the revolutionary era. The reason was not only that that was the law applied by the two English law officers, but that it was the law Americans insisted upon, and they did so expecting it would shield them from parliamentary innovations. "It is," the Stamp Act Congress asserted, "from and under the English constitution, we derive all our civil and religious rights and liberties." Although the kingdom of England no longer existed, the Congress's claim of the *English* constitution was not anachronistic. The men drafting that statement meant the same set of principles referred to by the people of Boston when they thanked their whig lawyer, James Otis, "for his undaunted Exertions in the Common Cause of the Colonies from the beginning of the present glorious Struggle for the Rights of the British Constitution." They all meant English rights and British constitutionalism.[34]

CHAPTER TWO

THE OTHER TAXES

A final introductory point to be made also pertains to the constitutional heritage that the colonies shared with their mother country and helps to explain the magnitude of the constitutional issue posed by Parliament when it attempted to tax Americans for purposes of raising a revenue. From the perspective of English constitutional history, the significance of the constitutional crisis thrust upon the British Empire by the introduction of parliamentary taxation in the form of the Stamp Act cannot be overstated. The Stamp Act controversy was no rite of passage of a people coming to age. In the context of the history of English and British constitutional liberty, it may be extravagant to term it the greatest threat to English freedom since the Norman Conquest, but surely it was the greatest any people claiming English constitutional rights had faced since Charles I's attempt to impose prerogative taxation. "A subject of greater importance than ever engaged the attention of this house!" William Pitt told the Commons of the Stamp Act, "that subject only excepted, when near a century ago, it was the question, whether you yourselves were to be bound, or free."[1] Pitt was referring to the ship-money crisis. Ship money was Charles I's attempt to impose a tax by prerogative degree, that is, without consent of Parliament. There were a number of such taxes sanctioned by constitutional custom and Charles sought to extend one of these, ship money, by collecting it more universally and more frequently than established practice warranted, introducing an innovation or departure from usage.

There are two aspects concerning the ship-money controversy that deserve the attention of students of the American Revolution. One is the fact that the arguments against the constitutionality of ship money were exactly the same as those against the constitutionality of the Stamp Act. The constitutional case developed by colonial whigs was, in many instances, a word-for-word echo of the constitutional case developed over a century earlier by such English lawyers as Oliver St. John, lead counsel for the defense in the major ship-money prosecution, and Henry Parker, one of the best constitutional writers on the parliamentary side of the controversy. The second aspect to be noted is that during the 1760s American whigs were not the only British subjects to raise questions about unconstitutional taxes. The ship-money issue of prerogative taxation was not yet dormant in the mother country. George III, acting much as Charles I had once acted — on the principle of necessity — imposed taxation by proclamation upon some of the islands ceded by France to Great Britain at the end of the Seven Years War. As it was the eighteenth century rather than the seventeenth, the king made a sincere effort to avoid giving constitutional offense; the proclaimed taxes were scheduled to remain in force only until local assemblies could be elected. Yet even this justification did not assuage the constitutional fears of people apprehensive of any manifestation of the royal prerogative. "I hope," a correspondent wrote the *North Briton*, "I may now, without offence, say, that a king of Great Britain has no such prerogative. It is a prerogative of the subjects of Great Britain to tax themselves; a prerogative committed in trust by them to their representatives; and is, perhaps, the only prerogative they have, effectually to secure their independence as a branch of the legislature. If this is once given up, all pretence to liberty and property afterwards must be ridiculous.[2]

That statement in the *North Briton* made two points about taxation without representation: that prerogative taxation threatened the constitutional viability of government by elected representatives, and that it jeopardized constitutional liberty. It must be kept in mind that these arguments were made not by an opponent of Charles I or by an American whig. They were made by a defender of parliamentary sovereignty during the reign of George III. Yet the principles stated were the same as ones pertinent both to Parliament's seventeenth-century struggle against ship money and the American whigs' eighteenth-century struggle against parliamentary taxation. Ship money, Oliver St. John told the House of Lords, "makes *Parliaments* to be nothing; This sets up the *Judges* above the *Parliament*. . . . If they may overthrow the proceedings of that Parliament of *3. Car.* [i.e., the petition of right] they may by the same Reason overthrow the Actions of this and all Future *Parliaments.*" Henry Parker also thought that ship money threatened representative government, because if the Crown could impose it at discretion, it could create a tyranny that "hath a controlling power over all Law, and knowes no bounds but its owne will." A century and a quarter later, Americans would be saying the same thing. "For if the Privilege of not being taxed without their Consent, be once taken from them," a committee consisting of future loyalists wrote in a statement adopted and published by the Connecticut legislature in 1764, "Liberty and Freedom are certainly gone with it. That Power which can tax as it shall think proper, may govern as it pleases; and those subjected to such Taxation and Government, must be far, very far from being a free People."[3]

It is important to stress that the loyalists just quoted were speaking of "Liberty and Freedom" as those words were defined in the eighteenth century. Today we think of their emphasis upon property as a defense of the material and tend to forget how much the concept of liberty in the seventeenth and eighteenth centuries depended upon property — upon the right to property and the right to security in property. We no longer think of property in the manner that people did in the revolutionary era, nor do we use the word "property" as they did, and it is sometimes forgotten that liberty itself was spoken of and thought of as property. Constitutional rights of individuals — the right to trial by jury, for example, or the right to be taxed only by consent — were possessions that English citizens owned, that were vested in them by inheritance from their ancestors.

We could wish that eighteenth-century Britons and Americans had been more precise in their arguments, that they had taken greater care to define terms like "property," especially when using them to explain constitutional rights. Their failure to do so, however, does not matter in most instances, as we can follow their meaning. Even when "property" meant "money," it was property in the constitutional sense only if no one could lawfully take it without the possessor's consent or the consent of the possessor's representative. The right that you had to that property was constitutionally similar to the right you had to liberty, to representation, to trial by jury, and other civil entitlements generally called civil rights. Because the erosion of one right could lead to the erosion of all rights, eighteenth-century lawyers and libertarians were defending more than their physical possessions when they resisted arbitrary taxation — whether it was taxation of British subjects by the royal prerogative or parliamentary taxation of unrepresented Americans.

It is now time to turn from the concept of property that was being

defended against the claims of parliamentary taxation and consider the
constitutional arguments upon which that defense was based. But first
it is necessary to outline the taxes that, in addition to the Stamp Act, gave
rise to the constitutional controversy leading to the American Revolution.

THE SUGAR ACT

The first tax laid upon the Americans to which they objected on constitutional grounds has been known by several names including the "Molasses Act," the "American Revenue Act," and, most commonly, the "Sugar
Act." The redrafting of a taxation statute passed in 1733 at the instiga-
tion of Great Britain's West Indian sugar islands, it could also have been
called the second Molasses Act or second Sugar Act. That earlier law, the
first Sugar or Molasses Act, imposed a duty of sixpence a gallon on foreign molasses imported into the colonies. Amounting to about 100 per-
cent *ad valorem*, it was less a tax than a prohibition, an attempt to give
the sugar planters of the British West Indies a monopoly on the North
American trade at the expense of molasses that could be purchased more
cheaply in French islands.[4]

Although North Americans were annoyed that the Sugar Act of 1733
was designed to benefit West Indies planters at their expense, they did
not raise constitutional objections against it, probably because they did
not think of it as a tax. After all, the tariff was practically a dead letter,
a duty on molasses so high that it amounted to a prohibition on the legitimate trade, leaving business to merchants willing to be smugglers.[5]
Most were willing because they had no choice. John Huske confessed to
the House of Commons in 1764 that "He had resided 24 years in America
and lived in a mercantile way with a gentleman who practised every
species of smuggling." The Sugar Act of 1733, he claimed, had "created
smuggling even by force. Smugglers of molasses instead of being infamous are called patriots in North America. Nothing but a low duty can
prevent it." Huske, speaking during the parliamentary debates on redrafting the Sugar Act, wanted his fellow legislators to realize that the molasses trade deserved special consideration as the well-being of several
North American colonies depended upon it. Cargoes of "the superfluous
lumber of our provinces and other things," purchased by the French
islands, were paid for in molasses. That molasses was then carried to the
mainland and distilled into rum. Next, he explained, "30 ships go from
New England every year laden with nothing but rum, and bring back
gold dust, elephants' teeth and slaves for the sugar planters." Huske thought

the duty should be lowered to two pennies a gallon. That tariff, he said, would be "much better than 3d., as there will be less temptation."[6]

George Grenville, not John Huske, determined parliamentary policy that year. During the very months when New York and Massachusetts leaders were writing their agents in London to work for repeal of the act of 1733, Grenville was sending orders to imperial officials in North America, including for the first time the navy, to enforce the law. The news, Governor Francis Bernard reported, alarmed New England more than had the fall of Fort William Henry during the last war. Grenville was implementing a policy earlier espoused by William Pitt and Charles Townshend. Pitt had wanted to enforce the Sugar Act to stop American trade with the French; Townshend had promised the Commons a new source of tax income. "Mr. Townshend," Edmund Burke later recalled, "in a brilliant harangue on this subject did dazzle them by playing before their eyes an image of a revenue to be raised in America." The *Political Register* in 1767 blamed the influence of the West Indian planters. They had clamored unsuccessfully for the law's enforcement, "till at length, in the year 1764, under a pretence of increasing the revenue, which was impracticable, they prevailed upon the ministry to enforce this law by Admiralty Courts."[7]

The new policy of enforcement was quickly followed by a new law that Parliament also expected would be enforced. The Sugar Act of 1733 was replaced by the Sugar Act of 1764. The duty on foreign molasses was lowered from six to three pennies a gallon and additional authority was vested in the customs service to collect the tax and adjudicate forfeitures.[8] The new legislation has been described as "the first statute distinctly to tax the colonies rather than to regulate trade."[9] In addition to reducing the molasses duty by half, the act of 1764 forbade import of foreign rum, and put importation charges on many other items including some, such as Madeira wine, hitherto free of taxes. "These duties," a London magazine assured its readers, "are all to be paid into the Exchequer, and reserved for defraying the charges of protecting the *British* colonies in America."[10]

THE TOWNSHEND DUTIES

The Sugar Act of 1764 was the first of four statutes that raised the issue of Parliament's constitutional authority to tax the North American colonies. The second was the Stamp Act, passed in 1765 and repealed in 1766. Third was the Townshend duties of 1767, named for Charles Townshend, the chancellor of the exchequer who was, said Burke, a "person of the first rate abilities, of ten thousand talents, who had a desire to please everybody. . . . [I]n order to please other respectable persons, [Townshend] produced a plan of taxation for America. He never gave as the reason that those duties were intended as a test of America. The reasons he gave were that it was in order to establish a police in America — to strengthen and fortify the government of America."[11]

Townshend's announcement that he would tax the colonies attracted much greater attention than had Grenville's first mention of the Stamp Act. "Mr. C[harles] T[ownshend]," a subminister reported to a friend, "has most certainly pronounced, in the H[ouse] of C[ommons] the doctrine of the distinction between internal & external Taxation, to be Nonsense & Absurdity." A London correspondent, writing to Philadelphia and quoting Townshend from memory, also recalled the word "nonsense" — "That that distinction of *internal* and *external* taxes was nonsense." Three months later, when Townshend again addressed the question, a reporter taking his words down as they were spoken quoted Townshend's explanation that he intended "to lay taxes upon America, but not internal taxes, because though he did not acknowledge the distinction it was accepted by many Americans and this was sufficient."[12]

Townshend was formulating a tax package based on the belief, shared by many members of Parliament, that Americans had constitutional objections to internal taxes such as the Stamp Act, but accepted as constitutional "external taxes,"[13] a term generally not defined but frequently assumed to include customs duties on either imports or exports. Like most of his colleagues, he thought "the distinction between internal and external taxes as not founded in reason," but if the colonists believed it made a constitutional difference that was justification enough for it "to be adopted in policy." As explained by Connecticut's London agent to the colony's governor, Townshend declared that, although "he knew no difference between internal and external taxes, (which, by the way, is a doctrine very generally adopted here,) yet since the Americans were pleased to make that distinction he was willing to indulge them, and chose for that reason to confine himself to regulations of trade, by which a sufficient revenue might be raised in America."[14]

The Townshend duties were part of a large legislative package that included creation of an American board of customs commissioners and reforms in the procedures, jurisdiction, and powers of the colonial vice-admiralty courts. We are concerned only with taxation, a matter easily summarized, for the duties were imposed on but four categories of British-manufactured products imported into the colonies. They were glass (five grades), painters' colors (including red and white lead for use in paint), paper (sixty-seven grades), and tea. There was hardly any discussion in Parliament of the merit of these duties, perhaps because "external" taxation was so widely believed to be constitutional in American legal theory. Surely few of Townshend's colleagues understood that his duties were a return to Grenville's policy of American taxation, a program most of them had repudiated the year before when they repealed the Stamp Act. The very first words of Townshend's preamble—"it is expedient that a revenue should be raised, in your Majesty's dominions in America"—left no doubt that the Townshend duties were intended to raise money and not merely regulate trade.[15]

Although Townshend expected his duties to raise about £40,000, with perhaps half coming from the tax on tea, the anticipated or actual income never became an issue, for American objections would be to the constitutionality of the duties, not their amount. Yet there was a secondary consideration to cause concern: the potential of expanded taxation. The Townshend duties could be open-ended; the belief in Bristol and London, a British writer informed a Boston correspondent, was that more goods would soon be added to the taxable list.[16]

THE TEA TAX

As a revenue measure, the Townshend duties were a failure—£13,202 was collected the first year, £5,561 the second, and the act was repealed in the third. This resulted not from any inherent defect in the legislation, but from American perceptions that the duties were unconstitutional: nonimportation associations were organized; British products were boycotted; and there was such a decline in importation that revenues decreased drastically. For several reasons it was decided to repeal most of the duties. Toward the end of 1770 the taxes on glass, paper, and painters' colors were abolished, leaving only the duty on tea. The tea tax was retained more as a symbol of Parliament's authority than to raise money. Had every duty been repealed Americans could have argued that Parliament had accepted their contention that the Townshend duties had been unconstitutional. Because the tax on tea was so high, the colonies ceased to fuss—they were getting their tea from smugglers and not paying the customs. Lord North, the leader of the ministry in 1771, could sincerely assert that the imperial crisis had abated. "Trade flourishes in all parts of the kingdom," he assured the Commons; "the American disputes are settled; and there is nothing to interrupt the peace and prosperity of the nation, but the discontents which a desperate faction is fomenting."[17] Then came the Tea Act of 1773.

Lord North was responsible for shattering the political and constitutional peace of which he had bragged. The East India Company was in financial trouble and he sought to help it avoid debt and dispose of its surplus tea. "The Comp[any]," Benjamin Franklin explained, "have accepted Bills, which they find themselves unable to pay, tho' they have the Value of Two Millions in Tea and other India goods in their Stores, perishing under a Want of Demand." One reason was that Americans, smuggling from Dutch sources, were not purchasing from the company. "[A]ltho' it is known, that the American Market is lost by continuing the Duty on Tea, and that we are supply'd by the Dutch, who doubtless take the Opportunity of Smuggling other India Goods among us with the Tea, so that for the 5 Years past we might probably have otherwise taken off the greatest Part of what the Comp[any] have on hand, and so have prevented their present Embarrasment, yet the Honour of Government is suppos'd to forbid the Repeal of the American Tea Duty. . . . Can an American forbear smiling at these Blunders?" Lord North thought Americans should not only not be smiling, but should also bail the East India Company out of its difficulties. To save it from collapse, and, incidentally preserve the government's share of the company's dividends, legislation was enacted permitting the company to dispose of its surplus tea in the colonies by shipping the tea in its own vessels and selling it through its own factors. The original Townshend duty on tea remained in force, but because a rebate was allowed on the tax paid on importation into Great Britain, the tea sold in America was not only to be cheaper than it had been previously, it would also be cheaper than at home and even cheaper than that smuggled from the Netherlands.[18] There was the rub: Americans would certainly purchase the company's tea and, as a result, for the first time they would pay in substantial amounts a tax imposed by Parliament for the purpose of obtaining revenue. "The East India Company," a New Hampshire writer would bemoan, "have procured an act to ship their rotten and infected teas to America, which liberty they never could obtain before as a Company, nor would they now have done it, if it had not been by that means to support the British act of taxing America."[19]

CHAPTER THREE

THE INTERNAL-EXTERNAL CRITERION

There were occasions during the revolutionary controversy when British imperialists and American whigs simply did not understand one another. They listened to the words spoken, believed they were in communication, but what one side said the other did not comprehend. There was perhaps no error more egregious than the frequent assumption by British officials that when American whigs objected to internal taxation they were saying that taxes not internal — external taxes whatever they might be — were constitutional. The error led to a misunderstanding that devolved into a belief that external taxes were constitutionally acceptable to the colonists. Charles Townshend compounded the mistake when he told the Commons there was a way to tax the colonies that conformed to American constitutional theories. As mentioned in the previous chapter, he thought the distinction between internal and external taxation "ridiculous in every body's opinion except the Americans," and enjoyed poking fun at the idea.[1] He was, however, willing to utilize any form of tax that the colonies would pay without raising a constitutional fuss.

Townshend's mistaken belief that Americans regarded internal taxes as unconstitutional and external taxes constitutional was of vital importance in the history of events leading to the Revolution. It explains not only why he so miscalculated and resurrected the controversy over taxation, but also, because so many members of Parliament had the same misunderstanding, why the Townshend duties passed through the Commons with very little discussion at a time when one might have expected London to have been more sensitive about taxing the colonies. Even Thomas Whately, drafter of the Stamp Act, believed that if his tax had not been internal the colonies would not have protested. John Huske, a New Hampshire native, who was supposed to be knowledgeable about American thinking, encouraged Townshend, assuring him "that by a regulation of the trade of America . . . you may have a sufficient revenue to pay all Great Britain's expence for her colonies and in manner perfectly agreeable to both."[2] As Lord North later told the Commons, recalling the repeal of the Stamp Act, "the doctrine then laid down was, that *external* duties was *your* right, *internal* taxes *theirs*."[3] The supposition seemed self-evident.

The Usage of "Internal"

If any individual can be said to have persuaded British opinion that external taxes imposed by Parliament were constitutional in colonial legal theory, both eighteenth-century observers and later historians agree that individual was Benjamin Franklin. The most renowned American in London, there as agent for Pennsylvania, he was invited to testify before the Commons during the debate on repealing the Stamp Act. He supposedly made the distinction between internal and external taxation the central theme of his testimony.[4] "[B]efore 1763," Franklin was reported explaining, "persons in Philadelphia had made a distinction between internal taxes and duties . . . the general conclusion was that the Parliament could not lay internal taxes upon them because it was not right nor constitutional. . . . That there is a distinction between internal and external taxes, that a man is left to his option more in paying one than the other." A pamphlet printed in London, Philadelphia, and Boston, gave Franklin's testimony wide circulation.

> Q. Did you ever hear the authority of parliament to make laws for America questioned till lately?
> A. The authority of parliament was allowed to be valid in all laws, except such as should lay internal taxes. It was never disputed in laying duties to regulate commerce.
> . . . .
> Q. Was it an opinion in America before 1763, that the parliament had no right to lay taxes and duties there?

A. I never heard any objection to the right of laying duties to regulate commerce; but a right to lay internal taxes was never supposed to be in parliament, as we are not represented there.

Q. On what do you found your opinion, that the people in America made any such distinction?

A. I know that whenever the subject has occurred in conversation where I have been present, it has appeared to be the opinion of every one, that we could not be taxed in a parliament where we were not represented. But the payment of duties laid by act of parliament, as regulations of commerce, was never disputed.

A persuasive argument has been made that Franklin's testimony "was shrewdly evasive," that the external-internal criterion "allowed him to evade the question of whether or not his countrymen were in principle denying Parliament's right to tax them." That, in fact, is what he should have done. As a colonial agent, his job was to lobby for repeal of the Stamp Act, and to do so he had to avoid making constitutional claims that would have offended the Commons.[5]

If Franklin did in fact draw a distinction between internal and external taxation and said that American whigs thought only internal taxes were unconstitutional, he was wrong. No colonial assembly rested the American constitutional case on the principle that internal taxes as opposed to external taxes were unconstitutional. It would have been out of character to have based their claim to constitutional rights upon a criterion that would not have provided a sound rule of law and could not have served as a constitutional principle marking a line between the legal and the illegal. One very practical reason was definition. Even today, after decades of debate among scholars, there is no agreement as to what people in 1765 meant by "external" when they drew a constitutional distinction between internal taxation and external taxation. One reason is that what was essentially a constitutional principle has been wrenched out of context, with the consequence that shades of differences have been swept aside. Arguments made by whigs much in the tradition of a lawyer writing a brief have been analyzed much as if they were stump speeches. It is necessary to appreciate that when the word "internal" was employed during the Stamp Act debate it was used forensically. Americans stressed "internal" to underscore the constitutional fact that the Stamp Act was the *first* internal tax ever imposed by Parliament on the colonies. That fact, if true, made the Act constitutionally vulnerable. To stress its internal feature was to concentrate the legal argument on the contention that it was contrary to custom, unprecedented, and an innovation, any one or all of which made the Stamp tax constitutionally dubious if not unconstitutional. Few Americans, remember, claimed the Stamp Act was illegal, only that it was unconstitutional.

It is one thing for a lawyer or an eighteenth-century whig to argue that a tax was unconstitutional because it was internal. It is quite another for us to assume that because internal taxes were condemned as unconstitutional, the lawyer or whig making the argument was conceding that external taxes were constitutional. That is not the way lawyers argue, nor was it the way eighteenth-century people stated constitutional principles. They could well contend that internal taxes were unconstitutional and, if asked, admit that there was no constitutional distinction between internal and external taxation. Indeed, they might admit that if one was unconstitutional so was the other. Yet they would still attack the constitutionality of the Stamp Act on the grounds that it was an internal tax because, by isolating the otherwise meaningless internal aspect they were able to narrow the factual issue to whether the Stamp Act was contrary to constitutional custom, was constitutionally unprecedented, and was a constitutional innovation.

Daniel Dulany furnishes the best illustration. A lawyer, he wrote the most widely read pamphlet attacking the constitutionality of the Stamp Act. His argument has been criticized for being a dull lawyer's brief, but that was probably its strength. Dulany attempted to demonstrate that the Stamp Act, as an internal tax, was unconstitutional. Never once did he use the phrase "external taxation." Those words were immaterial to his case. Yet, because he employed the word "internal," Lawrence Henry Gipson cited Dulany's pamphlet as evidence that Americans based their constitutional argument on the distinction between internal and external taxation.[6]

To clarify the constitutional argument made against internal taxation, therefore, it is necessary to look at some of the specific words and contexts in which that argument was framed. There is no better place to begin than with Franklin who, Gipson said, "made a very sharp distinction between the internal and external taxation of Americans by Parliament." For his evidence, Gipson cited only Franklin's testimony before the House of Commons, some of which we have already seen. In Franklin's answers quoted above, the term "internal taxes" was used twice. In each instance the counterdistinction Franklin drew to internal was not external, but "duties to regulate commerce" and "duties laid by act of parliament, as regulations of commerce." If Franklin chose his words as carefully as he has been credited with doing, then he did not mean taxes laid on imported goods for the purpose of revenue (Gipson's definition of external taxation), but duties imposed for the purpose of regulating commerce. It was only when members of Parliament asked about the validity of external taxation that the distinction entered into Franklin's testimony.[7]

The topic came up twice. The first occasion occurred when Franklin was asked to clarify the "difference between the two taxes to the Colony on which they may be laid." The difference, he replied, "is very great," explaining that Americans could refuse to pay a custom duty by not purchasing the product assessed, "[b]ut an internal tax is forced from the people without their consent, if not laid by their own representatives." The second reference to external taxation occurred when someone pointed out that Americans questioned the constitutionality of the Stamp Act on the ground it was taxation without representation. Why, Franklin was asked, did they not apply the same principle against "the parliament's right of external taxation." He answered that they "never had hitherto" but that they might soon do so if persuaded by the many arguments "lately used here to shew them that there is no difference, and that if you have no right to tax them internally, you have none to tax them externally." This answer, as well as answers in which he insisted that resolutions passed by the Pennsylvania and Massachusetts assemblies objected only to internal taxes and not to custom duties, may be evidence that Franklin drew the distinction between the two types of taxes. But what was the distinction? "By taxes," he said, the Americans "mean internal taxes; by duties they mean customs." He was asserting that the colonial resolutions had objected to only the first as unconstitutional. He was not saying, at least not in his testimony before the Commons when speaking as a colonial agent and not writing anonymous articles for newspapers, that another type of tax, customs duties imposed for the purpose of raising income in the colonies, was constitutional. In fact, he was asked that question and had to give an answer. Although Franklin avoided denoting as unconstitutional customs duties imposed to obtain revenue, he did not admit their validity.[8]

The distinction Franklin drew in his testimony to the Commons had only one meaning in law. It was not between unconstitutional internal taxation and constitutional external taxation. It was between unconstitutional taxation without consent and the constitutional regulation of commerce in which customs duties were applied for purposes of regulation, not for purposes of raising a revenue. While it can reasonably be surmised that Franklin stressed the word "internal" only as part of a strategy to suppress discussion of the larger constitutional issues,[9] a better view is that he and other colonial agents used the term "internal" to narrow the debate to a constitutional issue they could more reasonably manage and had a better hope of winning. If, as previously noted, Americans could demonstrate the Stamp Act was unconstitutional on some principle other than the broad ground of Parliament's sovereign power, their case would not only be easier to argue, it would also give less offense to the people who had to be persuaded, the members of Parliament. It is necessary, then, to ask why American whigs sometimes used the term "internal" even when it is obvious that they were not distinguishing between internal and external taxes.

One reason has already been suggested: cosmetic disguise or constitutional politeness — using the term "internal" to soften the implications of an assertion that, if phrased bluntly, would have implied complete autonomy from Parliament. The freeholders of Providence, Rhode Island, in resolutions that were adopted verbatim by the Rhode Island Assembly, seem to have had this objective in mind. They stated unequivocally that Parliament had no authority to impose taxes upon them and slipped the word "internal" into the text twice, not as a qualification, or for any obvious purpose except to soften their argument — to soften, that is, the impression the argument made on the minds of British readers who already believed that there were external as well as internal taxes. First they stated that the "People of this Colony have enjoyed the Right of being governed by their own Assembly in the Article of Taxes and internal Police," and argued that taxation by any authority other than the colony's General Assembly would be "unconstitutional." Next, after having asserted an unequivocal right to self-taxation, the Rhode Islanders introduced the term "internal Taxation" but in such a context that, although appearing to qualify their constitutional objection to the Stamp Act, did not qualify the statement just quoted that only the General Assembly possessed constitutional authority to tax British subjects domiciled in the colony. "That his Majesty's liege People, the Inhabitants of the Colony, are not bound to yield Obedience to any Law or Ordinance, designed to impose any internal Taxation whatsoever upon them, other than the Laws and Ordinances of the General Assembly aforesaid."[10] Given the entire text of the resolutions the phrase "internal taxation" had a political purpose, not a constitutional meaning. It made the Rhode Island claim appear less offensive to Parliament; it did *not* say that there were kinds of taxes other than internal that Parliament had constitutional authority to impose on the colony.

Another purpose for calling taxes "internal" during the revolutionary controversy was to focus attention on the division of government power we now refer to as federalism. To say that authority was "internal" was to say it was local and properly within the jurisdiction of the separate colonial legislatures. To say it was "external" was to say it was imperial and subject to the authority of Parliament. To speak in terms of "internal" and "external" was to speak of spheres of government for an empire in which federalism was only vaguely perceived as a constitutional doctrine. When the Providence resolves quoted above claimed that "the Article of Taxes and internal Police," and when the Maryland Stamp Act resolves claimed that "the Articles of Taxes and internal Polity" were in the exclusive purview of the local legislature, they were making a statement about federal limits on imperial power. They were not conceding to Parliament something called "external" taxes, surely not the Maryland legislators. In the same set of resolutions just quoted, it was also voted that the imposition of "any Tax on or from the Inhabitants of Maryland" by any authority other than their elected representatives "is Unconstitutional."[11]

The final and chief reason the colonists used the term "internal tax" when protesting the Stamp Act has already been mentioned: it was an innovation. One purpose was to isolate the Stamp Act from previous imperial imposts or taxes, all of which had been or were customs duties. A second purpose was to call attention to an aspect readily objectionable as a matter of constitutional law. Unlike the Sugar Act and other customs levies, the Stamp Act was new, unprecedented, and contrary to custom.

"[C]an you name any act of assembly, or public act of any of your governments, that made such a distinction?" Franklin was asked of the external-internal distinction.

"I do not know that there was any," Franklin replied. "I think there was never an occasion to make any such act, till now that you have attempted to tax us; that has occasioned resolutions of assembly, declaring the distinction, in which I think every assembly on the continent, and every member in every assembly, have been unanimous." In other words, the fact there had never before been an internal tax imposed by Parliament on the colonies was what made the "internal" aspect of the Stamp Act significant. As an "internal" tax the Stamp Act was a legislative innovation, an innovation of such magnitude to make it if not unconstitutional, at least constitutionally questionable. John Lind, a ministerial hack writing to refute American arguments in 1775, explained the constitutional doctrine as clearly as could any colonial whig. "If the right of [parliamentary] supremacy in general," he said of parliamentary taxation of the colonies,

> had never been *claimed* till the commencement of the present contest, the claim made at so late a period, might with reason be condemned as novel and unconstitutional. If having long ago been exercised or claimed, it had all along been *contested*, it might at least be looked upon as doubtful.[12]

THE DOCTRINE OF INNOVATIONS

The constitutional grievance against government innovations was closely related to two other constitutional doctrines which are important enough to merit separate chapters. They are the doctrine of precedent and the authority of custom. In fact, it is often difficult to distinguish between the constitutional complaint that an action is an innovation and the constitutional complaint that it is unprecedented. The difference is not so much in kind as in the method of proof and the formulation of argument. One objection to innovations was that they could eventually be cited as precedents. A Massachusetts legislative committee protested the change in the imperial constitution when London began paying the colonial governors' salaries by calling it "a most dangerous Innovation, as it affords a Precedent for future more extensive Evil of the same kind." Conversely, to justify some action, government often had to find a "precedent" for what otherwise might indisputably be an innovation. Due to the timeless quality of England's ancient constitution, though, this task was not as incongruous as it may first seem. Connecting innovation and custom was a technique at which common lawyers were especially adept. One lawyer in 1760, for example, suggested that Parliament debate the approaching treaty of peace with France, a constitutional innovation that would have trespassed on one of the king's most important prerogatives. "It may be thought," he argued, "that the Method proposed is not strictly constitutional. To those who are but little versed in Antiquity, the Revival of antient Custom may bear the Appearance of modern Innovation."[13]

The connection between innovation and custom was less close than between innovation and precedent. An action that was an innovation was also contrary to custom in a negative sense. The doctrine of custom condemned an innovation that was a departure from custom because it was something that had not been done before. The harm was in the departure from customary practice. To claim that the same action was an innovation might require evidence of harm independent of the fact it had not been done before. Generally, however, the harm of innovation was found in the fact of being an innovation, that is, constituting a change in or an alteration of familiar law.

"In general," the Massachusetts House of Representatives contended, "innovations are dangerous." The House was only saying what Englishmen had always been saying. "Innovations in all states are dangerous," Sir John Suckling wrote the Commons in 1628, "especially where there is a diminution of the laws, or a fear to execute justice." The members of Parliament agreed. "[T]he hearts of your people," they told Charles I, "are full of fear of innovation and change of government and accordingly possessed with extreme grief and sorrow." Quoting "an ingenious political writer," a Boston newspaper, during the Stamp Act crisis, explained the theoretical case against constitutional innovation.

> [T]he first article of safety, in Princes and States, lies in avoiding all councils *or designs of innovation, in ancient and established forms and laws,* especially those concerning *liberty, property* and *religion:* which are the possessions men *will ever have most at heart,* and be most tenacious of retaining: By avoiding the *designs of innovation,* they will leave the channel of *known and common Justice* clear and undisturbed.

The doctrine restrained government power. After all, to complain against an action as an innovation was to say that the innovator was at fault and, in most constitutional situations, the innovator was the government. Applying that legal truism to the revolutionary controversy, a London reviewer wrote in 1774: "The Americans . . . desire only to live in the state of subjection in which they have hitherto continued, without the imposition of new claims over them; if these new claims produce disagreeable consequences, they are justly chargeable on the innovators."[14]

Legal theory demonstrated peril and peril justified action. The Sons of Liberty of New London, Connecticut, agreed "to associate, advise, protect, and defend each other . . . not in the least desiring any alteration or innovation in the grand bulwark of their liberties and the wisdom of ages." Their purpose was to prevent constitutional innovations, the very reason *Amicus Publico* praised the crowds that had recently rioted against the Stamp Act in New York City. Mobs they may have been, but mobs showing "timely zeal for the true interest of the British Constitution; by endeavouring to prevent any innovations being made on the rights, liberties and properties of his Majesty's loyal subjects in North-America."[15]

There were two reasons why innovations had to be opposed. One was the doctrine that acquiescence converted innovation into precedent. "[I]t is the language of reason," the Massachusetts House of Representatives argued, "and it is the opinion of the greatest writers on the law of nature and nations, that if the Parliament should make any considerable change in the constitution, and the nation should be voluntarily silent upon it, this would be considered as an approbation of the act." The second reason was that it took but one innovation to create a precedent: if suffered to remain as statute, practice, or policy, what had been an innovation could become constitutional dogma. That reality explains colonial hostility to imperial innovations; those innovations were seen as threats to the constitutional, not to the economic or political, status quo. "The time to guard against corruption and tyranny," Thomas Jefferson realized, "is before they shall have gotten hold of us. It is better to keep the wolf out of the fold, than to trust to drawing his teeth and claws after he shall have entered." Edmund Burke referred to this constitutional alertness when he said that Americans "augur misgovernment at a distance and snuff the approach of tyranny in every tainted breeze."[16]

It is important to notice the emphasis of American whigs. Always it was on the newness, the innovation. "In the year 1764," the Massachusetts House reminded the colony's agent in London, "the Parliament of *England* first declared its determination to . . . grant to his Majesty a revenue out of the property of his *American Subjects*."[17] The colonial whigs were claiming that they had "enjoyed the Right and Priviledge of being governed by their general Assembly, in the Article of Taxing and internal Police" until the Sugar Act of 1764 and the Stamp Act of 1765. Aspects of these statutes that introduced "some late innovations in our system," as Thomas Pownall told the Commons, were, first, that both were intended to raise a revenue, and, second, that the Stamp Act was an internal tax. The colonists could use various words to call attention to their unconstitutional aspects of being innovations. One was to call "these taxations," as did the voters of Weymouth, Massachusetts, "NOVELTIES." Another word, when discussing the stamp tax, was "internal," as when the voters of Boston thanked Parliament for repealing the Stamp Act, "whereby our incontestable Right of Internal Taxation still remains to us inviolate."[18]

Whether the Stamp Act was the constitutional innovation American whigs claimed is a question that will be discussed in the chapter dealing with precedent. For the moment, it is enough to appreciate that not only did most colonists think it was, so too did the man who was expected to enforce it in the province where resistance was the strongest, Governor Francis Bernard of Massachusetts. "It must have been supposed," he wrote London at the height of the crisis, that

> such an innovation as a *Parliamentary taxation* would cause a great alarm, and meet with much opposition in most parts of *America:* it was quite new to the people, and had no visible bounds set to it; the *Americans* declared that they would not submit to it, before the Act passed. . . . Was this a time to introduce so great a novelty as a *Parliamentary* inland taxation into *America?*[19]

There is no need to make an exhaustive survey, to list the New England towns that voted the new taxes "grievous Innovations,"[20] or the numerous British writers who agreed.[21] What can be noted, however, is the strength of the rule against constitutional innovations. There were many forceful assertions of the doctrine during the revolutionary era,[22] few statements questioning it.[23] Although the principle belonged to the constitutional past, not the constitutional future, it retained a surprising hold on the constitutional imagination of British subjects, and would continue to do so throughout the controversy down to the time Americans declared their independence.

CHAPTER FOUR

THE TRADE REGULATION
CRITERION

Occasional American writers of the 1760s insisted there was no constitutional difference between internal and external taxation. The Stamp Act Congress made no distinction in the various pronouncements that it issued, nor did most of the colonial assemblies. As an anonymous London pamphlet in 1766 said of the constitutional argument: "Their unanimous Behaviour on the occasion [of the Stamp Act crisis], and the Remonstrances of several of their Assemblies, sufficiently declare they do not admit that the Parliament of *England* has any right to tax them without their consent."[1] That single sentence states the American whig constitutional position regarding the constitutionality of parliamentary-imposed taxes. Colonial whigs denied without qualification the authority of Parliament to tax them. Still, they used the adjective "internal" and occasionally the adjective "external," thereby sowing confusion sufficient to lead contemporary critics such as Chief Justice Thomas Hutchinson to chide them for their foolishness and later commentators to insist that because the distinction had been drawn it surely meant something.[2]

Hutchinson defined external taxation as "duties upon trade to be imposed for the sake of regulating trade," and was puzzled why anyone thought it better than internal taxation. "How," he asked, "are the Privileges of the People less affected [by external taxation] than by an internal tax?" "Is it any difference to me whether I pay three pounds ten shillings for a Pipe of wine to an officer of Impost or whether I pay the same Sum . . . to an excise Officer?"[3] For once during the revolutionary controversy there were many American whigs agreeing with Hutchinson. "[S]uppose for Instance," Samuel Adams suggested, "that some time hereafter under the Pretext of Regulating Trade only, a revenue should be design[e]d to be rais[e]d out of the Colonys, would it signify any thing whether it be called a Stamp Act or an Act for the Regulation of the Trade of America." William Hicks, a Pennsylvanian, had no doubts that the distinction was insignificant. "The one is precisely determined, while the other is more uncertain and eventual; but, in proportion to the sum raised, the effect will be exactly the same. It is taken for granted that the collection of a stamp duty would drain us of all the specie which we receive as a ballance in our *West-India* trade. If an exorbitant duty laid upon sugar and molasses produces the same effect, in what does the difference consist?"[4]

THE DICKINSON DISTINCTION

John Dickinson, the Pennsylvania farmer and lawyer, agreed with Hutchinson, Adams, and Hicks and also offered a solution to the problem they posed. Customs duties levied on Americans "*with intention to raise a revenue from us only,*" he wrote, "are as much *taxes* upon us as those imposed by the *Stamp-Act.*" He then asked the same question Hutchinson and Adams had asked and answered it as Hicks had answered it. "What is the difference in *substance* and *right*, whether the same sum is raised upon us by the rates mentioned in the *Stamp-Act*, on the *use* of paper, or by these [Townshend] duties on the importation of it [paper]. It is nothing but the edition of a former book, with a new title page." Both taxes were unconstitutional and should anyone argue one was legal because it was external, "I answer, with a total denial of the power of parliament to lay upon these colonies any 'tax' whatever."[5] To claim, however, that all parliamentary taxes on the colonies were unconstitutional was not the same as saying all customs duties imposed on America by Parliament were unconstitutional because not all customs duties were taxes. Dickinson thought the distinction could be drawn by asking the purpose for which specific customs duties were imposed.

Dickinson's distinction, offered in 1768 to explain why the Townshend duties were as unconstitutional as the Stamp Act, had previously been formulated during the Stamp Act crisis by Daniel Dulany of Maryland. "A Right to impose an internal Tax on the Colonies, without their Consent *for the single Purpose of Revenue*, is denied," Dulany asserted; "a

Right to regulate their Trade without their Consent is admitted. The Imposition of a Duty, may, in some Instances, be the proper Regulation." The question to be asked was whether the duty was levied for the purpose of trade regulation or for revenue. "[T]here is a clear and necessary Distinction between an Act imposing a Tax *for the single Purpose of Revenue*, and those Acts which have been made for the Regulation of Trade, and have produced some Revenue *in Consequence of their Effect* and Operation as *Regulations of Trade.*"[6]

Dulany's basic constitutional doctrine was clear: internal taxes for the purpose of revenue were unconstitutional; duties on trade for purpose of regulation were constitutional. He has, however, been criticized in some quarters for leaving unanswered the query whether duties imposed on trade for the primary purpose of raising a revenue were constitutional or unconstitutional. Dulany left the question open because he was a lawyer discussing the constitutionality of the Stamp Act. The matter of customs duties imposed to raise a revenue was irrelevant to the Stamp Act issue. It was not irrelevant to the constitutionality of the Townshend duties, however, and lawyer John Dickinson, unlike Dulany, had to address it. The Stamp Act, he claimed, had been the first tax the British Parliament had ever imposed on the colonies for the purpose of raising a revenue and for that reason it was unconstitutional. Further, the Stamp Act was an innovation in that it had been an internal tax. The Townshend duties were not new in that respect; customs tariffs had long been laid by Parliament upon the colonies. The Townshend duties differed from all customs duties previously promulgated by Parliament, Dickinson argued, because of the purpose for which they were imposed.

> Here [in the Townshend duties] we may observe an authority *expressly* claimed and exerted to impose duties on these colonies; not for the regulation of trade; not for the preservation or promotion of a mutually beneficial intercourse between the several constituent parts of the empire, heretofore the *sole objects* of parliamentary institutions; *but for the single purpose of levying money upon us.*

To make his constitutional objection, Dickinson employed familiar constitutional language: "This I call an innovation; and a most dangerous innovation."[7]

Dickinson's primary objective in formulating his distinction was to settle the imperial controversy by drawing a line of demarcation beyond which Parliament's authority to tax was not to extend. If he had a secondary objective, it was to end forever the idea that there was a constitutional difference between internal and external taxation.

This language is clear and important. A "TAX" means an imposition to raise money. Such persons therefore as speak of *internal* and *external* "TAXES," I pray may pardon me, if I object to that expression, as applied to the privileges and interests of these colonies. There may be *internal* and *external* IMPOSITIONS, founded on *different principles*, and having *different tendencies*, every "tax" being an imposition, tho' every imposition is not a "tax." But *all taxes* are founded on the *same principles*; and have the same tendency.

James Iredell later elucidated: "Taxes are the proper name for impositions, where money alone is the object. At the time of the Stamp Act this branch of the subject was not accurately canvassed."[8]

APPLICATION OF THE CRITERION

The trade-regulation criterion was the product of political expediency and constitutional practicalities. Dickinson, Dulany, Iredell, and other American constitutional commentators, wanting to remain part of the British Empire and to avoid parliamentary taxation, had to take a stand somewhere and a formula based on acknowledging the right to collect customs duties for the purpose of regulating trade provided a practical if not a foolproof solution. Imperialists such as Governor Bernard ridiculed the distinction. "The only difference," Bernard wrote, "between the Port duties declared to be for raising a Revenue, & those of which no such declaration is made is that in one the Intention is explicit; in the other it is implied."[9] Not so, Dickinson replied; the matter might turn on judgment but the distinction was real.

> The *nature* of any impositions laid by parliament on these colonies, must determine the *design* in laying them. It may not be easy in every instance to discover that design. Wherever it is doubtful, I think submission cannot be dangerous; nay, it must be right; for in my opinion, there is no privilege these colonies claim, which they ought in *duty* and *prudence* more earnestly to maintain and defend, than the authority of the *British* parliament to regulate the trade of all her dominions.[10]

Although Dickinson said it would not be difficult to ascertain when duties were constitutional, he suggested no specific test. Dulany had thought that the criterion could be the amount of revenue produced by the customs duty, but he also did not formulate a detailed scheme.[11]

One reason Dickinson and Dulany did not think the criterion posed practical difficulties was that both believed the constitution vested in Parliament the right to regulate colonial trade, a legal rule with which most colonial whigs would eventually disagree.[12] A second reason Dulany and Dickinson assumed that the distinction between duties for regulation of trade and duties for revenue would prove workable in practice was that they were lawyers. Both had read at the Middle Temple and were aware that much law turned on distinctions no more precise. Moreover, they knew that there was precedent for their distinction. Chief Baron Fleming, in one of the most famous taxation decisions of the seventeenth century, had upheld the right of King James, acting on his own and not with consent of Parliament, to increase the duty on imported currants. Without elaborating a specific rule, the court, much like Dickinson in the next century, found a distinction between the authority to tax and the authority to regulate trade and held the increase of the duty, a step that would have been questionable if exercised under the first authority, was constitutional as a trade regulation.[13]

Despite its soundness in common-law precedent, the American whig constitutional case against the Townshend duties, like the Dickinson distinction, failed to impress the British public, in part because it was misunderstood. There was a connection to this dual misunderstanding. After all, the Townshend duties were both the reason Dickinson formulated the distinction and its primary application. The duties were, as Governor Josiah Lyndon of Rhode Island told the king, "not for the regulation of commerce, merely, but for the express purpose of raising a revenue." That fact was beyond dispute, as it was stated in the very first clause of the statute's preamble. The duties were imposed in order "that a revenue should be raised, in your Majesty's dominions in America, for making a more certain and adequate provision for defraying the charge of the administration of justice, and the support of civil government in such provinces . . . and towards further defraying the expences of defending, protecting, and securing the said dominions."[14]

The constitutional issues with which the Townshend duties confronted Americans will be discussed in a following chapter. We are concerned here only with how the trade-regulation criterion was applied. There were fewer instances of its use than may be thought. One is provided by the New Hampshire House of Representatives and its belief that the British ministry designed the Townshend duties to avoid controversy, hoping that an indirect tax, a tax collected at the port of entry, would prove less objectionable than a direct tax such as the Stamp Act. No matter what the Townshend duties were called, the New Hampshire legislators pointed out, they were intended to raise a revenue, and raising revenue, not direct-indirect, was the constitutional test. "[T]he Duties Imposed by the late

Acts of Parliament, on some of the most necessary articles of Commerce, for the sole and express purpose of Raising a Revenue, are Equivalent to the most Direct Internal taxation." Georgia's Commons House of Assembly agreed, saying that the Townshend duties were an "Imposition of Internal Taxes."[15]

There could be hard cases, however. William Knox postulated one when he asked how the criterion would apply to a parliamentary tax placed on American manufacturers for the purpose of making colonial products more expensive than competing British goods: would that be legal as a regulation of trade? There was no answer to the question and none was relevant. American whigs had not formulaed the trade-regulation criterion to solve every potential controversy. Pragmatic and flexible, it could work only if Parliament avoided experimenting with new forms of taxes, did not expand the familiar and accepted operations of the customs service, and did not attempt to raise money in the colonies except incidentally to authentic trade regulation. Had these practicalities been heeded by Parliament, constitutional controversy could have been avoided, or so *Pelopidas* implied when he accused British writers of "playing with words" for saying there was a difference between internal and external taxation.

> I would ask these gentlemen whether they know why the colonies have in times past more strenuously opposed an internal than an external taxation, if they do not, I shall charitably inform them: an internal taxation has commonly been designed to raise a Revenue, and therefore could not by any means be fixed by the British Parliament upon the Americans without militating with a fundamental principle of British government, viz. that *no man can be taxed without his consent, either by himself in person, or by his representative;* whereas external taxation has been only designed for the regulation of trade, and if at any time an external tax is laid for the purpose of raising a Revenue, it is nothing better than an internal taxation.[16]

THE UTILITY OF THE CRITERION

Dickinson's distinction did not solve the imperial crisis over the authority of Parliament to impose taxation upon the North American colonies. Whether it could have remains speculative, for it never had a chance. The doctrine simply was not understood in London. Up until the very eve of the Revolution there were members of Parliament and pamphleteers who continued to insist that Americans accepted the constitutionality of external taxation, no matter that no one bothered to define the word; when American whigs said that any taxation for purposes of a revenue was unconstitutional, they were charged with being inconsistent.[17] Even Charles James Fox, speaking against the ministry and for the colonies, told the House of Commons that Americans had been compelled to abandon the original distinction between internal and external taxation once they realized that external taxes could be made "to answer all the purposes, and to produce all the mischiefs, of internal taxation." The same month Fox spoke, March 1775, a vote was taken in another legislative body of the British Empire, the New York Assembly. That vote is indicative of the persistence with which the word "internal" turned up in official colonial statements, a persistence helping to explain why people in Great Britain continued to think that the criterion turned on externality rather than on the purpose for which the levy was imposed. The Assembly was debating a petition to the House of Commons which contained a sentence that read, "An exemption from internal taxation, [etc.] . . . we esteem our undoubted and unalienable rights as Englishmen." A member moved to amend by striking the work "internal." The motion was defeated sixteen to eight. Anyone reading of that vote might reasonably conclude that the majority of New York's Assembly objected only to internal taxation and that external taxation, however defined, was constitutional. That supposition would be wrong. The New Yorkers refused to strike the word "internal" because they intended it to mean "illegal" or "unconstitutional," not because they were willing to accept an "external" tax imposed by Parliament for purposes of raising revenue, a fact they had demonstrated three weeks earlier when the same house that later refused to delete the word "internal" voted

> that his Majesty, and the Parliament of Great Britain, have a right to regulate the trade of the colonies, and to lay duties on articles that are imported directly into this colony from any foreign country or plantation, which may interfere with the products or manufactures of Great Britain, or any other parts of his Majesty's dominions; Excluding every idea of taxation, internal or external, for the purpose of raising a revenue on the subjects in America, without their consent.[18]

Responsibility for the confusion may lie with the word itself. In the beginning of the revolutionary controversy, American whigs, objecting to what can redundantly be termed an unprecedented innovation contrary to established imperial custom, had stressed the word "internal," and in time the expression "internal taxation" came to mean unconstitutional. Yet the term remained vague and, for a mere adjective, was ex-

tremely mischievous. Even when Americans unequivocably stated a different test, there were imperialists such as William Knox who inevitably
returned the discussion to internality. In the earliest statement of constitutional principles issued in the name of a majority of the colonies,
the Stamp Act Congress enunciated a constitutional rule to which American whigs would adhere until the Declaration of Independence eleven
years later. "That it is inseparably essential to the freedom of a people,
and the undoubted right of Englishmen, that no taxes should be imposed
on them, but with their own consent, given personally, or by their representatives." The statement was as clear as one could expect of law, yet
Knox did not cite it to inform his readers of American whig opposition
to parliamentary taxes imposed on them. "Here," he complained, "is no
distinction of taxes internal or external, regulation or revenue; all sorts
(if indeed there can be more than one sort) are alike unconstitutional,
old ones as well as new."[19] Colonial whigs, Knox was saying, were insincere and inconsistent concerning the internal-external distinction.

Even though misunderstood and misrepresented, the trade-regulation
criterion was not without effect. The earl of Hillsborough, secretary of
state for colonial affairs, came very near making it official British policy
in 1769 when he informed the colonial governors that the ministry had
no intention "to propose to Parliament to lay any further Taxes upon
America for the purpose of raising a Revenue." Hillsborough's promise
was nothing more than Dulany's formula, nothing less than Dickinson's
distinction. Although one can never be certain, it is difficult not to believe that the promise would have eased the constitutional crisis had Lord
North appreciated its utility and not enacted the tax on tea. By the time
North did make the final concession and adopted Hillsborough's promise
as official policy, it was too late to resolve the constitutional issue by settling the question of taxation only. In 1778, Parliament, groping for a
way to end the war, decided that Dickinson had been correct all along,
and passed a statute entitled "An Act for removing all Doubts and Apprehensions concerning Taxation by the Parliament of *Great Britain* in
any of the Colonies, Provinces, and Plantations in *North America*." The
preamble provided that to restore peace "it is expedient to declare that
the King and Parliament of *Great Britain* will not impose any Duty, Tax,
or Assessment, for the Purpose of raising a Revenue in any of the Colonies, Provinces, or Plantations." In the body of the act the promise was
made that no duty, tax, or assessment would be levied "except only such
Duties as it may be expedient to impose for the Regulation of Commerce."
The last occasion when the trade-regulation criterion, or any criterion
for that matter, had an opportunity to affect the crisis, at least for one
colony, occurred in 1780 when the British temporarily reestablished royal

government in Georgia. Meeting the loyalist assembly, Governor James Wright urged the legislators to accept the statute of 1778, to accept, that is, the constitutional rule for which another loyalist, Daniel Dulany, had pleaded fifteen years before.

> The point of Taxing America is wholly given up by the King and Parliament, and only a Power reserved to impose such Duties, as may be expedient for the regulation of Commerce (which Power even the warmest Zealots for America never denied to Parliament) and the Nett Produce of those duties, are in every instance to be applied to the use of the Province.[20]

The constitutional formula was familiar but too late.

CHAPTER FIVE

THE SECOND ORIGINAL CONTRACT

The lesson of the internal-external material leads to one conclusion. Most American whigs claimed that the colonies enjoyed an absolute immunity from parliamentary taxation imposed for the purpose of raising a revenue. The next question to be asked is what were the constitutional grounds upon which this immunity was based. The answer is that American whigs, knowing they were engaged in constitutional litigation, argued as lawyers, in the alternative. Among the several legal theories upon which they based their constitutional claim of not contributing to an imperial tax were English rights, the authority of custom, the doctrine of precedent, and the principle of consent. These topics will be covered in the following several chapters. The first to be discussed relates to the various defenses arising from the constitutional right of contract.

The extent to which the language of contract colored political debates during the eighteenth century is remarkable. Almost every issue could be analyzed in terms of the elements of consent, obligation, and expectation, and arguments could be phrased with such words as "debt," "compact," "purchase," and "consideration." Appreciation of this vocabulary and its meaning is important both because it clarifies what was being said and because to the extent that contracts were argued we are furnished some evidence with which to measure the importance of natural law during the revolutionary era. When eighteenth-century people based claims to rights upon contract they were relying on constitutional authority more positive than natural law. As the Reverend Jonathan Lee said when delivering Connecticut's 1766 election sermon, "Dominion, or right to rule, is evidently founded neither in nature or grace, but compact, and consideration." That constitutional principle was especially true for the colonies, the governor of Rhode Island thought, as the first settlers "came out from a kingdom renowned for liberty, from a constitution founded on compact." It was, in fact, a constitution founded not only on compact but by compact. "By this most beneficent compact British subjects are to be governed only agreeable to laws to which themselves have some way consented, and are not to be compelled to part with their property but as it is called for by the authority of such laws."[1]

As remarkable as the extent to which the language of common-law contract was employed in revolutionary political discussion was the ease and versatility with which it slipped into the debates. Its use may be implicit evidence that the participants were conscious of the fact that they were dealing with a crisis as much constitutional as political, one that could be solved if a satisfactory constitutional formula could be agreed on. The object was "to establish a form of government, a compact, between Great-Britain and its Colonies, wherein the power of the former, and the liberties of the latter, shall be fairly and clearly ascertained." When war with France threatened in 1771, Edmund Burke used the concept of contract to warn of the national peril unless the imperial squabble was resolved. "[T]he quarrel is as far from being compromised as ever," he said of the constitutional crisis; "before America, therefore, can heartily concur in any measures which it may be necessary for Britain to take, her grievances must be redressed; and he who shall advise hostilities against the Bourbon compact, till a compact shall take place between Britain and her Colonies, is a foe or a driveller."[2]

It would not do to think only of bargain and exchange. The terms of the contract did not have to be arrived at by formal negotiation. They could be implied from events, circumstances, or silence. In 1766, for example, a "British American" warned the colonists not to rejoice over repeal of the Stamp Act if the repeal was "not *at least a tacit compact that the parliament of* Great Britain *will never again use the right of taxing us without our* consents." The terms could also be explicit, spelled out in specific details with an offer and acceptance. In 1775, when Parliament proposed renouncing the right of taxation in return for colonial payments of requisitions, Governor William Franklin urged the New Jersey legislature to accept the offer and bind the contract. Parliamentary taxation, he promised, would not be exercised "so long [as] the Colonies shall perform their Part of the Compact."[3]

With such language shaping the substance of ideas, it cannot be surprising that colonial whigs not only thought of their quarrel with Great Britain in terms of promise, obligation, and breach, but premised their defense against some of London's constitutional demands in contract theory. There were at least four, if not five, contracts that were postulated and argued on each side of the revolutionary debate. They were separate contracts and it is important they be kept separated, as failure to do so could lead to confusion. For example: the first contract, the social compact, was hardly ever cited during the revolutionary era; but because some commentators have confused it with the second or the original contract (and also because it is a natural-law doctrine), it has been accorded a significance that would surely baffle people of the eighteenth century.

The five contracts argued in support of either the colonial whig or the imperialist side during the revolutionary constitutional debates were: (1) the social compact under which individuals formed themselves into a society; (2) the original or constitutional or government contract between ruler and ruled, and, in the special situation of North America, between the Stuart kings of England and the first settlers of the colonies; (3) the second original contract, a novation of the original contract; (4) the imperial contract providing that Americans would contribute financially to imperial defense in return for Great Britain's military protection; and (5) the commercial contract, in answer to or in novation of the imperial contract, stipulating that Great Britain exercised a monopoly over and enjoyed the profits of the colonial trade in lieu of receiving any further compensation for providing imperial defense.

The Original Contract

A book dealing with the revolutionary controversy over the constitutional authority of Parliament to tax the colonies for purpose of revenue is not the place to discuss in detail either the social contract or the original contract. The social contract simply did not contribute to the debates in any significant manner. The original contract, although the most important of the five contracts argued, was also not material to the debate over taxation; it was raised primarily against Parliament's claim to possess constitutional authority to bind the colonies by legislative decree and consideration and therefore is best postponed to a volume on the legislative causes of the American Revolution.[4] For the purposes of this book, then, it is more useful merely to summarize the theories behind the two contracts and illustrate their use by noting arguments advanced on the few occasions they were applied to the issue of parliamentary taxation.

The social contract was a legal fiction explaining how individuals came together and formed society. The constitutional or government contract — called the original contract in the eighteenth century — was an implied agreement between ruler and ruled from which the powers and limitations of government were inferred.[5] The first is a theory of the origin of government, the second a theory of the constitution of government. It would be unnecessary even to mention the social contract had it not been rendered important by nineteenth- and twentieth-century writers confusing it with the original contract, a mistake seldom committed in the eighteenth century. After the Revolution had begun and Americans, creating new political arrangements, had to think about the nature of government, the social contract assumed some importance in both constitutional and political theory. That period and those issues should not be confused with the revolutionary era. The social contract had a place in the debates over constitution making, not the debates about the constitutional authority of the British Parliament.

Examples of revolutionary constitutional arguments based on the social contract are rare. In the Boston Declaration of 1772, a document that is probably the one official statement adopted by a government agency (the town meeting) controlled by American whigs that depended more on natural law than on constitutional law for authority, the creation of both a social contract and an original contract are claimed as natural rights. The famous resolves of the town of Abingdon, Massachusetts, condemned for radicalism in the House of Commons, are even more revealing; they provide as clear and detailed a comparison and contrast of the social and original contracts as can be found anywhere in the revolutionary literature. In the first paragraph, the people of Abingdon defined the social contract; in the second, they described in remarkable fullness the original contract as they interpreted it. They began by declaring that nations and individuals while in the state of nature were "naturally free."

> Voted, as the opinion of this town, that mankind, while in their aforesaid natural state, always had, and now have, a *right* to enter into compact and form societies, and *erect* such kind of government as the majority of them shall judge most for the public good.
>
> Voted, as the opinion of this town, that the right of sovereignty over the inhabitants of this province, claimed by any former British King, or by his present Majesty, by succession, was derived to them, and is derived to him, by recognition of the forefathers of this coun-

try, of his then Majesty, as their sovereign, upon the plan of the English constitution: who accordingly plighted his royal faith, that himself, his heirs and successors, had, and would grant, establish, and ordain, that all and every of his subjects, which should go to, and inhabit this province, and every of their children which should happen to be born there, or on the seas in going thither, or in returning from thence, should have and enjoy all *liberties and immunities of free and natural subjects*, within any of their dominions, *to all intents, constructions, and purposes whatsoever*, as if they, and every of them, were born in the realm of England.[6]

The distinction between the two contracts should be kept in mind because although the social contract was seldom mentioned when Americans discussed the authority to tax,[7] the original contract was utilized in arguments that cannot be comprehended if the two are confused and the social compact is thought of when the original contract was meant. The warning is for us, not the eighteenth century. We tend to think of only one contract, the social contract, and forget the original. During the revolutionary era usage was generally unambiguous because facts about the contract were stated. If attention is paid to what was said, the contract referred to is evident. Here are three samplings of the language employed. The first was written when the Stamp Act was still only a rumor and is a clear reference to the colonial original contract, an element of which, providing evidence of the terms, was the charter of government. "As to those that hold under charter," a Rhode Islander asked of the proposed tax, "would it not be a direct breach of that compact and those conditions, on the faith whereof the adventurers embarked their lives and fortunes." Maryland's Daniel Dulany raised the same issue after the Stamp Act had become a reality: Americans claimed exemption from taxes imposed without their consent, he argued, "upon Principles on which their Compact with the Crown was originally founded." And when repeal of the law was being debated, William Pitt also referred to the same contract. "You have," he warned the Commons, "broken the original compact if you have not a right of taxation."[8]

Unlike the social contract, the original contract did not depend on theories about the state of nature or natural rights. It was implied from historical events and based upon principles of government that the person citing the contract either hoped to establish or wanted continued. In the case of the original American contract, the historical event was the departure of seventeenth-century English people from the mother country and their emigration to the colonies. Those first settlers, Governor Hopkins explained, "removed on a firm reliance of a solemn compact and royal promise and grant that they and their successors forever should be free, should be partakers and sharers in all the privileges and advantages of the then English, now British constitution." What the original contract said and how it was employed in constitutional forensic has to be deferred to consideration of the authority of Parliament to legislate for the colonies as it was on that question that its various provisions were discussed and analyzed. To clarify the meaning of the original contract as it related to the taxation controversy, a brief summary of its stipulations, as explained by a London magazine, is useful.

> Before their [the first settlers in the colonies] departure, the terms of their freedom, and the relation they should stand in to the mother country, in their emigrant state were fully settled, they were to remain subject to the king, and dependant on the kingdom of *Great Britain*. In return they were to receive protection, and enjoy all the rights and privileges of freeborn *Englishmen*.[9]

Related to the question of parliamentary taxation, the original contract connoted that the first settlers of the colonies "undertook and affected the settlement of *America*, with an assurance that they could not be divested of their property and liberty without their consent given in their respective assemblies." That assurance was implied from the fact under the contract that they were to enjoy the rights and privileges of freeborn English citizens. And that right, the right not to be taxed without consent, was not only an English right, it was stipulated in the original contract that the English people had earlier concluded with their kings. "It is a fundamental maxim of English law," a London magazine writer explained in 1770, "that there is a contract between the crown and subjects; if so, the crown cannot lay on any tax, or any other burden, on the subject, but agreeable to the original contract by authority of parliament; neither can the lords properly concur, or the commons frame a tax-bill for any other purpose but the support of the crown and government, consistent with the original contract between that and the people." What was stipulated in the original English contract in Great Britain, the town of Boston instructed, was carried over and incorporated into the original American contract.

> The Constitutional Mode by which Legislation and Taxation are conducted in Great-Britain, being nothing more or less than the Exercise of the Power of the People by their Representatives: This form of Government is extended by sacred Compact to the English Dominions in America, therefore the Privileges and Powers of the Commons of this Colony respecting Legislation and Taxation, are to all

> Intents and Purposes, as full, express, and uncontroulable within the
> *Colony*, as those usually exercised by the Commons of Great-Britain,
> within the *Realm*, and *alike* subjected to the Revision of the King.[10]

An important point that must be emphasized if the original-contract doctrine is to be understood properly is that it was not formulated to solve the Stamp Act crisis. Also worth reiterating, even though obvious, is that it did not originate in or depend upon natural-law theory. It not only was part of, but often had been pleaded as a central doctrine of, the ancient constitution of both England and Great Britain. Nor was the principle of taxation only by consent a new stipulation in the original contract. It too was a familiar constitutional maxim long before commencement of the revolutionary debate over parliamentary taxation, as is illustrated by two examples, one from the colonies in 1691, the other from the English bar in 1725. The first, contained in a sentence written to justify the New England revolution of 1688 against the governor appointed by James II, argued that taxation by consent was part of the original contract and defined both doctrines just as American whigs would from 1764 to 1776.

> [T]here was an *Original Contract* between the King and the first
> Planters in *New-England*, the King promising them, if they at their
> own cost and charge would subdue a Wilderness, and enlarge his
> Dominions, they and their Posterity after them should enjoy such
> Priviledges as are in their Charters expressed, of which that of not
> having Taxes imposed on them without their own consent was one.

The second illustration is provided by a common lawyer explaining the original contract in common-law terms and relating it to the authority of taxation. It was, he wrote,

> an implied original Contract betwixt the Governors and governed.
> For as no Man is by an Law intended to part with any Part of his
> Property without a Promise from the Receiver to give him an adequate Return, whence the very parting with a Shilling's worth of
> any merchantable Commodity is sufficient to entitle the Party, without proof of any express Promise for that Purpose, to recover an adequate Recompence. Is not the Reason much stronger to admit a tacit
> Contract amongst the Members of a Voluntary Society, and to suppose they did not part not only with a Part but all their Properties,
> even with their Liberty (if it can be parted with) and for nothing too?[11]

It was on the basis of this familiar and established constitutional doctrine that Americans contended that the Stamp Act was a breach of the "compact between K[ing] and subject," depriving them of "Power and Privileges . . . secured to our Ancestors by solemn Covenant between them and the King of England, and perpetuated by the Charter to their latest Posterity." Because the "principal privilege implied" in the "original contract," as the Massachusetts House explained, "is a freedom from all taxes, but such as they shall consent to in person, or by representatives of their free choice and election," the Virginia House was confident it could state the exact terms of that contract. It was

> their ancient and inestimable Right of being governed by such Laws respecting their internal Polity and Taxation as are derived from their own Consent with the Approbation of their Sovereign or his Substitute: A Right which as Men and Descendants of *Britons*, they have ever quietly possessed since first by Royal Permission and Encouragement they left the Mother Kingdom to extend its Commerce and Dominion.[12]

THE SETTLEMENT CONTRACT

The third contract argued during the taxation part of the revolutionary controversy was an alternative version of the original contract and could be called the second original contract, the second constitutional contract, the second government contract, or, if a descriptive title will help, the settlement contract. It was based on the factual assumption that since the colonies had been settled at English expense and sustained during their early years by English taxpayers, Americans owed in return a debt that was to be repaid by acceding to parliamentary taxation. The debt was premised on several theories — gratitude,[13] duty,[14] reasonable expectations,[15] and justice[16] — but in the most frequently stated and fully developed argument it rested on contract, a contract based on a benefit conferred analogous to the *quid pro quo* of the common-law action of debt. The mother country, it was argued, had supported the colonies "at considerable expence" during their infancy, and they "owed" her for "the blood and treasure which it has cost her to defend and establish them." William Knox explained:

> They were unable to subsist, much less to protect themselves. The bounty, the confidence, and humanity of individuals in England were freely exercised towards them; and the power of the state, raised and maintained at the sole expence of the people of England, was fully exerted in their behalf. The people of England have, therefore, a right to reap advantage from the success of the adventurers.

In its most extreme, the second original contract provided grounds for the claim not only of a debt, but of ownership. "I still *call them our Colonies*," one writer asserted as late as 1776. "They are ours by Birth, by Nutrition, Tuition, Support and Protection!—They are ours by dear bought Purchase of many Millions of Money and Rivers of Blood, shed in their Defence!"[17]

The second original contract was most memorably interjected into the revolutionary debate when George III cited it as justification for augmenting the armed forces his ministry was ordering to North America to quash colonial efforts to establish an independent nation. "I need not dwell upon the fatal effects of the success of such a plan," the king told Parliament in a speech from the throne. "The object is too important, the spirit of the British nation too high, the resources with which God hath blessed her too numerous, to give up so many colonies which she has planted with great industry, nursed with great tenderness, encouraged with many commercial advantages, and protected and defended at much expence of blood and treasure." Thomas Jefferson, reading the speech in Virginia, became so upset that he wrote a long refutation of the argument, perhaps intended for publication, that takes up seven pages of the most recent edition of his papers. A year later, in the "Original Rough draught" of the Declaration of Independence, Jefferson claimed that colonial settlement was "effected at the expence of our own blood & treasure, unassisted by the wealth or the strength of Great Britain."[18] American whigs reading these words did not ask for proof; they long had been convinced. Of all the factual arguments drawn from history there was none they sustained more successfully than that the contention that "the colonies were planted and nursed at the expence of the British nation" was "an untruth."[19]

The American answer to the British claim of a second or counter original contract was based entirely on fact. Concisely stated by the people of Ipswich, Massachusetts, the argument was that "when our Fathers left their Native Country . . . they came of their Own accord and at their own Expense and took possession of a country they were obliged to Buy or Fight for and to which the Nation had no more Right than the Moon." Pennsylvania, its House of Representatives asserted, had been settled and expanded "without the least Expence to the Mother State," and Virginia, the people of Fairfax County pointed out, "was not Settled at the National expence of England, but at the private expence of the Adventurers, our Ancestors, by solemn Compact with, and under the auspices and protection of the British Crown." The same facts were argued from the commencement of the revolutionary controversy to the very end. "Hath the government of England," a Rhode Islander asked in August 1764, "been at any expense in supporting the colonies of *New England?* No.— Is one farthing balance due unto them, in the whole account from the first planting of *New England* to this time? No!" "Those who began the Settlement of New England," another Rhode Islander was still arguing, over a decade later, "were unsupported & lost half their Number the first Winter they were in America and the Survivors carried on the Settlement at their own Expence."[20]

American whigs were so confident of their case that they not only challenged the imperialists to produce some record of public grants made by the British government to the first settlements,[21] they were even willing to concede a few important facts. New York perhaps, depending upon how one interpreted the evidence surrounding its conquest from the Dutch, and Georgia and Nova Scotia certainly, had received financial support at the time of their settlement.[22] Georgia, the most important exception as it had received annual subsidies for almost two decades, could be explained away as a departure from precedent, an outpost in Britain's wars against Spain,[23] or by claiming the funds were designed more for Parliament's spoils system than to benefit Americans.[24]

As the champions of parliamentary taxation pleaded the second original or settlement contract in novation of the American whigs' reliance on the original contract, the whigs only had to deny the facts of the second contract. For the most part, they did just that, pointing out that first England and then Britain spent nothing on the early colonies, built no forts, maintained no troops, and patrolled none of the coast.[25]

An alternative answer to denying the facts of the second original contract was to assert that the facts proved no contract: "that the bounties which *Great Britain* is said so lavishly to have bestowed upon us, are meted out in the common political measure, with an evident intention *finally to promote her own particular* benefit"; "That, whatever assistance the people of Great Britain might have given to the people of the colonies, it must have been given either from motives of humanity and fraternal affection, or with a view of being one day repaid for it, and not as the price of their liberty and independence." But what if an imperialist changed the argument and cited either fraternal affection or expectation of repayment as consideration for the contract? American whigs had an answer: neither was sufficient to create a contract. "Ought not gratitude to oblige them to submit?" A.M. asked. "This is the first instance of a tax being laid on gratitude or of ingratitude being declared *High Treason*, otherwise, God knows where rebellion would end." Or why not a contract in the nature of the civil law's quasi-contracts arising from the relationship between the parties? "From Infant Establishments, entitled to all the Indulgencies which a fostering Mother could grant, they were now grown into great and flourishing States. Reason therefore on the Side of the Mother Country, warranted the Exaction of some Compensation for her past Services."[26] American whigs could have answered by simply denying the facts, as some did. A remarkable effort, however, was also made to develop a legal defense. To the extent that this plea can be analogized to the *quantum meruit* count in common-law assumpsit, American whigs replied that the *quantum meruit* was canceled by the debt Great Britain owned the eighteenth-century colonists for what their seventeenth-century ancestors had done: that the settlement contract was set off by the settlement debt.

THE SETTLEMENT DEBT

American whigs' answer of law to the British claim for a *quantum meruit* or a repayment for services rendered at the time of settlement, was based on the contractual theory that they had placed Great Britain in their debt. After all, London probably would not have been so brash as to attempt to tax the colonies in payment for past services "had not the good services of the colonies been very strangely forgotten. Services, in which the colonists, at a vast expence of blood, toil, and treasure, have greatly contributed to the wealth, power, and glory of the British empire: By which they have, at their own costs, added to it a vast territory, much larger than the isle of Great-Britain." From these premises it followed that the early settlers, rather than putting themselves into England's debt by being supported by the mother country and, as a consequence, losing the right of self-taxation, instead merited the "Favour" of Great Britain. They merited it "by giving an almost boundless Extent to the *British* Empire, expanding its Trade, increasing its Wealth, and augmenting that Power which renders it so formidable to all *Europe*."[27]

The debt Great Britain owed to the colonies for the toil and hardships of the first generations of settlers could be explained by various legal theories. As the debt alleged was almost always pleaded in defense of what the colonists called "the rights of Englishmen," it would be repetitive to explore the implications of the theory at this point. It would be more useful to sum it up by quoting an instance of the settlement-debt argument applied to the issue of parliamentary taxation. The existence of the settlement debt was often explained in the contractual language of payment as consideration. Here was how the Pennsylvania House of Representatives stated the doctrine:

> That the Colonists here have paid a valuable Consideration to the Crown for the said Charter and Laws, by planting and improving a Wilderness, far distant from their Mother Country, at a vast Expense, and the Risk of many Lives from the savage Inhabitants, whereby they have greatly encreased the Trade and Commerce of the Nation, and added a large Tract of Improved Country to the Crown, without any Aid from, or Expence to, *Great-Britain* in the said Settlement.

The obligation created by the consideration paid was less an executory contract than a debt.

> It was but a debt due to these brave adventurers, and their immediate descendants that the right of taxation should be vested in people upon the spot, who in the nature of things must be supposed, to know the affairs of the province better than the people at the distant of four thousand miles, between whom and them, there runs an incessant and tempestuous ocean.

Of course, it was possible to state the same idea without invoking the language of contract or debt. It could be put in terms of reasonable expectation, an argument not that Parliament had no authority to tax but why Parliament should be reluctant to tax. "I will only remind you," Jared Ingersoll told Thomas Whately when asked to comment on the proposed Stamp Act, "that our people dont yet believe that the British Parliament really mean to impose internal taxes upon us without our Consent, especially the people of this Colony who beside their Charter of Priviledge granted them by K[ing] Ch[arles] 2d have, they say, planted themselves & subsisted hitherto without one farthings Expence to the Crown."[28] This argument for Connecticut could have been made on behalf of at least ten other of the whig colonies.

CHAPTER SIX

THE IMPERIAL CONTRACT

The fourth contract contributing to the revolutionary debates along with the social contract, the original contract, and the settlement contract was the imperial contract. On the matter of Parliament's authority to tax the colonies, the imperial contract was perhaps the most important and certainly the most frequently mentioned of the contracts, and, in fact, was seldom if ever cited to support any constitutional argument other than that authority. Stated simply in nonlegal terms, the contract exacted colonial payment for imperial protection.

> [I]f the COLONIES constitute Parts and Portions of the BRITISH EM-PIRE, frequently claiming, and as often enjoying the powerful PRO-TECTION of the LEGISLATURE, at an immense Expense of Blood and Treasure, to the main Body of the Kingdom; it follows, as clear as the Sun, that the same COLONIES ought to be subject to A MODERATE TAXATION, imposed by the supreme Legislature upon them in common with their Fellow Subjects, for the Protection and Safety of the whole; and for the Relief of the main Body, from the Burthen incurred on their Account.

As originally stated, the claim that the British were owed support by the colonies — a claim of quasi-contract alleging an obligation great enough to justify direct imperial taxation — consisted of two counts. The first count alleged that current taxes in Great Britain were unusually heavy because "a great part of the national debt" had been "contracted" by the mother country "protecting" the North American settlements "from the arbitrary attempts of their implacable enemies." The second count asserted that this huge debt had been contracted during the Seven Years War when imperial forces had made the continent safe for British America.[1]

Although many writers on the imperial side of the revolutionary debate assumed the validity of the imperial contract, few who gave its existence any thought were willing to state it as a constitutional absolute and say, as did Henry Goodricke, that its existence and terms were "not of dispute." Most of those invoking the imperial contract attempted to develop some contractual theory to establish its legality. "[T]he first and great principle of all government, is, *that support is due in return for protection*," was probably the explanation with the widest acceptance. "*On this acknowledged principle*," it was said, "the *stamp-act was planned*." That claim seems to be correct; George Grenville, the minister responsible for the Stamp Act, made the argument several times. "Protection and obedience are reciprocal," he told the Commons. "Great Britain protects America; America is bound to yield obedience." By obedience he meant the payment of taxes, and why not? The Americans were obligated to reciprocate. "When they want the protection of this kingdom, they are always very ready to ask it. . . . The nation has run itself into an immense debt to give them their protection." It was only proper, then, that they contribute a small share toward the public expense, an expense arising from themselves.[2]

There were several other grounds or alternative arguments upon which the imperial-contract claim was based. The simplest, as might be expected, was moral obligation.[3] Another was equality; the British taxpayers were said to be bearing an unequal share of the financial costs of defending the Empire.[4] A third was equity; "The people of *England*," one writer reasoned, "are taxed in Consequence of the last *American* War; is it not equitable that the *Americans* should bear their Part?" Governor William Franklin seems not only to have thought so, but to have felt the equity strong enough to give rise to an equitable contract. Do not forget the benefits received from the mother country, he told the New Jersey Council and Assembly, bidding his listeners "to acknowledge that it is to her Support, held forth at the Expence of her Blood and Treasure, that they principally owe that Security which hath raised them to their present State of Opulence and Importance. In this Situation, therefore, Justice requires that they should, in Return, contribute according to their respective Abilities to the *Common Defence*."[5] The theory of an equitable contract could be explained not only in terms of both justice and equity — it

was "just and equitable" that Americans "contribute a reasonable proportion for the support of that government, by which they are protected"
— but also in terms of equality, or a theory of equitable equality. "[W]ill
not the government become *unjust* and *oppressive*," John Shebbeare asked,
"if the supreme authority of this realm suffer the *Americans* to remain
untaxed, whilst we groan under the burthen of seventy millions of debt,
raised to support them in the last war? A war, begun, in order to settle
the confines of the colonies, and concluded in freeing *them* from their
Canadian foes."[6]

The strongest arguments for the imperial-contract theory were those
analogizing the contract to a common-law obligation, utilizing either the
benefit-conferred rule of the action of debt, the detriment-suffered test
of *indebitatus assumpsit*, or the unjust-enrichment doctrine of quasi-
contracts. The benefit conferred or the *quid pro quo* of the debt is obvious. Either the war Great Britain had fought on the colonies' behalf
had been so costly "that those who had reaped the chief Benefit, should
contribute a Portion towards defraying the Expence which had attended
the Acquisition," or "[t]he advantages the colonies obtained by the peace,
and the debt incurred by the late war, undertaken for their defence only,
with other considerations too numerous to be mentioned here, required
some retribution from them." An argument made in 1776 relied upon
both the benefit-conferred and the detriment-suffered theories. "We have
fought, we have conquered for the Americans. We have restored Peace
to their Possessions at Home, and freed them from Apprehensions of Disturbances from Abroad. In so doing we have contracted a Debt too heavy
for English Shoulders to bear."[7]

A distinctive aspect of an unjust-enrichment doctrine is that it was used
almost exclusively to prove a contract imposed by law. "[N]o man," Samuel Johnson explained, "has a right to security of government without
bearing his share of its inconveniences. Those who increase the expenses
of the public ought to supply their proportion of the expenses increased.
The payment of fleets and armies may be justly required from those for
whose protection fleets and armies are employed." The same contract could
also be theorized on grounds of offer and acceptance. All one had to
assume or prove was that the colonies had requested protection, the mother
country had provided it, and the imperial contract was implied.[8]

DEFENSES OF LAW

Allegations about the imperial contract upset American whigs much
more than its strength as constitutional law would seem to warrant. They
went to great lengths to disprove the implied obligation, not only postu-

lating the fifth or the commercial contract as a plea in novation, but also marshaling elaborate legal theories and detailed factual evidence to deny the imperial contract in both law and fact. There is no clearer gauge of the concern felt by colonial whigs than that, from the very start to the very end of the revolutionary era, they framed legal and factual arguments supporting their side of the case. Both the Massachusetts House of Representatives during the Stamp Act crisis and Benjamin Franklin while he was a delegate to the second Continental Congress devoted surprising amounts of time to the effort.[9]

The chief legal defense focused on the Seven Years War, the conflict that had burdened Great Britain with the debt Parliament wanted the colonies to share. One American answer in law was that the war had not been entirely a British affair; there had been reciprocal duties. Although the colonies had received help, they had also furnished aid to the imperial armed forces and thus had contributed their fair share to the war effort.[10] The argument appears at first glance to be an argument of fact, as it was, but just as significantly it was also one of law. It was an argument of fact because it reduced the British claim of defending the colonies to a contributing role, denying that the mother country alone had won the imperial victory. As an argument of law it provided a legal answer to that element in the imperial contract resting on the proposition that Americans should pay for their own defense. The colonies were denying the contractual obligation not only on the grounds that there was no contract, but also that they had paid and were paying all that legally could be demanded. "On no Occasion," the New York Assembly insisted, "can we be justly reproached for with-holding a necessary Supply, our Taxes have been equal to our Abilities, and confessed to be so by the Crown; for Proof of which we refer to the Speeches of our Governors in all Times of War."[11]

In terms of law, American contributions to the war effort could be argued to sustain several legal arguments. One was that British protection had been part of a joint or imperial struggle for which no debt was owed unless Britain also owed the colonies a debt: that there was a legal set off, both sides having made contributions proportionally fair. The same evidence was also used to substantiate two tests Americans applied to prove they owed no debt. The first test was that the colonists had provided to the war effort everything asked by the London government. The legal conclusion was so obvious that it was not always stated: since the colonies had done everything they were asked to do and since they had not been asked or expected to make the same war effort Britain had made, they could not legally be charged with a debt.[12]

The second legal test Americans applied from the evidence was that the British were estopped from alleging that a debt was owed because the British had previously acknowledged that none was due. That fact was "apparent, from the several Grants of Parliament, to reimburse them [the colonies] Part of the heavy Expences they were at in the late war in America." Surely the House of Commons never would have voted these sums had the British people not believed the Americans had contributed more than their part to the war effort. "We call upon you yourselves, to witness our loyalty and attachment to the common interest of the whole empire," the first Continental Congress demanded of the British people. "Did you not thank us for our zeal, and even reimburse us large sums of money, which, you confessed, we had advanced beyond our proportion and far beyond our abilities." Thomas Hutchinson thought so, for he said that the contributions were so far beyond colonial abilities "that the Parliament was convinced that the burden would be insupportable" and that was why it voted reimbursement. Acting "under that Conviction" that "our Contribution surpassed our Strength," the New York Assembly told the Commons, Parliament "thought it but just to take off Part of the Burthen, to which we had loyally and voluntarily submitted." Daniel Dulany, giving the argument a different emphasis, suggested that if in fact there was a debt owed for protection, the practice of reimbursement estopped Britain from collecting it. "The Faith of *Great Britain*," he argued, "hath been engaged in the most solemn Manner, to Repay the Colonies the Monies levied by internal Taxations for the Support of the War.— Is it consistent with that Faith to tax them towards sinking the Debt in Part incurred by that Re-payment?"[13]

Another argument at law was the contention that the imperial contract was not a valid ground for justifying parliamentary taxation of the colonies because military protection could not be cited to raise a binding debt since such protection was due the Americans from the mother country under the original contract between the king and the first settlers. "Before their departure," the government of Rhode Island insisted, "the terms they removed upon, and the relation they should stand in to the mother country, in their emigrant state, were settled. They were to remain subject to the King, and dependent on the kingdom of England; in return, they were to receive protection, and enjoy all the privileges of free born Englishmen."[14]

The argument that could be described as "the most legal" of all those American whigs made against the validity of the imperial contract was that, as a matter of law, the imperial contract was not a legal contract. Two grounds supported this contention. The first related to the claim explained in the last paragraph: under the original contract, Great Britain had a legal duty to protect the colonies. "[I]t is often urged that the nation hath been at a vast expence in defending us," a *New Englander* wrote in the *Providence Gazette.* "I grant it: but at the same time I aver it to have been their duty. The nation, in consideration of our subjection, and our country being part of the dominions of the crown, were bound by the laws of God and Nature to protect us and our properties, if able." Eleven years later, Franklin made much the same argument though he thought the consideration was that the colonies had joined Britain in all her wars and were not permitted "to keep peace with any power she declared her enemy." "Under such circumstances," Franklin asked, "when at her instance we made nations our enemies, whom we might otherwise have retained our friends, we submit it to the common sense of mankind, whether her protection of us in these wars was not our *just due,* and to be claimed of *right,* instead of being received as a *favor?*"[15]

The other ground for contending there was no imperial contract was the legal argument that protection alone, without a promise of repayment, could not impose an obligation. "[A]dmitting that much British blood was spent in the defence of those Colonies," a London writer asked, "[a]re the Americans *ungrateful* or *rebellious,* because they have been protected, to suffer for this reason, impositions that are unjust? Has a man, because he grants you a favor, therefore a right to do you an injury, and deprive you of your indubitable birthrights?" A Massachusetts lawyer thought the answer was no. "Put the case," Oxenbridge Thacher suggested, "that the town of *Portsmouth* or any other seaport had been besieged and the like sums expended in its defence, could any have thought that town ought to be charged with the expense?"[16] More commonly, the colonies were analogized to European nations. "The mother-country has spent her blood and treasure in supporting, at different times, *France* against *Spain,* and *Spain* against *France, Prussia* against *Hungary,* and *Hungary* against *Prussia,* and so on, without end. Does this give our parliament a right to tax all Europe?" The answer was always the same. "If Britain has protected the property of America, it does not constitute her the owner of that property. She has, for her own sake, protected, in their turns, almost every country in Europe, but that does not make her the proprietor of those countries, or give her a power of taxation over them."[17]

There was one other objection at law to the imperial contract. The payment that it stipulated — i.e., the right of Parliament to impose taxes on the colonies for purposes of raising revenue — was constitutionally exorbitant for the consideration rendered. "Did the protection we received annul our rights as men, and lay us under an obligation of being miserable?" Samuel Adams asked. A Connecticut governor told the earl of Hillsborough that after having entered the war and contributing to it "beyond our abilities," the discovery that Parliament planned to tax the colonies for the cost of the war was "peculiarly grievous and afflicting."[18] The Americans had expected that their contribution to the war would provide them security, the London agent of the Massachusetts House of Representatives noted. "How great then was their surprize to find their liberties taken from them, under a pretence of providing for that very security." The constitutional price asked was far too high for the imperial contract to be enforceable.[19]

DEFENSES OF FACT

A surprising aspect of the imperial-contract controversy is that American whigs spent as much time refuting the facts of the contract as they did the law. They did so, Maryland's Dulany explained, for political reasons. The scheme of drawing taxes from the colonies was popular in Great Britain where little thought was given to the justification. "It is affirmed to those who cannot detect the Fallacy of the Assertion, that Millions have been expended *solely* in the Defence of *America*. They believe it, and thence are easily persuaded that the Claim of a Contribution from the Colonies is just and equitable, and that any Measure necessary to secure it, is right and laudable."[20] The burden of persuasion was undertaken then as much for political as constitutional purposes.

The first part of the American case was that they had contributed their fair mite to the war effort. They made the argument not only by pointing to their own "very grievous burden of Debt" as just noted, but also by repeated citation of their war record. It was "chiefly by" the "vigorous efforts" of Massachusetts, the first Continental Congress bragged, that "Nova-Scotia was subdued in 1710, and Louisburg in 1745." During the last war, the Massachusetts House boasted, all the northern colonies "exerted themselves in full Proportion to that of *Great Britain*. This Province in particular had in one Campaign on Foot seven Thousand Troops. This was a greater Levy for a single Province, than the three Kingdoms have made collectively in any one Year since the Revolution."[21] In fact, John Mitchell claimed, Britain's victories were due to the colonies "who first beat the *French* at Lake *George*, and put a stop to the progress of their victorious arms; they afterwards maintained from 20,000 to 25,000 men, without which we could not have expected any of the successes we met with."[22] A bit more emotional were claims that although Britain might be staggering under a large debt, New England had made a sacrifice that could never be repaid. "[W]hat restitution," the people of Bristol, Rhode Island, asked, "has been, or can be made, for the flower of the land, who were slain in battle? and the charges consequent thereon, have been, and still are, a burthen to this town; as there are several widows of those who were either slain in battle, or died in the service of their King and country, who have, and still are, supported by the town."[23]

The issue most extensively disputed was the reason France and Great Britain had gone to war. The British contention was that because the Seven Years War had begun in North America, it had been fought for "[t]he security of our American colonies," that is, for "the defence and protection of the British provinces in America, and the security of their commerce." The proposition seemed so obvious to them that its mere statement provided all the proof necessary. The British were being taxed to "pay the interest of [sic] money, which was expended in the defence of America," a national debt not "contracted upon *your own accounts*," but incurred solely, "in defending and protecting these Americans, avenging all their Quarrels, and extending their Boundaries far beyond the Lines of Prudence, and perhaps of Justice."[24]

The American answer was argued more factually than the British assertion, probably because it was far less self-evident. William Pitt had called the Seven Years War "my German war," and that, Arthur Lee asserted, was just what it had been. "What was the mighty aid given to the Colonies?" Lee asked, then prefaced his answer by quoting King George II. "'Proper *encouragement* has been given to the several Colonies to exert themselves in their own defence, and in the *maintenance of the Rights and Possessions of Great Britain.'*— It seems then, that the Americans were not only to defend themselves, but the rights and possessions of this Country."[25]

One could even admit it was an American war, forget the European fighting, and still call it Great Britain's struggle. "[I]f the last war began about American boundaries," one writer contended, "it was only because America is a British territory . . . it would equally have begun in whatever part of the dominion the encroachment had been made."[26] Benjamin Franklin would not concede that the conflict had concerned "American" boundaries. "It began about the limits between Canada and Nova-Scotia," he told the Commons, "about territories to which the Crown indeed laid claim, but were not claimed by any British Colony; none of the lands had been granted to any Colonist; we had therefore no particular concern or interest in that dispute." "The war," Samuel Adams agreed, had been "waged in defence of lands claimed by the crown, and for the protection of *British property*."[27]

The meaning of Adams's reference to British property was explained by Franklin. The first attack may have occurred in Ohio country, but that did not make the war an American affair. The cause of the first fighting had been the Indian trade, claimed by the British under the treaty of Utrecht and disputed by the French. British, not American, property had been seized. "The Indian trade," Franklin wrote, "is a British interest; it is carried on with British manufactures, for the profit of British merchants and manufacturers; therefore the war, as it commenced for the defence of territories of the Crown, the property of no American, and for the defence of a trade purely British, was really a British war."[28]

THE QUESTION OF THE BENEFIT

There were two ways British writers refuted the American defense. The first was to marshal additional counterevidence to show that the war had been an American struggle. In 1769 William Knox devoted over 24 pages of a 207-page pamphlet to printing evidence dating from 1754 that the colonies needed, wanted, and actively sought British protection against the French. The second was to admit that the mother country had been fighting for herself, but contend that the purpose did not matter. The Americans had an obligation to repay because, as the facts proved, a benefit had been conferred that the colonies could not deny. "[W]hatever benefit England might propose to herself in the prosecution of the late war, the colonies themselves have been incomparably the principal gainers by it. Now they enjoy a peace and tranquillity, which they scarcely ever knew before." Put more extremely, "while we paid all . . . they reaped all the fruits." In addition to the benefit conferred on the Americans, the colonial obligation might be proven by the detriment suffered by the British. "A war enter'd into by Great-Britain," one writer summarized in 1778, "in consequence of the earnest supplications of her American subjects, from which this country derived empty fame, and *they* solid advantage; a war by which they were *enriched, strengthened, secured;* while we were *impoverished, weakened, endangered.*"[29]

The Americans, of course, answered that they had not been the gainers. "We reap nothing," the Massachusetts House of Representatives contended, "except a more immediate Security." Two possible exceptions might be the fishery and the fact that the Indians were not "any longer under French Influence to our Prejudice."[30] But even these gains were slight, if gains at all,[31] and some colonial whigs were bold enough to argue that the Americans not only gained nothing by the war, they actually had lost. The French may have been ousted, but Great Britain took all the territory, all the commerce, and a monopoly of the Indian trade, leaving the colonists with a decrease in the value of their lands. Worse, even though the Americans had fought and incurred expenses to bring about the British conquests, "they have been deprived of them since the peace." A proclamation issued in 1763 prohibited settlement beyond the mountains and the territories drained by the Ohio River had been added to the jurisdiction of Quebec, governed by London for the advantage of Great Britain. "The immense tracts of land subdued," Governor Stephen Hopkins argued, "and no less immense and profitable commerce acquired all belong to Great Britain, and not the least share or portion to these colonies, though thousands of their men have lost their lives and millions of their money have been expended in the purchase of them."[32]

CHAPTER SEVEN

THE COMMERCIAL CONTRACT

The colonial factual argument against the imperial contract was not as strong as American whigs would have liked. Although it is not possible in a constitutional history to evaluate the strengths and weaknesses of both sides, a point to be noted is that neither side persuaded the other. The argument, after all, was forensic, and lack of persuasion did not have to be fatal if there was yet a counterargument to be offered. American whigs and their British supporters, realizing they had not proven their factual case against the imperial contract, attempted to nullify its implications with a novation or yet-another contract. That contract, the fifth, or what can be called the commercial contract, was based on a deceptively simple contention. If Great Britain had, in fact, gone to war to protect the colonies, she had not done so "out of disinterested regard for them; but to secure the profits of their trade; a trade, which, had they become subjects to *France*, must have been lost to *England*." What had Britain been protecting, David Hartley inquired of the Commons in 1775, "yourselves or them?" The trade of the colonies was controlled by the mother country for the profit of the British people. Even if London provided the colonies with protection, what difference did it make, the commercial-contract argument asked? "Have they not paid for it by the benefits of their commerce?"[1]

There were various theories upon which the commercial contract could be propped. Daniel Dulany cited the general benefits the colonies contributed to Great Britain's economic prosperity and the principle of equity, Virginia's House of Burgesses cited the restrictions that the mother country placed on colonial trade and the principles of justice or reasonableness, and South Carolina's Commons House of Assembly cited American purchase of British manufactures to the exclusion of those of other nations and the principle of fair exchange. No matter what the consideration — Great Britain's legislative monopoly over the trade of the colonies, the profits of American exports that by law had to be shipped to Europe through the mother country, or the additional strength American numbers brought to the British military — the debt owed under the imperial contract was continually being repaid. "By these means, the colonies not only pay for their own protection, but help to protect all his Majesty's dominions, in all parts of the world. It is upon this trade to the plantations, that the safety of the whole nation depends, and more particularly of *Great Britain* itself."[2]

THE BENEFIT CONFERRED

The refutation of the imperial contract on the basis of commercial considerations was rationalized in a variety of ways. Samuel Estwick, agent for Barbadoes, barrister, and future member of Parliament, made it an issue of constitutional dogma. "[C]ommercial colonization," he contended, "by historical authority, by fact, by reason, by the definition of the terms themselves, excludes the very idea of taxation." Isaac Barré thought it less a legal than a moral obligation. "When I stand up an advocate for America," he explained, "I feel myself the firmest friend of this country. We owe our greatness to the commerce of America." The Continental Congress elaborated: "It is universally confessed, that the amazing Increase of the Wealth, Strength, and Navigation of the Realm, arose from this Source; and the Minister, who so wisely and successfully directed the Measures of Great-Britain in the late War, publicly declared, that these Colonies enabled her to triumph over her Enemies." The argument was generally stated as a benefit, for the additional wealth had resulted from the fact that America "purchased our goods, increased the revenue *by that purchase* — enriched our merchants — employed our men — raised seamen for our fleets." Because of these "solid benefits," the mother country had never thought of taxing the colonies. As the member for Liverpool told the Commons, "Our advantage from America arises from their buying our manufactures."[3]

According to the American whig perception of the trade laws, at least when arguing the commercial contract, all the benefits were conferred on the British, all the detriments were suffered by the colonists. The mandate that most colonial products could be sold nowhere but within the Empire or to the mother country meant not only that British merchants obtained goods more cheaply, but also that they had a monopoly of resale to the remainder of the world. The reverse rule, that the colonies could not import products from anywhere but Great Britain, meant higher prices for Americans and higher profits for British merchants. The Massachusetts House of Representatives, when stating these facts, was careful to stress that it was "not, at this time, complaining of this policy of the mother state." The objection was not to the regulation of trade but to being taxed in addition and, even worse in the case of the Townshend duties, being taxed on products that could be purchased from no market other than Great Britain.[4]

The commercial contract might not merit so much attention had it been argued mostly in pamphlets and newspapers. A measure of the seriousness with which it was perceived comes with the realization that it was primarily pleaded by official bodies in America and supported in the mother country by members of the House of Commons. "[T]he product of our labor and our trade," the governor of Connecticut wrote Lord Hillsborough, "naturally and necessarily tends to and centers in Great Britain, and if our wealth should be ten times greater than it is, the bulk of it would be expended in purchasing her manufactures." "*Britain*, by Means of her Colonies, enjoys an extensive Trade . . . that . . . rebounds to her Benefit," the acting agent of Massachusetts asserted during the Stamp Act crisis. "That Trade alone is sufficient to possess *Great-Britain* of all that can possibly by any and every Means be drawn from her Colonies." From the Stamp Act Congress that same year to the Continental Congress on the eve of independence, the colonial representative bodies reminded Great Britain not only that it controlled American trade, but also that it restrained it "in every way that could conduce to your emolument." As a result, "we eventually contribute very largely to the revenue of the crown"— strong "Reasons," the New York Assembly thought, "for leaving us free from ungranted Impositions."[5]

The claim stated more than a moral obligation. American whigs believed that they were asserting contractual consideration. Because "the profits of the trade of these colonies ultimately center in Great-Britain," the Stamp Act Congress insisted, "they eventually contribute very largely to all supplies granted there to the crown."[6] For some whigs, the value of the consideration was established beyond dispute. According to a Virginian, "The Balance against America proves clearly on which Side the Advantage has been." The "monopoly of the American trade," a member of Parliament wrote, "stood in the place of taxation, and was a full equivalent." In fact, it stood for more. It was, as he told the Commons, a debt for which "the least that we owe to them in return is protection." His meaning was clarified by another member who termed the "Protection" furnished to the colonies by Great Britain the "Compensation" paid in return for the monopoly of colonial trade.[7]

THE DETRIMENT SUFFERED

William Pitt had complete confidence in his opinions. Unlike just about every other participant in the revolutionary debate, he was certain he could measure the "ample compensation" paid the mother country by her monopoly of America's commerce in exchange for military protection. "I will be bold to affirm," he told the Commons, "that the profits to Great Britain from the trade of the colonies, through all its branches, is two millions a year." More to the point, Pitt insisted that just as this sum was gain for Britain, it was loss for the colonies, a detriment constituting contractual consideration. "This is the fund that carried you triumphantly through the last war," he asserted. "You owe this to America. This is the price that America pays you for her protection."[8]

The consideration Pitt raised — the detriment suffered by Americans due to the commercial contract — provided opponents of parliamentary taxation with an argument stronger than that derived from the benefit conferred on Britain by the contract. That argument took two forms. In Great Britain it was usually stated that Parliament should not tax the colonies for purposes of revenue unless it first relinquished the commercial monopoly. In America the possibility of accepting taxes as a substitute for trade regulation was presented more as a political than a constitutional solution. Parliamentary taxation of the unrepresented colonies would have been unconstitutional no matter who regulated their trade — the legislature in the mother country or each provincial assembly. Some Americans asserted that if Great Britain abandoned the monopoly the colonists would more willingly contribute to imperial defense. They would do so, however, in what they regarded the constitutional manner, contributions to the Crown voted by each assembly, not by taxation imposed by Parliament.[9]

THE SUBROGATE TAX

A revealing alternative way of describing the commercial contract, perhaps more accurately thought of as an alternative to arguing the commercial contract, contended not that Britain's monopoly of colonial trade was the *quid pro quo* America paid as its share of the common defense in lieu of taxes, but that the monopoly in itself *was a tax*. The contention went back at least to Robert Walpole, Britain's chief minister in the early decades of the century. According to a story frequently retold during the revolutionary era, when it was suggested to Walpole that Parliament tax the colonies, he answered that "the colonists, by the profits of our trade with them, *enabled* us to pay *our* taxes, which was the same as paying taxes to the mother country; and that, by the restrictions, under which we have laid their commerce, all their money comes to the mother-country; and the mother-country can at most have but their all." One explanation, then, was "that by confining our colonists to trade only with us, we make them pay our taxes, without directly laying upon them any *internal* tax." It was to describe this theory that colonial whigs employed the phrase "indirect taxes" or "secondary taxes."[10]

There were two ways of theorizing the subrogate-tax defense. One told the British that Americans "help . . . to pay your taxes by purchasing your manufactures,"[11] that is, "by compelling them in a manner to take our goods at our own price, and obliging them to send their goods here, to be sold in effect at our price, we lay upon them a large share of our taxes."[12] The same argument, coming from the colonies, was that these payments were "nearly the same as being taxed ourselves, and equally beneficial to the crown." A significant factor was that the Americans could purchase products nowhere else, as a result of which the British government was collecting that much more when it taxed goods manufactured at home but sold to colonists. "[D]o not the Americans pay taxes to government, by purchasing articles *on which it has imposed Taxes*," a critic of Samuel Johnson's anti-American polemics asked. A second critic answered yes by posing a second question. "If," he wrote, "your *monopoly* of American traffic supplies a good part of those [British] taxes, is it just to say, that America does not contribute; or that she is not entitled to protection from any part of them?"[13]

A second way of theorizing the subrogate-tax argument, besides claiming that it paid British taxes, was to stretch the definition of taxation and assert that Great Britain's trade monopoly, beyond being a financial detriment to the colonies, was a tax: a real tax, as much a tax as the Stamp Act had attempted to impose. "It is said," the duke of Grafton told the House of Lords, "that America is not taxed. I answer they pay Taxes in taking your Manufactures." The fact that the colonists were customers who could purchase only from a monopoly was, the Massachusetts House agreed, "in reality a tax." The marquis of Rockingham had this definition of taxation in mind when he told the Lords "that the only sure *con-*

stitutional taxes which could, or ought to be drawn from the Colonies, would be the monopoly of their trade."[14]

THE IMPERIAL ANSWER

Although William Knox agreed that the trade monopoly was in essence a tax, he thought the argument led to an opposite conclusion. That Parliament taxed the colonies by regulating their commerce was not a contract barring parliamentary taxation, Knox reasoned, but precedent for taxing them directly. Others viewing the question from the imperial perspective also thought the American evidence did not add up to the commercial contract.[15] There were, of course, some who insisted the Americans' argument was fallacious either because the colonies suffered no trade disadvantages or because "the Advantages of trade simply Considered . . . are mutual." Others put the argument on the grounds that the detriments were mutual or that the advantages to the colonies were more substantial than those to Great Britain.[16] Americans, it was said, belonged to an extensive empire and reaped all the bounties that the mother country lavished upon her distant dependents. "Were there no other ground to require a revenue from the colonies, than as a return for these obligations, it would alone be a sufficient foundation." The commercial contract could even be argued in reverse. If the colonies had prospered under Great Britain's trade laws — "under the advantage of a greater commerce" — then they should "contribute something considerable toward the necessary support of the state."[17]

Another imperial answer was that the commercial contract did not prove what American whigs said it proved. Colonial arguments, Thomas Townshend told the Commons,

> proved too much, or proved nothing; they proved Ireland and America were taxed, because they purchased certain commodities in this country, nay, that every foreign nation in Europe, contributed to our burthens, because they are the consumers of some of our manufactures. In point of absentees and residents, the same arguments held good; for he knew no part of the dominions of the British crown for which there were no persons constantly residing in London and other parts of England. . . . [H]e did not know a county in England that might not urge the same plea with equal weight and plausibility.[18]

Townshend's contentions had substance to the extent that the commercial-contract argument claimed that the colonies enriched Great Britain by purchasing products and by paying duties on those products.[19] They did not answer the part of the commercial-contract argument that asserted Great Britain regulated, monopolized, and received the profits of American trade.

The monopoly count in the commercial contract did not go unchallenged, however. British imperialists pleaded in replication that control of trade generated expenditures as well as profits and that the expenditures may have been greater than the profits, certainly greater than anything Americans were asked to pay in taxes. "Ungrateful people of America!" George Grenville charged. "Bounties have been extended to them. When I had the honour of serving the crown, while you yourselves were loaded with an enormous debt, you have given bounties on their lumber, on their iron, their hemp, and many other articles."[20] There is no need to consider the many bounties or trade indulgences that Grenville had in mind.[21] One example is sufficient, the one most frequently cited and which some British critics thought answered Americans' contractual claim. It was the criminal sanction imposed on anyone in the mother country or in Ireland who grew tobacco. "This surely," John Lind contended, "was no mean sacrifice to the welfare of America, and the system of *monopoly* is not *entirely* in favor of England."[22] These bounties were employed as evidence that the commercial contract served the mutual benefit of both parties, that it conferred greater benefits on the colonies, or that the consideration paid by Great Britain for her monopoly of American trade was imperial support of American agriculture, not exemption from imperial taxation.[23]

Opponents of American taxes were not persuaded. "The gentleman boasts of his bounties to America!" William Pitt replied to Grenville. "Are not those bounties intended finally for the benefit of this kingdom? If they are, where is his peculiar merit to America?" In fact, it was pointed out, most bounties were on products such as pitch, tar, indigo, and hemp, and were intended "to get those commodities cheaper from the Colonies," divert Americans from manufactures, free Britain "from the clutches of foreign Extortioners," and end the navy's dependence on foreign countries for essential supplies.[24] Even the restriction on tobacco growing was dismissed, as its purpose had not been to benefit Virginia, but to protect the collection of import duties and preserve a commercial monopoly.[25]

> [T]he only true reason for prohibiting the cultivation of tobacco in these kingdoms, is in the preamble of the act itself declared to be, *"that by planting thereof, your Majesty is deprived of a considerable part of your revenue, arising by customs upon imported tobacco;"* for which reason its cultivation has been likewise prohibited in France, where the government cannot be supposed to have any particular solicitude for the prosperity of Virginia.[26]

No matter how vast the amounts Great Britain spent on the colonies, or what restrictions she placed on her own inhabitants, the opponents of colonial taxation always found reasons why the bounties and the statutes benefited Britain more than America.[27] That fact summarizes the probative nature of all the contracts argued during the revolutionary debates. They served to strengthen the conviction of the person arguing them; they did not convince the other side.

There is good reason the various contracts did not provide definitive solutions to the taxation dispute dividing the North American colonies from Great Britain. Only one of the contracts, the original contract, was "constitutional" in the sense that it was familiar to constitutional lawyers, for it alone of the revolutionary contracts was based on doctrine from the ancient English constitution. As previously mentioned, however, the original contract contributed very little to the debate over imperial taxation. The three other contracts were major considerations in the taxation controversy. Except for the doctrine of taxation-by-consent, no other issue contributed as many words to the debate as did the question of contract. But all three — the second original contract, the imperial contract, and the commercial contract — were new; they were not known to the ancient constitution but *sui generis* to the imperial constitution. Because the second original contract was a colonial version of the original contract, its constitutional associations could not be missed and the evidence indicates it was generally treated as a legal contention even by those who thought it invalid. The imperial and commercial contracts, however, were constitutionally novel, and that novelty surely deprived them of the authority of more traditional constitutional doctrines such as parliamentary supremacy or taxation only by consent, which were supported by constitutional law and precedent. There was some legal theory but no constitutional precedent supporting the imperial and commercial contracts. An American whig convinced by the evidence supporting the imperial contract or an imperialist persuaded that the commercial contract was proven in fact could ignore them in law, treat them as politically convincing reasons why the colonies should or should not be taxed but irrelevant to the question of the constitutionality of parliamentary taxation. A second reason the contracts were not conclusive arises from the very element that helped to make them so extensively argued — they were easily debated. The evidence employed to prove their terms was not difficult to develop. Although it often purported to be historical evidence, it was more often forensic, used with little regard to any consideration but whether it would support the contention being argued. All too often it seemed convincing to the person adapting it because that person was already convinced.

We cannot be certain, but the failure may have been a failure of persuasion rather than of doctrine. What must be remembered is that there was both a political side and a constitutional side to each contract argument. The political purpose of arguing the imperial contract, for example, was to persuade others that it was fair for Parliament to tax the colonies, that it was reasonable to expect the Americans to pay for the protection they received from the mother country. An individual convinced of Parliament's constitutional authority to tax Massachusetts because of sovereignty or supremacy or a combination of reasons other than the imperial contract might still argue that contract, not to establish the constitutional right but to persuade others of the political expediency. Indeed, such a person might argue the imperial contract without realizing it was a constitutional doctrine and without thinking it relevant to the issue of the constitutionality of Parliament's authority to tax the colonies. What cannot be determined is what percentage of those pleading the imperial contract, or, on the other side, the commercial contract, thought it more a political than a constitutional argument. All that can be said with certainty is that many arguing one contract or the other did believe the matter in contention constitutional; they spoke of "right" and "obligation" and of "being bound." It may be that most participants in the revolutionary debate thought of the contracts as one of several alternative arguments or at best a mere collateral factor. It is possible they believed that although the authority to tax could not be based on contract alone, nonetheless either the imperial or commercial contract or both were constitutional doctrines. It is not unreasonable to guess that that was why some American whigs took so much trouble to refute the imperial contract and why imperialists marshaled arguments against the commercial contract. A person convinced by the imperial contract could not sneer at the theory underlying the commercial contract. An imperialist might need no persuasion that the premise that Americans should pay for the protection of the mother country stated a stronger obligation than did the idea that the colonies purchased that protection by permitting Great Britain to monopolize their commerce; but that imperialist, arguing that the imperial contract justified parliamentary taxation, had to give some heed to the commercial contract. One such person may have been George Grenville. No one put greater emphasis on the imperial contract than Grenville, who justified the constitutionality of the Stamp Act in part on it, yet even when doing so he may have acknowledged the claim of the commercial contract. A Scottish periodical reporting the first discussion in Parliament of colonial taxation does not indicate the speaker quoted, but as Grenville's program was being explained he may have been the one. The message was clear: the Commons was told to look to the colonies for new taxes but warned not to proceed as if North America were part of Great Britain. After pointing out that colonial taxation might have to be limited because the colonists were already paying the costs of local government and defense, the speaker brought up the commercial contract. "We ought," he said, "likewise to consider, that the people of that country are still kept under many restraints in their trade, for the benefit of their mother country as supposed, though I doubt much if it be so; therefore it should be unjust to make them contribute to the general public expense equally, that is to say, proportionately, with the people of this island."[28]

A decade later, after the battle of Lexington had been fought and the Continental army was facing British troops in Boston, the commercial contract would have been forgotten had it been only a slice of propaganda thrown into the debate by Americans bent on independence for economic or nationalistic reasons. However, it was still recalled. When the ministry sent the colonies London's final proposal for compromising the taxation controversy, the Continental Congress thought the commercial contract still relevant when explaining why Americans could not agree. So, too, did Virginia's House of Burgesses.

> Because, on our agreeing to contribute our proportion towards the common defence, they [Commons and Lords] do not propose to lay open to us a free trade with all the World: whereas to us it appears just that those who bear equally the burthens of Government, should equally participate of its benefits. [E]ither be contented with the monopoly of our Trade, which brings greater loss to us and benefit to them, than the amount of our proportional contributions to the common defence; or, if the latter be preferred, relinquish the former, and do not propose, by holding both, to exact from us double contributions.[29]

CHAPTER EIGHT

THE TAXATION-LEGISLATION DICHOTOMY

When Charles Townshend was in the opposition in the House of Commons, attached to the leadership of William Pitt, he became discouraged over his chances of ever advancing schemes for taxing the North American colonies. "Mr. Pitt," he mourned to the duke of Newcastle, "I find is against *all* taxation." Pitt not only was opposed to all taxation of the colonies, his opposition was also the most important of any voiced by a member of Parliament. The reason was not only that he was the most influential statesman of the day and his words inspired Americans more than could those of any other British politician, but also because he articulated a constitutional theory of why the mother country could not legally tax her colonies.

Pitt's theory was based on four premises: the definition of property; the logic of federalism in the British Empire; the terms of the commercial contract; and the contention that under the British constitution taxation and legislation were distinct and separate government powers. The first, the definition of property, was the most familiar as it was closely connected with the doctrine that to be constitutional taxation had to be with consent of the taxed. London, Pitt insisted, "had no right whatever to tax *America*," because "it is contrary to that essential, unalterable right in nature, ingrafted into the *British* constitution as a fundamental law,

85

that *what a man has honestly acquired is absolutely his own*, which he may freely give, but which cannot be taken from him without his own consent."[1]

Pitt's second two authorities — the nature of federalism within the Empire and the commercial contract — were closely related, and both owed much to the way in which he viewed and defined property. Parliament, he believed, possessed supreme authority over all parts of the British Empire, but that supremacy was not absolute. "[T]his supreme power," Pitt told the House of Lords, "has no effect towards internal taxation; for it does not exist in that relation. There is no such thing, *no such idea in this Constitution, as a supreme power operating upon property.*" From this theory of the constitutional division imposed by imperial federalism upon legislative authority over private property, Pitt moved easily to the commercial contract. "Let this distinction, then, remain forever ascertained," he pleaded on behalf of the Americans. "Taxation is theirs; commercial regulation is ours." Pitt wanted the colonists to recognize Britain's "supreme right of regulating Commerce and Navigation." He wanted the British to accord Americans "their supreme, unalienable right in their Property, a right which they are justified in the defence of, to the last extremity."[2]

Pitt's fourth premise — a constitutional dichotomy between the authority to tax and the authority to legislate — was the most important because, although he did not originate the constitutional doctrine upon which it was based, its significance to the revolutionary legal debate would have been far less but for its association with him. In what may have been the most widely circulated speech of the controversy over the Stamp Act, Pitt attempted to solve this constitutional crisis by returning to a basic principle of the British constitution and drawing from it the taxation-legislation dichotomy.

> Taxation is no part of the governing or legislative power. The taxes are a voluntary gift and grant of the Commons alone. In legislation the three estates of the realm are alike concerned, but the concurrence of the peers and the crown to a tax, is only necessary to close with the form of a law. The gift and grant is of the Commons alone. . . . [T]his House represents those Commons, the proprietors of the lands; and those proprietors virtually represent the rest of the inhabitants. When, therefore, in this House we give and grant, we give and grant what is our own. But in an American tax, what do we do? We, your Majesty's Commons of Great Britain, give and grant to your Majesty, what? Our own property? No. We give and grant to your Majesty, the property of your Majesty's commons of America. It is an absurdity in terms.

That statement summarizes William Pitt's solution to the taxation part of the revolutionary crisis: separate the power to tax from the power to legislate and—in theory—from the orbit of government itself.[3]

THE TAXATION-REPRESENTATION CONNECTION

It is indicative of how much we have lost the constitutional mentality of the eighteenth century that it is difficult to reconstruct the Pitt dichotomy in twentieth-century language. Contemporaries, though, had little trouble understanding it, and no one summarized the doctrine better than a critic attempting to ridicule it. "The Honourable Gentleman has told us," an anonymous writer reported, "that England has no right to tax America, because Taxation is no part of the governing or legislative power; because the Taxes are the gift and grant of the Commons alone; and because in the British House of Commons the Americans are not virtually represented." By way of contrast, a later biographer and other historians have assumed Pitt's division was between internal and external taxation or that he had anticipated the Dickinson distinction between duties imposed for the regulation of trade and to raise a revenue. Even constitutional historians seem to have been confused; one quoted Pitt's argument with approval as late as 1863, when surely it was no longer viable, and another recently dismissed it as having "more common sense than logic," a description that would seem more accurate from the political than the constitutional perspective.[4] Constitutionally, Pitt's division between taxation and legislation was neither illogical nor *sui generis*. It was derived from a constitutional function of the House of Commons. Its political, not its constitutional, application was what most contemporaries thought faulty.[5]

"Pitt's dichotomy" is in fact a misnomer; the doctrine, based on familiar constitutional principles, had been injected into the Stamp Act debates well before Pitt was heard from, endorsed by distinguished members of Parliament including Charles Pratt, judge of the Common Pleas, recently elevated to the House of Lords as Baron Camden, and soon to be appointed Lord Chancellor of England. Camden commanded more prestige among the general public than any other common lawyer, and was described by a contemporary as "the people's lawyer." One of the biographers of England's judiciary estimated that he "acquired more popularity than any other who ever sat on the bench." As Lord Chancellor, Camden would become the titular leader of the common-law bar. His words, therefore, received both professional and political respect.[6]

Camden not only stated the dichotomy, he also stated it more emphatically than Pitt. He placed it on a different foundation — representation — although it is likely he thought representation just a variation of the doctrine of consent. Camden told the House of Lords that he had given the matter much thought. Years later, Lord Campbell described what Camden said as "a set speech, upon which he had taken immense pains,— which has been rapturously praised, and some passages of which are still [second half of the nineteenth century] in the mouths of schoolboys."

> My position is this — I repeat it — I will maintain it to my last hour,— taxation and representation are inseparable; — this position is founded on the laws of nature; it is more, it is itself an eternal law of nature; for whatever is a man's own, is absolutely his own; no man hath a right to take it from him without his consent, either expressed by himself or representative; whoever attempts to do it, attempts an injury; whoever does it, commits a robbery; he throws down and destroys the distinction between liberty and slavery. Taxation and representation are coeval with and essential to this constitution.

It would be difficult to imagine a more extreme statement by a Lord Chancellor of England. To Camden the British constitution was a constitution of absolute prohibitions derived from natural law. His words just quoted were probably the most drastic assertion of natural law uttered during the entire revolutionary debates. Surely no American whig of any consequence put so much reliance on that authority. Camden took the contemporary definition of property and pronounced it "an eternal law of nature," about as far as it was possible to go short of divine injunction. Parliamentary taxation of the colonies, he maintained, was "illegal, absolutely illegal, contrary to the fundamental laws of nature, contrary to the fundamental laws of this constitution," a "constitution grounded on the eternal and immutable laws of nature." Nor did Camden hesitate to embrace revelation. The doctrine, he asserted, was not new, "'tis as old as the constitution; it grew up with it, indeed it is its support; taxation and representation are inseparably united; God hath joined them, no B[riti]sh P[arliamen]t can separate them; to endeavour to do it, is to stab our very vitals."[7]

Without stressing the dichotomy between taxation and legislation, Camden stood foursquare with Pitt. The taxation-representation connection, after all, was but another way to the same principle. Pitt had made the taxation-representation connection part of his formula when first stating it, although, interestingly, he put more emphasis on the constitutional and less on the metaphysical than Camden. "Rep[resentatio]n and Taxation," he said in his denunciation of the Stamp Act, "go together and always have in this Country." Sir Fletcher Norton, the Solicitor General, expressed astonishment. "I thought that argument had been beat out of the House," he remarked, and just about every lawyer who joined the debate disparaged it — except, of course, Lord Camden. He not only embraced it, he almost caricatured it. The explanation probably is that he shared with Pitt an inordinate reverence for the principle of representation and consent in British constitutionalism — a representation, however, of property rather than of persons.[8]

It will not be necessary to analyze Camden's taxation-representation doctrine. It is so closely connected to the principle of taxation-only-by-consent-of-the-taxed that to say more runs the risk of seeming repetitious when that vital yet lengthy topic is discussed. The taxation-representation connection has been mentioned here in part because it was argued in support of Pitt's taxation-legislation dichotomy theory. It was not based on precedent or immemorial custom as was the taxation-by-consent doctrine, nor did it arise from the historical practice of the constitution as had the legislation-taxation dichotomy. Rather, it owed something to natural law and, like Pitt's distinction, a good deal to the peculiar aspects of a constitutional institution. For Pitt, that institution was the House of Commons. Camden went a bit further and narrowed the emphasis to a special aspect of the Commons — its capacity as the representative institution of British government. What made these arguments basically different from the fundamental American contention of consent was that Pitt, Camden, and their supporters insisted that Parliament was absolutely sovereign over the colonies in all respects except taxation, a proposition colonial whigs rejected. Pitt maintained that the sovereign power could not tax the colonies because under the British constitution taxation was distinct from legislation. The former was an authority derived from consent; the latter was an authority derived from sovereignty. Lord Camden argued that Parliament could not tax as long as American property was not represented. Colonial whigs denied Parliament's authority both to tax and (in most cases) to legislate because they were not represented.[9]

THE IRISH ANALOGY EXPLANATION

The most striking feature of the Pitt-Camden thesis was that it boldly embraced a contradiction that most other British supporters of American claims to immunity from parliamentary taxation either ignored or rejected. That contradiction was explicit in Camden's statement that "the legislative supremacy" belonged to Great Britain but that supremacy did not encompass taking private property without consent of the owner. The proposition was so uncomplicated that its inconsistency was immediately apparent, making it an easy target for ridicule. It was dismissed in such terms as "downright nonsense," "a burlesque upon common sense," and "mere flummery and declamation."[10]

American whigs also ridiculed the Pitt dichotomy, but for more pragmatic constitutional reasons. Not only did they have to guard against one element of Pitt's dichotomy—that legislation was part of the absolute power of sovereignty—they also had to reject the all-or-nothing concept of sovereignty. They had to do so because of the way sovereignty was argued by the imperialists who too rejected the dichotomy. The imperialist contention was not only that taxation was part of the legislative power but also that the authority to legislate could not be diluted without surrendering sovereignty. Carried to its ultimate conclusion the imperialist contention was that the Pitt dichotomy "laid the foundation of a total separation between Great-Britain and the Colonies, and in them, of an absolute independence of the Mother Country." Well over a year before Pitt first spun his theory of the dichotomy between taxation and legislation, the New York Assembly anticipated the ultimate imperial contention, considered its merits, and insisted that exemption from legislative taxation did not mean independence. "For the Experience of near a Century, has fully envinced, that our Subjection to *Great-Britain*, and her Laws, and our strenuous Efforts upon every publick Emergency, have not been the less Conspicuous under an Immunity from Taxes, imposed by a *British* Parliament."[11]

This 1764 answer to the contention that self-taxation meant independence implied substantive arguments that would be refined but not changed throughout the remainder of the revolutionary debate. The Assembly had pointed to its own experience. Near a century of taxing itself had not meant independence. Supporters of the Pitt dichotomy made the same case by citing analogies on the Continent[12] or the Irish comparison. "It is equally true," Governor George Johnstone tried to persuade the Commons, "that legislation may exist without the power of taxation. The Kingdom of *Ireland*, within our own Dominions, is a proof of what these learned gentlemen assert to be so impossible." A month after Johnstone spoke, Pitt told the Lords the same thing. "This country superintends and controuls their trade and navigation," he said of the Irish; "but they *tax themselves*." Charles Garth, member for Devizes and South Carolina's agent, thought Ireland furnished evidence not only that Pitt's dichotomy could work successfully without leading to independence, but that it was supported by constitutional precedent found in both custom and juridical opinion. "Lord Coke and other great Lawyers," he claimed, "have in their time denied the power of Parliament to lay Taxes upon the people of Ireland for want of Representation therein, and in almost the same breath have asserted the Legislative Authority of the Parliament to bind the Subjects and Inhabitants of that Island."[13]

It will be necessary to evaluate the meaning and application of the Irish analogy when considering the doctrine of consent, but that is not the question now being discussed. Here, we are concerned with the constitutional status of Ireland as an analogy for the Pitt dichotomy—not for the principle of taxation by consent but for the rule that taxation was a government power separate from legislation. "Subordinate to another, yet free within ourselves, so far as freedom consists in the power of taxation," was how a writer for an Irish magazine described the status in 1775. In a sense, the scheme was little more than a federal arrangement of imperial power. Whether or not one agreed with Pitt that taxation and legislation were distinct functions of government, one could still isolate taxation from legislation by treating it as a local authority in a federal system. Ireland, with its own Parliament, was taxed "according to our constitutional rule" of consent, a British writer observed. "It is," he added, "very evidently deducible from these authorities, that, however diffuse and general the power of our Parliament may be for the purposes of commercial regulation, yet in respect to Taxation, the constitutional rule has made it, in this point at least, entirely local." Ireland, then, was testimony to the fact that self-taxation need not mean independence —"that the exclusive privilege to be taxed by their own representatives, may exist with the dependency of the people upon the supreme legislature" —or, as the New York Assembly contended: "The Fidelity and Dependance of the Kingdom of *Ireland*, and the Colonies have always been firmly secured, though untaxed by the Parliament of *Great-Britain*."[14]

The Constitutional Explanation

The Irish analogy was not the main legal authority supporting the taxation-legislation dichotomy. Its chief prop was the British constitution. There were some observers who thought the distinction had always been part of the constitution and others who believed it was more a doctrine of the imperial than of the British constitution. Again, federalism was a factor. "Taxation, as exercised by the *English* Parliament over the Colonies, is a Law by which the Makers of it are not governed." In other words, one part of the Empire taxes another part but those legislating are not taxed. Statutes not concerned with raising revenue, that is, "general Laws for the Punishment of Crimes, or the Prevention of Inconveniences, bind those who are concerned in making those Laws, equally with those who are not concerned in making them." Taxation in an imperial situation, then, can be different from other types of legislation and, being "partial" rather than "general," held the likelihood of being "oppressive."[15]

A more traditional constitutional explanation for the taxation-legislation dichotomy, or what a writer called the "very material difference between the laws of England and the laws of taxation," was one "founded upon the very nature of our constitution," a constitution in which "Monarchy, Aristocracy, and Democracy, are blended together in certain Proportions." Under this blending, "the *Granting of Supplies*, or *Laying* Taxes, is deemed the Province of the House of Commons, as the Representative of the People." The Crown and the Lords could only assent or reject the taxes; they could not propose them or change the amount the Commons voted.[16]

It was from this constitutional arrangement of taxation that the Stamp Act Congress and other official bodies speaking for American whigs claimed privileges under the taxation-legislation dichotomy even before Pitt was heard from. Their case was based on the same right upon which "the House of Commons Found their Practice of Originating Money Bills." They claimed the same "Distinction, the House of Commons has always contended for and enjoyed," that is, "the constitutional Right of originating all Money Bills." As Pitt explained to the Commons: "To impose the Tax belongs to the Legislature but this house only grants the Money. That is the ground-work on which the Legislature proceeds. Your first Act is to vote that a Supply be granted and till that is done the whole Legislature Stagnates." Expressed somewhat more clearly by the New York Assembly, the constitutional doctrine was that in Great Britain taxes were voted by the Commons, "consented to by the Lords, and accepted by the Crown, and therefore every Act imposing them, essentially differs from every other Statute, having the Force of a Law in no other Respect, than the Manner thereby prescribed for levying the Gift."[17]

The association of the taxation-legislation dichotomy with the constitutional doctrine that money bills had to originate in the House of Commons is more important than may be thought. That doctrine was one of the most cherished in contemporary British constitutionalism, providing the popular branch of government with both its most effective security from and its chief check against prerogative power. In order to "secure their freedom, and their independence as a branch of the legislature," theory held, "[t]he greatest or only privilege the commons of Great Britain have reserved to themselves . . . is the power of granting money for the use of government; of appointing the manner in which it shall be raised, and the purposes to which it shall be applied: which includes also a right to be informed afterwards how it has been disposed of."[18]

These rules, that all money bills had to originate in the Commons and that the Lords could not amend them, were more than merely practices of parliamentary procedure. They were basic doctrines of constitutional authority, perhaps the most rigid and jealously guarded of any constitutional principles during the eighteenth century. It was because they were so fundamental that Pitt confidently asserted that they proved "that Legislature and Taxation were seperable," and other writers could contend that there was "a material difference between money bills and all other laws." After all, "[h]ad the right of taxation belonged to parliament as a necessary part of its legislative authority, this right might have been exercised with equal justice by either house, and it would doubtless have been equally exercised over all those who were subject to its legislative authority."[19]

In addition to serving as the constitutional source of the taxation-legislation dichotomy, the rule that money bills had to originate in the House of Commons could be authority in itself for asserting that the colonies could not be taxed constitutionally by Parliament: one need only agree why the Lords were barred from touching money bills — any explanation would do — and American immunity would follow. If, for example, it was decided that the Lords were excluded because "they have not a knowledge of the circumstances of the people sufficient" for making decisions about what property could best bear taxation and how it should be collected, the same reasoning could be applied to the colonies. The rule would only have to be applied to the Commons as well as to the Lords. The conclusion would be "that the British House of Commons cannot order a bill to be prepared and brought into their house for imposing a tax upon the people of our colonies in America."[20] Or there was Franklin's assumption that the Lords were not allowed to originate money bills because they paid but a small proportion of all taxes, yet "may put a Negative upon a Money-Bill, merely because otherwise, they might alledge, they are taxed against their Will." By "Parity of Reason," Franklin asked, ought not "Three Millions of People . . . to have the Power of rejecting a Bill for taxing them, because otherwise they too may alledge, they are taxed against their Will?"[21]

THE CONSTITUTIONAL THEORY

Despite the antiquity and the central place in the British constitutional system of the doctrine that money bills were the exclusive purview of the Commons, most participants in the revolutionary debates could not be persuaded that the doctrine had any bearing on whether Parliament possessed authority to tax the colonies for purposes of revenue. Critics of Pitt's

dichotomy continued to insist that there was no constitutional distinction between the power of legislation and the power of taxation. They
insisted that they could "see no difference between the raising [of] taxes
and imposing laws of any other kind."[22] The constitutional procedure of
money bills originating in the Commons was said to prove nothing; the
constitutional rule, after all, was that the other two branches of the legislature had to consent for taxes to be enacted.[23] Pitt thought some of
his critics carried their contentions too far for their own constitutional
safety. In one of the first of many arguments during the revolutionary
debates tying colonial rights to British governmental institutions, he
warned his doubters not to endanger their own constitutional privileges
for the sake of American taxes. "The distinction between legislation and
taxation is essentially necessary to liberty," he contended. "The crown,
the peers, are equally legislative powers with the commons. If taxation
be a part of simple legislation, the crown, the peers have rights in taxation as well as yourselves: rights which they will claim, which they will
exercise, whenever the principle can be supported by power." Although
the argument was not ambiguous and the average contemporary could
appreciate the implications, Pitt's warning was not convincing. Most members of Parliament, indeed most of the public, had no constitutional fears
of admitting that taxation was part of the legislative authority. They
understood that since the Commons' privilege of originating money bills
was supported by constitutional custom, not by the taxation-legislation
dichotomy, there was no danger to British liberty if Parliament taxed the
colonies for purposes of revenue. Sir Gilbert Elliot, a Scots advocate,
turned Pitt's argument around, wondering whether the Commons might
not endanger its cherished constitutional position in money matters if
it did not tax the colonies. "[T]he commons," he told the House, "have
maintained and asserted the right against the crown, and against the
Lords, of solely voting money without the controul of either, any otherwise than by a negative: And will you suffer your colonies to impeach,
to attack those rights, to impede the exercise of them, untouched as they
now are, by the other branches of the legislature?"[24]

None of Pitt's critics worried about the privileges and powers of the
House of Commons. Once they applied the doctrine previously discussed,
the indivisibility of sovereignty, they dismissed Pitt's warning (and the
dichotomy itself) as a constitutional impossibility. Pitt's "argument is made
up of a direct contradiction," an anonymous writer observed. "For without a right to tax, there can be no sovereignty.— Sovereignty comprehends
legislation, and government; without which, it cannot exist. And wher-
ever the right of legislation and government is, there alone, exists the

supreme right to tax. Wherefore, to have a right to the sovereignty, and yet no right to tax, is a political absurdity."[25]

That theory, the current theory of absolute sovereignty, doomed whatever chance Pitt's dichotomy might have had. Because a power that could not tax also could not legislate, Governor James Wright reminded the Georgia Commons House of Assembly, "the authority of the British parliament must be full and complete, or does not operate at all." The rule that *"the supreme Legislative Body of every Kingdom, however constituted, is the supreme Taxing Power, while it preserves its Authority over that Kingdom"* was "almost the only universal Principle that runs through all Governments, indiscriminately, good and bad, despotick and free, barbarous and polite.—That Power only which can give Laws, can impose and Levy Taxes."[26] George Grenville had flung this doctrine back at Pitt the very first time Pitt spoke on American taxation and defended the taxation-legislation dichotomy. "That this Kingdom has the sovereign, the supreme legislative power over America, is granted," Grenville asserted, "and taxation is a part of the sovereign power; It is one branch of the legislation. It is, it has been exercised over those who are not, who were not represented."[27] One writer even claimed that the power to tax was "the very essence of Sovereignty," an evaluation with which Grenville apparently agreed when he claimed that "[i]f Great Britain under any Conditions gives up her Right of Taxation she gives up her Right of Sovereignty which is inseparable from it in all ages & in all Countries." It was precisely on that constitutional theory that some members of Parliament opposed repeal of the Stamp Act, most notably Lord Mansfield, of whom it was said: "[H]e looked upon it to be a tacit relinquishing of the supreme authority of this country over America." Guided by the same constitutional argument, Grenville discouraged Knox from proposing that Great Britain repeal its taxes on the colonies in return for requisitions set by Parliament but raised in each colony by whatever means the local assembly thought proper. The scheme would be impossible to enforce, he thought, for "no man would think it worth while to make a Quarrel with the Colonies for a Sum of money when the Right of Taxation & consequently that of Sovereignty from which it has been & ever must be inseparable has in effect been surrendered."[28]

If we think the sovereignty argument smacks too much of constitutional formalism we must avoid dismissing it as rigidity carried to extremes. The theory belonged to the practical world of eighteenth-century politics and constitutional law. Americans understood and accepted it, one reason the taxation-legislation dichotomy had little support in the colonies. "To deny that the parliament of Great-Britain have any right to dispose of our acquired property, and at the same time to assert their power to restrain our *natural liberty*, is really advancing such a paradox in policy, as I shall never attempt to reconcile," William Hicks wrote in a widely circulated pamphlet. "[O]ur liberty must be ideal," another American thought, "and our privileges chimerical, while the omnipotent of parliament can 'bind our trade, confine our manufactures, & exercise every power whatever except that of taking money out of our pockets without our consent'."[29] Sovereignty was simply too strong a notion for some American whigs to ignore.

CHAPTER NINE

THE DEFENSE OF CHARTER

When the Sugar and Stamp Acts began to menace the constitution under which they and their ancestors had lived for a century and a half, American whigs swiftly developed a consensus of opposition. Voiced in New England town meetings, the declarations of middle-colony grand juries, the resolutions of southern trade associations, and the petitions of legislative assemblies — official and quasi-official statements — the main defense of American rights took shape, and the first line of defense upon which whigs made their stand was the charter of incorporation by which most colonies were governed.

"We have ever supposed our Charter the greatest security that could be had in human affairs," the people of the town of Weymouth, Massachusetts, lamented shortly before the Stamp Act was to become operative.[1] The claim was extreme. Most American whigs would not have made it — the charter defense was the weakest of the constitutional arguments upon which colonial rights could be asserted. Nonetheless, it deserves our attention if for no other reason than that it was so frequently cited and effectively argued.

"[A]ll acts," the Massachusetts House of Representatives resolved the same month as the voters of Weymouth, "made by any power whatever, other than the General Assembly of this province, imposing taxes on the inhabitants, are infringements of our inherent and unalienable rights, as men and British subjects; and render void the most valuable declarations of our charter." If the claim was more modest than that of Weymouth, it was also more familiar. Nothing new was being asserted, certainly not in Massachusetts, where, as a British critic noted, the defenders of local rights, from the earliest period of settlement, "in their public Proceedings, as well as in their private Writings, [had] been constantly holding out to us their first Charter Rights, and the Original Terms of their Colonization." As far back as 1689, another year in which Massachusetts' tradition of self-government had been under imperial attack, the charter was described by the colony's defenders as "the hedge which kept us from the wild Beasts of the field." And in 1728, also thinking of a protecting rather than confining fence, *The New-England Weekly Journal* called the charter "the great Hedge which Providence has planted around our natural Rights, to guard us from an Invasion." Now, during the Stamp Act crisis, that defense was renewed. Put in the strongest terms, the legal claim was that the charter had established "a constitution" that was violated by the Sugar, Stamp, and Townshend Acts. Based on that premise, the argument contended that parliamentary taxation for purposes of raising revenue was an unconstitutional "invasion upon charter rights and privileges."[2]

Although the theme of this chapter is that the charter defense was constitutionally inconclusive, a preliminary exception should be noted. It appears that at the commencement of the revolutionary crisis, at least in 1764, there were some people who expected much from the charter defense. Governor Horatio Sharpe of Maryland, for example, reported the popular belief that "the Judges will never in case of a Dispute with the Collectors of such [Parliament-imposed] Taxes give Judgment against the express words of the Charter in which the King has declared that neither he nor his Successors would ever lay any Impositions or Taxes on the Inhabitants of the province."[3] That such a belief would filter up to impress a royal governor tells us much about popular notions concerning colonial rights. Some people not only took charter privileges seriously, they thought them good pleas at common law against imperial statutes. It would not be long, however, before American whigs realize this assumption was erroneous.[4]

THE WORDING OF CHARTER

There was reason for the people of Maryland to expect that their judges would treat imperial taxation as a nullity: their charter contained a clause pledging that the king would not tax them. "We, our Heirs, and Successors, at no Time hereafter," the Maryland charter stipulated, "will impose, or make or cause to be imposed, any Impositions, Customs, or other Taxations, Quotas, or Contributions whatsoever, in or upon the Residents or Inhabitants of the Province aforesaid . . . or upon any Tenements, Lands, Goods or Chattels." American whigs, whether defending all the colonies against parliamentary taxation or only Maryland, summoned this proviso to support their case. They might as well have never mentioned it, however, because the clause not only caught whigs in a tactical quandary, it was also inconclusive in both meaning and constitutional relevance. It was inconclusive in meaning because it said nothing more than that the grantor, James I, and his heirs and successors would not tax Maryland. Did the promise mean only taxes imposed by the Crown or did it include parliamentary taxes? It was constitutionally inconclusive because there was no tribunal except Parliament itself to which the issue could be appealed and if the question had been left to Parliament the ruling would have been that the Maryland charter proscribed only prerogative taxes—those promulgated by the Crown.[5]

For American whigs to have cited the Maryland exemption as authority forbidding parliamentary taxation of other colonies entailed several risks. The charter of Pennsylvania seemed to say the opposite of what was stipulated in the Maryland charter; it not only provided for imperial taxation, it also specifically mentioned parliamentary taxation by providing that the people of the colony had authority to tax themselves, "Saveing unto us, our heires and Successors, such impositions and Customes, as by Act of Parliament are and shall be appointed." There appear to have been no attempts by American whigs to construe these words to mean export and import duties only. Franklin, during his testimony before the Commons at the time of the Stamp Act debates, was asked if there was in the Pennsylvania charter "an express reservation of the right of parliament to lay taxes there." Instead of drawing fine distinctions, he simply denied the fact. "I know," he admitted, "there is a clause in the charter, by which the King grants, that he will levy no taxes on the inhabitants, unless it be with the consent of the assembly, or by act of Parliament."

"How then," he was asked, "could the assembly of Pennsylvania assert, that laying a tax on them by the stamp-act was an infringement of their rights?"

"[B]y the same charter," Franklin replied, "they are intitled to all the privileges and liberties of Englishmen; they find in the great charter, and the petition and declaration of rights, that one of the privileges of English subjects is, that they are not to be taxed but by their common consent."

Franklin was next asked if there were "any words in the charter that justify that construction," and gave what many listeners must have regarded as an evasive answer: "The common rights of Englishmen," he said, "as declared in Magna Charta, and the petition of right, all justify it."[6]

Franklin was following instructions of the Pennsylvania Assembly which had directed its agents to take their stand on the general provisions of the colony's charter and claim that it incorporated British and English rights going back at least to Magna Carta. No mention was made of the embarrassing clause in the charter authorizing parliamentary taxation. Implicit in the instructions was the argument that general constitutional rights took precedence over specific words limiting those rights. This was a rule of construction lawyers understood, strong in that it favored constitutional rights, but failing to answer the contention that since the first settlers of Pennsylvania had accepted the charter with its taxation clause, their successors should be so bound. Five years later, a writer in London spun a theory demonstrating one argument supporting the Assembly's method of charter construction. There was, he pointed out, "a power *implied* in the British parliament to tax" Pennsylvania, but not a power expressed. "In the same charter where this power of parliament is *implied*," the writer reasoned, "*British privileges* are *granted* expressly. Here there is a contradiction; which then shall we give up, the *positive grant*, or the *implication?* Certainly the implication."[7]

Although the Pennsylvania rule of construction was plausible in British constitutional law, its strength depended upon how specific the words of the reservation were and the words in the Pennsylvania charter reserving to Parliament the right to levy "impositions and Customes" were reasonably specific. But just as American whigs did not argue that the reservation was limited to import and export duties because they did not intend to concede the validity of any taxes, few on the imperial side stressed specificity, as they did not want to imply that Parliament's jurisdiction could be determined by the wording of a colonial charter. It was safer, they thought, to cite the reservation as a fact and draw a general conclusion. Conclusions, however, could be drawn in opposite directions. One writer, for example, tested the exemption from taxation in the Maryland charter against the general principle of parliamentary supremacy, a principle contrary to that relied on by the Pennsylvania Assembly. As applied by him, the principle of parliamentary supremacy meant that Parliament could tax unless a colony was "particularly exempted by grant or compact." Because Maryland alone was exempted from parliamentary taxation by this test, it followed that all other colonies could be taxed. The same general principle of supremacy could also be applied to the Pennsylvania charter to reach the same conclusion — the direct opposite of that reached by the Pennsylvania Assembly. "The charter of Pennsylvania," John Wesley noted, "has a clause admitting, in express terms, taxation by Parliament. If such a clause be not inserted in other charters, it must be omitted as not necessary; because it is manifestly implied in the very nature of subordinate government: all countries which are subject to laws, being liable to taxes." Wesley's argument asked too much: that Americans of all colonies admit that a clause in Pennsylvania's charter gave Parliament authority to tax them. "[I]s it not more reasonable," an Irish magazine asked Wesley, "to imagine *this* clause was *inserted in* the one charter *as necessary*, then *omitted* in the *others* as *not* necessary; especially when it is a clause, intending to *deprive* a set of people of a natural and particular *right?* — else, why was it inserted in any charter?"[8]

A second example of the same evidence leading to opposite conclusions is furnished by the exemption clause in the Maryland charter. "Suppose it is true," Samuel Johnson surmised, "that any such exemption is contained in the Charter of Maryland, it can be pleaded only by the Marylanders. It is of no use for any other province." The argument was based on the imperialist rule of construction, again reading charters from the presumption of parliamentary supremacy rather than of English rights. If, as John Lind suggested, Maryland alone was exempted from parliamentary taxation, "all the other provinces are, as to this point, in the same situation, as if no charter had been granted."[9]

When arguments such as these are added to the evidence of the Pennsylvania charter, it can be seen why American whigs did not make much of the Maryland exemption clause. If the colonists had contended that the Maryland exclusion was binding on Parliament, why was the Pennsylvania inclusion less binding on the colonies? Whigs discovered that, often as not, the charter defense had them on the defensive, explaining away the Pennsylvania provision. The most common and, from a legal perspective, the most persuasive argument they employed was the doctrine of nonuser; that is, to interpret the Pennsylvania inclusion by examining the constitutional practice of the imperial government during the century since the charter was granted and the colony settled. Nonuser was established by historical evidence, "the contemporary and continual construction which they [the colonies] have received from the conduct of Parliament, which best knew its own intentions, and which did not tax them: insomuch that the non-user may be better argued to be a tacit renunciation of taxation as to Pennsylvania, where the power was reserved."[10] The American whig effort to explain away the Pennsylvania provision was no more successful than imperialist attempts to explain away the Maryland exemption.

CARL A. RUDISILL LIBRARY
LENOIR RHYNE COLLEGE

THE LIMITS OF CHARTER

If the vagueness of charter puzzles us it is probably because we think charters something different from what they were. Charters were not organic laws, colonial constitutions, or blueprints for action. They were documents of incorporation, providing outlines of power. Although they were argued as authority for both sides of the taxation controversy because they appeared to support both sides, they were in legal fact authority for neither. Looking at both the first Virginia and first Massachusetts charters, William Knox concluded that the early colonist might have been taxed constitutionally "by the King's *sole prerogative*, for the *use* and *benefit* of the crown only, and in no case . . . taxed by themselves, or their representatives elected by themselves; for these charters convey no such powers to the companies, or to their council." However, someone else writing in the same year as Knox thought the charters proved the exact reverse.

> The Colonies, by their respective Charters, have not uniformly the same privileges, or the same constitution. But tho' they differ, in many particulars, they are alike, in the following; namely, That the inhabitants of every one of them, have a right to tax themselves, by their representatives, in their provincial assemblies; that none of them vote for representatives, in the British Parliament; and that all of them are to enjoy the freedom, of British subjects.[11]

It cannot be said that Knox was right and the second writer wrong or vice versa. It was a matter of probativeness, and the colonial charter was not very probative as constitutional authority. Franklin was perfectly consistent, at least from the perspective of constitutional advocacy, when he dismissed the wording of the Pennsylvania charter by citing that charter's general principles and condemning as "an ungrateful and barren Argument" the "flimsy Apology for the Right of taxing the unrepresented Colonies" that imperialists drew "from the Tenor of some of their Charters." He was criticizing the assumption "that the Charters granted the original Colonists are the only Foundation on which their respective Constitutions rest." They were, rather, but one of several foundations of the American constitutional case and from one perspective were not even that. For taken in their most common and useful function, the charters were less sources of constitutional authority than evidence of the constitution—"evidential" primarily, as John Dickinson put it, "of the rights and immunities belonging to all the King's subjects in America" and of the original contract between the first settlers and the Stuart kings.[12] That reality explains why the charter was a much greater factor in arguments over the authority of Parliament to legislate for the colonies and the rights of Americans than it was in the debate about taxation.[13]

The realization that the charter was evidence of constitutional rights rather than the constitution itself did not preclude American whigs from making arguments treating charters much as later state constitutions were treated: as organic acts. The Connecticut House of Representatives, for example, may have been claiming exemption from taxation on the strength of charter alone when it resolved: "That it is the just right and privilege of his Majesty's liege subjects of this Colony, to be governed by their General Assembly in the article of taxing and internal police, agreeable to the powers and privileges recognized and confirmed in the royal charter aforesaid, which they have enjoyed for more than a century past, and have neither forfeited nor surrendered." The Massachusetts House apparently was making much the same claim when it contended "that the charter of the province invests the General Assembly with the power of making laws for its internal government and taxation; and that this charter has never yet been forfeited."[14]

The last point raised by both houses provides a final explanation of why the charter was not an authority for claiming immunity from parliamentary taxation. Both Connecticut and Massachusetts said that their charters had not been forfeited, indicating that forfeiture was a constitutional possibility. In fact, a charter not only could be forfeited in a court of law, it could be revoked by Parliament. "The subjects who can produce no better title to liberty than a royal charter," an anonymous pamphlet correctly observed, "hold it by a very precarious tenure. A charter itself however beneficial to those who receive it, is an undeniable evidence of *absolute power* in the grantor."[15]

The legal mechanics of forfeiture were by no means so simple, but American whigs were aware that charter was tenuous ground on which to stand and that was one reason — the revocability of charter, along with the vagueness of charter and the realization that charters were not organic laws — they not only did not stand on that ground but took pains to shift themselves from it. That certainly was what the Maryland Assembly did. At the time of the Stamp Act crisis, when Maryland was the one colony with a promise of no taxation in its charter, its lower house may have thought that the charter was enough to protect the colony when it resolved: "That it is the Unanimous Opinion of this House, That the said Charter is Declaratory of the Constitutional Rights and Privileges of the Freemen of this Province." Six years later, however, when the dispute was whether the governor could promulgate official fees, the lower house sought a much broader and firmer constitutional base than merely the defense of charter.

This Principle of the *English* Constitution hath been declared, confirmed and secured by divers Statutes . . . the Fees of an Office are a Tax upon the Subject. The good People of this Province are undoubtedly entitled, as *English* Subjects, to all the Rights, Liberties, Privileges and Immunities of his Majesty's liege Subjects, born and residing within his Kingdom of *England*, and therefore need not recur to the royal Charter of this Province for the Establishment of their Rights, Liberties and Privileges.[16]

CHAPTER TEN

THE DOCTRINE OF CONSENT
TO TAXATION

Unlike the plea of charter and the argument of contract, the doctrine that taxation was unconstitutional without consent was central to the revolutionary controversy. Thomas Hutchinson noted early in the period that the whig slogan was "No representation, no taxation." After the Revolution had begun, the clause in the Declaration of Independence charging George III with "imposing taxes on us without our consent" was referred to by a London reviewer as "the grand foundation of the contest," and the pamphleteer who answered the Declaration for the ministry referrred to the doctrine of consent as "originally the *apparent* object of [the] contest."[1]

The ministerial hack was correct. Before the Stamp Act was even passed by Parliament, Rhode Island's Governor Stephen Hopkins noted that all American pamphlets agreed "That it is the incontestable right of a subject of *Great-Britain* not to be taxed out of parliament, and that in parliament every subject dwelling within the kingdom of *Britain*, is represented." He might have made his statement much stronger had he noted that the declarations of official American governmental bodies also agreed. As early as January 1764, a committee of the Massachusetts House of Representatives protested the new vigor London was putting into enforcement of the Sugar Act of 1733, saying it could not concede "to the

Parliaments having a Right to Tax our trade which we can't by any means think of admitting, as it wou'd be contrary to a fundamentall Principall of our Constitution vizt. That all Taxes ought to originate with the people." In May, the Boston town meeting made what has been called the first public denial of Parliament's authority to tax without consent. The next month the Massachusetts House of Representatives reacted to news that Parliament was considering the Stamp Act by warning other colonies that stamp taxes imposed by the imperial legislature would deprive Americans "of some of their most essential Rights as British Subjects and as Men particularly the Right of assessing their own Taxes and being free from any Impositions but such as they consent to by themselves or [by] Representatives." And before the year had ended the burgesses of Virginia had informed separately each of the three branches of Parliament that for them to impose taxes on North America would violate colonial rights. They petitioned the king "to protect your People of this Colony in the Enjoyment of their ancient and inestimable Right of being governed by such Laws respecting their internal Polity and Taxation as are derived from their own Consent, with the Approbation of their Sovereign." They remonstrated to the Commons that it was "essential to *British* Liberty that Laws imposing Taxes on the People ought not to be made without the Consent of Representatives chosen by themselves." And they memorialized the House of Lords that it was "a fundamental Principle of the *British* Constitution, without which Freedom can no Where exist, that the People are not subject to any Taxes but such as are laid on them by their own Consent, or by those who are legally appointed to represent them."[2]

A CONSTITUTIONAL DOGMA

It cannot be said flatly that Americans were not represented in Parliament. Colonial whigs said it, of course, because by their definition of representation they were not represented. The British definition of representation, though, differed from the American and most participants for the imperialist side of the taxation debate believed the colonists were legally and constitutionally represented in the House of Commons. What everyone acknowledged was that no member of Parliament was elected by the people of a colony, and most persons in Great Britain would have agreed with the Massachusetts House of Representatives that Parliament's taxing of the colonies would mean taxes levied "without the Voice or Consent of one *American* in Parliament." In order to understand the American argument against parliamentary taxation, the British definition of representation should be set aside for the moment. The American argument is more familiar, for it is closer to twentieth-century concepts of representation in both the United States and the United Kingdom. It was the criterion employed by the Pennsylvania Assembly when it resolved "[t]hat the only legal representatives of the inhabitants of this province, are the persons they annually elect to serve as members of assembly."[3]

The American definition was not complicated, nor was its application as a test for determining the constitutionality of the Stamp Act. "[T]he Consent of the Inhabitants of this Colony," the Connecticut lower house pointed out, "was not given to the said Act of Parliament personally or by Representation, actual or virtual, in any Sense or Degree, that at all comports, with the True intendment, Spirit, or equitable Construction of the British Constitution." The two arguments were blended into one by South Carolina's Commons House of Assembly. "[T]he only Representatives of the People of this Province," it resolved, "are Persons chosen therein by themselves; and . . . no Taxes ever have been, or can be, constitutionally imposed on them, but by the Legislature of this Province." The issue was constitutionality, and the American whig conclusion was that parliamentary taxation of the colonies was unconstitutional. "Resolved therefore," the Pennsylvania legislature asserted, "That the taxation of the people of this province, by any other persons whatsoever than such their representatives in assembly, is UNCONSTITUTIONAL, and subversive of their most valuable rights."[4]

Maryland's Lower House of Assembly gave four reasons the colonies could be taxed only by their local legislature: (1) the emigration theory;[5] (2) guarantees contained in Magna Carta, the Petition of Right, and the Bill of Rights; (3) the colonial charters, especially Maryland's, with its exemption clause; and (4) custom. Although not every assembly stated the same grounds, Maryland's four explanations were typical in that they did not rely on natural law. Although it may have been possible to base the right of taxation by consent only on natural law, there was no need to do so. Had any official body done so, it surely would have been the Boston town meeting. Bostonians often mentioned natural rights when asserting the privilege of consent to taxation, but generally meant those particular natural rights favored by American whigs: natural rights based not on nature as much as on the British constitution or the most peculiar "natural rights" of all, those promulgated by acts of Parliament. "If," the town meeting declared in 1767, "the people of this province, are by nature, and by the royal charter, intitled to all the rights of natural born subjects . . . all property taken from them, by any manner or way without their consent, must be an infringement of their natural and constitutional rights." The next year, the same voters claimed that parliamentary taxation was "in Violation of the said Royal Charter; and . . . in Violation of the undoubted natural Rights of Subjects, declared in the aforesaid Act of Parliament, *freely* to give and grant their own Money for the Service of the Crown, with their own Consent, in Person, or by Representatives of their own free Elections."[6] The act of Parliament to which the Bostonians referred was the Bill of Rights. Although it may be that the voters of Boston interpreted that statute as merely declaratory of preexisting natural law, the way the claim is worded indicates that they thought the taxation-only-by-consent doctrine a natural-law principle dependent on the authority of positive law.[7]

Although the source of the doctrine might be ambiguously explained, its principle was as clear as any doctrine pleaded during the revolutionary era. "[I]t is," Pennsylvania's Assembly insisted, "the inherent birthright, and indubitable privilege of every British subject, to be taxed only by his own consent, or that of his legal representatives." Or, as a neighboring legislature said, the people of New Jersey "ought to be protected" from parliamentary taxation, "by the acknowledged principles of the constitution, that Freemen cannot be legally taxed but by themselves, or by their Representatives."[8]

When Americans claimed that parliamentary taxation was "a violation of their rights, [and] is contrary to the constitution," they generally did not identify which constitution. It was understood that they meant the British constitution. The principle that taxation could be imposed only by consent or representation had never been an American constitutional doctrine and never would be, at least not under the federal constitution. Revolutionary colonial whigs asserted it as a British right to which they had a claim as valid as that of subjects in the mother country: it was "the indubitable Right of all the Colonists as *Englishmen*." The word "Englishmen" was emphasized because the doctrine had been incorporated into the British constitution from the old English constitution where, the New York Assembly pointed out, it had been "a fundamental principle . . . declared by magna charta, and confirmed at the glorious revolution, by the petition and bill of rights." Americans were thus asserting their entitlement to one right, no taxation without consent, on the basis of another right, equality. Again, the legal theory was enunciated by the freeholders of Boston. It was, they insisted, a matter both of equality and constitutionalism, for under the British constitution "it is established no Man shall be govern'd nor taxed, but by himself or [by] Representative. . . . In open violation of these fundamental Rights of Britons, Laws & Taxes are imposed on us to which we have not only not given our consent but against which we have most firmly Remonstrated."[9]

The principle was stated as strongly as language permitted. It was not only a "fundamental" law of the British constitution "that no Englishman is to be taxed without his own consent," it was an "essential" right, "the very essence of the British Constitution."[10] As we are dealing only with the question of the authority of Parliament to tax British North America, it would be premature to enter into a discussion of comparative rights. It is enough to note that the privilege of not being taxed except by consent was regarded as one of the highest rights in the British constitution. Many constitutional theorists ranked it with trial by jury as one of the two most valuable privileges possessed by British subjects,[11] and some thought it the most important.[12] It was called the "grand aphorism of the British constitution," "so invaluable" that "no other can exist without it."[13]

Although numerous similar quotations could be offered of colonial assemblies repeating the same assertions — the claim, for instance, that among the many rights Americans possessed "The principal of these (and which is the only Security free Subjects can have for the rest) is the sole Right of levying Taxes upon themselves"[14] — the words of Virginia's House of Burgesses are typical and can serve to sum up for all the others.

> [T]he fundamental and vital Principles of their happy Government, so universally admired, is known to consist in this: that no Power on Earth has a Right to impose Taxes upon the People or to take the smallest Portion of their Property without their Consent, given by their Representatives in Parliament; this has ever been esteemed the chief pillar of their Constitution, the very Palladium of their Liberties. If this Principle is suffered to decay, the Constitution must expire with it, as no Man can enjoy even the shadow of Freedom; if his property, acquired by his own Industry and the sweat of his brow, may be wrested from him at the Will of another without his own Consent.[15]

It is by keeping in mind how much American whigs considered the right to be taxed only by consent to underlie all their constitutional privileges that we can understand their fierce, hostile reaction to parliamentary taxation. It explains what a writer in December 1765 meant when he said of the ministers who had sponsored the Stamp Act that "[b]y one single Stroke of political Legerdemain, They have unhing'd the whole Constitution"; why the voters of Providence instructed their representative that they were "not bound to yield obedience" to any tax enacted by Parliament; and why Benjamin Welsh, who presumably considered himself a law-abiding man, felt it proper to publish in a Maryland news-paper a notice "to all Officers whatever, that may be appointed by Virtue of that most grievous and unconstitutional [Stamp] Act (to prevent them Trouble) That I will pay no Tax whatever, but what is laid upon me by my Representatives."[16]

CHAPTER ELEVEN

THE STATUS OF THE DOCTRINE

Two constitutional contentions supported the claim that Americans could not be taxed without consent. One was that the rule requiring consent for taxation had always been constitutional law. The second was that in Great Britain the rule still was constitutional law: that subjects "born within the Realm of England have a Property in their own Estate, and are to be taxed only by their own Consent, given in Person or by their Representatives." The validity of the doctrine was so widely assumed that most writers relying on it did not cite any authority to support its authenticity. It was even suggested that since the doctrine "is so well established" as one of the highest rights Britons possessed, "it is unnecessary to attempt a Demonstration of it to *Englishmen*, who feel the Principle firmly inplanted in them diffusing through their whole frame Complacency and Chearfulness," a claim that may not have been an exaggeration. The doctrine of consent to taxation, the historian of the revolutionary press found, was the constitutional rule most commonly mentioned in British newspapers and periodicals. It was, a magazine writer asserted, a legal principle "which no writer of any credit had disputed in this country, since the [Glorious] Revolution, until our controversy with the Colonies seemed to require the propagation of doctrines less favourable to freedom and the just rights of mankind."[1]

Due to the nature of the British constitutional system, the question of whether taxation without consent was constitutional was seldom litigated in the courts or referred to the attorney general for an official opinion. For contemporary testimony of how the principle stood in Great Britain during the 1760s and 1770s, therefore, we must turn to the popular literature as well as to constitutional-law texts. When we do, evidence is readily found not only that the doctrine was considered basic law in Great Britain, but that it was Irish constitutional law as well.[2] Indeed, it was stated as much as a self-evident truism in Britain as in America, and would continue to be throughout the remainder of the century, after the American Revolution had been fought and lost.[3] It was also enunciated in writings and speeches during the revolutionary era that were not concerned with colonial affairs,[4] even by lawyers who insisted that Parliament could constitutionally tax the unrepresented Americans. Those lawyers often admitted that for Parliament to do so was unconstitutional, but they contended that Parliament, as sovereign, had sovereign (and therefore lawful) power to refuse to accord the colonists whatever constitutional rights it pleased, even the right not to be taxed without consent.[5]

The variety of ways in which the doctrine of taxation only by consent was stated as a component of the eighteenth-century constitution in Great Britain is well worth our attention because it helps explain the confidence with which American whigs relied on the doctrine. One way was to promulgate the doctrine as a fundamental principle. Even Richard Price — a critic of how deceptively the doctrine operated in practice because of defects in how the word "representation" was defined in contemporary Britain — termed the doctrine of taxation only by consent "the fundamental principle of our government" and "the *principle* on which our government, as a *free* government, is founded."[6]

Lord Shelburne, who had presided over the Board of Trade and was secretary of state for colonial affairs during a brief period after the Stamp Act was repealed, believed that the right of the people to grant their own money was the most important privilege possessed by the British. He was reported to have said that Great Britain was robbing the Americans of this right, agreeing with a parliamentary writer who asserted that to tax the colonies without consent "would be an attempt to deprive them of that privilege which is the chief privilege enjoyed by all British subjects in any part of the British dominions, because it is the only privilege we can depend on for the preservation of all the privileges and immunities we have a right to." Before concluding that this argument was a bit overblown, it would be well to note that the premise upon which it rested was little different from one on which William Blackstone, generally thought of more as a tory than a whig, fixed his imprimatur; in the *Commentaries* he had only a short catalog of personal rights, but one unequivocally and clearly stated was the right not to be taxed except by consent.[7]

A second method of expressing the doctrine was to place it within the general standards of liberty. A good example was furnished by a writer in 1769 who was not discussing the colonies, but was interested in the theory of liberty, a concept he defined largely in terms of the right to be taxed only by consent. There was, he concluded, only one nation in Europe where liberty was firmly established. "Great Britain is that happy kingdom, and her people, in preference to the subjects of all other states, can most truly say — we are free, we have a property we can call our own, we can freely dispose of it agreeable to our inclinations without controul, it is not liable to be seized by rude violence."[8]

A third way to formulate the doctrine was to stress the concept of representation; that is, taxation by representation or consent by representation. As previously discussed, Lord Camden built his theory of taxation on a connection with representation. "I challenge any one," he told the Lords, "to point out the time when any tax was laid upon any person by P[arliamen]t, that person being unrepresented in P[arliamen]t."[9] His friend, William Pitt, expressed the same principle positively. "To be taxed without being represented," he argued, "is contrary to the maxims of law and the first principles of the constitution." Stated negatively, as a restraint on government, the principle was that not to tax unrepresented persons "is one of those sacred rules, by which the supreme legislature itself is bound to act." One writer even found "language" in "the Constitution of the British government" that read "*No right of Representation granted, no Taxation by Parliament.*"[10]

A fourth way that the doctrine of taxation only by consent was stated was to present it less as a matter of constitutional law or a rule of government than as an attitude of conduct inherent in the British character. On behalf of the party of Rockingham whigs, Edmund Burke proposed telling the king in 1777:

> We assure your Majesty, that, on our parts, we should think ourselves unjustifiable as good citizens, and not influenced by the true spirit of Englishmen, if, with any effectual means of prevention in our hands, we were to submit to taxes to which we did not consent, either directly, or by a representation of the people, securing to us the substantial benefit of any absolutely free disposition of our own property in that important case.[11]

Yet another way eighteenth-century Britons discussed the doctrine was to depict it as a constitutional privilege belonging to Parliament. It was, after all, a right that Parliament had reserved to itself following the Glorious Revolution. "For no subject of England," Blackstone explained, "can be constrained to pay any aids or taxes, even for the defence of the realm or the support of government, but such as are imposed by his own consent, or that of his representatives in parliament." To state the rule in that fashion, which in an eighteenth-century context can be described as the constitutionally positive, was to say that Parliament "is uncontestably vested with the sole right of levying money." In contrast, a writer taking what can be termed the constitutionally negative, put the doctrine into a wider historical context going back to the Stuart kings of the seventeenth century by stating it not as a privilege of Parliament but as a restraint upon the monarchy; that is, that under the British constitution, the Crown could not impose a tax without the people's consent. [12]

If an educated guess is permitted, it might be conjectured that most persons in eighteenth-century Great Britain thought the doctrine primarily a barrier against prerogative taxation rather than a constitutional rule implementing either the principle of representation or the principle of consent. That likelihood will be considered in the next several chapters. The point to note now is that the British emphasis on the doctrine as a check against monarchy, rather than Parliament, remained a lively constitutional concern despite the greatly curtailed power of the house of Hanover. The only occasion when the doctrine arose as a constitutional issue in Great Britain during the prerevolutionary period, aside from Parliament's attempt to tax the Americans, involved not the legislature but the Crown. Following the war against France, imposts had been levied on the ceded islands — St. Vincent, St. Dominica, Grenada, and the Grenadines — by proclamation issued in the king's name without sanction of Parliament. The ministry justified these taxes on the principle of the right of conquest. Rejecting that argument, a writer for the *North Briton* urged his readers not to misunderstand the issue. "For the question is not, What the inhabitants of those islands may, or may not have reason to complain of? but the true and important questions in this case are In what hands has the British constitution intrusted the power of levying money?" The answer, of course, was Parliament, a fact that helps explain why the American appeal to the same doctrine failed to impress some in Great Britain, for the colonists were contesting Parliament, not the king. The principle was quite the same, however, as the writer implied, when contending that "[t]he great, perhaps only, privilege the Commons have to support their independance, is . . . the power of raising money. . . . If this should once be gone, all must go with it, and a dissolution of the government ensue." As long as the Commons retained the privilege "all will be done that may appear necessary, or expedient for the preservation of our excellent constitution."[13]

SPECIFICITY OF THE DOCTRINE

To reject the American whig argument, imperialists did not have to deny the doctrine of consent for taxation. They could admit that parliamentary taxes on the colonies were unconstitutional, but still defend them as a legal exercise of sovereign power, or they could assert that although the doctrine was valid the colonists interpreted it incorrectly. "To say," Allan Ramsay explained, "that no Englishman is to be taxed, without his consent, either in person, or by his representatives, is merely sound without sense, and not true in fact; but must be limited, by the constitutional mode of taxation, which only requires, that no Englishman shall be taxed, without the consent of a representative body of men, in parliament." That was one meaning of the doctrine — a limitation on prerogative taxation: British subjects could be taxed only by consent of Parliament, precisely the institution by which Americans were being taxed. How, it was asked, could the doctrine of taxation only by consent be interpreted to mean that a person could not be taxed unless he voted for a representative who was a member of the legislative body imposing the tax when one-twentieth of the inhabitants of the mother country had no right to vote for members of Parliament? Those who could not vote were taxed the same as those who could. Besides, when colonial whigs abandoned generalities and depended on specific authorities, they frequently cited the Bill of Rights, a statute that could be read as limiting the consent doctrine not just to consent by representation but to one type of representation: representation in the British Parliament. "The levying money," it provided, "for or to the use of the Crown by pretence of prerogative, without grant of Parliament, for longer time, or in other manner than the same is or shall be granted, is illegal."[14]

One aspect of the consent-to-taxation principle in the revolutionary era, evidenced by several of the statements quoted in this and the last chapter should now be clear: contemporaries in the mother country often stated the doctrine without limiting it to consent by Parliament. The mayor, aldermen, and livery of London, for example, told the king that "They esteem it an essential, unalterable principle of liberty, the source and security of all constitutional rights — that no part of the dominion can be taxed without being represented." They did not say "without being represented in Parliament," because they meant taxation by representation, not just taxation by Parliament. The Bill of Rights Society expressed the same concept by urging that the Commons "restore to America the essential right of taxation by representatives of their own free election," a principle that George Grenville had recognized lay at the heart of the dispute even before passage of the Stamp Act.[15] Although a larger number of writers did use the word "parliament," examination of their meaning shows that many, in fact most, intended it to refer to any representative assembly within the Empire, not just the houses of the British legislature sitting at Westminster.[16] "It will not avail," Richard Henry Lee explained, "to say that these restrictions on the right of taxation, are meant to restrain only the sovereign, and not Parliament. The intention of the constitution is apparent, to prevent unreasonable impositions on the people; and no method is so likely to do that, as making their own consent necessary, for the establishment of such impositions."[17]

Daniel Dulany elaborated on this argument, giving specific attention to the contention that the Bill of Rights, when it codified the consent doctrine, intentionally and constitutionally limited both the doctrine and the meaning of consent to Parliament. That the statute referred to Parliament by name, Dulany insisted, was hardly surprising; Parliament, after all, was the institution giving consent of the British people to taxation. For Parliament alone to have been mentioned in the Bill of Rights did not disprove but rather "effectually establishes the very Principle contended for by the Colonies."

> Is not this a new Kind of Logic, to infer from Declarations and Claims, founded on the necessary and essential Principle of a Free Government, that the People ought not to be Taxed without their Consent, that therefore the Colonies ought to be Taxed by an Authority, in which their Consent is not, nor can be concerned; or, in other Words, to draw an Inference from a Declaration or Claim of Privilege, subversive of the very Principle upon which the Privilege is founded?[18]

A revealing point that has so much to do with the role of Parliament in the eighteenth-century British Empire that a full examination of its implications must be deferred until the topic of legislation is taken up should nonetheless be noted now: one of the major difficulties leading to the revolutionary war was the inability of the British imperialists and American whigs to reach a compromise on the doctrine of parliamentary supremacy. Part of the reason was that the British believed that the constitutional settlement, arrived at in the aftermath of the Glorious Revolution, had resolved all questions and could not be disturbed; current liberty was established in the doctrine of parliamentary supremacy, a doctrine whose orbit included the principle that taxes could be constitutionally levied only by consent. To the British, then, parliamentary consent was constitutional consent because for them the only danger of taxation without consent arose from the potential of prerogative taxation as indicated by reaction to the proclamation imposing taxes on the ceded islands. Contemporaries had not raised the issue of taxation by consent in so many words, but rather had exclaimed against Crown taxation or taxation without authority of Parliament. "The power of levying money," a typical reaction to the Crown's promulgation of taxes on the ceded islands warned, "never was, nor ever can, in a free government, be with safety placed in the hands of the supreme executive."[19] Because prerogative taxation was the only threat they could imagine and because they believed parliamentary taxation eliminated that threat, British constitutionalists generally could not accept or even appreciate the contention of Americans, when objecting to parliamentary taxation of the colonies, that they were raising the same constitutional issue that English and British whigs had raised when opposing prerogative taxation.

Richard Watson, regius professor of divinity and future bishop of Llandaff, preaching at Cambridge University less than two months before the Declaration of Independence, both noted the connection and associated it directly with the doctrine of taxation by consent. "Those who entertain high notions of the omnipotency of Parliament, will see no resemblance between the causes, which brought on the dissensions then, and now," Watson wrote, comparing the American conflict to the English Revolution against Charles I; "others will think, there is no difference except in this; that it was a part of the nation, which then resisted the King, because he would have taken from them their property, without their consent given by themselves or their representatives; and now, it is a part of the empire, which resists the Legislature for the very same reason." American whigs had been attempting to make this argument persuasive ever since the Stamp Act crisis eleven years earlier. "[H]ow is our case (in point of representation)," a writer had asked Connecticut's *New London Gazette*, "better than if this [Stamp] Act was imposed on us by *Royal Prerogative* only; which all will allow to be Unconstitutional?" Benjamin Franklin made the point for a London newspaper in terms no one with the least superficial knowledge of English constitutional history could have misunderstood when he said that Americans then faced "the same Oppression" that Britons would face if an attempt was made to tax them "by Royal Edict." Colonial resistance, he thought, could be compared to "the Conduct of the brave Hampden, who thought it his Duty to resist the lawful Sovereign's illegal Demand of three Shillings and Four-pence, for the single Reason, that he had no Hand, either personally, or representatively, in consenting to the Tax of Ship Money."[20]

Colonial whigs were asserting as a constitutional truism what appeared to be a political contradiction: that although only Parliament could constitutionally tax British subjects, Parliament could not constitutionally tax British subjects in North America due to the doctrine of consent. The argument was premised on the colonial definition of representation: if colonists were not permitted to vote for members of Parliament, then, in American theory, the members of Parliament did not represent them. That was the reason the name of John Hampden was so often invoked. For if the colonists were to be taxed by that Parliament in which they were not represented, "their rights as subjects under the government of the *English* constitution, are as clearly invaded as they were in the case of *ship-money;* and the province of Massachussets [*sic*] Bay now stands in the same situation in behalf of the rights of all the people in *America,* as Mr. *John Hamden* [Hampden] did for all the people of England in the last century."[21]

The constitutional principle that Americans had a right not to be taxed without consent and that they could be taxed with consent only by a legislative body to which they chose representatives was the most basic and widely understood of any argument made during the revolutionary controversy. "There is nothing more certain," Thomas Cushing and Samuel Adams insisted in 1765, "than that every English Subject, has a Right to be represented in the same Body which exercises the Power of levying Taxes: Now this [stamp] Act lays an *internal* Tax upon many Thousand Freeholders, who are not & cannot be represented in Parliament."[22]

DENIAL OF THE DOCTRINE

Cushing and Adams claimed that nothing was more certain than that British subjects could be taxed only by consent; although it would appear from what has been said in this and the previous chapter that every knowledgeable person agreed, that conjecture would be incorrect. There were individuals on both sides of the Atlantic during the revolutionary era who denied that the doctrine of consent was part of either the British or the imperial constitution.

Various arguments were used by persons doubting the constitutionality of the requirement of consent for taxation. They can be reduced to two basic contentions. The first insisted that the doctrine could not exist in the form and to the degree American whigs claimed — a constitutional barrier prohibiting parliamentary taxation — because of the principle of the absolute nature of sovereignty. The second simply denied that the doctrine existed in the imperial constitution, some writers denying it ever had existed in the British constitution.

The first denial, based on the sovereignty of Parliament, is similar to the argument previously discussed, one of the objections to the taxation-legislation dichotomy: that taxation was part of the sovereign power and sovereignty could not be divided, restrained, or limited. The same objection could be applied with equal force to the contention that Parliament could not tax people without their consent through representation. "The Right of raising and applying the public Revenues," it was asserted, "is a Part of that Power, and in order to its due Execution must be vested in the Sovereignty or first Authority of the State."[23] Even some of the most cherished constitutional phraseology in the English language, to say for example "free gifts" instead of "taxation," gave way to the superior claims of sovereignty.

> [B]y the principles of the British Constitution, neither individuals, nor subordinate communities, such as the colonies, are justifiable in asserting, that all aids from them for Public Services, should be their own free and voluntary gifts. According to the fundamental principles, and to the whole texture of the British constitution, Public Supplies granted for the support of the state are always of duty; or, in other words, the right of taxation in the British state is not in the people at large, but in the Supreme Superintending Power, who prescribes the Duty. It is the General Superintendance that gives a right to taxation, by implying the necessity of being supported; and where the constitution of the state has placed that superintendance, it, of necessity, places the right of demanding supplies, and regulating the mode of raising them.

One version of this argument contended that sovereignty encompassed the doctrine of consent and was not a rejection of it. Under the sovereign power, William Knox explained, every person enjoying the protection of that sovereignty and possessing property under it consented to "all taxes imposed by it, inasmuch as he *consents* to the authority by which they are imposed; and this conclusion will hold equally good when applied to the people in the Colonies, as it does for the people of Great Britain." Knox received this principle from his mentor, George Grenville, who believed that the doctrine of consent to taxation did not require representation but was correctly stated by the rule that "no man can be tax'd without his own Consent or the Consent of those whom the Society has empowr'd to act for the whole"— in other words, "empowered" by the sovereign power — which in turn meant that everyone was deemed to have consented to the rule that "[t]he supreme legislature represents all the subjects of the state."[24] From the same perspective of absolute sovereign power, consent could also be unnecessary as taxation would not be a taking of property. "[T]he supreme power has a right to *some part* of a subjects' property, because it cannot subsist without *it.*" The supreme power, or the government, was not entitled to all property for it did not need all, but what it needed already belonged to it — belonged, that is, not as potential acquisitions only but as property presently owned. The "commons are invested with the whole property of the kingdom, in trust," John Lind explained, and had authority to "apportion and distribute" it for support of the government. The Commons also had the duty to secure "to each man his share of the remaining parcel; which share *alone* is his property, and to be disposed of as he pleases."[25]

The second ground taken by imperialists to counter American whig claims that they could not constitutionally be taxed in Parliament when not represented in the Commons was to deny that the doctrine of consent to taxation was part of the British constitution.[26] A variation of this contention was the assertion that although the doctrine was an important constitutional principle, it was not fundamental constitutional law.[27] Some imperialists termed the doctrine a "sophism" without foundation in law. A few rejected it on the bold argument that representation was not a constitutional imperative for taxation.[28] It is interesting, however, that in both Great Britain and the colonies hardly any of the people who doubted the constitutionality of the doctrine were lawyers. One lawyer who did deny it was Attorney General Yorke, and even he, although saying that lack of representation did not affect the power to tax, admitted that for Parliament to exercise that power might give Americans a claim to be represented at Westminster. A second lawyer denying the doctrine was Lord Mansfield, who maintained that since Parliament could take private property without consent, it followed that Parliament could tax without consent.[29]

One point deserves emphasis: only a small percentage of writers for the imperial side of the controversy and an even smaller percentage of members of Parliament who spoke on the issue of taxation denied the constitutionality of the doctrine of consent to tax. Many of those who professed to do so, such as Grenville, really did not. Although they contended that consent was not necessary for constitutional taxation, they also claimed that Americans were virtually represented, indicating that if they were confident that consent was not necessary they knew that others in Britain were not. Hence, they reinforced their argument with the doctrine of virtual representation. In fact, most educated persons in Great Britain who said anything on the subject believed that consent was constitutionally necessary for taxation. Typical was a writer for the *Monthly Review* who was astonished to find anyone denying it. "An assertion so contrary to the letter and spirit of numerous acts of state," he observed, "as well as repugnant to all that has been *written and believed* of English rights or of English government, would seem at least to require one *sub-stantial* proof." Evidence that not everyone taxed had the right to vote was not convincing. To "prove that taxes are not of the nature of gifts, as Englishmen have at least always fondly considered them," it was not enough to show that there were "particular persons and places in Great Britain, who are taxed without their consent." The reason was "that it is unjust to deny the existence of a great fundamental principle of the English constitution, because either from the alterations of time, or the occurrence of natural obstacles, the operation of this principle is not every where equally extensive."[30] For this writer, and, indeed, for most of his contemporaries, the status of the doctrine was as substantive as it was for the most militant American whigs: the only taxes that could constitutionally be imposed on British subjects were those promulgated by the consent of the people taxed or their representatives.

The real question, then, is not which of the two perceptions of the eighteenth-century constitution — that of those who insisted that people could not be taxed without consent or that of those who denied the doctrine — was correct. Rather, it is necessary to ask the authority for the doctrine and the reason so many British subjects on both sides of the Atlantic believed that taxation required some form of actual or virtual representation. The answer is to be found in the apparatus of constitutional advocacy, in precedent, in analogy, and in generally honored constitutional conventions. To resolve the issue, therefore, we must turn first to the theory of constitutional precedent and then consider the history of the doctrine of consent in Great Britain, analogies to taxation of the colonies, the weight of specific precedents of parliamentary taxes imposed on North America, the argument of virtual taxation, and the principle of custom.

CHAPTER TWELVE

THEORY OF PRECEDENT

Sometime before May of 1764, a Rhode Islander wrote a letter to the *Providence Gazette*. "It is true," he said, referring to news that Parliament was considering a stamp tax for the North American colonies, "the one proposed would be small and equal, therefore in itself not an object for opposition; but should this internal tax be effected, it might in any future times be a dangerous precedent, in the hands of a bad ministry, for laying insupportable burthens, to the privation of that liberty and property claimed by every Briton as his birth-right." In February of the next year, before the Stamp Act had been passed by Parliament, Thomas Whately, member for Ludgershall and private secretary in the treasury of George Grenville, contemplated passage of the Stamp Act by considering the same legal principle that had occurred to the Rhode Islander — the principle of precedent. "The great Measure of the Sessions is the American Stamp Act," Whately declared. "I give it the appelation of *a great measure* on account of the important point it establishes, the Right of Parliament to lay an internal Tax upon the Colonies."[1]

After the stamp tax had been enacted and before it went into effect, people in the colonies continued to write of it in terms of the theory of precedent. The Stamp Act, a September issue of the *New York Post-Boy* warned, "must be considered as an *entering wedge*, or introduction to future oppressions and impositions." Thirteen days later, the inhabitants of Boston agreed when they voted instructions to their representatives in the General Court. "[T]his Act," they asserted, "if carried into Execution, will become a further Grieveance [*sic*] to us as it will afford a Precedent for the Parliament to Tax us in all future Time, and in all such Ways and Measures, as they shall Judge meet without our Consent." The *Boston Evening-Post* repeated the theme over a month later. "And why," it asked, "may not this act, in subversion of the privileges of our charters, in future time, be improved, as a precedent against Magna Charta itself, and the other charters in England, to the ruin of their Privileges, with equal and stronger forces than the Post Office is used in this case?"[2]

The *Evening-Post* referred to two different precedents. One was the Post Office Act of the ninth year of Queen Anne, a statute we will have to look at in some detail when examining specific, statutory precedents of parliamentary taxes levied on the colonies, because it had been relied on as a precedent establishing Parliament's right to impose the Stamp Act. The second precedent was the Stamp Act itself. As all the people just quoted said, it could be used as a precedent for other taxes and other parliamentary mandates. It could become a precedent in two distinct senses: first, the very fact of having been enacted by Parliament and entered on the British statute books; second, by operating as a parliamentary tax and being paid by Americans to the British treasury. Colonial whigs had that second aspect in mind when they took to the streets and prevented execution of the stamp tax. A *tenable* precedent furnished by London's claim of the right to tax North Americans, made a more *persuasive* precedent by Parliament's assertion of that right when it passed the Stamp Act, could have become an *irrefragable* precedent had many colonists in fact paid taxes. Under the doctrine of precedent, had Americans purchased the stamps they would have provided imperial authorities with evidence acknowledging the legality of parliamentary taxation. Put in more legal terms, failure to have resisted the Stamp Act would have given London the argument that the Americans had waived the claim of unconstitutionality.[3]

FUNCTION OF PRECEDENT

The theory of precedent may be better understood by contrasting it to the theory of innovation previously discussed. The doctrine of innovation warned that an action was legally dubious because it had not been done before. Precedent was evidence of legality or constitutionality because something had been done before. Since the stamp tax was enacted by Parliament, payment of it by Americans would have furnished the imperial government with a precedent for future taxes. The fact that prior to the Stamp Act Parliament had never imposed on the colonies a direct, internal tax was not a precedent but evidence of a third legal doctrine closely associated with the doctrine of innovation and the doctrine of precedent: the doctrine of custom.[4]

A reviewer for a London magazine in 1766 provided an indication of the importance of precedent in the eighteenth century when he complained that although everyone extolled the constitution, commentators "have been unwilling to rest on its own most admirable and solid foundation, namely, the fitness and utility of it; and considering this obvious argument as insufficient, have imagined themselves under a necessity of supporting it merely by precedents, and the authority of ancient custom." What the writer did not understand was that precedents were "the very life" of the constitution because they provided authority by which disputes could be accommodated. As Daniel Dulany explained:

> The use of precedents must be perceived, when the inconveniences of contention, which flows from a disregard of them are considered and especially when they are severely felt: when we reflect, that the intercourse of the members of political bodies, the measures of justice in contests of private property, the prerogatives of government, and the rights of the people are regulated by them.

Another critic of precedents, or at least of how lawyers used them, was a Rhode Islander commenting on the Stamp Act.

> I am in doubt if there be so much in the matter of *precedents* as some would have. I know, that the *lawyers* have carried the authority of *precedents* so far, that if a point be to be gained, nothing is required or sought after but a *precedent*, and if that can be found among the various and contrary resolutions, they form a conclusion that the point is *clearly established;* whether the *precedent* be footed on justice and reason, or on whim and arbitrariness.

Like the London reviewer, the Rhode Islander missed the point of the doctrine of precedent as employed in the seventeenth- and eighteenth-century constitution. He was troubled that "*Precedents* of infringing the liberties of the subject are to be met with plentifully in history." That fact, although true, was not characteristic of precedents in British constitutionalism. They were primarily used to restrain government and to establish "ancient" liberties. It was, after all, the government that most often attempted to initiate change and people like the American whigs who invoked the theory of precedent to resist change. Sovereigns and ministries were not only forced to find precedent to justify actions, they were even on occasion forced to produce that peculiarity of English legalism, a precedent for an innovation.[5]

There were no rules or standards for judging the persuasiveness of precedents. Much depended upon personal preference and subjective evaluation. Quite often precedents cited for one cause or another were not relevant to the issue at bar. John Lind, for example, attempted to defend the Stamp Act with an analogy that was not analogous: the tax for Americans was "without a precedent; but long since had it been established among their fellow-subjects in Great Britain." Another frequently employed argument cited negative proof, alleging that something that had not occurred was precedent much as if it had occurred. William Knox found a precedent for parliamentary taxation of the colonies that way: in 1713 the New York Assembly had refused to enact certain provincial taxes that London had requested; the British government threatened that if the Assembly did not act, Parliament would; the Assembly then passed a tax bill. Although Parliament had not taxed New York, Knox thought this event precedent for parliamentary taxation because Parliament had clearly indicated that it believed it had the power to do so. Conversely, Governor Thomas Pownall thought that Parliament, by not taxing any colonies before 1765 and by accepting grants from them in the form of requisitions, had created a precedent against itself.[6]

Time was an important consideration in proving precedents, although not in a manner we might think. Duration was significant; in some cases sequence was not. *Junius* dismissed precedents of arbitrary commitments for contempt of the Commons as being "of too modern a date to warrant a presumption that such a power was originally vested in the house of commons." South Carolina's Commons House of Assembly, contrary to the ministry's instructions and to constitutional practice in Great Britain and all other colonies, asserted the authority to order money from the colonial treasury, and supported its claim with what it considered to be valid precedent. England's Attorney General William de Grey did not agree. The Commons House might be able to prove that it had exercised the privilege previously, he admitted, but that evidence did not deserve the weight of legal precedent. A practice so contrary to British constitutional norms under which only the executive could order money disbursed, the attorney general ruled, was not "warranted by the modern practice of a few years, irregularly introduced, and improvidently acquiesced in." A sufficient duration of time, therefore, could make a precedent when used to prove that a practice had become established and accepted as a rule of government. Time was, however, not necessarily a factor when viewed from the perspective of the chronology of events. In 1776, to free British soldiers for service in North America, the ministry stationed Hanoverian troops at Gibraltar, a step some members of Parliament claimed violated the Bill of Rights. The secretary at war, Lord Barrington, disagreed. "[T]he Bill of Rights," he argued, "never was, nor could be intended to extend further than the kingdom: he instanced, in proof of his assertion, the garrisons of Dunkirk and Tangier, in Charles II.'s time, and that of Calais at a much earlier date." What Barrington did was interpret the Bill of Rights with precedents from the period before the Bill of Rights had been enacted, precedents not related to any of the reasons why the bill was passed.[7]

USES OF PRECEDENT

John Dickinson, who believed that the authority to take property for the purpose of raising revenue was a distinct constitutional power, did not think that parliamentary statutes such as the Hat Act precedent for the stamp tax or for other taxes. However, he deemed them precedent for what they did do — restrict colonial manufacturing. "*Great-Britain* has prohibited the manufacturing *iron* and *steel* in the colonies," Dickinson noted, referring to the Iron Act of 1750, "without any objection being made to her *right* of doing it. The *like* right she must have to prohibit any other manufacture among us. Thus she is possessed of an undisputed *precedent* on that point."[8]

Dickinson stated two concepts. One was that Great Britain possessed so clear a precedent on the point of her authority to prohibit colonial manufacturing that it was "undisputed." The second was the statement or implication that part of the reason the precedent was undisputed was that when the Iron Act was passed by Parliament, no objection had been made by the colonies. Richard Henry Lee agreed with this theory of how precedents acquired legal persuasiveness. After enactment of the Townshend duties he wrote Dickinson, scolding him because the Pennsylvania legislature had not "expressed, even the least dislike to the late duty act, although all England now agrees, its principal intention to be, to establish a precedent for American taxation, by the British Parliament." Most of the colonies had vigorously protested the Stamp Act and it had been repealed, Lee pointed out. To have protested the first tax and not to have protested the second could lead to the conclusion that the Townshend duties, having received (like the Iron Act) colonial acquiescence, were a valid precedent. "[S]ilence in this case must, by all the world, be deemed a tacit giving up our rights, and an acknowledgement, that the British

Parliament may, at pleasure, tax the unrepresented Americans." Dickinson replied that he agreed with Lee's argument. Protests, the Pennsylvanian wrote, had to be made or consent would be implied and a precedent established.

> Claims so unreasonable in their nature, made on private persons, may be past over in silence and contempt. But in affairs of a higher dignity, transacted between different states, or different orders of the same state, the preservation of mutual respect, and the fatal tendency of precedents, seem indispensibly to require objections, at once firm and respectful to be made, where the parties have a right or a cause to object.[9]

The concept that precedents had to be guarded against provided American whigs with a program for action. The topic of avoidance of precedent is elaborated on in a later section, when it will be seen that many legislative bodies in the colonies were on the watch to avoid exactly what Dickinson and Lee warned about: the creation of precedent by the British ministry. When they either failed to object or were unable to do so, the assemblies or other bodies tried to discount the implication that they had acquiesced. Maryland's Lower House of Assembly, for example, protested to the governor that since he had not called them into session from the time the Stamp Act was first proposed until after it had been enacted, people in Great Britain could be told that Maryland had accepted the constitutionality of parliamentary taxation.

> It is incumbent on us, as the Representatives of a Free People, to Remonstrate against that Measure; especially as it prevailed at a Time so very critical to the Rights of *America;* at a Time when the good People of this Province ardently wished for an Opportunity to express, by their Representatives in Assembly, their Sense of a Scheme, then entertained by the *British* House of Commons, of imposing Stamp-Duties on the Colonies; and for want of which, their involuntary Silence, on a Subject so Interesting and Important, has been construed, by a late Political Writer of *Great-Britain,* as an Acquiescence in that intended Project.

The Marylanders made this argument in 1765 at the start of the revolutionary controversy. Nine years later, there had been so many potential precedents to protest that the voters of Providence, Rhode Island, thought the burden of proof should be shifted. Rather than an assembly having to state for the record that it had not had an opportunity to object, they said, the British should not be permitted to imply acceptance. "We lament," the Providence town meeting resolved, "any seeming acquiescence which hath at any time heretofore been made in these colonies, under parliamentary usurpations of our liberties; but as any such tacit concessions were made through fear, inattention, or without a due consideration of our rights, we strongly protest against any precedent being made thereby, to our disadvantage."[10]

CREATION OF PRECEDENT

Creation of precedent was a very lively enterprise during the Stamp Act crisis and not only in the obvious way that the Stamp Act could become a precedent for parliamentary taxation of the colonies. Even before it had a chance to reach that stage, people were attempting to manipulate events in order to change, strengthen, or modify the precedent. A letter from London written in March 1764 and published in several newspapers urged the colonists to take the initiative and alter the potential precedent by assenting to the tax before it was, as it surely would be, enacted by Parliament.

> [T]he several Assemblies should signify their Assent and Desire to that Tax, under the present Exigencies of the State, and the Necessity of the Case, by which they avoid every Appearance of an Infringement of their Liberty, and shew their Inclination to pay their Obedience to a British Parliament, which has the Power to make every Part of its Dominions submit to such Laws as they may think proper to enact; by this Means they will prevent a Precedent from internal Taxes being imposed without their Consent, which will inevitably be the Case next Session, if they withhold their Assent to the Stamp Tax.[11]

George Grenville even held out to the colonial agents the idea that prior consent would permit their assemblies to create a precedent against Parliament, a limited precedent of being consulted whenever future taxes were contemplated. The plan, William Knox explained, was to give colonial legislatures a chance "to establish a precedent for their being consulted before any tax was imposed on them by parliament"; should they consent to the stamp tax in principle before enactment, it "would afford a forcible argument for the like proceeding in all such cases." At least one agent, South Carolina's Charles Garth, passed on the proposal, suggesting that prior consent might "establish a precedent, of being previously consulted" before future taxes were enacted, and pointing out that if the colonies did not consent and "should an opposition prove fruitless, it may make a consultation upon future occasions appear not so proper."[12]

There was no chance that the South Carolina Commons House or any other colonial assembly would take Grenville's bait. The precedent of being consulted was simply not a gain when contrasted to the loss from the precedent of parliamentary taxation created by the Stamp Act. "Every Mention of the parliam'ts Intention to lay an Inland Duty upon us," a Virginia legislative committee advised that colony's agent, "gives us fresh Apprehension of the fatal Consequences that may arise to Posterity from such a precedent." In fact, Daniel Dulany argued, Grenville's proposed precedent would not have been a modifying precedent but, as a colonial admission of Parliament's authority to tax, a further precedent strengthening the imperial claim of legislative supremacy. "How would the Precedent have been established," he asked, "or, if it had, what would have been the Advantage? This Conduct would have admitted, that the Colonies might be Taxed at any Time, and in any Manner, without their Consent; and consequently, would at once have been an effectual Surrender of all their Privileges as *British* Subjects." Four years later, Samuel Adams raised a similar consideration when he answered an argument that the colonies should have asked Parliament to postpone the Stamp Act's operation while they pleaded their case against its constitutionality.

> But does he not consider, that in *pleading* our cause, as he terms it, we implicitly put it in the power of others to be the judges whether they shall tax us without our consent. . . . And supposing that after having pleaded our cause . . . we should not have prevailed upon them to have receded from their purpose of taxing us . . . would they not have . . . told us that we ought not surely to complain, since in pleading our cause before them, we left it to their sole judgment and decision, whether they had not the right to tax us. . . . This it must be own'd would have afforded a happy precedent for all futurity.[13]

Although Grenville's modifying precedent was never adopted, the doctrine of precedent remained a factor in the Stamp Act debates in at least two other respects. One was the argument that once the tax had been proposed and American whigs had objected to its constitutionality, it had to be enacted; had Parliament not passed the Stamp Act after colonists publicly, loudly, and frequently called it unconstitutional, the failure to act could have been argued as precedent that Parliament had acknowledged that it did not have authority to tax the colonies internally.[14] The second was that repeal of the act would become precedent for the same rule. "I have not the least doubt," Grenville lamented, "that our brethren in America will express great joy at the repeal of the Stamp Act, especially if they understand by it, as they justly may . . . that they are thereby exempted for ever from being taxed by Great Britain."[15]

DANGER OF PRECEDENT

Grenville had been apprehensive of the danger posed by permitting an unfavorable precedent to be established. Sharing the same English legal traditions, American whigs were also watchful for dangerous precedents. Thomas Cushing missed the seriousness of the British government's decision in 1763 to collect the customs imposed by the Sugar Act of 1773, but he did understand why his colleagues in Massachusetts General Court would not join him in suggesting that the tariff be lowered. They were opposed to "any duty at all, as of Dangerous precedent." Everyone, however, seemed to realize the danger threatened by the Townshend duties. It was not economic. The financial burden imposed by the duties was little more than a nuisance on American pocketbooks. It was the precedent created for further taxes that aroused opposition. The Townshend duties, the general committee of Charles Town, South Carolina, explained, were "more ruinous in their Precedent, than fatal in their present operations." The Townshend tax "is *only* designed to be a PRECEDENT, whereon the future vassalage of these colonies may be established," John Dickinson wrote, warning Americans not be to deceived just because the duties were not heavy.

> A conduct more dangerous to freedom . . . can never be adopted. Nothing is wanted at home but a PRECEDENT, the force of which shall be established, by the tacit submission of the colonies. With what zeal was the statute erecting the post-office, and another relating to the recovery of debts in *America*, urged and tortured, as *precedents* in support of the *Stamp-Act*, tho' wholly inapplicable. If the parliament succeeds in this attempt, other statutes will impose other duties.[16]

The major confrontation that American whigs had with precedent as a danger involved neither the Stamp Act nor the Townshend duties but the tea tax. When all Townshend duties except the tariff on tea were repealed, colonists knew why. The tax had been "retained upon tea for the avowed purpose of establishing a precedent against us."[17] The situation became more perilous when Parliament lowered the tax on tea and gave the East India Company a monopoly on the North American market.

Interestingly, the act of doing so also altered the charter of the company, causing protests in Great Britain that raised the same legal issue in London that was agitating the colonies. If the bill was passed, the company's general court had warned, it would destroy vested privileges "and must therefore prove a precedent dangerous to the property of the people at large." After the enactment of the Tea Act, dissentient lords repeated the warning. "[T]he provisions and precedent of this bill," they protested, "render the public faith of Great Britain of no estimation, the franchises, rights, and properties of Englishmen precarious."[18]

Maryland's deputy governor, Robert Eden, attempted to allay colonial apprehension by telling "the reasonable people" that the Tea Act could not be precedent for further taxation. It merely lowered the duty on tea, he pointed out; it did not impose that duty. At most the Tea Act could "only serve as a precedent for any future Act that may operate in the same manner it does, which is as a relief . . . tea being now much cheaper than it was before." The argument, he admitted, "has not the weight I could wish." Tea was cheaper because even though a duty was imposed at the American port of entry, a drawback of an even higher amount had been allowed the company against the tax paid when the tea had originally been imported into Great Britain. "The insidious Purpose," some New York citizens realized, "of levying the Duty in America, and taking off a much greater in England, is . . . nothing less than to establish the *odious* Precedent of *raising a Revenue in America.*"[19]

American loyalists tried to persuade whigs that although the precedent might be of a tax it could not possibly have amounted to a serious danger. "Shall we move Heaven, and Earth, against a trifling Duty, on a Luxury?" Jonathan Boucher asked. The whig answer was yes. "[T]he late Exportation of tea by the East India Company," the first North Carolina provincial congress resolved, "was intended to . . . establish a precedent highly dishonorable to America and to obtain an implied assent to the powers which Great Britain had unwarrantably assumed of levying a tax upon us without our consent." At the other end of the continent several Rhode Island towns were saying the same: that the East India Company Act was "designed as a precedent for establishing taxes, duties and monopolies, in America."[20]

The danger posed by the creation of this precedent — a danger which acquired additional force by the statutory mandate that once the tea was landed the duty would be paid whether tea was sold to the public or was just left to rot — explains why whigs felt compelled to stage various tea parties. As an unknown whig said to the Boston merchants who had been appointed consignees of the tea by the company, "if we allow them [the imperial government] a fair opportunity of pleading precedent by a successful execution of the tea act, under your auspices, we may bid adieu to all that is dear and valuable amongst men."[21] The danger of this particular precedent may have been overstated, but the principle was not. Few legal doctrines were so well understood or more frequently acted upon during the revolutionary era. Whigs felt that they had no choice but to act, and that both the British constitution and English legal history supported them. "What," John Dickinson asked, "would the liberties of the people of *England* have been at this time, if precedents could have made laws inconsistent with the constitution?" George Mason warned that had American whigs failed to act against the creation of precedents, the dangerous consequences would not have been felt only in the colonies. "Can the foundations of the state be sapped and the body of the people remain unaffected?" he asked a committee of London merchants. "Are the inhabitants of Great Britain absolutely certain that, in the ministry or parliament of a future day, such incroachments will not be urged as precedents against themselves?"[22]

Avoidance of Precedent

It would be tedious to recount the many steps taken by American whigs to avoid precedents that London might have used in support of the constitutionality of parliamentary taxation for purposes of raising revenue. The most famous actions of avoidance have been mentioned: the crowds that took to colonial streets in 1765 to prevent implementation of the stamp tax and the crowds of 1773 and 1774 that prevented tea from being unloaded in every American seaport except Charles Town, South Carolina. Only two other incidents, both of which occurred during the Stamp Act crisis, merit attention because they illustrate the extent to which American whigs were on their constitutional guard against the creation of taxation precedents.

At the height of the Stamp Act crisis, at a time when colonial crowds were forcing stamp distributors to resign and taking other steps to prevent the law from becoming a precedent for parliamentary taxation, the governor of North Carolina, William Tyron, met with about fifty gentlemen of Brunswick, New Hanover, and Bladen counties to propose a plan to end the violence. Tyron "offered to pay himself the whole Duty arising on any Instruments executed on Stampt Paper, on which he should have any Perquisite or Fee; such as Warrants and Patents for Land." The gentlemen to whom the offer was made had to reject it. Americans could not permit any aspect of the Stamp Act to function and it did not matter who paid the tax. The explanation, drafted by a committee of the gentlemen, explains why: avoidance of precedent. "[T]he Submission," they contended, "to any Part of so oppressive and (as we think) so unconstitutional Attempts [at parliamentary taxation], is opening a direct Inlet for Slavery, which all Mankind will endeavour to avoid."

> For these Reasons, it is with great pain we are obliged to dissent from what your Excellency has been pleased to mention, of your paying the Stamp Duties . . . nor can we assent to the Payment of the smaller Stamps: An Admission of Part, would put it out of our Power to refuse, with any Propriety, a Submission to the whole; and as we can never consent to be deprived of the invaluable Privilege of a Trial by Jury, which is one Part of this Act, we think it a more consistent, as well as securer Conduct, to prevent, to the utmost of our Power, the Operation of it.

Later that same year, the governor of Maryland ordered the colonial printer to print copies of the statute repealing the Stamp Act and of the Declaratory Act in which Parliament reserved the authority to tax the colonies. The two branches of the colonial legislature quarreled over whether to reimburse the printer. At a conference, lower-house conferees told conferees for the upper house that the lower house could not pay the printer's claim because:

> Publication of the Acts of Parliament in this Province, by Proclamation, is without Precedent; and the Allowance contended for, would probably induce, for the future, the like Publication of all Acts of Parliament to be made hereafter, and, as constantly, Charges similar to the present. That this House are apprehensive their making such Allowances, might hereafter furnish an Argument, that this House acquiesce, contrary to their former Resolutions, and present Opinion, in the British Parliament's having a Constitutional Right to impose internal Taxes on her Colonies.

Neither the gentlemen in North Carolina nor the lower house of Maryland's Assembly was concerned with immediate effects; in the first instance, the governor had offered to pay for the stamps and in the second, the cost of printing two statutes was so minor it could not have been a consideration. What troubled them was precedent. They were acting on a legal theory familiar to eighteenth-century nonlawyers as well as lawyers. It was also one that the Maryland legislators overstated somewhat when contending that a single payment to the printer would have given the governor a precedent allowing him to print what he pleased in the future or that to print the statute repealing the Stamp Act would imply

acquiescence of Parliament's authority to tax the colonies. What is striking is not the legal reality but the fear, not whether caution was needed
but the precaution that was taken. Both the North Carolinians and the
Marylanders anticipated legal risk and took steps to prevent it; put another way, both acted to avoid a precedent.[23]

CHAPTER THIRTEEN

HISTORICAL ASPECTS
OF THE DOCTRINE

History and precedent should not be confused. History is evidence, and precedent is authority; to mix the two can produce misleading distortions. They are, of course, not unconnected: history provides evidence of precedent and is one of the sources from which precedent is drawn, a source in which precedent and custom blend. History also can clarify precedent by illustrating the roots of the legal doctrine that the precedent supports, a consideration especially pertinent to the consent-for-taxation principle since its origins, well understood in eighteenth- and twentieth-century Great Britain, have become clouded in the United States due to a misplaced emphasis upon John Locke. Failure to consider the English and British constitutional antecedents of the American Revolution can lead to the error of assuming that principles such as the right to be taxed only with consent come not from positive law but from commentators on law.[1] It is true that an eighteenth-century British lawyer, Lord Kames, attributed the doctrine to Locke and thought its acceptance due to his "respectable authority," but Kames was a Scots advocate and judge who was not trained in English law and may not have been too well versed in English constitutional history. It also is true that some common lawyers on both sides of the Atlantic — Lord Camden, John Dickinson, James Otis, and Arthur Lee among them — mentioned or quoted

Locke when explaining or defending the doctrine, but none of them confused commentary with origination. They knew Locke was defining an old constitutional doctrine, not promulgating something new. "His principles," Camden said of Locke's statement of the taxation-by-consent maxim, "are drawn from the heart of our constitution." Lee, in a letter to *Junius*, prefaced a reference to Locke by noting, "The mode only of *giving it* [property] *by representation* is a creature of the constitution."[2]

Certainly the authority that Americans had in mind when they claimed the privilege of taxation only by consent was not speculative law, theoretical law, or natural law, but rather constitutional law. Besides charter rights, they depended on the laws and statutes of the mother country. As the Maryland legislature asserted, "it was granted by *Magna Charta*, and other the good Laws and Statutes of *England*, and confirmed by the Petition and Bill of Rights, that the Subject should not be compelled to contribute to any Tax, Tallage, Aid, or other like Charge, not set by common Consent of Parliament." In 1775, an Edinburgh magazine listed the "law-authorities" colonial newspapers cited "against the authority of Britain to tax America": Sir Edward Coke, the *Journal of the House of Commons*, "Opinion of the judges of England, 20th of Henry VI," "Opinion of the judges of England, 2 Richard III," William Pitt, and Lord Camden. Locke was not mentioned.[3]

Perhaps had it not been for the unfortunate emphasis on Locke's influence, there might be no need to consider the constitutional history of the taxation-by-consent doctrine. Even so, it is not necessary to conduct a comprehensive survey of the origins since what concerns us is what eighteenth-century people in Britain and America, especially those who cited the doctrine as a rule of law, thought about its authority as established by constitutional custom and proven by history. They traced it back to time immemorial, even to the gothic constitution when the doctrine was "a fundamental part of all European constitutions."[4] In one respect, the quoted Maryland resolutions were unusual; few contemporaries thought of the privilege as a grant. It was instead a right; a right not derived from governmental grace but rather a limit on governmental power. "The Law of England, whereby the Subject was exempted from Taxes and Loans, not granted by common Consent of Parliament," John Pym, speaking on behalf of the Commons, told the Lords, "was not introduc'd by any Statute, or by any Charter or Sanction of Princes, but was the antient and fundamental Law, issuing from the first Frame and Constitution of the Kingdom."[5] Pym spoke in 1628.

The distinction was important because, as previously noted, the doctrine was as much a check on government as it was a civil right. It had been their ancestors' wisdom, contemporaries thought, "to circumscribe the regal authority, and to give to the body of the people the greatest, or rather the most important share in the government, by allotting to their representatives the exclusive right of disposing, in the first instance, of their property." Governor George Johnstone, pleading the colonies' case in the House of Commons, explained the doctrine's theory and mentioned some of the highlights of its history that will be traced in the remainder of this chapter.

> The great and only secret yet found out for preserving the liberties of mankind from encroachments of their power which is necessary for the executive in large kingdoms, is the power of the purse. This was the subject of contention in the Civil Wars of Charles the first: it is this privilege alone which makes the House of Commons respectable; This was the point which Hampden obtained for us.[6]

BEFORE THE STUARTS

John Pym, addressing the opening of Parliament in 1640, claimed that it was "a fundamentall truth, essentiall to the constitution and government to this kingdome, an hereditary liberty and priviledge of all the free-borne subjects of the land, that no tax, tallage, or other charge, might be laid upon us without common consent in parliament." Pym believed that the doctrine had been incorporated into the original contract between William I and the English people—"acknowledged by the Conqueror, ratified in that contract which hee made with this nation upon his admittance to the kingdome, declared and confirmed in the lawes which he published." And since Pym twelve years earlier traced the principle of consent to the laws of the Saxons, it was clear that he did not mean that the doctrine came from William's royal favor. Even during the feudal era that followed the Norman Conquest—a system "by no Means the most favorable to Liberty"—the fundamental principle had been "that no Freeman could be governed or taxed, unless by his Consent."[7]

To prove the claim that the post-Conquest era knew the consent-to-tax doctrine, participants in the revolutionary debates cited the analogies that will be discussed in the next chapter and the historical evidence being summarized in this. After the implied contract with William I, the most important event was the explicit contract with King John: Magna Carta. It provided that no scutage or aid should be imposed unless by the common counsel of the realm, with the exception of the three aids prescribed by the law of feudal tenures.[8] William Pitt thought that Magna Carta supplied historical evidence directly applicable to the North American colonies, and other participants in the revolutionary debates cited Magna Carta as but the first of several documents in which the monarchs of England pledged not to tax without consent.[9] The reign of Edward I was the period most frequently mentioned, both because that king's confirmation of the great charter contained the rule that feudal aids would no longer be collected without consent and because of the famous statute *de tallagio non concedendo.* The statute was attributed to the year 1297 when, according to David Hume, opposition from the nobility secured the country "for ever against all impositions and taxes without consent of parliament" and "the English nation had the honour of extorting, from the ablest, the most warlike, and the most ambitious of all their princes, who was thus bereaved of the power which he and his predecessors had hitherto assumed, of imposing arbitrary taxes on the people."[10] It was understood by Hume and his eighteenth-century contemporaries that with *de tallagio non concedendo* the English people for the first time became "entirely emancipated" from prerogative taxation. Edward had pledged that "No Tallage or Aid shall be taken or levied by us, or our Heirs, in our Realm, without the Good-will and Assent of Archbishops, Bishops, Earls, Barons, Knights, Burgesses, and other Freemen of the Land" or that "No Officer of ours, or of our Heirs, shall take Corn, Leather, Cattle, or any other Goods, of any manner of Person, without the Good-Will and Assent of the Party to whom the Goods belonged."[11] The importance of tallage and aid was that they were two incidents of feudal tenure that previous kings had claimed were not included in the prohibition of Magna Carta; and when Edward I renounced them it could be said that prerogative taxation was at an end.[12]

Unfortunately for the historical knowledge of the eighteenth century, *de tallagio non concedendo* was not a statute, nor had it been adopted by Edward I. People thought it had, however, and that is what is important. Blackstone could dismiss subsequent prerogative taxes by saying "this fundamental law had been shamefully evaded," implying that kings subsequent to Edward I who collected prerogative taxes had acted unconstitutionally. Jean Louis De Lolme was much bolder. In his influential study of the constitution, first published in London the same year as the Battle of Lexington, he placed *de tallagio non concedendo* even ahead of the Petition of Right as a fundamental source of constitutional liberty. "In conjunction with Magna Charta," he boasted, it formed "the basis of the English constitution."[13]

The historical misunderstanding rewrote history only by about half a century. The question that *de tallagio non concedendo* was supposed to have settled in the reign of Edward I was, in fact, settled in the reign of Edward III. It was then that the Crown surrendered its right to tallage and to some other charges, a "surrender" thought of during the revolutionary era not as a surrender of royal rights but as a confirmation of ancient law. In 1780, then, John Cartwright would quote from Sir John Fortesque, who wrote in the reign of Henry VI that "No king of England can change or make laws, or raise taxes, without the assent or consent of *his whole kingdom* in parliament expressed."[14]

THE TUDORS AND THE STUARTS

Even after the rise of the strong national state under the Tudor monarchs, the consent-to-taxation doctrine remained an essential component of English governance. It may have been frequently breached, especially during the reign of Elizabeth I, but it also seems to have been so much taken for granted that contemporaries assumed its validity although they did not frequently discuss it.[15]

The doctrine received its most serious challenge during the reigns of James I and Charles I. The issue between the first two Stuarts and the people, it was said in 1772, was "whether taxes, aids, and subsidies can be assessed by the King, as sole Judge of the occasion, and the quantum — or whether they must be granted by Parliament."[16] James, who believed taxes could be imposed by Crown decree, was reminded by the Commons that whenever the issue had been raised in the past his predecessors had "agreed that this old fundamental Right should be further declared and established by Act of Parliament; wherein it is provided that no such charge should ever be laid upon the people without their common consents; as may appear by sundry Records of former times."[17]

Events during the reign of Charles I gave American whigs and their British supporters their most frequently cited historical parallels to Parliament's attempts to tax the colonies for purposes of revenue. "Was not," a correspondent of the *New London Gazette* asked in 1765, "the raising taxes by ship money, &c. without the consent of the good people of England who were to pay them, and arbitrary courts of trial, contrary to the rights of Englishmen and the common usages of the land, principal grievances and causes of civil war in the reign of Charles I?"[18] Why had Charles been opposed? an anonymous London pamphleteer asked eleven years later. "To secure to the People the right of making for themselves those laws by which they were to be governed, and the right of laying that taxation upon themselves which they themselves were to pay." "If our ancestors," a second London pamphlet explained, "had not resisted in the days of Charles the First, the constitution of this country would have been subverted, and an unlimited power of arbitrary taxation vested in the prince, on the same principles on which we claim a right to tax America." The eighteenth-century perception that the king's attempt to raise money without authority of Parliament had constituted "treason against the constitution" had been shared by Charles's contemporaries. Thomas Wentworth, earl of Strafford, had been convicted and executed for, among other crimes, "having, by his own authority, commanded the laying and assessing of soldiers upon his majesty's subjects in Ireland, against their consents." And the Reverend Roger Manwaring, chaplain to Charles I, was proceeded against in the Commons for preaching that the king's "Royal Will and Command in imposing Loans, Taxes, and other Aids upon his People, without common Consent in Parliament, doth so far bind the Consciences of the Subjects of this Kingdom, that they cannot refuse the same without peril of eternal Damnation."[19]

The same session of Parliament that accused Manwaring resolved that: "it is the undoubted right of the subjects of England that they have such a propriety in their goods that they are not to be taken from them, nor to have levies, taxes, and loans set upon them without assent of parliament." American whigs remembered that 1628 Parliament as the petition-of-right Parliament, where Coke made the boast that "The Lord may tax his Villain high or low, but it is against the franchises of the land, for Freemen to be taxed, but by their own consent in Parliament." Coke incorporated the doctrine in the Petition of Right. After reciting the *Statutum de Tallagio non Concedendo* and other familiar precedents, the Commons told Charles that "your subjects have inherited this freedom, that they should not be compelled to contribute to any tax, tallage, aid or other like charge not set by common consent in Parliament." The numerous violations of the doctrine by the king were mentioned, and the petition concluded with the prayer "that no man hereafter be compelled to make or yield any gift, loan, benevolence, tax, or such like charge without common consent by act of Parliament."[20]

The beheading of Charles I ended the possibility that prerogative taxation would become the constitutional norm in England. During the period of Cromwell's commonwealth, various attempts at writing a constitution for the nation included the doctrine of taxation by consent,[21] but with the Restoration these efforts came to an end. The doctrine rested as it had before on constitutional custom,[22] custom now made stronger by the defeat of Stuart absolutism, no longer the bone of contention between Crown and Parliament but stated in the legal literature of the time as a constitutional absolute. The doctrine was stated generally as a right vested in Parliament but occasionally stated, as American whigs would have stated it, as a right protecting property against any arbitrary taking. Andrew Marvell anticipated colonial language in 1677 when he insisted that "No Money is to be Levied but by the common consent." A couple of years later Edward Chamberlayne provided another example: "Two things especially, the King of England doth not usually do without the consent of his Subjects, *viz*, make *New Laws*, and raise *New Taxes*."[23]

The Doctrine in the Seventeenth-Century Colonies

The consent-to-tax doctrine was so much a part of the governance of the early colonies that a separate volume would be necessary to do the topic justice. Here only a brief survey of some highlights will be attempted. The first point to be noticed is that the doctrine was known in British America from the very beginning of settlement. Just two years after the colonization of Massachusetts Bay, the Puritan magistrates were compelled to share power with elected representatives because some towns objected to being taxed without their consent. "If magistrates," one leader asked, "should *ex officio* practise such a power over mens proprieties, how long would Tyrany be kept out of our habitations?" The same question must have occurred to the first North Carolina legislature convened under a royal governor. The governor, following London's instructions, attempted to settle executive fees by Crown authority, but the lower house, equating fees with taxes, protested that it was "the undoubted Right and Priviledge of the People of England that they shall not be taxed or made lyable to pay any sum or sums of money of Fees other than such as are by Law established." Although the legislators did not make good their contention, they and their counterparts in other colonies kept up the argument until it became part of the constitutional controversy that produced the Revolution.[24]

In contrast to North Carolina, Virginia faced the issue of taxation, not fees, and successfully asserted the right to consent. "[T]he governor," an early statute provided, "shall not lay any taxes or impositions upon the colony, their lands, or commodities other way than by the authority of the general assembly, to be levied and employed as the said assembly shall appoint." After the original company lost its charter, Virginians sought to have the doctrine of taxation by consent incorporated into a second charter. Later, when the Commonwealth demanded that they acknowledge the parliamentary authority of Cromwell's government, the colonists did not "surrender" until they had exacted, in writing, this agreement: "That Virginia shall be free from all taxes, customes and impositions whatsoever, and none to be imposed on them without consent of

the Grand Assembly."[25] The pledge was reiterated by Charles II sometime after his restoration when he issued a declaration affirming that
"Taxes ought not be laid upon the Inhabitants and Proprietors of the Colony but by the common Consent of the General Assembly, except such
Impositions as the Parliament should lay on the Commodities imported
into *England* from the Colony."[26]

Due to the nature of the judicial process in the eighteenth century, few
opinions were written by judges and those that were remained manuscripts
since no reports were published. Consequently, we cannot expect to find
many statements by colonial jurists explaining legal theory about the
consent-to-taxation doctrine. At least one, however, is extant and it is both
sufficiently well known and sufficiently theoretical to merit quotation.
Written by Samuel Symonds, it explains a judgment in the court of Massachusetts's Essex County. The plaintiff refused to pay an assessment levied
by the town of Ipswich and when a constable distrained "his pewter dishes
or platters" to satisfy the rate, he sued the official. Symonds's reasoning
in ruling for the plaintiff reveals a great deal about how the doctrine of
taxation by consent was perceived in the seventeenth-century colonies.

> That every subject shall and may enjoy what he hath a civell right
> or title unto, soe as it cannot be taken from him, by way of gift or
> loan, to the use or to be made the right or property of another man,
> without his owne free consent.
>
> $\cdot$ $\cdot$ $\cdot$ $\cdot$
>
> Secondly, This to me is some strengthning to induce my apprehen-
> sion in this case, viz. That notwithstanding in England, it cannot
> be denied, but that mens estates were sometymes unduly taken from
> them: Some by force, some by fraud, some by sinister wresting of
> evidences, yea, and sometimes of lawe itselfe as about knighthood-
> money, shipmoney, &c. yet I dare say, if search be made into histo-
> ries, lawyers bookes of reports, records &c. it cannot be made to ap-
> peare that in the most exorbitant times any man hath had his estate
> taken from him as by the guift of others, under colour of lawe, or
> countenance of authority. Noe, noe, lawyers would have blushed to
> have given such a construction of lawes; and suddenly their faces
> would have waxed pale. . . .
>
> This I say further, and I doe argue it from the greater to the lesse.
> That if noe kings or parliament can justly enact and cause that one
> mans estate, in whole or in part, may be taken from him and given
> to another without his owne consent, then surely the major part of
> a towne or other inferior powers cannot doe it. But shew us any man
> that can produce any footstep for such a way, either directly or in-
> directly.[27]

The judgment, of course, pertained only to the assessment of a single town, but the theory behind the principle could be applied just as readily to parliamentary taxation of the colonies. That was surely what the members of the Massachusetts General Court meant four years after Symonds's opinion when they declared: "We conceive any imposition prejudicial to the country, contrary to any just law of ours (not repugnant to the laws of England) to be an infringement of our rights." Cotton Mather, writing in 1690, may have intended not just to state the same constitutional doctrine, but to emphasize its English origins when he reported that several years earlier England's attorney general had "told the King [Charles II] that he could no more grant a Commission to leavy money on his Subjects there [in the colonies] without their consent by an Assembly, than they could discharge themselves from their allegiance to the English Crown."[28]

Charles II did not attempt to alter the customary colonial constitution, but his successor, James II, precipitated the constitutional crisis of the century when he revoked the charters of the seven most northern colonies and created the Dominion of New England. Edmund Andros was appointed governor to rule — even though the English attorney general gave his opinion that to do so was illegal — without an elected assembly, promulgating prerogative taxes as well as prerogative ordinances. In 1681, the New York court of assizes had complained to James, then duke of York, about Andros, saying that as governor he was acting without a legislature and that "a Yearly Revenue is Exacted from us against o[u]r Wills." With the creation of the Dominion of New England it was the turn of the people of the former province of Massachusetts Bay to complain. Contemporary evidence clearly indicates that a major reason for their rebellion was taxation without consent.[29] "[O]ne of the Crimes objected against Sir E. A[ndros] and his Complices" was "*that they levied moneys on the King's Subjects in* New-England, *contrary to the fundamentals of the English Government,* which doth not allow the imposition of Taxes without a *Parliament*"; that "They made Laws for the *Levying Moneys without the consent of the People either by themselves or by an Assembly*";[30] and that when "true English men" opposed "these Illegal Taxes" they were arrested, and "the Prisoners pleading *the priviledges of English men* not to be taxed without their own consent, they were told that *the Laws of* England *would not follow them to the end of the Earth.*"[31] The English "rights" these defendants enumerated were the "statute of 25 Ed[ward] I Tallagio non concedendo that says 'Taxes shall not be imposed without consent of the Commons'," and "the priviledges of Englishmen according to Magna Charta." Or, as the selectmen of Ipswich resolved, "it is against the Privileges of *English* Subjects to have Money raised without their own Consent in an Assembly or Parliament."[32]

Andros was sent back to England, and the Dominion of New England dismembered. Massachusetts was recreated with a new charter and its General Court passed "An act setting forth general priviledges." It sought to insure that "the rights and liberties of the people . . . shall be firmly and strictly holden and observed," and the statute's text "reads like a summary of all the charges which the people had made against Andros." Of nine "rights and liberties" specified, the fourth provided that

> No aid, tax, tallage, assessment, custome, loan, benevolence or im-
> position whatsoever shall be laid, assessed, imposed or levied on any
> of their majesties' subjects or their estates, on any colour or pretence
> whatsoever, but by the act and consent of the governour, council and
> representatives of the people, assembled in general court.[33]

THE DOCTRINE IN THE EIGHTEENTH-CENTURY COLONIES

In 1765, it would have been impossible for anyone with knowledge of eighteenth-century colonial history to have claimed that the consent-to-taxation doctrine had been formulated by American whigs in response to the Stamp Act. Colonists had not only insisted upon the doctrine as a basic constitutional right all throughout the century,[34] they had also claimed it on every premise that would later be argued during the revolutionary controversy. One premise frequently cited was the right to be free of prerogative taxation. The defense of consent was raised on several occasions, notably by the Massachusetts General Court in 1728 when it refused to obey royal instructions that the colony establish a permanent revenue for paying the governor's salary, by the Virginia House of Burgesses during the famous "pistole fee" dispute in the 1750s, and by the lower house of Maryland's Assembly when it protested executive fees on the eve of the Revolution.[35]

A second consideration stressed was popular control of the revenue. The notable colonial lawyer Andrew Hamilton emphasized that fact when retiring after many years as Speaker of the Pennsylvania Assembly. "The taxes are inconsiderable," he explained, "for the sole power of raising and disposing of the public money is lodged in the Assembly."[36]

Property was a third basis used to formulate the doctrine in North America during the sixty-five years of the eighteenth century before the revolutionary controversy began. "Resolved," the New York Assembly voted during the reign of Queen Anne, "that the imposing and levying of any monies upon her Majesty's subjects of this colony, under any pretence or colour whatever, without consent in General Assembly, is a grievance and violation of the people's property."[37]

A fourth source from which the doctrine derived its theoretical authority was liberty. The "Right inherent in the People by the *Constitution*, to judge (by their Representatives) of their own Taxes," A *Freeholder* told the *Maryland Gazette* in 1748, "is the great Hinge upon which Liberty hangs; and whenever that is weakened or thrown down, Liberty must be proportionably weakened or fall with it." It was, he explained,

> one of the most distinguishing Marks of *British* Liberty, nay the very Soul and Essence of it, for the People, or (which is the same Thing) the Representatives of the People, to be possess'd of the Power of keeping their Purse in their own Hands, to be the sole Judges how much is necessary to be raised upon them, and to direct the Disposal of it.[38]

There were other grounds, such as English precedent and charter rights,[39] upon which the doctrine of consent to taxation was claimed, but the main one was constitutional law. When Governor John Penn vetoed a tax bill, saying that it subverted the colony's mode of taxation, Pennsylvania's Assembly replied that all the bill did was "take away the Power of the Justices of the Peace and the Grand Jury of taxing those who do not choose them." The bill would have replaced an "unconstitutional" mode of taxation. "According to the English Constitution, no person whatsoever has a right to take away the property of another without his consent, given in person or by his representative."[40] This was but one of many examples of the doctrine setting the rule for constitutional conduct by colonial legislatures in policy decisions not directly connected with the revolutionary controversy over parliamentary taxation.[41] New England assemblies, for example, sometimes refrained from taxing towns that had not sent delegates; and, in 1769, when the Georgia governor refused to permit representation to four new parishes, the legislature did not tax them.[42]

No matter the grounds on which the doctrine was placed, it was always stated in the same principles and to the same purpose whether in the colonies or the mother country, in the seventeenth or eighteenth century. It was defined by individuals publicizing their views about freedom as well as by public bodies taking a stand on the question of parliamentary taxation. The New York lawyer William Livingston summed up the doctrine in 1752 as concisely as it had ever been stated. "It is a standing Maxim of *English Liberty*," he wrote, "that no Man shall be taxed, but with his own Consent."[43] A quarter of a century later, a British clergyman took a few more words to explain the same principle. "He must," Caleb Evans observed, "be extremely ignorant of the nature of the English Constitution, who does not know, that the *granting our own property*, and not having it disposed of without our consent, is considered as the very Soul and vital Spirit of it, the grand palladium of British Liberty, and the bulwark of freedom."[44]

CHAPTER FOURTEEN

THE AUTHORITY OF ANALOGY

During his examination before the House of Commons in 1766, Benjamin Franklin was asked whether Americans were acquainted with the English Bill of Rights and if they knew "that, by that statute, money is not to be raised on the subject but by consent of parliament." "They understand that clause to relate to subjects only within the realm," Franklin answered. "The Colonies are not supposed to be within the realm . . . and they are in that respect in the same situation with Ireland. When money is to be raised for the Crown upon the subject in Ireland, or in the Colonies, the consent is given in the parliament of Ireland, or in the assemblies of the Colonies. . . ."[1]

It is the method of Franklin's argument that deserves attention. He utilized an authority of law that was related to, but should not be confused with, the doctrine of precedent: the principle of analogy. The use of analogy to establish propositions under the eighteenth-century British constitution generally took one of two forms, proof by past analogy and proof by current analogy, with the former further divided by analogies drawn from ancient history and analogies drawn from English or British history.

Ancient analogies were quite common. It was fashionable for writers when commenting on the North American colonies to draw comparisons with colonies of other times and nations, particularly ancient Greece and Rome. This technique, however, was largely irrelevant to the constitutional controversy as participants on both sides well knew. "The reasoning about the colonies of Great Britain, drawn from the colonies of antiquity," Lord Mansfield pointed out, "is a mere useless display of learning; for, the colonies of the Tyrians in Africa, and of the Greeks in Asia, were totally different from our system." American whigs agreed. "The form of the British government, and the nature of our connection with it," William Hicks observed, "are so essentially different from every colonization with which we are acquainted, that we cannot be directed by precedents drawn from any former establishment."[2]

Past analogies drawn from English or British history were a different matter. They could be argued as authority when shown to be on point. "If the king is to *take* at his pleasure, what have we to give?" James Burgh asked, noting that that question "was the common argument against *Ch*[arles] Ist's raising money without consent of parliament; and may, with equal propriety, be used by our colonists against their being taxed by the *British* parliament, in which they have no representation." What Burgh meant by the colonists "using" the opposition to Charles I was that such history was relevant as a legal analogy. The passage of time and the changed circumstances may have weakened the persuasiveness of the analogy as a historical analogy, but such considerations had much less weight in legal reasoning. Burgh's analogy was a valid legal analogy because American whigs were raising the same constitutional issue, taxation without consent, that the opponents of Charles I had raised.[3]

Current analogy had fewer similarities to precedent than did past analogy. More truly an appeal to analogy *per se*, it was premised on the principle that a constitutional privilege enjoyed by one part of the Empire should be enjoyed by the other equal and comparable or analogous parts. "[T]here has not been," Caleb Evans wrote in a typical instance of the technique, "one argument yet brought, to prove the right of the English parliament to tax the Americans, but would equally serve to prove their right to tax the Irish, or the right of the King to tax us all, without asking the representatives of the people any thing about the matter." Besides Ireland, current analogies supporting the American constitutional case of immunity from parliamentary taxation for purposes of revenue included the Isle of Man, Guernsey, Jersey, and even the mother country. The last may seem at first glance to be a past, not a current analogy. It was, however, a current analogy to James Burgh, who, if attention is paid to the next quotation, will be seen to have appealed not to past analogy but to what was for him a current analogy: Great Britain.

Magna Carta, and the Bill of Rights, prohibit the taxing of the mother-country by prerogative, and without consent of those who are to be taxed. If the people of *Britain* are not to be taxed, but by parliament; because otherwise they might be taxed without their own consent; does it not directly follow, that the colonists cannot, according to *Magna Charta*, and the bill of rights, be taxed by parliament, so long as they continued unrepresented; because otherwise they may be taxed without their own consent?[4]

Theory of Analogy

The authority of analogy was one of the oldest maxims of English common law. Bracton had explained it as early as the thirteenth century. "If any new and unwonted circumstances shall arise," he wrote, "then, if anything analogous has happened before, let the case be adjudged in like manner, proceeding *a similibus ad similia*."[5] The chief test of an analogy's authority was relevance. A British clergyman, for example, drew an analogy between the right of the colonies to tax themselves and the right of English parishes to assess rates on their congregations that he thought relevant to the question of whether Parliament could tax Americans: the parishes had a privilege "to cess" themselves in order to meet their expenses, just as each colony taxed its inhabitants to support local government; but since payment of parish rates by parishioners did not excuse them from parliamentary levies to support the national government (what he called the general expenses of government) so payment of colonial taxes by Americans did not excuse them from parliamentary levies to support the general expenses of the imperial government. A second British clergyman objected that the analogy was not relevant because English parish rates were not comparable to American colonies' taxes. The "analogy" was not analogous because it was based on the false premise that "the colony-rates to pay the salaries of their *governors*, their judges, and other officers, and in the late war, to raise, clothe, and maintain troops, &c.— were only *private colony-rates*, like our *parish-rates*, — they had no relation at all to the *general expenses of government*."[6]

The main theoretical underpinning for the authority of analogy, at least when used to prove that Parliament lacked constitutional power to tax the colonies for the purpose of raising revenue, was the principle of equality. If other parts of the Empire, especially Ireland, were free from parliamentary taxation, then the provinces of North America should be also. "*Ireland*," the Massachusetts House pointed out, "is a conquered

Country, which is not the case with the Northern Colonies, except *Canada:* Yet no Duties have been levied by the *British* Parliament on *Ireland.* No internal or external Taxes have been assessed on them, but by their own Parliament." The right asserted was as much equality as consent to taxation. Although the claim to equality was especially evident when the analogy was to current practice, as in the case of Ireland, it was also being asserted when past analogy such as the former right of the English clergy to tax themselves was cited. The Stamp Act Congress was demanding equality for Americans with both past and present analogies when, petitioning the king, it argued:

> The invaluable Rights of Taxing ourselves, and Trial by our Peers . . . are not, we most humbly conceive Unconstitutional; but confirmed by the Great Charter of *English* Liberty. . . . [T]he First of these Rights . . . [is] a Right enjoyed by the Kingdom of *Ireland,* by the Clergy of *England,* until relinquished by themselves, a Right, in fine, which all other your Majesty's *English* Subjects, both within, and without the Realm, have hitherto enjoyed.

The argument was still being made a decade later, as when Arthur Lee joined the past analogies of Chester, Wales, and Calais to the present analogies of "England" and Ireland and associated them all with the principle of equality: "The practice of every free state, especially of England; the practice of Ireland, Chester, Wales, and Calais, as members of the empire; the constitution of the church, and the very nature of all property, all conspire to shew, that this principle is the essential right of the subject in every part of the dominion."[7]

EVIDENCE FROM PAST ANALOGIES

When participants in the revolutionary controversy sought authority in past analogies, they were generally careful to distinguish between precedents for taxation and precedents for legislation. Both sides acknowledged that precedents in analogies were more readily established for nontaxation statutes binding territories not represented in Parliament than they were for taxation. In fact, supporters of the dichotomy between sovereignty and taxation, championed by William Pitt and Lord Camden, sometimes utilized evidence by analogy to prove the distinction. "Had the right of taxation always followed the supreme authority," one writer reasoned, "there would have been no need of an act of union for taxing of Scotland. But the people of that country possessed the right of being taxed only by representatives of their own choosing, and they would not part with their privilege, without a just share in the assembly that was to tax them for the future; and their proportion of taxation, was made the very measure by which that of their representation was settled." A second writer argued:

> [I]f taxation had been a simple act of legislation, or if it had been true as our author [Samuel Johnson] asserts, that 'a tax is a payment exacted by authority,' there could have been no pretence for the Commons to claim these exclusive privileges, respecting money bills; nor is it possible to believe the Peers would have submitted to a claim so injurious and unreasonable: neither would the clergy, whilst subject to the legislative authority of parliament, have been exempted from the taxes imposed by parliament, and allowed the exclusive privilege of taxing themselves, which they enjoyed, until a share in the popular representation was granted them in the reign of Charles II. We find by the roll of the 4th of Richard II . . . that when the House of Commons proposed to grant an aid, provided the clergy would pay one third of it, as possessing one third of the realm, the clergy answered they were not to grant aids by parliament; and desired the Commons to do their duty, and leave the clergy to perform theirs. And here we have a strong proof that the powers of legislation and taxation are essentially distinct by the English constitution, because we find that with respect to the clergy they could not be exercised by the same persons.[8]

Even if the author was correct in saying the clergy precedent was "strong proof" of the taxation-legislation dichotomy, it was a questionable analogy for the matter of parliamentary taxation of the colonies. At no time, it was contended, were the clergy not represented; they had always enjoyed direct representation in the Lords by those of their estate who were bishops and could vote for members of the Commons even when they formed a separate convocation. That fact, however, was disputed, and some participants in the revolutionary debates believed that the clergy had not voted until taxed by Parliament and had been granted the vote in order to be taxed constitutionally. Recent scholarly research indicates that during the reign of Charles II the clergy consented to be taxed by Parliament and in return "obtained the right of voting at elections," but that is irrelevant to the weight accorded the analogy in the eighteenth century. That weight depended upon what individuals believed or wanted to believe. Even those who accepted the argument as established truth probably would have cited the analogy not as conclusive authority, but rather as one piece of evidence that needed reinforcement from other evidence of a similar nature to become persuasive.[9]

Evidence more conclusive to the eighteenth-century legal mind than the clergy analogy was provided by analogies drawn from other units of local government within the Empire, particularly the Palatinate counties of Chester and Durham and the principality of Wales. It may be that no other facts cited to prove arguments of law during the revolutionary period were so frequently mentioned. For many in the mother country, the controversy had commenced when, in the most memorable exchange of the Stamp Act crisis, Pitt and Grenville debated the meaning of the Chester-Durham analogies. Pitt had begun the exchange by startling the ministry with the legislation-taxation dichotomy. Grenville, who could not believe such a theory was being taken seriously, tried to prove it constitutional nonsense by arguing analogy. "[T]axation is a part of that sovereign power," he contended. "It was exercised over the palatinate of Chester, and the bishopric of Durham, before they sent any representatives to parliament. I appeal, for proof, to the preambles of the acts which gave them representatives: the one in the reign of Henry 8, the other in that of Charles 2." Grenville "then quoted the acts, and desired that they might be read"— a remarkable indication not only of how well he was prepared for a constitutional debate, but also of the importance of the Palatinate analogies in English constitutional history and eighteenth-century British constitutional thought. Just as revealing, Pitt answered Grenville in kind. asserting that Grenville's analogies proved the opposite: Parliament could not tax the colonies. "I would have cited them," he explained, "to have shewn, that, even under arbitrary reigns, parliaments were ashamed of taxing a people without their consent, and allowed them representatives." Pitt also reminded the Commons of yet a third analogy, one with which his listeners were so familiar he simply mentioned it, assuming that everyone understood its relevance. "Why did the gentleman confine himself to Chester and Durham?" Pitt asked. "He might have taken a higher example in Wales; Wales, that never was taxed by Parliament, till it was incorporated."[10]

The hundreds of later references to the analogies of Chester and Durham generally reiterated the arguments of Grenville and Pitt. The evidence was considered so important that the preambles to both statutes were printed several times in the British press. The longer, the law granting representation to Chester, was most frequently quoted, but for our purposes the shorter one for Durham is sufficient.

> Whereas the inhabitants of the county palatine of *Durham* have not hitherto had the liberty and privilege of electing and sending any knights and burgesses to the high court of parliament, although the inhabitants of the said county palatine are liable to all payments, rates and subsidies granted by parliament, equally with the inhabi-

tants of other counties, cities and boroughs in this kingdom, who
have their knights and burgesses in the parliament, and are therefore concerned equally with others the inhabitants of this kingdom,
to have knights and burgesses in the said high court of parliament
of their own election, to represent the condition of their country, as
the inhabitants of other counties, cities and boroughs of this kingdom have.

There was little dispute about what the statutes meant. Pitt and Grenville agreed, as did their followers, and so have subsequent historians.
"It was found," as one writer explained in 1774, "that the people of those
districts were taxed and not represented, and the language of the legislature is the same to them all.— If you pay duties and taxes it is your right
to be represented, and partake in the choice of those that lay them upon
you, and therefore we grant you representatives to all future parliaments."
As Pitt said in the debate with Grenville, the Wales analogy seemed
stronger since Wales had not been taxed until it was granted representation. For those who believed Wales had been granted representation in
order to be taxed, the analogy was even stronger.[11]

Lawyers were in general agreement about the facts, but not about what
inference should be drawn from them. There were three interpretations.
For the attorney general of England and the other law officers, the evidence that Chester and Durham had been taxed before they had had
representation provided precedent that Parliament could tax without consent. For supporters of American claims to exemption from parliamentary taxation, the fact that the statutes granted representation after citing taxation without consent as a grievance was evidence that Parliament
had acknowledged the constitutional right of subjects not to be taxed except by a legislature in which they were represented. A third interpretation was that even though these analogies supported the authority of
Parliament to tax the colonies, they were evidence that taxation without
consent, admittedly legal as an exercise of sovereign power, was nonetheless unconstitutional and therefore wrong. The conclusion was either that
Parliament should cease its attempt to tax Americans until they were represented or that Americans had no complaint until they applied for and
were denied representation.[12]

EVIDENCE FROM CURRENT ANALOGIES

Other analogies were drawn from current constitutional parallels with
various territories and political subdivisions within the Empire. They

ranged in significance from the Isle of Man, an analogy of little importance, to Ireland, an analogy of more or less significance depending upon how much one was persuaded by arguments distinguishing the constitutional status of Ireland from the constitutional status of the colonies.

The Manx analogy was mentioned only at the beginning of the revolutionary controversy. Governor Stephen Hopkins cited Man as a unit of the Empire not taxed because not represented in Parliament. It was current analogy, but not for long. In 1765, the year of the Stamp Act, Man was purchased from its lord, vested in the Crown, and incorporated into the kingdom with representation in the Commons. It then became a past analogy, of less interest to Americans because of the consent-to-tax doctrine than the fact it had been united to Great Britain to end smuggling and "increase the revenue to a prodigious degree."[13]

Guernsey, Jersey, Alderney, and Sark — taxed by their own assemblies and not by Parliament — were current analogies of more weight than Man because their status remained unchanged throughout the period. "The islands of Guernsey, &c.," a typical commentator explained, "are not taxed by the British parliament at all, they still have their own states, and I never heard that the British parliament ever offered to hinder them to lay on their own taxes, or to lay on additional ones, when they are not represented."[14] These analogies were not much discussed, even by those who thought them significant, probably because they were overshadowed by Ireland, an analogy of such magnitude it alone could make or break the argument.

Revolutionary writers gave the Irish analogy detailed discussion, sometimes using Ireland as an example to warn Americans of the potential abuses of British rule, as John Dickinson did in a long analysis, or as an anonymous correspondent to a Boston newspaper did in 1773 when arguing that the power of parliamentary taxation meant the power to confiscate American property. That, after all, was what had happened to Ireland, "once a rich and flourishing Isle; but being charged beyond her abilities, with the payment of excessive sums, to worn out panders and whores, she is now sinking beneath the infamous load; and must, ere long, die a martyr to the absolute control of the parliament of Great-Britain."[15]

Another tactic was to use the Irish analogy to argue that what few rights belonged to the oppressed people of Ireland surely also belonged to the free people of British North America. "Ireland was our Example," James Iredell told the British in 1777. "We saw no reason why we should not live with you upon as cordial terms as that Kingdom." The thesis was that Parliament had never claimed nor exercised the authority of taxing the Irish, that it had not done so because it did not have the right, and by analogy it should also not have the right to tax North America. To prove the argument, ancient history and musty documents were uncovered, analyzed, and debated, even in the House of Commons.[16]

The evidence was less persuasive than we might think. Indeed, it was not very conclusive at all. For one thing, it was often incorrect or just plain wrong, although error was never raised as an issue.[17] What was important was the nature of the evidence. Like all history used in constitutional advocacy, proof by the Irish analogy was bound to be inconclusive, for there was not only generally a contrary conclusion that could be drawn from the facts, but other facts were always available to prove the opposite case.[18]

One fact disproving the argument against Parliament was that Parliament could, if it wished, tax Ireland. Charles Jenkinson, who served as secretary to the treasury and held the position of vice treasurer of Ireland, told the Commons "that the right of taxing it had always been maintained, and *exercised* too, whenever it was thought expedient, and ought undoubtedly always to be so, whenever the British parliament judged proper; having no other rule in this respect but its *own discretion*." Jenkinson was saying not merely that the analogy did not exist, he was also saying that even if it did exist, it would be constitutionally irrelevant because Parliament, in its sovereignty, could disregard it. Even people who took the analogy seriously could argue the last point, either by maintaining that the analogy could not bind the sovereign power or by contending that there was no constitutional principle giving Americans the right to claim equality with the Irish. The latter distinction was one Americans were not likely to argue. They may have wanted Ireland to be an analogy for parliamentary taxation, but not for much else. To have pushed the argument of equality with the Irish further could have led to a lessening of American rights, not their security. As Governor William Pitkin of Connecticut observed, "It is painful to hear the Colonies compared to Ireland, who are subjected by conquest, and by their conduct forfeited those immunities we are justly entitled to."[19]

The fact that Ireland was a conquered country also produced contrary conclusions about its value as an analogy for American constitutional rights. Lord Mansfield thought that conquest alone made it irrelevant. "Ireland is too tender a subject to be touched," he warned the House of Lords. "The case of Ireland is as different as possible from that of our colonies. Ireland was a conquered country; it had its *pacta conventa*, and its *regalia*." American whigs and their British supporters agreed that Ireland's conquest made the analogy less exact than it otherwise might have been, but turned the argument around by insisting that conquest made America's case even stronger. "The Colonies," a lord mayor of London told the Commons, "are more free than Ireland, for America had not

been conquered; on the contrary, it was inhabited by the conquerors."
There were two arguments drawn from the fact, both reaching the same
conclusion. One was that Americans, not having been conquered, should
have possessed greater rights than the conquered Irish. That expectation,
however, was belied by the analogy of Irish taxation. That the Irish taxed
themselves meant they enjoyed rights the colonists were denied. *"The people of the colonies,"* one such argument pointed out, *"left their native
country with the strongest assurances, that they and their posterity, should
enjoy the privileges of free and natural born English subjects.* And now
they are contending for a privilege, in the possession of a *conquered* people under the same government with themselves." A second conclusion
drawn from the fact of conquest was that the Americans' claim to taxation by consent was stronger because, as descendants of English settlers,
they could assert it as a right of inheritance, while the Irish, as a conquered people, claimed it not by constitutional right but from the pleasure of the conqueror. "The parliament of *Ireland,*" a Scots lawyer who
had been admiralty judge in Ireland explained, "had their rights and
privileges granted them by the king and parliament of *England,* after
they were conquered by them, and so by the right of conquest might
prescribe what rules they thought proper." America, by comparison, had
not been conquered or, if conquered, had been conquered by "private
people."[20] A clergyman thought the latter contention disproven by Ireland's constitutional status: although Ireland had been conquered, it "was
annexed to the dominions of the Kings of England *not as a colony,* but
sister kingdom." If the distinction was taken seriously, it would have provided a legal reason for not drawing analogies between Ireland and the
North American colonies. A second clergyman, the only revolutionary
writer known to have taken the trouble to refute the distinction, rejected
it not on the grounds of law but of absurdity of facts.

> True, Sir, the IRISH were our inveterate enemies, massacred in cool
> blood thousands upon thousands of English protestants, and would
> never have submitted to the government of Great Britain if they could
> have helped it: and it was therefore *highly proper* to allow *them* to
> have their own representatives and to tax themselves. But to allow
> these privileges to COLONISTS, to our *younger brothers,* to those who
> ought to be addressed as *freeman,* — is, it seems, quite preposterous.
> For *them* to claim the prerogatives of the *Irish* is such a "stretch of
> lawless liberty" as is perfectly shocking to think of.[21]

Although both sides appealed to the Irish analogy for proof either that
Parliament could or could not tax the colonies, neither side could persuade the other because the evidence was not conclusive. It may well be

that the analogy was used most effectively when it was cited for political rather than constitutional purposes. Robert Nugent stressed the political dimension when he warned the House of Commons that should Parliament let Americans have their way on the issue of taxation, a spirit of resistance would be infused into the Irish. Benjamin Franklin had a more constitutional argument in mind when he imagined Ireland as an analogy not for the colonies but for Great Britain and wondered what "the people of England" would think if the Irish Parliament claimed over them the same authority that the British Parliament claimed over Americans.

> Should it happen, through the revolutions of time, that some future king should make choice of Ireland for his seat of government, and that the parliament of that kingdom, with his majesty's concurrence, should assume the right of taxing the people of England, would the people of England quietly acquiesce, or implicitly pay obedience to laws made by virtue of an assumed right? And yet, as there is no law in being to prevent his majesty from making any part of his dominions the seat of his government, the case is by no means foreign to the present question.[22]

CHAPTER FIFTEEN

PRECEDENTS FOR TAXATION

The General Assembly of Pennsylvania, combining an argument of both custom and precedent, maintained that until 1765 there was no statutory precedent for parliamentary taxation of the North American colonies. "This Right in the People of this Province," it asserted, "of being exempted from any Taxations, save those imposed by their own Representatives, has been recognized by long established Usage and Custom, ever since the Settlement thereof, without one Precedent to the contrary, until the passing of the late Stamp-Act." Although supporters of Parliament's right to tax the colonies claimed they were "exceedingly surprized" by the assertion, they should not have been; the argument had been made from the very start of the controversy. "33 laws," Richard Hussey told the Commons during the Stamp Act debate, "have been passed by Parliament in relation to North America. None of them have laid an internal tax, at least no internal tax which can so fairly be called so as this Act." The opposite had also been argued. Grenville's supporters insisted that there were many precedents of internal taxation of the colonies by Parliament, and even cited some. "They . . . urge," Jared Ingersoll wrote the governor of Connecticut, "that the only reason why America has not been heretofore taxed in the fullest Manner, has been merely on Account of their Infancy and Inability; that there have been, however, not wanting

Instances of the Exercise of this Power, in the various regulations of the American Trade, the Establishment of the post Office &c."[1]

The issue was not whether Parliament believed it had power to tax the colonies, but whether it had ever exercised the power; whether, as Daniel Dulaney said, the Stamp Act was "the first statute that hath imposed an internal tax upon the colonies *for the single purpose of revenue.*" Dulany thought the Stamp Act was the first revenue statute laid on North America by Parliament. Edmund Burke and John Lind thought the first revenue statute had been the second Sugar Act, passed the year before the Stamp Act. Lind, arguing that there was precedent for the Stamp Act, claimed that the Sugar Act was the statute by which Parliament first added the authority of taxation to the several powers it had previously exercised over the colonies.[2] Many other contemporaries — making arguments discussed in this chapter — traced parliamentary taxation of the colonies to the reign of Charles II, sometimes even to the Commonwealth when Cromwell ruled, and occasionally, although infrequently, back to James I.

The reason for such wide variation in the arguments of precedents to taxation is not that the evidence was vague, but that the evidence was subject to subjective factual and legal interpretation about which people of goodwill could differ. Answers to questions for the 1760s were being sought from the 1730s or 1670s or 1640s, which meant that precedents from times when imperial government was new, weak, or experimental were to be guides for the revolutionary period, when Parliament was conscious of its authority and the British customs service had agents scattered throughout all of the colonies. Even more difficult were statutes promulgated by Parliaments that were not aware that those statutes would one day be cited as precedent for the authority of later Parliaments to tax the colonies for the purpose of raising revenue. Parliament in the seventeenth century may have assumed that it possessed the constitutional power to tax the colonies, but it is more likely that, as a collective body, it never thought about the issue. Yet what earlier Parliaments said, as well as the revenue laws they did promulgate, were cited in the 1760s as evidence relevant to the question of whether there were constitutional precedents for the Stamp Act, the Townshend duties, and the Tea Act.

RELEVANCE OF PRECEDENTS

Of the many constitutional topics discussed and debated during the revolutionary controversy, none was as extensively researched according to the accepted premises of legal scholarship as the question of whether there were precedents for parliamentary taxation of the colonies. How deeply the investigation was conducted depended upon the way in which the person making the argument perceived the matter of proof and legal authority. For a few people it was sufficient to establish precedent by analogy. "The less is included in the greater," Samuel Johnson explained. "That power which can take away life, may seize upon property. The parliament may enact for America a law of capital punishment; it may therefore establish a mode and proportion of taxation." William Blackstone thought that the analogy to property alone should establish the power. "We have in many instances affected the property of the colonies," he contended, pointing to parliamentary statutes "determining that debts due from the Colonies may be proved by affidavit here" and to an "Act imposing [a] penalty of £5 on a person who cuts timber of certain descriptions in North America." The Stamp Act, Blackstone said, was "a penalty rather than a taxation"; somewhat in contradiction, he was also reported as insisting that "All Penalties are Taxations, for [the] Stamp Act is but a penal Law as almost all Revenue Laws are." William Knox drew the same analogy to a parliamentary statute for recovering in North America debts owed creditors resident in Great Britain. "[C]an any man," he asked, "who admits the power of parliament to take away the lands of the people in America (the most sacred part of any man's property) and dispose of them for the use of private persons, inhabitants of Great Britain, question the parliament's having sufficient jurisdiction to take away a small part of the products of those lands, and apply it to the public service?"[3]

The precedent-by-analogy argument was not the same as the "sovereignty argument." Blackstone and Knox were not saying that Parliament had the right to tax the colonies because it possessed supreme sovereign power; they were saying that if Parliament could take colonial property to satisfy British creditors, it could by analogy take colonial property for purposes of taxation. The contention was persuasive as far as the analogy was valid. Pitt and those who agreed with him that there was a constitutional dichtomy between legislation and taxation believed the analogy to be irrelevant. Had Blackstone and Knox taken the dichotomy theory seriously, they might have answered that the analogy proved the dichotomy idea false because the substance of taking for taxation was the same as taking for creditors: both actions were a taking of property. Stronger grounds for saying the precedent-by-analogy argument was irrelevant came from the constitutional thesis that taxation was not a taking of property but rather a free gift granted the government by consent of the property owner. As long as American whigs adhered to the language of free gifts they could distinguish taxation from any analogy whether it was a debtor statute or an act such as the one authorizing British troops to be quartered at colonial expense.

More persuasive would have been precedents of direct parliamentary taxation upon the colonies to which Americans had acquiesced and which they had paid. People disagreed not about whether such precedents were relevant but about whether these precedents existed. Ministerial supporters were confident there were many such precedents. Some imperialists even compiled long lists of various legislation, including statutes for trying pirates in the colonies, regulating coinage, and forbidding land banks. American whigs rejected these out of hand: statutes dealing with piracy, coins, and creditors were not precedents for parliamentary taxation of the colonies and irrelevant to the question whether such taxation was constitutional.[4]

More difficult to dismiss were statutes regulating trade and imposing customs duties. They were often cited as precedents for taxation and because they involved the payment of duties, American whigs treated them with more respect than they did statutes of internal legislation not imposing financial penalties. If a semantic distinction may be drawn, the revenue-raising customs statutes were "less irrelevant" to the issue of taxation than were statutes that generated income for the royal treasury. The question of their degree of relevance was ardently debated. There were two main grounds of disagreement. One turned on interpretation of the purposes of specific legislation and the intent of Parliament. The second concerned the meaning of words and whether certain statutory phrases were formulary.

Daniel Leonard, a Massachusetts lawyer and loyalist, asserted that the test should be the purpose for which a law was passed, and that that purpose could be ascertained from the content of the statute.

> There has lately been a most ingenious play upon the words and expressions, *tax, revenue, purpose of raising a revenue, sole purpose of raising a revenue, express purpose of raising a revenue,* as though their being inserted in, or left out of a statute, would make any essential difference in the statute. This is mere playing with words; for if, from the whole tenor of the act, it is evident that the intent of the legislature was to tax, rather than to regulate the trade, by imposing duties on goods and merchandise, it is to all intents and purposes an instance of taxation, be the form of words, in which the statute is conceived, what it will.

A different criterion used to answer the same question asked whether the duties generated by a customs statute "were appropriated to particular uses." If so, the purpose of the law could be more for raising revenue than for regulating trade and would be a precedent for parliamentary taxation.[5]

Chief Justice John Marshall, writing long after the Revolution had ended, rejected the last test on the premise that the general purpose of British trade statutes was to police imperial commercial activities. "[A]ll the duties on trade were understood to be imposed, rather with a view to prevent foreign commerce, than to raise a revenue." It did not matter that some income was assigned for specific purposes. The general purpose of trade regulation overrode secondary purposes, and trade laws, even those producing substantial amounts of money for the imperial treasury, were not precedents for parliamentary taxation.[6]

Benjamin Franklin thought that the distinction lay more in how the statute operated than the purpose that its drafters had had in mind. In an argument similar to one he made during his examination by the House of Commons, Franklin explained to a London newspaper that parliamentary laws for regulating commerce and navigation were materially different from the Stamp Act and therefore not precedent for taxation of the colonies. Trade regulation, he contended, "lay duties on the importation of goods, which people may buy or let alone. . . . But the stamp act *forces* the money from the country under *heavy penalties*, and denies *common justice* in the courts, unless they will submit to part with it."[7]

A final approach, the one Daniel Leonard called "mere playing with words," considered what the statute said and, more significantly, what expressions or legislative formulas were included or not included. Using this technique, David Ramsay counted twenty-nine regulations of monopoly and trade enacted between 1660 and 1764 and concluded:

> Although duties were imposed on America by previous acts of Parliament, no one title of "giving an aid to his Majesty," or any other of the usual titles to revenue acts, was to be found in any of them. They were intended as regulations of the trade, and not as sources of national supplies. Till the year 1764, all stood on commercial regulation and restraint.[8]

LEGISLATION OF CHARLES II

Throughout the revolutionary controversy, people on both sides of the Atlantic compiled lists of North American taxes promulgated by the British Parliament. A frequent starting point was the reign of Charles II.[9] Although occasional references were made to statutes or ordinances from earlier times, these generally tended to show that Parliament believed it possessed constitutional authority to tax the colonies, not that it had exercised that authority. [10]

What everyone sought were precedents of constitutional significance, the older the better from the imperialist point of view. The oldest of any importance — enacted by the first Restoration Parliament — was the grant to Charles II of tonnage and poundage. This law was cited as the "first instance of taxation" of the colonies because it specifically provided that the duties were payable upon commodities "not only imported into the realm of England, but also into the dominions thereunto belonging." [11] Despite the words of the statute, however, tonnage and poundage had never been collected in America. As a result, tonnage and poundage were more precedent for what Parliament thought it constitutionally could do than precedent of a tax imposed on and collected from the colonists. It was, however, a piece of evidence that could be used to support a general proposition. "Did not," one writer asked when citing it, "the parliament, at that time, much more than a century past, possess the supreme legislative power of *taxing America?*" [12]

William Knox, who made the most persistent and persuasive arguments about precedents supporting Parliament's authority to tax the colonies, did not think tonnage and poundage a precedent. Rather, he argued and many others agreed that the Navigation Act of 1673, also passed in the reign of Charles II, "is the first which *lays taxes in the Colonies, for the sole purpose of revenue.*" That statute imposed duties on the exportation from the colonies to England of sugars, tobacco, cotton, indigo, ginger, logwood, fustic and other woods used to manufacture dyes, and cocoa nuts

> to be levied, collected and paid at such places and to such collectors and other officers as shall be appointed in their respective plantations to collect, levy and receive the same, before the lading thereof, and under such penalties both to the officers and upon the goods, as for nonpayment of or defrauding his Majesty of his customs in England. [13]

There were many American whigs who agreed with Knox that the Navigation Act was the first parliamentary statute "that ever imposed duties on the colonies, for any purpose." However, because its purpose was not to raise income but to regulate trade, they denied that it was a precedent for taxation. [14] For proof, they pointed to the preamble, which stated that an earlier statute had permitted free trade among the colonies, and complained that many colonists had abused the privilege.

[N]ot contenting themselves with being supplied with those commodities for their own use, free from all customs, (while the subjects of this your kingdom of *England* have paid great customs and impositions for what of them hath been spent here) but contrary to the express letter of the aforesaid laws, have brought into divers parts of *Europe* great quantities thereof, and do also daily vend great quantities thereof, to the shipping of other nations who bring them into divers parts of *Europe*, to the great hurt and diminution on your Majesty's customs, and of the trade and navigation of this your kingdom.

It is apparent that the act sought to prevent violations of the trade laws forbidding the colonists to trade with foreign nations or to ship colonial products by foreign vessels and, to that extent, the objective of the law was the regulation of trade. However, one consequence of contemporary practice had been that products were being shipped directly to Europe, bypassing English ports "to the great hurt and diminution of your Majesty's customs." To the extent that Parliament sought to have American goods unladed in England so that they paid a duty there, the purpose of the law was revenue. True, the duties imposed by the act to be paid on exportation from a colony would not have been for revenue. They were to regulate imperial commerce; they only indirectly aided revenue by limiting shipment to England as goods destined for English ports were not charged with the duty in the colony. John Lind, a ministerial writer who insisted that the navigation statute was "an act laying a *tax* for the purpose of *raising a revenue,*" admitted that the purpose was not clearly stated. "The act was worded very *incorrectly,*" he noted. "Of two constructions, the colonists very naturally embraced that which was most favourable to themselves. They considered the payment of these duties, as a discharge from giving the securities not to go to any *foreign* market."[15]

Some lawyers arguing for the constitutionality of parliamentary taxation were not troubled by the vague terminology of the Navigation Act. They thought its general nature too clear to allow dispute, or found proof in particular items; the statute's imposition, for example, of "duties upon the Commodities of the Plantations before they could export them; which is undoubtedly, to all intents and purposes, a clear *Revenue Tax.*" Knox emphasized two particulars that he thought demonstrated that the act had been intended for more than trade regulation. The first was that only one duty — the duty on logwood — could have been imposed for purpose of prohibition. The second was that rates laid on other products were the same as those set on goods exported from England, where the charges were undisputably for the purposes of revenue. He sought to make the first point by asking a question.

[I]f parliament had only intended these taxes as *regulations of trade,* that is to say, as prohibitory of the exportation to *foreign parts,* or *from one Colony to another,* of any of the products or commodities, upon which the taxes were laid; why did it impose a tax, of only one shilling and six-pence the hundred weight, upon muscovado sugar, which was then worth more than *twenty shillings* in the Colonies, and at the same time tax a hundred weight of logwood, which was not worth near so much, at five pounds? The same question may be asked, in respect to all the other commodities, and the answer can only be, that the high tax, in the one case, was intended for a pro-hibition, and in all the others, the taxes were *expected to be paid,* and to raise a revenue, in the Colonies, from their trade, for the gen-eral service of the state.

Knox's second particularization was based on the assumption — he termed it his belief — that the duties imposed on colonial products exported "to foreign parts, or from one Colony to another" were "the *same* as were then paid in England, upon the importation of those products into that kingdom."

The plain and obvious intention of parliament, therefore, appears to have been, that the people, in the Colonies where the respective commodities were not produced, should pay the same taxes for us-ing them, as were paid by the people of England for using them; and that such of those products, as were carried to foreign countries, should also pay the same taxes; as well to prevent foreigners from having them cheaper than the people in England, or in the Colonies could have them, and thereby cutting them off from any preference in the market, as also to raise a revenue to the state, out of what was consumed by foreigners.[16]

American whigs found both of Knox's particularizations unconvinc-ing for the same reason: they proved the intention of regulating trade as much as they evinced the purpose of raising revenue. Logwood was prohibited, but the charges placed on the other colonial goods were set at rates intended to insure that they would be exported to English rather than to foreign or colonial ports. Knox had said that Parliament sought both to have duties equal throughout the Empire and to prevent foreign-ers from buying colonial goods more cheaply than they sold for in England — in other words, a mixed purpose, partly regulation and partly reve-nue. American whigs answered that since the revenue purpose was directed as much at protecting the revenue raised in England as at ob-taining additional revenue from the colonies, the Navigation Act had not been designed to raise money. To clinch the point, they offered as a final bit of proof the fact that the law did not appropriate to any use the income collected from the duties imposed. Knox dismissed the last point, saying that "it was not *then* the practice of parliament, to appropriate all revenues that were to arise, from the taxes it imposed, either in England or in the Colonies; they were given to the King generally, and without account for the public service of the state."[17]

Some imperialists thought Knox's argument proved the Navigation Act a precedent for parliamentary taxation because it showed that the act was intended to raise some income and that Parliament did not have to appropriate to specific purposes any income raised for that income to be taxation revenue.[18] Other imperialists agreed with American whigs that appropriation was necessary to stamp customs duties with the legal character of revenue rather than regulation. Admitting that the original Navigation Act had not been a revenue-raising measure, they claimed that it had been converted into one in 1714 by a second statute directing that "the plantation duties" be paid "into the said receipt of [the] Exchequer, for the purposes in this act expressed."[19] There was, in addition, another statute that some supporters of parliamentary taxation said confirmed either that the Navigation Act had been intended for revenue purposes or that a revenue purpose had been incorporated into the Navigation Act retroactively. The explanation of Thomas Pownall is of special interest, as he had interpreted the original Navigation Act as a trade regulation, not a revenue measure. He had been persuaded that the original act was not a revenue law by its provision stipulating that if a bond was posted to guarantee that a ship's cargo would be unladed in England and Wales, duties did not have to be paid on exportation from the colonies. It was only after an act of 1696 repealed that provision, Pownall contended, that "we find, for the first time, these duties converted into a revenue: they are directed to be paid whether bond is given or not." John Lind thought that the repeal proved even more: that the intent of the Navigation Act had always been to obtain revenue and not to regulate trade.

> [T]he former [1696] Act affords a corroborating proof, that the duties imposed by that [navigation] act were intended to raise a revenue. And as a still farther proof we may observe, that the officers to whom these duties are to be paid, are called "the officers for collecting and managing his majesty's *revenues.*"[20]

THE FIRST SUGAR ACT

Another statute frequently cited as a precedent (by some as the *first* precedent) for parliamentary taxation was the Sugar Act of 1733. It was seen as both less and more important than the Navigation Act; less important because it was of a much later date and hence not a precedent of long standing, more important because it was the first parliamentary imposition of custom duties upon the colonies using what lawyers called words of donation, "the technical words of '*give*,' and '*grant*.'"[21]

The Sugar Act provided that "the commons of *Great Britain* assembled in parliament have given and granted unto your Majesty the several and respective rates and duties herein after mentioned." The conclusion of supporters of imperial taxation was unqualified: "Here then at least, one would think, was clearly a duty imposed for the purpose of *raising* a revenue."[22]

Because of the thrust of the imperialist argument, discussion as to whether the first Sugar Act was a precedent for the Stamp Act and Townshend duties generally turned on two considerations: the particular words "giving" and "granting," and whether the general purpose of the statute was revenue or trade regulation. The two could and often were combined in a single analysis of statutory interpretation. "In this act," Richard Price admitted, "the duties imposed are said to be GIVEN and GRANTED by the Parliament to the King; and this is the first *American* act in which these words have been used. But notwithstanding this, as the act had the appearance of being only a regulation of trade, the colonies submitted to it; and a small direct revenue was drawn by it from them."[23]

Edmund Burke also combined the two arguments. He admitted that the Sugar Act was the first revenue statute imposed on the colonies containing the clause "give and grant," but explained the words away by stressing other words, particularly the words of the title: "An act for the better securing of the trade of his Majesty's sugar colonies in America." Moreover, he argued, the "Act was made on a compromise of all, and at the express desire of a part, of the colonies themselves. It was therefore in some measure with their consent; and having a title directly purporting only a *commercial regulation,* and being in truth nothing more, the words were passed by, at a time when no jealousy was entertained and things were little scrutinised." In a pamphlet apparently commissioned by the ministry, John Lind answered Burke by ridiculing both Burke's contention that the words in the title of the first Sugar Act should be accorded more weight than the words of donation in the text and his conclusion that the title of the act "considers it merely as a regulation of trade." "So then," Lind wrote, "the stamp act would have been good, and constitutional, provided Mr. Grenville had bethought himself to intitle it 'an act to regulate the transfer of property in his majesty's colonies and plantations in America." Lind also took issue with Burke's argument that the Sugar Act of 1733 had been a compromise accepted by "all" colonies, even desired by some. In an astute twist, he pointed out that if the act was indeed a compromise then it must have been agreed to; and if agreed to it was taxation by consent.[24]

Consent could be implied only if one concurred with Burke that the first Sugar Act had been a compromise and that the colonies of the North America mainland had been parties to the compromise. There had been two earlier versions of the act passed by the Commons, both of which would have protected the trade of the British sugar islands with the continental colonies by prohibiting any commerce at all with the French West Indies. The Lords rejected these bills and it may be for that reason that in 1733 the supporters of the British sugar islands introduced a less excessive version, substituting high taxes discouraging trade in place of outright prohibition. This change was what Burke meant by compromise. It was for him proof that the purpose of the act had been trade regulation, not revenue. North Americans, however, had not supported the change. Even Lind admitted that "[p]age after page in the [Commons] Journals is filled with their objections to the principle of the act." In fact, what was said in the House in 1733 became the chief point of departure when determining whether the Sugar Act furnished precedent for parliamentary taxation. The agent for Rhode Island had protested that even the compromise bill would divest the colonists "of their rights and privileges as the King's natural-born subjects and Englishmen, in levying subsidies upon them against their consent, when they are annexed to no county in Great Britain, have no representative in Parliament, nor have any part of the legislature of the kingdom." As Americans were reminded at the very commencement of the revolutionary controversy, "the bare mention" of this argument had caused one member of the Commons to take "fire."[25] The Rhode Islanders were saying that the sugar bill violated their charter, Sir William Yonge pointed out. "This is something very extraordinary, and in my opinion looks mighty like aiming at an independency, and disclaiming the authority and jurisdiction of this house, as if this house had not a power to tax them, or to make any laws for the regulating of the affairs of their Colony."[26] Thomas Winnington, a lawyer and like Yonge a supporter of the ministry, was quoted as saying much the same. "I hope," he told the Commons, "they have no charter which debars this House from taxing them as well as any other subject of the nation." The speeches of both men were cited to show that "the sentiments of the whole House" understood that Parliament had constitutional authority to tax the colonies.[27] Perhaps these words were evidence of what the Commons thought in 1733 but the point is by no means certain. Yonge was arguing why Rhode Island's petition should not be received and Winnington was only partly quoted. "I am sure they can have no such charter," he had added, "but if it were possible, if they really had such a charter, they could not say that the bill now before us were any infringement of it, because the tax to be thereby laid on, is no tax upon them, but a tax which is to be laid upon the French only."[28] Winnington was saying that although Parliament had authority to tax the colonies, the sugar bill, if enacted, would not be an exercise of that authority. A careful analysis of his words provides another example of the inconclusiveness of much of the evidence upon which each side depended. On the one hand, the ministry could say that the debate helped make the Sugar Act precedent for taxation because rejection by the Commons of Rhode Island's petition indicated that the House believed the purpose of the bill was to tax the colonies. On the other hand, American whigs could use the same debate to show that the Commons did not understand that the sugar bill imposed a tax.

The lesson of inconclusiveness can be carried further. Sir John Bernard had scoffed at Winnington's argument "that the Bill now before us is a Bill for Taxing the *French* only. . . . Does the Gentleman imagine that the Tax paid in this Island [Great Britain] upon *French* Wine, is a Tax upon the *French?* Does not every Body know, that the whole is paid by the Consumers here?" Bernard, therefore, would seem to be rejecting Winnington's argument that the sugar duty, if enacted, would not be a tax on the colonies. In fact, he was agreeing with it, but on grounds more substantive and persuasive.

> The duties to be laid on by this Bill are so far from being duties for the supply of the Government, that I do not believe that even those Gentlemen, who appear so fond of the duties to be laid on by it, so much or expect or wish that any money shall be thereby raised for the use of the public; the Bill is not intended for any such end; it is rather in the nature of a prohibition.[29]

Bernard's understanding seems to have reflected that of the House. The purpose of the sugar bill as seen by those who enacted it was to protect the British sugar islands from French competition by making French molasses too expensive for the North American colonies. That is certainly a fair historical judgment, endorsed both by scholars of the American Revolution and historians of British taxation, one of whom concluded that the Sugar Act of 1733 was not even a tax but "amounted merely to a regulation of trade." The intention of the 1764 Parliament when it restructured the customs system by enacting the second Sugar Act is a different matter which will be examined in a separate chapter dealing with the revolutionary issues raised by that statute. For the moment it is sufficient to note that the possibility that the first Sugar Act would not be perceived as a tax measure may explain why Thomas Whately attempted to prove the constitutionality of the second Sugar Act by observing of the first that "the Amount of the Impositions has been complained of; the Policy of the Laws has been objected to; but the Right of making such a Law, has never been questioned."[30] The Americans did not question parliamentary regulation of the trade. They questioned Parliament's authority to tax them for purposes of revenue — something they did not think the first Sugar Act was intended to do.

THE GREENWICH HOSPITAL TAX

Another precedent cited by some writers as proof that Parliament could and had taxed the colonies before the Stamp Act, although not mentioned by most supporters of the imperialist side, was the Greenwich hospital tax.[31] A law dating from the reign of William III, it imposed a tax of sixpence a month on British seamen for their own support should they become disabled or impoverished. If the original act did not apply to colonial seamen, an amendment of Anne extended it to them and a further amendment of George II provided for collectors in North America.[32]

During the revolutionary controversy it was claimed by supporters of Parliament's authority to tax the colonies that the fee imposed on mariners by the Greenwich Hospital Act not only was a tax but a precedent for parliamentary taxation of North America. It was also said to be an especially strong precedent as the "tax has always been, and still is *levied in the Colonies*," and — or so a former governor of Massachusetts asserted — "there never was an instance in America" when payment was "refused or disputed." Perhaps as pertinent was the fact that the hospital fee was levied on mariners living in Jersey, Guernsey, Alderney, Sark, and Man, places to which Americans drew analogies when claiming a constitutional right not to be taxed.[33]

Colonial whigs did not — and could not — deny the existence of the Greenwich hospital statute but they did deny that it was a precedent proving Parliament's authority to tax them. Their demurrer turned on facts rather than on law. Americans said they had not paid the tax, that the tax had not been collected before the 1760s, that if paid it had been paid under protest, and that, as it was raised for a special, limited purpose, it was not a tax, or, at least, not a tax imposed for the purpose of revenue. A second argument distinguished between merchant seamen and commercial fishermen. American whigs admitted that the hospital rates had been assessed against merchant seamen serving on crews of ships engaged in the international or intraempire trade, but argued that the withholding of sixpence a month from seamen's salaries by the owners of vessels engaged in such commerce did not constitute a precedent for an internal tax on the colonies. "Mariners are not inhabitants of any part of the dominions," James Otis pointed out: "the sea is their element till they are decrepit, and then the hospital is open to all mariners who are British subjects without exception."[34] At most, American whigs contended, the hospital fee was precedent for parliamentary authority in an area that colonists admitted was constitutional: regulation of the imperial trade.

A different question was whether the hospital tax had ever been collected from fishermen. Payment by fishermen sailing from and returning to a single colonial seaport in which they generally lived and contracted for hire could have proven a precedent more relevant to parliamentary taxation than payment by mariners on merchant vessels. Not surprisingly, American whigs showed more concern about the fishermen precedent than about the seamen analogy, and argued that fishermen had never paid the Greenwich hospital fee, "from the first settlement of the country to this day, and with good reason, as no one of them ever has or can expect an admission into that hospital."[35]

The factual issue was never resolved, and the debate continued throughout the revolutionary era.[36] One change, however, did occur. After the customs system was reformed by Charles Townshend in 1767, substantial sums were collected, at least in Massachusetts, where high-ranking officials of the imperial revenue were stationed.[37] Although these payments damaged the American evidence to some extent, they did not provide significant support for the imperialist case because they occurred too late to constitute an indisputable precedent.

Post Office Revenue

The parliamentary statute that most supporters of imperial taxation thought an indisputable precedent of a colonial tax and the one that most troubled American whigs was the act of Queen Anne's reign extending the British postal system to other parts of the Empire. George Grenville reportedly told the House of Commons that "even if there had been no precedent of a revenue from America granted to the Crown by Act of Parliament," the Post Office Act was "sufficiently declaratory thereof." Put another way, the act was a declaratory precedent or a precedent by implication. Other defenders of Parliament's authority to raise a revenue in North America were much more positive. "Shall we," George Boucher asked, "refuse to obey the Tea Act, not as an oppressive Act, but as a dangerous, a sole Precedent of Taxation, when every Post-Day shews us a Precedent, which our Fore-Fathers submitted to, and which we still submit to, without murmuring?" John Lind was even more certain of the precedent.

> The act for the establishment of a general post-office, is clearly an act imposing duties for the purpose of raising a revenue. The subjects in America, are by this act, put under the same restraints as the subjects of England: they must send their letters by the messengers employed by *one* common post-master; must pay the rates ordered, and apportioned by the same legislature.[38]

Two aspects of the post-office statute were stressed by those who claimed it was a precedent proving the authority of Parliament to tax the colonies: that it imposed an "internal" charge on Americans, and that one of its various purposes was to raise revenue.

"This is an *internal* tax," it was said of the North America Post-Office Act; it "partakes of the nature of a general tax upon its inhabitants" and "raises an internal revenue."[39] For imperialists, this was an unquestionable precedent supporting the constitutionality of the Stamp Act. "The postage was an *internal* tax on *paper folded* like letters; the stamp-act on *paper unfolded.* Wherein lies the difference? If the *latter* was an *internal* tax, the former was the same."[40]

The postal act did more than impose internal charges upon American residents. It was a dramatic manifestation of British legislation controlling and ordering events in the colonies, entailing the promulgation of extensive executive orders and including several provisions providing for criminal punishments. Not only did the act mandate the death penalty for any postal official who destroyed or stole mail, but, as William Knox stressed when arguing that it was a precedent for colonial taxation, "the ferrymen, and owners of ferries in North America, are required to give up their dues for ferriage, and to carry over the post without payment, under a heavy penalty."[41]

These aspects of the Post Office Act, though, were generally regarded by American whigs as irrelevant to the issue of Parliament's authority to tax the colonies. If precedent for anything, they were precedent for the authority to legislate, not to tax, and could be explained away as exigencies of imperial regulation which the colonists had accepted either by reason of practical necessity or by implied consent.[42]

Imperialists disagreed. Thomas Whately, writing on behalf of the Grenville administration, postulated a theory explaining why the penal and regulatory features of the statute should be considered precedent for the authority to tax: whether by prohibiting colonists from carrying mail for profit, imposing penalties, or requiring free ferriage, they cost Americans money. "[C]ertainly Money levied by such Methods, the Effect of which is intended to be a Monopoly of the Carriage of Letters to the Officers of this Revenue, and by means of which the People are forced to pay the Rates imposed upon all their Correspondence, is a public Tax to which they must submit, and not meerly a Price required of them for a private Accom[m]odation."[43]

The second aspect about the Post Office Act that imperialists claimed made it a precedent for direct parliamentary taxation was that revenue had been one of its purposes. The statute extending the British postal establishment to North America had stated that its objectives were "to raise a present supply of money for carrying on the war, and other her Majesty's most necessary occasions"[44] and "that the business may be done in such manner as may be most beneficial to the people of these kingdoms, and her Majesty may be supplied, and the revenue arising by the said office, better improved, settled and secured to her Majesty, her heirs and successors."[45] Other evidence proving the purpose of the act was provided by the legislative history of the post office. It was generally believed during the revolutionary period that the obtainment of revenue had been a prime reason Parliament, during the reign of Charles II, had made the delivery of mail a government monopoly. Charles assigned the income to his brother James, and when James succeeded to the throne, the profits of the postal service became part of the hereditary revenue. William III and Anne continued to collect it until 1711, when Parliament took control of a specified portion. After George III became King, as Whately pointed out, "the Post Office Revenues were carried with the others *to the aggregate Fund, to be applied to the Uses, to which the said Fund is or shall be applicable.*" "If all these Circumstances do not constitute a Tax, I do not know what do," he concluded. "The Revenue arising from the Postage in *America* is blended with that of *England* [and] is applied in Part to the carrying on of a continental War, and other public Purposes; the Remainder of it to the Support of the [British] Civil List; and now the whole of it to the Discharge of the National Debt by Means of the aggregate Fund."[46]

It must be stressed that many people in eighteenth-century Great Britain, when not thinking of or addressing the question of American taxation, described the post office as part of the public revenue. Blackstone, in his *Commentaries,* called it a "very considerable branch of the revenue." Even American whigs, at least during the early stages of the revolutionary controversy, occasionally lapsed into language indicating that they thought of postage as taxation. In 1764, for example, Rhode Island's government protested to the king about "duties on importations of divers kinds of goods, by the post office, by stamp duties, and other internal taxes."[47]

Whether the postal service in fact generated appreciable income from operations in the colonies was a separate question with little bearing on the constitutional issue. "It is ridiculous to call the Post Office an instance of an internal tax," Richard Hussey told the Commons. "What a financier that must be who could expect to draw money from the Post Office in North America! Till the last two or three years the Post Office has been out of pocket and now only produced £2 or 300 a year." It would appear that Hussey was largely correct. The post office provided so little revenue even in Great Britain that one historian concluded that it "can hardly be considered a form of taxation." In North America, the post office did not begin to yield a surplus until 1764, a change ironically credited to a militant whig, Benjamin Franklin.[48]

AMERICAN PERCEPTION OF THE POSTAL PRECEDENT

American whigs distinguished the post-office precedent on several grounds. Perhaps the most persuasive was the contention that although post-office fees might be a precedent for some sort of tax, they were not precedent for taxes on tea, glass, paper, or the other products assessed by the Townshend duties. Less persuasive was the related supposition that even if the post office was a precedent for taxation, it was not a precedent for taxation without consent because the colonists had given constructive consent to the extension of the British postal system to North America. Theoretically related to the notion of constructive or implied consent, but of much greater persuasion, was the argument that because Americans had perceived the Post Office Act as a statute dealing with commerce, not as tax, they had not anticipated it might be cited as a precedent for parliamentary taxation. As commercial legislation, it was a legitimate instance of regulation, a legislative role that by colonial acquiescence Parliament was permitted to perform. Daniel Dulany explained:

> This matter . . . of the post office may be referred to the general superintending authority of the mother country, the power of the provincial legislatures being too stinted to reach it. In this view, and upon the consideration of the general convenience and accommodation arising from the establishment, the people of America have not complained of it. But if this instance were more pertinent than

it is, it would only prove what hath been too often proved before: when men do not suspect any designs to invade their rights, and sub-dolous steps taken to that end are productive of immediate conve-nience without pointing out their destructive tendency, they are fre-quently involved in ruin before they are aware of danger; or that the conduct flowing from the negligence of innocent intentions may afford an handle to men of different dispositions for the commission of oppression.[49]

The distinction most frequently raised by American whigs turned on the question of purpose and the purpose most often mentioned was con-venience. In one respect, the argument was related to the notion of con-structive consent; that was certainly the sense made of it by Lord Mayor William Beckford when he dismissed the post office as a taxation prece-dent because it had been extended to North America "for the convenience of the colonies themselves."[50] That is, as a London pamphlet suggested, "the introduction of it into our Colonists was a mere thing of commercial convenience." The question was put directly to Franklin when he testi-fied before the Commons: did the Americans, he was asked, "consider the post-office as a tax, or as a regulation?" "Not as a tax," Franklin answered, "but as a regulation and conveniency." James Otis elaborated on the distinction when he contended that the post office "is for the convenience of trade and commerce: it is not laying any burden upon it; for besides that it is upon the whole cheaper to correspond in this way than any other, everyone is at liberty to send his own letters by a friend." That was an-other way of viewing the precedent: that the tax, if it was a tax, was paid voluntarily. "[T]he Post Office," Franklin reasoned, "is not so much a tax as a regulation, as it compels no person to send letters by it, as he may send it by a private messenger." Put another way, payment of a postal fee was "merely a *quantum meruit* for service done, and which every man may do in another way, if he thinks it cheaper and safer, i.e. he may send his letter by a special messenger, or by his friend." Even the statu-tory imposition upon ferrymen that they transport letter carriers with-out charge was not a tax because Americans "do not consider it as such, as they have an advantage from persons traveling with the post."[51]

From the colonial whig perspective of the purpose for which the British post-office system had been extended to America, it was irrelevant whether the postal system raised a revenue or not. "[A]lthough this Institution may produce a Revenue," Richard Jackson reasoned, "as well as Laws for regu-lating Trade neither can properly be called Tax Laws any more than Penal Laws can be called so, which yet may produce a considerable Revenue to the Gov[ernmen]t." As a second member of the Commons put the same argument, the Stamp Act was "intended to be laid upon very different principles." Benjamin Franklin summed up all these positions:

> The Post-Office, say the Grenvillians, is, in Effect, a Tax upon America, which they never have complained of. The advancing of so frivolous an Apology for their Injustice and Oppression, shews the Difficulty they find in patching up an indefensible Cause. They might as well have drawn a Defence of their Policy from the establishing of Tolls at Turnpikes. Will any Man of common Sense attempt to force a Comparison between a Regulation evidently for the Benefit of the Colonies, and of our Merchants trading with them, and whose Effect is a saving of Money to the Colonists, and a Scheme, whose declared Intention is, to take from them their Property, and to increase the Revenue at their Expence, and contrary to their Inclination?[52]

We may be certain that these arguments persuaded a number of American whigs that the Post Office Act was not a precedent proving Parliament's authority to tax the colonies. Still, many were so troubled by the potential force of the precedent that they either dismissed it for inapposite reasons or, when discussing it, avoided discussing the merits. Thomas Jefferson's dismissal was almost flippant. "The act . . . for establishing a post office in America," he wrote, "seems to have had little connection with British convenience, except that of accom[m]odating his majesty's ministers and favorites with the sale of a lucrative and easy office." Silas Downer's reasons for dismissal, although no more convincing than Jefferson's, had greater originality. He admitted that the Post Office Act imposed a tax, but contended that it was not a precedent for parliamentary taxation because it had been enacted by an inappropriate legislature.

> In the 9th. of *Anne*, the post-office act was made, which is a tax act, and which annually draws great sums of money from us. It is true that such an establishment would have been of great use, but then the regulation ought to have been made among ourselves. And it is a clear point to me that let it be ever so much to the advantage of this country, the parliament had no more right to interfere, then they have to form such an establishment in the electorate of *Hanover*, the King's *German* dominions.[53]

The difficulty that the Post Office Act gave American whigs is perhaps best demonstrated by an unknown Rhode Islander who seems to have felt that although it might be a precedent it was an "unfair" precedent.

[L]et it be osberved, that such an institution, if not made too expensive, is so manifestly for the convenience of a country, that it is not
to be wondered at that the colonists put up with an undesigned bor-
dering too close upon a meer right, which might arise from want
of due attention to it, when instead of evil consequences, there sprung
a general convenience. It is well known by all, who are but a little
versed in history, by what silent and almost imperceptible degrees
the liberties of subjects may be encroached upon, and how much
they will endure before they will make any general complaint; and
it is unfair to cite as a *precedent* our submission to an unconstitutional proceeding, although then unattended with any evil consequences. But it is now apparent that that measure, by only being
brought into *example*, hath been of *dangerous* consequence; and very
likely the colony of *South-Carolina*, who, I am told, would never
permit the postmaster-general to exercise any authority there, fore-
saw the evil tendency of such a *precedent*.[54]

The South Carolina story may have been only parabolic when this
Rhode Islander told it in 1765, but it presaged the future. By 1774, American whigs were so troubled by the post-office statute and evidence it
provided of precedent for parliamentary taxation that, to depreciate the
"certainly unconstitutional" post office, they established a rival system,
"a post-office upon constitutional principles" or "what is called a constitutional Post-Office."[55] Since the former post office had been created by
Parliament, Boston's committee of correspondence explained, the revenue that it raised was "equally as obnoxious as any other revenue Act."

We are fully sensible that the Post Office upon the present footing
is unconstitutional, and a usurpation of the British Parliament no
longer to be born. The Act which originated this Office is to all intents and purposes a Revenue Act, and is formidable and dangerous
to the liberties of America, as the Officers have it in their power to
intercept our communications, to extort what they please, and to
apply them to divide us, and then to inslave us — it is a power that
extends thro' all the Colonies, and is unsafe in the hands of those
who have for a long time convinced us, that a regard to the rights
of Mankind, is not the principle upon which they act.[56]

Historians who doubt constitutional explanations think that there may
have been another reason why the "constitutional" postal system was created. It has been argued, for example, that the motivating purpose "was
much less an attempt to resist a revenue producing act of Parliament than
it was part of the committee's over-all effort to see a reliable union es-

tablished among the colonies."[57] That may be so, but it is doubtful. The realization that the Post Office Act was a precedent, perhaps the only precedent, for parliamentary taxation upon the colonies was surely a major consideration in creating the new system. The words of individual participants furnish the best clue to motivations. Francis Lightfoot Lee received a letter in October 1775 from Landon Carter upon which postage had been paid "to the *hated* Post Office." "As the constitutional post now goes regularly," Lee replied, "we may with a safe conscience say how d'ye to each other." Over a year earlier, a man in New York wrote that the post office was a matter in which "the Cause of American Freedom is deeply concerned" because it was a precedent "upon which every other unconstitutional Act has been grounded." If the colonies set up their own system and abolished that created by the British Parliament "it will put an entire Stop to their laying any further unconstitutional Burdens upon us." Finally, the *Boston Evening-Post* reported that "a considerable fund is already raised for the support of new Posts at Philadelphia and Baltimore, and the citizens at New-York are determined to open subscription books for the like purpose, as soon as the town of Boston has given a sanction to the capital design of annihilating that fatal precedent against us — the POST-OFFICE."[58]

WEIGHING THE PRECEDENTS

There were several other statutes that writers on the imperial side of the revolutionary controversy cited as precedents supporting Parliament's authority to tax the colonies. They were mostly of secondary significance, imposing duties on exports or imports, acts American whigs could distinguish from revenue measures on the grounds they were intended to regulate trade or had been enacted after the revolutionary controversy had commenced. An example was the Quartering Act requiring colonies to furnish supplies to British troops stationed within their territory, a measure frequently challenged as an unconstitutional tax. The only serious precedents to parliamentary taxation therefore were those discussed above and the legal weight they should be accorded depends on the answers to two questions: whether the Navigation or Sugar Acts had been intended to raise revenue and whether postal rates, regardless of the revenue they did or did not raise, were a form of taxation. Not to be forgotten, however, was the constitutional question mentioned earlier about the relevance of these precedents. Thomas Hutchinson, for example, agreed with whigs that before the second Sugar Act there had been no precedent of taxation by Parliament of the colonies but thought that proved nothing about Parliament's constitutional authority. Taxation was part of the sovereign's legislative power, Hutchinson pointed out, and since Parliament was sovereign, there were no constitutional grounds upon which its authority could be disputed.[59]

For the majority of Americans, loyalists as well as whigs, and for the predominant number of their fellow citizens in Great Britain who did not accept the new jurisprudential notion that sovereignty meant arbitrary power without restraint, precedent was still a vital component of constitutional authority. For some, the precedential evidence was conclusive. "These acts of the legislature," John Shebbeare wrote on behalf of the imperialist side, "prove the certainty of their [British] rights to tax them [Americans], for much more than a hundred years. Their application to parliament, and the obedience to these acts, by the colonists, prove that they entertained no doubt of the legislature having a just right to tax them." John Adams, writing for the other side of the debate, examined the same precedents as Shebbeare and found them just as conclusive. "As for duties for a revenue," he argued, "none were ever laid by parliament for that purpose, until 1764, when, and ever since, its authority to do it has been constantly denied." Adams challenged imperialists to cite a statute prior to the second Sugar Act "in which the word revenue is used, or the thought of raising a revenue, is expressed." Daniel Dulany, scoffing at the "artificial painted precedents which have been produced," did not consider the second Sugar Act a precedent because it was not for taxation only but also had been intended to regulate the molasses trade. Writing of Ireland as well as of the American colonies, Dulany insisted that there was not "one instance before the Stamp Act of a tax imposed by Parliament upon either for the *unmixed* purpose of revenue."[60]

A different perspective from which to employ these precedents or the lack of precedent for taxation was posed by the issue why Americans had not protested parliamentary taxes before 1764. "They never," a leading lawyer told the Commons during the Stamp Act debates, "disputed the Right of this Country in Taxation first by Prer[ogative], now by Parl[iamen]t." There had been no dispute, American whigs replied, because there had been nothing about which to dispute, a point they proved by noting the absence of precedents. A variation of this argument for people persuaded that the Greenwich hospital fee or the Navigation Acts were precedential taxation statutes contended that they were unimportant precedents. "Taxes for the purpose of raising a revenue had hitherto been sparingly attempted in America," Burke was quoted by colonial newspapers as arguing. "Without ever doubting the extent of its lawful power, parliament always doubted the propriety of such impositions. And the

Americans on their part never thought of contesting a right by which they were so little affected." Robert Carter Nicholas conceded even more weight to the evidence of precedents, while agreeing with Burke that they meant nothing. "That America," he admitted, "hath acquiesced in and paid former Duties, and some of these merely internal, I do not deny; but she did not discover their dangerous Tendency till, within these few Years, her Eyes were clearly opened by farther Encroachments." An opposite argument, though, could explain the paucity of relevant precedents equally well. "In the preceding reigns," a London magazine writer observed, "the Americans were as yet in their infancy; no duties were laid, because we were convinced of their incapability of paying them; but now, opulent, why should they not assist that government, to whom they are indebted for their very existence?"[61]

All in all the debate, though joined and pursued by both sides, was inconclusive. There was just enough evidence for the imperialists to claim a few precedents, but they were so innocuous that some American whigs and their British supporters felt confident treating them with scorn. "To assert that America has been always subject to the taxing power of a British parliament," a London publication complained, "was the least we could have expected from men, who seem resolved to carry their point at any expence; but to bring forward . . . a long string of *duties* upon the various articles of *American commerce* . . . [is] a most daring mockery and insult upon the good nature of Englishmen." Supporters of Parliament's right to tax the colonies for the purpose of raising revenue, the *Boston Post-Boy* noted with contempt, had searched everywhere for precedents and "they could find nothing that even *their* unlimited Audacity could dare to call *Precedents* in this Case, but the Statute for establishing a Post-Office in *America*, and the Laws for regulating the Forces here, during the late War."[62]

CHAPTER SIXTEEN

DOCTRINE OF CUSTOM

When Samuel Adams contended that the Greenwich hospital fee had not been paid by American fishermen "from the first settlement of the country to this day," he was not teaching a lesson of history but making an argument of law. Adams was casting doubt on the constitutionality, even on the legality, of efforts to collect the hospital tax in the colonies. So, too, voters of Providence, Rhode Island, believed they were making a statement of law when they declared that their "particular Rights as Colonists" were "precisely known and ascertained, by uninterrupted Practice and Usage from the first Settlement of this Country, down to this Time." They were instructing the town's representatives to ignore the Stamp Act because, among other reasons, Rhode Islanders had since the colony's founding "enjoyed the Right of being governed by their own Assembly, in the Article of Taxes," a right that had "never been forfeited." As a result of that continuous, uninterrupted enjoyment, the Assembly was said to possess "the only exclusive Right to lay Taxes and Imposts upon the Inhabitants of this Colony: and . . . every Attempt to vest such Power in any Person or Persons whatever, other than the General Assembly aforesaid, is unconstitutional, and hath a manifest Tendency to destroy *British*, as well as *American* Liberty." The colony's Assembly made the same argument, also using words like "right," "power," and "unconstitutional."[1]

Adams and the voters of Providence were saying that legal rights had been created either because certain actions had always been performed by defined institutions or in defined ways or because actions had been abstained from. The authority of custom for which they contended is clear and the evidence generally uncomplicated, yet there are few other legal doctrines of the revolutionary era so misunderstood.

Two examples should be sufficient to illustrate how custom has been misstated and colonial arguments of custom have been dismissed. One is from the writings of George Louis Beer, the other from a biography of Samuel Adams. "From the legal standpoint," Beer observed, Parliament's claim of authority to tax the colonies "was unassailable. It was somewhat vulnerable from the historical standpoint, as Parliament had hitherto not exercised all its legal powers, notably that of taxation." One of the biographers of Samuel Adams wrote that even though Adams "could find no legal precedents for [his] contention" that American assemblies alone had the constitutional right to tax the colonies, "he could find ample justification for it in the facts of colonial history. For decades, the Americans had enjoyed self-government not by virtue of any formal grant of power, but by prescriptive right, and nothing is easier for the emotional enthusiast than to confuse custom with law."[2] Eighteenth-century common lawyers would not have understood either of these observations. For them Adams and his fellow whigs were appealing to the authority of custom, not to history, and custom had authority because in many situations custom was law.

There was no misunderstanding in revolutionary Great Britain. Educated laity as well as common lawyers knew the legal theory upon which colonial whigs rested this part of their argument against parliamentary taxation and appreciated that the theory was constitutional, not political or historical. American whigs, the *Political Register* noted, were appealing to the authority of custom, claiming that the right to be taxed only by the consent of representatives chosen by themselves was "a privilege to which they think they are intituled, in common with their fellow-subjects in Britain, both by their birth-right, by their charters, and by constant usage and custom, the foundation of all the laws of the realm." It would be error to accept the last assertion too literally; custom was no longer the authority for all law. Command of the sovereign, though, had not yet become the sole basis of legal sanction. A remarkably large school of legal theory during the revolutionary era still accorded custom equality with, even superiority over command. "There are some old-fashioned People," Arthur Lee boasted, "who will be constant in thinking, that what has prevailed from the Beginning of the Colony, is Part of the Constitution; and that ancient and undoubted Rights are of all other the most sacred and valuable." Lee was writing in 1774, toward the end of the revolutionary controversy. Ten years earlier, before the Stamp Act had been enacted, the Connecticut Assembly summed up the colonial claim to constitutional autonomy when it made what everyone then understood to be an argument of law.

> [T]hese Powers, Rights, and Privileges the Colony has been in Posses-sion of for more than a Century past. This Power of Legislation nec-essarily includes in it an Authority to impose Taxes or Duties upon the People for the Support of Government and for the Protection and Defense of the Inhabitants, as, without such Authority, the gen-eral Right of Legislation would be of no Avail to them. These Privi-leges and Immunities, these Powers and Authorities, the Colony claims not only in Vertue of their Right to the general Principles of the *Brit-ish* Constitution and by Force of the Royal Declaration and Grant in their Favour, but also as having been in the Possession, Enjoyment, and Exercise of them for so long a Time, and constantly owned, ac-knowledged, and allowed to be just in the Claim and Use thereof by the Crown, the Ministry, and the Parliament, as may evidently be shewn by Royal Instructions, many Letters and Acts of Parlia-ment, all supposing and being predicated upon the Colony's having and justly exercising these Privileges, Powers, and Authorities: And what better Foundation for, or greater Evidence of, such Rights can be demanded or produced is certainly difficult to be imagined.[3]

AUTHORITY OF CUSTOM

A chapter dealing with Parliament's customary authority to tax the North American colonies is not the place to consider the jurisprudential underpinnings of the doctrine of custom.[4] The best that can be provided is a brief outline of the legal concepts. There are two preliminary points to be kept in mind: that law *qua* custom was positive law and must not be confused with natural law and that custom affected law on several levels.

On the most elementary level, custom provided law with a means of knowing which rules and practices operated successfully. Some protesting members of the House of Lords utilized this relationship when they de-scribed the legal principle upon which the repeal of the Stamp Act had been based as "nothing more than a return to the ancient standing policy of this Empire. The unhappy departure from it has led to that course of shifting and contradictory measures which have since given rise to such continual distractions." They were saying that had Parliament not deviated from the customary imperial constitution, the revolutionary controversy would have been avoided. Put in a different context, the same complaint utilized custom as a protection against arbitrary action. At least if custom was compared with promulgated command (whether by Crown or legislature) as a guide to law, custom was both safer and likely to be better. Nothing, after all, "would be more fatal to liberty than to judge individuals upon laws occasionally enacted, and arising suddenly out of the heat of the times, and the peculiar circumstances of the case under contemplation." One reason custom provided a quality of law better in application and less arbitrary than legislative command was that it reflected popular values. The very fact that a usage survived the stress of time over several generations was proof that people both accepted its utility and had conferred on it popular consent. According to Bishop Burnet, that supposition or rationalization of custom's authority meant that custom was a means by which "the common sense of all Men [gives] a just and good Title." It was also a way of providing law with a democratic base without having a democratic government. As Judge Davis theorized in the seventeenth century: "When a reasonable act once done is found to be good and beneficiall to the people, and agreeable to their nature and disposition, then do they use it and practise it again and again, and so by often iteration and multiplication of the act it becometh a *Custome;* and being continued without interruption time out of mind, it obtaineth the force of a *Law.*"[5]

Another use of custom, one falling just short of custom's main task of serving as the authority of law, was to provide evidence of law. "The law is not known but by usage, and usage proves the law," Judge Jenkins explained. One of the most surprising instances of this function occurred whenever the government, even though promulgating law by command, utilized custom as evidence to prove that law. An example of the technique comes from an episode in the history of the doctrine of taxation only by consent mentioned in an earlier chapter, Henry VI's decree declaring that Chester could not be taxed because it was not represented. The people of Chester and their ancestors, the king announced, "have not been charged before this time, with any fifteenth or subsidy granted unto us, or any of our progenitors, by authority of any parliament." As a result, Henry promised, "it is our full will and intent, that they be not charged with any such grant, otherwise than they, their predecessors and ancestors have been charged afore time. And that they have and hold, possess, and enjoy, all their liberties, freedoms, and franchises, in as ample and large form, as ever they had in our, or any of our said progenitors days."[6]

As Judge Davis said and as Henry VI implied, there was yet a more definitive level upon which custom affected law: custom was one of the chief sources for the authority of law and, as authority, was in fact law. The rule was stated by Thomas Wood in his *Institute of the Laws:* usage and ancient custom make law. There were even law writers in the eighteenth century who thought custom had more authority than parliamentary command. "[S]o great and omnipotent is the power of custom," a pamphleteer wrote in 1764, "that it not only creates laws, but has produced a Court, whose decisions controul, and render inoperative and of non-effect, acts authorised by the express words of the Legislative Power. . . . I judge it scarce necessary to say this is the Court of Chancery, whose jurisdiction is solely founded on custom."[7]

Perhaps the conceptual legal apparatus that made most colonists familiar with the authority of custom was common law. "By *Common Law*" was meant "those general Customs that bind the whole Realm, by an immemorial usage."[8] Common law was "the custom of the nation, approved good by many ages" and, in the seventeenth century, it was possible to claim that no other law could "have that validity which the custom of so many ages hath."[9] It is instructive that a law dictionary published at the start of the eighteenth century divided "the *Law of England*" into three parts, the first of which was common law. What remains of common law in the United States in the twentieth century can still, to a large degree, be defined as custom — or, at least, as the custom of the judiciary. But law itself is more likely to be defined as "[t]hat which is laid down, ordained, or established . . . a body of rules of action or conduct prescribed by controlling authority, and having binding legal force."[10]

The legal concept that is most difficult for people of today to comprehend is that the authority of the constitution once depended in great part on custom. At the time of the English Revolution, a royalist judge could claim that Charles I was entitled to "that which all his Ancestors, Kings of this Realm, have enjoyed: That enjoyment and usage makes the *Law.*" During the American revolutionary controversy an imperialist pamphleteer asserting Parliament's constitutional right to tax the colonies could claim that it was on the ground of custom and only custom that "the House of Commons defends its exclusive claim to the right of bringing in and framing all money-bills." All colonial constitutional procedures and many colonial constitutional rights were derived from custom, particularly legislative privileges and the standards of legislative representation. The writer of a 1767 London political pamphlet relied on the authority of custom when he told George Grenville that although Americans were not represented in Parliament, they had from their very first establishment, for more than 100 years, uniformly exercised and enjoyed the privilege of imposing and raising their own taxes, in their provincial assemblies, of which they choose the members. So that they look upon themselves now to be not only intitled thereto by the principles of the *British* government, but by an uninterrupted usage sufficient of itself to make a constitution.[11]

PROOF OF CUSTOM

There were many tests for determining the legal validity of a purported custom. In 1770, the King's Bench, the highest judicial authority in the common law except for the House of Lords, defined two "qualities" necessary "to constitute a legal custom."

[F]irst, a custom must import some general right in a district and not a few mere private acts of individuals; and, in the next place, such custom must appear to have existed immemorially. All customs operate (if they have any operation) as positive laws. The mere fact of usage will be no right at all in itself, but when a custom has prevailed from time immemorial, it has the evidence and force of an immemorial law. If the custom be general, it is the law of the realm; if local only, it is lex loci, the law of the place.

It should be added that there was one other important test of a custom: it had to be reasonable. Aside from reasonableness, however, the criteria stated by the King's Bench were the two that American whigs had to sustain if they were to prove that the right to be taxed only by consent of the local colonial assembly had been established as a binding custom in imperial constitutional law. The first test involved geographical evidence, the second evidence of duration.[12]

Geography posed the most difficult factual challenge for American whigs because there were burdens of proof they had to meet to provide satisfactory evidence of a customary constitutional exemption for parliamentary taxation. First, it was not enough for the custom to be local; it also had to be imperial. Second, relevant facts had to be argued to establish a custom as a doctrine of law. To prove the customary exemption, therefore, American whigs needed facts that showed that the custom had been accepted and acted upon by the imperial government. The doctrine of law was explained in 1764 by an English common lawyer whose words are of special interest because he belonged to the emerging school of jurisprudence that defined law as command, but nonetheless conceded that command could be superseded by custom: "contrary custom" could not "of themselves destroy a Law. . . . Yet the Power that makes a Law, may allow them to prevail against it. Then the Question is, how to know when the Law-giver is willing his Law shall submit to a contrary Custom? Answer. By his tacit consent, and secret Approbation."[13] American whigs, of course, did not accept this definition of law; they cited evidence of parliamentary acquiescence not to prove parliamentary consent, but to prove that the custom existed. The acquiescence of first the Crown and later of Parliament proved, they said, that the custom existed and that it was imperial. It was this legal principle that the New York Assembly expounded when it reminded the House of Commons that the colonies always had exercised

> the Powers of Legislation; in Virtue of which, the Right of imposing Taxes, hath been invariably and exclusively exercised by their Representatives in General Assembly convened: A Right strengthened by long Usage, and if not openly recognized by his Majesty and the Legislature of *Great-Britain, evidently* implyed in the Requisitions made by the Crown with the Consent and Approbation of Parliament.[14]

The second test of custom laid down by King's Bench was time: "No usage" could be part of common law, "or have the force of a custom, that is not immemorial." According to the doctrine of law extant in the seventeenth century and still prevalent in the eighteenth century, the binding force of common-law rights and of English constitutional conventions was roughly proportionate to their antiquity. Custom acquired its validity by having been followed and applied from time immemorial.[15] Today's lawyers and historians might surmise that this requirement of antiquity placed a burden of proof upon American whigs that they could not possibly have met: how, they might ask, could colonial experience be termed immemorial? The answer is that the test of immemoriality was variable, depending upon what law was being proven by custom. From every perspective, immemoriality in seventeenth- and eighteenth-century English law was a duration of imprecise measurement.

Although it would be reasonable to presume that a period of thirty-seven years would be too short a duration to establish as law a practice governing anything so important as taxation, an argument once had been made about the Irish constitution that might have been of use to the imperial side of the revolutionary controversy had Parliament possessed a precedent of colonial taxation for purposes of revenue of even that brief a time. It was claimed in 1698 that a custom "of Thirty seven years standing" had established in Irish constitutional law the right of the English parliament of "Taxing them without their Consent." In contrast, Earl Camden ruled that over twice that amount of time was not sufficient to create a constitutional privilege shielding a British minister from prosecution. In 1770 Camden was asked by the government to accept as law the right of a secretary of state to issue general search warrants on the grounds that such warrants had been issued by secretaries at least since the Glorious Revolution. The time span of eighty-two years was not enough, the judge held. "If the practice began then," he is reported by one source, "it began too late to be law now." "If it began then," another official account says, "it is too modern to be law." Or (in a version even more revealing for our purposes as it has Camden using the word "evidence") "it is much too modern to be evidence of the common law."[16]

It is not necessary to reconcile these varying tests of time. They illustrate that the proof of custom in English law was not an exact science, a difficulty for lawyers in the mother country that had no bearing on the revolutionary constitutional debate. When American whigs argued the constitutional custom of taxation only by local consent they sought to prove its validity by a time span that was absolute, not relative. Colonial proof of constitutional custom, especially the all-important custom of freedom from parliamentary taxation, could be traced to a "time immemorial" because it could be traced to the beginning of relevant time. A committee of correspondence of the colony of Barbados did so, for example, when it claimed that "we have enjoyed that privilege" of "an exemption from every other internal tax, than such as may be laid upon us by the representatives of our own people . . . ever since the first establishment of a civil government in this island to the present time."[17]

Assemblies on the North American mainland used the same evidence as the Barbados committee. When colonial legislatures claimed that by custom they alone had constitutional authority to raise revenue within their jurisdictions, they relied on absolute time to prove immemoriality. "Your Memorialists," Virginia's House of Burgesses contended, "have been invested with the Right of taxing their own People from the first Establishment of a regular Government in the Colony." It was "A Right which as Men, and Descendents of Britons, they have ever quietly possessed since first by Royal Permission and Encouragement they left the Mother Kingdom to extend its Commerce and Dominion."[18] Pennsylvania's lower house, claiming the right to consent to taxation as one which "they have possessed ever since this Province was settled,"[19] pointed out that "[t]his right in the people of this province, of being exempted from any taxations, save those imposed by their Representatives, has been recognized by long established usage and custom, ever since the settlement thereof, without one precedent to the contrary, until the passing of the late Stamp-act."[20]

The unusual quality of this proof — a date certain beyond which it was not necessary to trace back the continuity of a custom — was appreciated by contemporaries. John Dickinson marked the contrast between the uncertain standards of proof for custom in much of English law and the ease of proving the American assertions of constitutional right to taxation by local consent.

> The people of *Great-Britain*, in support of their privileges, boast much of their antiquity. It is true they are antient; yet it may well be questioned, if there is a single privilege of a *British* subject, supported by longer, more solemn, or more uninterrupted testimony, than the exclusive right of taxation in these colonies.

Since the argument rested on a comparison of a somewhat relative standard of proof with one that had a definite, limited measure of time, the assertion could even be made that the American privilege of the right to taxation by consent was supported by stronger constitutional evidence than was the same claim in Great Britain. It could be admitted that the colonists had not "been so long in possession of the same right of taxing themselves" as had the Scots, "but they have been longer in possession of it than any man's knowledge goes to the contrary; and the people of the *colonies* can say in vindication of their right, what cannot be proved by *England, Scotland* or *Ireland*, that they have been taxed by their own representatives ever since they have existed."[21]

THE AMERICAN ARGUMENT

There were always English legal writers, even in the seventeenth century, who questioned whether custom was law. Usually, however, they were not lawyers. By the 1760s, a few legal theorists were denying that custom could have equal weight as legal authority with the sovereign's command. The agent for the Massachusetts House of Representatives, for example, reported that during the Stamp Act debate there was not a member of the Commons prepared to support the legal theory that a right founded in custom could stand "against the right of Parliament to tax the colonies."[22] He exaggerated, not only because there were members of the Commons willing to defend American rights on the authority of custom, but also because few people, whether lawyers or not, doubted that custom had validity as law. Instead of disparaging American notions of custom as law, most supporters of imperial taxation sought to distinguish the evidence and questioned colonial whig legal conclusions.

They did this chiefly by adopting one of two techniques: they believed or affected to believe that the American argument was an argument of fact rather than of law or, they agreed that the American facts had been proven but disputed the American conclusion, saying that the facts proved either a different or a much narrower conclusion of law.

It was not difficult for British writers to ignore the legal substance of the American whig appeal to custom and treat the argument as one of fact. All one had to do was admit everything the colonists claimed and conclude: "be it so; this argument reacheth no farther than to the expediency of the Stamp-act, and not to the right of making it." A more sophisticated version of this technique was presented in a conversation between *Philodemus* and *Aristocraticus*. "But have we the less right because we have not exercised it before?" *Aristocraticus* asked about Parliament's authority over the colonies. "No," *Philodemus* answered,

> but when a right is disputed, its never having been exercised for a course of ages, is a strong presumption, where its existence is not necessary and certain, of its non-existence; especially if the occasions have been frequent, and the temptation strong to exercise it, if it did exist, and the power was not wanting, and the plea specious, and the acquiescence probable.[23]

Philodemus was wrong: that an action had been abstained from was not a presumption of fact, it was a presumption of law. Moreover, very few persons during the revolutionary controversy thought that the colonial whigs were making an argument of fact. Theirs was a legal argument the proof of which depended upon facts and most supporters of imperial authority knew that it had to be answered in law. For that reason, *Philodemus*'s contention contained no substance and is of interest only because it helps to delineate precisely what the debate was about. His second premise, however, was of greater significance because it was endorsed by George Grenville when he argued that proof of the custom depended not on the fact that Parliament had abstained from taxing the colonies, but on why it had abstained. Parliament had not taxed the colonies, Grenville admitted, but only because it had been waiting for the colonies to grow strong enough to bear the tax. Another way to put the argument, as John Lind did, was to agree that prior to the Sugar Act of 1764 only insignificant trade duties had been collected in America, "but as the riches of any part of the empire increases, so also ought their taxes to increase, so that all parts may pay towards the common security, in proportion to their wealth."[24]

Again, the argument did not directly answer the American whig citation of constitutional custom. It might have done so — or at least have had more weight — had imperialists provided proof that the government in London had always had plans to tax North America, plans postponed during the poverty of the colonies, and that there had been a general understanding that once Americans were strong enough, wealthy enough, or both, Parliament would tax them. Such facts would have provided evidence countering colonial whig facts that the colonies had not been taxed for purposes of revenue and using those facts to establish a custom of not being taxed. This argument, or at least a version of it, was made by Francis Maseres, attorney general of Quebec. Maseres reinterpreted colonial whig facts and drew a conclusion of law different from the whig conclusion. Because his conclusion was an argument of law, it provided a seemingly persuasive answer to the American whigs' case that constitutional custom exempted them from parliamentary taxation.

Maseres accepted the whigs' evidence that Parliament had not taxed the colonies for purposes of revenue and agreed that "this long forbearance" by Parliament amounted "in reason and equity, if not in strict law, to a renunuciation of its authority of taxing the Americans for these purposes, and a transfer of it to the American assemblies." Then, interpreting the evidence narrowly, Maseres drew a conclusion of law different from that drawn by colonial whigs. The colonies, he pointed out, had taxed themselves only for "the local purposes of their respective provinces." Any conclusion of law based on that fact had to be limited to local taxation. Put one way, the argument was that if Parliament had acknowledged by customary forbearance that colonial assemblies were vested with exclusive jurisdiction to collect local taxes, the custom was limited to local taxes. Put another way, the only taxes that the force of custom prohibited Parliament from imposing were those that raised money for local purposes. The customary constitution, therefore, did not exempt Americans from parliamentary taxes imposed for imperial — or what Maseres called "general"— purposes.[25]

Maseres's conclusion of law contained a good deal of persuasiveness. The American whig evidence of parliamentary forbearance could be limited to local taxation as that was the species of taxes that the colonies had collected as a result of being left to their own legislative authority. What Maseres did not mention was that forbearance was only part of the American whigs' evidentiary case. They did claim forbearance — that Parliament had never taxed them for the purpose of raising revenue of any kind — and that they had always been taxed for revenue purposes only by their local assemblies "lawfully convened according to the antient and established practice." But in addition, they also argued evidence supporting their customary constitutional right to raise taxes for general, imperial purposes. To prove that contention, they produced evidence of greater probative value than mere forbearance as it showed that the imperial government had knowingly taken actions acknowledging that by constitutional custom the colonial assemblies, not Parliament, imposed taxes for general revenue purposes. At times, especially during the recent war against France when in need of American aid to support imperial activities, London had not promulgated taxes directly upon the colonies. Instead, "Requisitions have been constantly made to them by their Sovereigns on all Occasions when the Assistance of the Colony was thought necessary to preserve the *British* Interest in America."[26] This evidence, colonial whigs insisted, was sufficient to prove their customary constitutional right of being assessed taxes for general, imperial purposes only by consent of their local, elected assemblies. That right was established by the fact that it had been tacitly implied in the requisitions made by the Crown, with the consent and approbation of Parliament. "[F]rom whence," it was concluded, Americans "cannot now be deprived of a Right they have so long enjoyed, and which they have never forfeited."[27]

The American whigs' position was unequivocal and contained no reservations distinguishing between taxes for local and for general purposes. They were claiming as a constitutional custom, in the words of Virginia's elected legislators, "That the sole Right of imposing Taxes on the Inhabitants of this his Majesty's Colony and Dominion of *Virginia*, is now, and ever hath been, legally and constitutionally vested in the House of Burgesses." That argument was made in 1769. Earlier, at the very commencement of the revolutionary controversy, the same legislative body had summed up (in the famous Stamp Act resolves that history associates with Patrick Henry) the entire American appeal to a customary constitutional right not to be taxed by Parliament.

> That his Majesty's liege People of this his most ancient and loyal Colony have without Interruption enjoyed the inestimable Right of being governed by such Laws, respecting their internal Polity and Taxation, as are derived from their own Consent, with the Approbation of their Sovereign, or his Substitute; and that the same hath never been forfeited or yielded up, but hath been constantly recognized by the Kings and People of *Great Britain*.[28]

CONCLUSION

As with every other principle of ancient English jurisprudence, the doctrine of custom did not exist separated from other rules of law. It was

closely associated in both substance and evidence with another legal argument previously considered, the theory of precedent. Both precedent and
custom could be proven by the same evidence and defended by the same
tactics. There was, of course, a substantive difference: precedent was not
law; it was only evidence of law. Precedent, or proof by precedent, also
provided evidence of custom, which in turn provided both evidence of
and authority for law. Custom was law and the constitution was custom.

In one respect, custom and precedent were similar. Just as legal rights
were defended by preventing the creation of adverse precedents, so customary rights were protected by preventing contrary precedents that might
be cited to prove a different custom or to prove that a custom was no
longer valid due to disusage. For that reason, when American whigs re-
sorted to crowd action to keep the Stamp Act from becoming a precedent
of internal colonial taxation for purposes of revenue, they were also defending the customary colonial constitution. By forcing every stamp distributor to resign, whig crowds not only denied to the British ministry
a precedent of parliamentary taxes collected for revenue, they also preserved an unbroken customary practice.

"The American stamp-act," a writer for London's *Monthly Review* observed in 1774, "was perhaps the most inconsiderate measure that government could have attempted to carry into execution, as it came at least
a century too late." He was referring to the constitutional fact that for
Parliament constitutionally to collect revenue from the colonies in 1765,
it should have established the right by a custom going back to 1665 if
not before. By 1765, when Grenville's administration made the attempt,
it was too late because too many British citizens in Great Britain as well
as in the colonies still defined and interpreted the constitution as a bun-
dle of customary rights and not as the command of Parliament. Under
that constitution, subjects in the colonies could be taxed constitutionally
only with the consent of their local legislatures. A common lawyer who
was agent for Barbados in London summed up the constitutional argument when he wrote of the colonial practice of taxation by consent of
elected representation:

> This is, this has been, and ever was the mode of practice: it has been
> sanctified by custom, more than doubling that limitation of time,
> which establishes custom into the common law of the land: it is now
> wedded to the constitution, making part of that great principle of
> representation, in which the very essence of the constitution consists;
> and being so engendered into existence, whilst the constitution lasts,
> it must remain.[29]

CHAPTER SEVENTEEN

ISSUE OF THE SUGAR ACT

Discussion of the authority of custom completes the survey of the constitutional arguments advanced by American whigs against Parliament's attempt to raise in the colonies taxes for purposes of revenue. The next four chapters consider how those arguments were applied to the Sugar Act, the Stamp Act, and other pieces of imperial legislation that American whigs protested as unconstitutional taxation.

It has been suggested that since the colonists raised fewer constitutional objections to the sugar duties than to the Stamp Act, they were indifferent to the constitutional principle.[1] The conclusion does not necessarily follow from the fact. Had the colonial whigs' complaint against British taxation been economic, we could expect that the colonists would have protested equally all parliamentary attempts at taxation, at least to the extent that taxes were equally burdensome. Had the quarrel been nationalistic, all British statutes, whether for taxation, regulation, or police, would have been objectionable. But to the extent that the dispute concerned the constitution and the legal exercise of authority, we should expect that American whigs would raise constitutional and legal issues. In doing so, they would not make the same case against every statute unless the constitutional premises of each statute were the same. We should not, therefore, expect to find the same arguments directed against the

Sugar Act that were directed against the Stamp Act unless American whigs perceived the constitutional objections against both to be the same. If Americans were sincere in claiming that constitutional rights, not economic interests, motivated them, and if they conceded to Parliament constitutional power to levy duties when regulating trade but not to tax them for revenue purposes, they would not formulate the same legal argument against a tax regulating their foreign trade that they would have against a penny tax on newspapers. They would not call unconstitutional a parliamentary tax in an area and for a purpose for which Parliament had been taxing them by long-established custom. They would protest that same tax as unconstitutional if it was an unprecedented innovation without foundation in constitutional custom.

Our lesson is that revolutionary imperial statutes, those that did not impose taxes as well as those that did, must be evaluated on the constitutional issues they raised. They should further be distinguished by specific objections raised against them by American whigs. Constitutional issues should not be confused or equated with nonconstitutional arguments. Following passage of the Sugar Act of 1764 and prior to passage of the Stamp Act, some writers still thought it realistic to argue that there were no constitutional issues to trouble Americans. "None of the Colonies," a minor British official correctly observed, "have as yet denied the Authority of the British Parliament to tax them, on the contrary several have expressly acknowledged it to be their Duty to obey at the same time that they have remonstrated against the Acts of the last year." He may have had in mind polemics such as one written in part by the governor of Connecticut and ordered printed by the colonial Assembly; it anticipated passage of the Stamp Act, protested its validity on constitutional principles, but did not so much as mention the Sugar Act.[2]

The task is to separate legal complaints from political or commercial objections. Distinctions have to be drawn or questions will not be clarified. Americans were unhappy with the Sugar Act; some colonies reinforced their agencies in London to combat it, and newspapers from South Carolina to New England printed the text of the statute despite the fact that it was so long that it could fill all the news columns of one edition and spill over into a second. What matters here, however, is less that Americans were troubled than what they were troubled about. Following repeal of the Stamp Act, both houses of the Georgia Assembly thanked King George III for the "speedy and necessary Relief," indicating that all colonial grievances had been corrected. And in a message to the governor, the Commons House of Assembly said that its members could not "sufficiently venerate and admire the Magnanimity and Justice of the British parliament in so speedily redressing the Grievances by them complained of."[3] Considering that only the Stamp Act had been repealed, a reasonable interpretation of these words is that the Georgia legislators either did not think the Sugar Act a grievance, or thought it a grievance of a different magnitude or quality than the grievance posed by the Stamp Act. All their constitutional complaints, it would seem, had been directed against the Stamp Act and all had been corrected by its repeal. The question that deserves attention, then, is how these Georgians and other Americans agreeing with them perceived the Sugar Act, why some colonists thought of it as a form of taxation as alarming as the Stamp Act and others did not think it a tax at all.

PERCEPTIONS OF THE SUGAR ACT

There are two preliminary points that must be stressed. The first is that there were American whigs who thought that the Sugar Act raised different constitutional issues than the Stamp Act. The two houses of the Massachusetts General Court, for example, protested that the Sugar Act "essentially affects the civil rights and the commercial interests of the colonies," but still "acknowledge it to be our duty to yield obedience to it while it continues unrepealed."[4] They would never acknowledge a duty to obey the Stamp Act. The second point is that in contrast to the stamp duty, which most Americans thought unconstitutional, colonial whigs did not perceive the Sugar Act in a uniform way. Some said it was a measure regulating trade and posed no constitutional issues; others said it was a tax levied upon the colonies for purposes of raising revenue and for that reason unconstitutional.

The initial question is why the Sugar and Stamp Acts were perceived differently. An obvious answer, based on eighteenth-century jurisprudence, is that the Sugar Act of 1764 was perceived as a continuation of the Sugar Act of 1733, an adaptation of an existing, long-accepted system, changed from a law exclusively regulating trade to one both regulating trade and raising incidental revenue; as such it was sanctioned by constitutional custom. The Stamp Act, by contrast, was a new tax without precedent; it was, therefore, an unconstitutional innovation. Although that explanation has been sometimes suggested, it can be supported by evidence only if that evidence is carefully selected and contrary evidence excluded. Many Americans, for example, confessed that at first they had misinterpreted the Sugar Act, particularly because it bore a "Semblance" to established methods of trade regulation. "We saw, in the preamble," John Dickinson explained, "something of the usual forms, 'for extending and securing navigation and commerce,' [and] were lulled into security." Dickinson could be read as saying that the new statute continued the old; more likely, however, he was saying that American whigs at first had been careless and read the second Sugar Act as narrowly as possible, because, as Edmund Burke surmised, they had been hesitant to think that Parliament had intended to impose a tax on them.[5]

There is little evidence that American whigs at first accepted the Sugar Act because, even though it raised revenue, it was not an innovation. The better view is that it was not protested as quickly as the Stamp Act because it was not as obviously a tax measure. The Sugar Act was susceptible to various readings. If that contention is hard to credit, consider the difficulty historians have had interpreting it. A few conclude that the Sugar Act was not an innovation; others say it was both a traditional trade regulation and the first attempt by Parliament to raise revenue in the colonies. Most historians apparently have thought that the Sugar Act was a revenue measure, but still disagree about whether it should be seen as not "oppressive" and hence without legal implications, whether it introduced important constitutional changes incidentally, or whether it was specifically intended by Parliament to reform and alter the imperial constitution in a drastic and fundamental way.[6] A good illustration of how interpretations have differed is provided by turning from the original act of 1764 to the revision of 1766, when Parliament reduced the duty on molasses from three pennies per gallon to one. Some historians say that this reduction set the tariff so low that the impost had been converted from a trade regulation into a revenue measure.[7] The opposite conclusion, though, is equally defensible: after the reduction, the duty on molasses was so low "it could be viewed as no more than a regulatory trade measure."[8]

The chief piece of evidence that the Sugar Act was designed to raise revenue, cited by contemporaries such as Dickinson and Burke, as well as by twentieth-century historians, is the statute's preamble.[9] It is a maxim of legislative construction that to find the intent of Parliament one should look to the preamble. The preamble of the Sugar Act provided:

> Whereas it is expedient that new provisions and regulations should be established for improving the revenue of this kingdom, and for extending and securing the navigation and commerce between *Great Britain* and your Majesty's dominions in *America*, which, by the peace, have been so happily enlarged: and whereas it is just and necessary, that a revenue be raised, in your Majesty's said dominions in *America*, for defraying the expences of defending, protecting, and securing the same; we . . . the commons of *Great Britain*, in parliament assembled, being desirous to make some provision, in this present session of parliament, towards raising the said revenue in *America*, have resolved to give and grant unto your Majesty the several rates and duties herein.

Edmund Burke, sundering these words much as a lawyer would, set about proving that the Sugar Act had introduced a new constitutional policy. "This Act," he told the Commons, "had for the first time the title of 'granting duties in the colonies and plantations of America;' and for the first time it was asserted in the preamble, 'that it was *just* and *necessary* that a revenue should be raised there.' Then came the technical words of 'giving and granting,' and thus a complete American Revenue Act was made in all the forms, and with a full avowal of the right, equity, policy, and even necessity of taxing the colonies, without any formal consent of theirs." By this language in the Sugar Act, a contemporary account of the same speech reported Burke as saying, Parliament "for the first time, asserted the right, equity, policy, and even necessity of taxing the colonies, without any formal consent of theirs." The Sugar Act was, Burke demonstrated, a radical departure from standard imperial practice as it

> opened a new principle; and here properly began the second period of the policy of this country with regard to the colonies; by which the scheme of a regular plantation parliamentary revenue was adopted in theory, and settled in practice. A revenue not substituted in the place of, but superadded to, a monopoly; which monopoly was enforced at the same time with added strictness, and the execution put into military hands.[10]

Some imperial officials agreed with Burke that the Sugar Act had been meant to raise revenue.[11] That idea was by no means dominant, however — not even in Parliament. The Sugar Act's duty on molasses, it was also said, "has been imposed" for "the advantage and emolument of our own islands, and not with any view to raise money upon the North Americans."[12] Rose Fuller, who had been chief justice of Jamaica, one of the islands that the sugar duties had been intended to aid, told the House of Commons less than a year after its enactment that it had been passed not "so much as a revenue [measure] as a means of inducing administration to tax them to prevent illicit trade with Holland, etc."[13]

How historians perceived the Sugar Act of 1764 sheds light on the way the statute and legislative intent has been interpreted. How the leaders of revolutionary Great Britain perceived the act tells us something of that legislative intention. The evidence, however, that will most help us to understand the constitutional causes of the Revolution is how American whigs perceived it and whether the Sugar Act awakened the same constitutional concerns aroused by the Stamp Act. Another way to put the question is to ask why some colonists did not perceive the Sugar Act to be as constitutionally objectionable as the Stamp Act. Many of them did, of course, but there were Americans, including some whigs, who at first did not think that the Sugar Act posed a constitutional threat.

One explanation, suggested previously, deserves a second look: the Sugar Act of 1764 was initially perceived by American whigs to have been the same constitutionally as the Sugar Act of 1733, the statute that the act of 1764 replaced. The 1733 law, the governor of Rhode Island pointed out, "was only to tax our foreign importations, which is a matter of general commerce, and can be regulated in parliament only." He wondered how anyone could "see no difference between such a law and a stamp duty." The point was well taken if the governor was writing about the first Sugar Act. It was possible, however, to see no difference between the second Sugar Act and the stamp tax if one concentrated not on the similarity of the 1764 law to the first act, but on the revenue that it raised. "The former acts imposing duties on molasses," merchants of Boston argued, "were intended only as a regulation of trade, and to encourage our own islands; and the duty was only on foreign molasses: But by these acts [1764 and amendments], it is imposed on all molasses, and expre[s]ly for the purpose of raising a revenue." John Dickinson disagreed. Although he soon changed his mind, he said that at first he had not perceived that the taxing aspects of the second Sugar Act departed in substance from the policy of the act of 1733 sufficiently enough to constitute a constitutional grievance. He explained the difference between the constitutional sugar duty and the unconstitutional stamp tax in terms somewhat similar to the explanation of the Rhode Island governor.

> First, That tho' the [sugar] act expressly mentions the raising a revenue in *America*, yet it seems that it had as much in view the "improving and securing the trade between the same and *Great-Britain*," which words are part of its title: [Dickinson next quoted the preamble copied above.] Secondly, *All* the duties mentioned in that act are imposed solely on the *productions and manufactures of foreign countries*, and [unlike the Townshend duties] not a single duty laid on any production or manufacture of our mother country. Thirdly, the authority of the provincial assemblies is not therein so plainly *attacked* as by the last [Townshend] act, which makes provision for defraying the charges of the "administration of justice," and "the support of civil government." Fourthly, That it being *doubtful*, whether the intention of the 4th *Geo*. III Chap. 15 [i.e., Sugar Act], was not as much *to regulate trade*, as *to raise a revenue*, the minds of the people here were wholly engrossed by the terror of the *Stamp-Act*, then impending over them, about the intention of which there could be no *doubt*.

John Dickinson may be misunderstood. There were Americans who distinguished the Sugar Act from the other parliamentary taxes on these grounds, especially the fourth. Dickinson, however, may not have been one of them. Perhaps passage of the Townshend duties changed his perception. After their enactment, nearly all colonial whigs recognized that the Sugar Act was a constitutional grievance. "Here first," Dickinson would argue in 1774 of the Sugar Act, "we find the Commons of *Great Britain* 'giving and granting' our money, *for the express purpose* of 'raising Revenue in *America*'."[14]

THE COMMERCIAL OBJECTIONS

There is another distinction to be drawn. Americans made many complaints against the Sugar Act, but not all had to do with law. Those that were economic must not be confused with those that were constitutional. It was not inconsistent for a colonist to say that Parliament's commercial policy was unreasonable or oppressive yet admit that it was constitutional. Even arguments that Parliament abused or misused its authority did not necessarily raise a constitutional issue. To avoid misreading an economic grievance as a legal grievance, close heed must be paid to what was said. An example was the often-raised complaint that the Sugar Acts had been passed to benefit the West Indian islands and that North Americans were forced to pay duties on foreign molasses for no other purpose than to promote the prosperity of British planters. That was an economic, not a constitutional, complaint. So too was the charge made against the Sugar Act that to raise money "for the general service of the crown, or colonies, by such a duty, will be extremely unequal, and therefore unjust,"[15] and the assertion that taxes must be imposed fairly and equitably. Although these three objections, and others like them, pose legal questions that would be constitutional issues in the twentieth-century United States, they did not state complaints that were of constitutional concern during the revolutionary controversy. Economic, not legal, questions were raised when people challenged Parliament's wisdom and impartiality rather than its authority. Numerous revolutionary sources, for example, described the Sugar Act not as a tax regulating trade but as a "prohibition" on trade, complaining that the duty had been set so high it left honest traders no alternative but to go out of business or to become smugglers. None of these factors, though, was raised as a constitutional rather than a commercial objection.

Although no scientific surveys have been conducted, it is reasonable to guess that most protests against the Sugar Act concentrated on economic considerations. Typical were the instructions sent by Pennsylvania's House of Representatives to its agent in London. He was told "to exert your Endeavors to obtain a Repeal, or at least an Amendment, of the

Act for regulating the Sugar Trade," and to point out how much the new statute increased the cost of doing business, but he was not instructed to appeal to constitutional right. The distinction is significant. Protests against both the Sugar and Stamp Acts which raised constitutional objections only to the Stamp Act were intended to question the constitutionality of only the stamp tax. An instance can be found in a petition submittted to the Crown by the governor of Rhode Island.

> The restraints and burdens laid on the trade of these colonies, by [the Sugar Act] . . . must ruin it. The commerce of this colony dependeth ultimately on foreign molasses, and the duty on that being so much higher than it can possibly bear, must prevent its importation; and by that means we shall be deprived of our principal exports, totally lose our trade to Africa, and be rendered unable to make remittance to Great Britain for the manufactures we cannot live without.

Nothing more was said about the Sugar Act. In the same petition, constitutional objections were raised against the Stamp Act and the jurisdiction of the vice-admiralty court, but not against the revenue aspects of the Sugar Act. Similarly, a petition of the New York Assembly a year later asserted that the stamp tax was unconstitutional, but raised only commercial objections to the Sugar Act. Perhaps the most persuasive illustrations are provided by the Stamp Act Congress. Although it protested on constitutional grounds that part of the Sugar Act that extended the jurisdiction of the vice-admiralty courts—"a manifest tendency to subvert the rights and liberties of the colonists"—its other objections to the Sugar Act were commercial, not legal, complaining that it was "burthensome" on trade not that it was an unconstitutional tax. That pattern of argument was even more pronounced in the petitions the Congress submitted to Parliament. The memorial sent to the House of Lords, for example, began on a constitutional note, acknowledging "a due Subordination" to Parliament and claiming "the Two fundamental and invaluable Rights and Liberties" of "Trial by Jury" and "Exemption from all Taxes, but such as are imposed on the People by the several Legislatures in these Colonies, which Right also they have, till of late, freely enjoyed." But when the revenue aspects of the Sugar Act were considered, the constitutional expressions disappeared and the grievance was stated entirely in economic terms.[16]

Although the larger argument that taxation for revenue was unconstitutional without representation was lost on many in Great Britain, at least on those who believed that American whigs objected only to internal taxation, the particular argument that trade regulation should not be constitutionally compounded with taxation was well understood. In 1775, John Lind, one of the most persistent British critics of colonial claims to constitutional rights, recalled that Americans had not protested the constitutionality of the Sugar Act before passage of the stamp tax.

> [F]or though they remonstrated, and with reason, against some of the provisions of this act, they at that time did not so much as argue against the principle. They conceived, and endeavoured to shew, that the power of parliament had been impoliticly exercised; but they did not *yet* go so far as to say, that the power itself was unconstitutional.

Ten years earlier the *Annual Register*, commenting on what was then current news, had printed a long account of the commercial difficulties imposed on North America by the Sugar Act. The story gave no hint that constitutional questions might be involved in the discussion until it was noted that the colonies had been

> put to the severest trial of their love and respect for the mother country, and it is but doing them justice to say, that . . . most of them bore this stroke of the supreme legislature of Great Britain with all that patience and submission, which the most indulgent parent could have expected from the most dutiful children. For, if some presumed to call in question her authority, they were excited thereto, not so much by any actual laws or regulations concerning them, as by a vote of the house of commons passed at the time of laying the new duties [i.e., Sugar Act] upon the foreign trade, "that, towards further defraying the necessary expences of protecting the colonies, it may be proper to charge certain stamp duties upon them."[17]

Constitutional Objections

There is a final distinction yet to be drawn — a distinction between constitutional arguments. They were not all the same. To find that an American whig thought that the preamble of the Sugar Act stated only a trade purpose and did not express the intent to raise revenue, for example, does not mean that that whig had no constitutional objections to the Sugar Act. Although he did not think that it violated the constitutional privilege of being taxed only by consent, he could still recognize that it raised constitutional considerations either in general principles or by a specific provision.

A general constitutional principle argued by American whigs against the Sugar Act was equality. A petition of Rhode Island to the Crown in November 1764 raised the principle in an argument that bears on the question of taxation. The petition objected to being taxed without consent not on the grounds that Rhode Islanders were deprived of the constitutional right of consenting to taxation, but on the grounds that they were denied a right belonging to fellow British subjects and therefore were being treated unequally. The petition raised the issue of equality in three regards — commerce, jury trial, and taxation — by asking

> that our trade may be restored to its former condition, and no further limited, restrained and burdened, than becomes necessary for the general good of all your Majesty's subjects; that the courts of vice admiralty may not be vested with more extensive powers in the colonies than are given them by law in Great Britain; that the colonists may not be taxed but by the consent of their own representatives, as Your Majesty's other free subjects are.[18]

Americans also protested — and protested angrily — as unconstitutional a specific nontax provision in the Sugar Act, the section vesting enforcement of the law's criminal parts in the court of vice-admiralty. Parliament's purpose had been to take jurisdiction away from the colonial judiciaries and place it with an imperial tribunal. More important, determination of guilt was transferred from the common-law jury to a civil-law judge appointed by the Crown, a constitutional grievance that the lower house of the Connecticut legislature described as "highly dangerous to the liberties of his Majesty's American subjects, contrary to the great charter of English Liberty, and destructive of one of their most darling rights, that of tryal by juries, which is justly esteemed one chief excellence of the British constitution."[19] Although this constitutional objection raised a nontax issue that more properly belongs in a study of colonial whig assertions of civil rights,[20] it merits mention at this point because it was as serious a constitutional issue during the revolutionary controversy as taxation without consent. It was raised as a constitutional objection to the Sugar Act both by groups saying that the Sugar Act violated colonial rights to taxation by consent,[21] and by groups that did not think of the Sugar Act as a revenue measure.[22]

In turning to the issue of whether the Sugar Act was unconstitutional taxation, a point made previously should be reiterated: most of the evidence we have of people reading the words of the statute narrowly enough to conclude that Parliament had not intended to raise revenue comes from the very earliest stages of the revolutionary epoch. After the House of Commons had passed the resolution claiming authority to tax Americans, perceptions in the colonies changed[23] and the constitutional aspects of the Sugar Act were seen more clearly.[24] Thomas Cushing provides an illustration. In November 1763, thinking in terms of the Sugar Act of 1733, already thirty years old and not perceived to be an unconstitutional tax, he wrote to the agent for Massachusetts suggesting that if the tariff on molasses were lowered "to an half penny or a penny per gallon" that "the Duty wou[l]d be chearfully and universally paid" and the Crown might obtain "considerable revenue." The agent interpreted these instructions to mean that there was no constitutional issue and when the Sugar Act of 1764 was being debated in Parliament he wrote Boston that "to make a Merit of our Submission," he had acquiesced in a duty of two pennies. By then Cushing had learned that more was involved than merely lowering established custom rates. The Massachusetts General Court, he wrote, would not consent to any duty, not even to "such as the trade wou[l]d bare." To do so would "be conceeding to the Parliaments having a Right to Tax our trade which we can't by any means think of admitting, as it wou'd be contrary to a fundamentall Principall of our Constitution vizt. That all Taxes ought to originate with the people."[25]

Those words would indicate that Cushing understood that the lower house wanted the Sugar Act challenged as unconstitutional, but many historians of the American Revolution deny that the Massachusetts legislature protested the sugar tax on constitutional grounds. Their explanation is that the House of Representatives drafted a petition to London saying "that we look upon those Duties as a tax, and which we humbly apprehend ought not to be laid without the Representatives of the People affected by them," but when the upper house was asked to join in the petition, Thomas Hutchinson persuaded his fellow councillors to soften the language from a stand on the constitutional right of taxation by consent to a prayer for the continuation of indulgences traditionally enjoyed, putting the plea on economic rather than constitutional grounds. The Council's revised petition was accepted, though apparently with reluctance, by the House of Representatives. That acceptance can fairly be interpreted as a backing away from the legal issue, though if done for political reasons it need not mean that the constitutional question was intentionally conceded. In fact, members of the lower house seem to have feared that a concession would be implied; upset that they had ever agreed to Hutchinson's strategy, they later wrote their agent in London to explain what they now wished they had said in the petition.

> The House of Representatives were clearly for making an ample and full declaration of the exclusive Right of the People of the Colonies to tax themselves and that they ought not to be deprived of a right

they had so long enjoyed and which they held by Birth and by Charter; but they could not prevail with the Councill, tho they made several Tryalls, to be more explicit than they have been in the Petition sent you.

The agent was reminded that just prior to the petition the house had sent him a copy of James Otis's *The Rights of the British Colonies Asserted and Proved* and had instructed him to use its arguments. "You will therefore collect the sentiments of the Representative Body of the People rather from what they have heretofore sent you than from the present Address." He was being told that despite the petition he should have opposed passage of the Sugar Act on the ground that Parliament could not constitutionally lay taxes on the colonies for purposes of raising revenue.[26]

Hutchinson certainly understood that he had annoyed the Massachusetts House with his tactics and that its members had tried to correct whatever damage he had done to their constitutional argument. "The Assembly of Massachuset's Bay," he wrote in reference to the instructions just quoted, "was the first that took any publick notice of the [Sugar] Act, and the first which ever took exception to the right of Parliament to impose Duties or Taxes on the Colonies, whilst they had no representatives in the House of Commons." He noted with a touch of annoyance that the letter of instruction had been published by the house "before it was possible" for the agent to have received it. Hutchinson knew what the whigs were doing and why they thought it important to set the public record straight; he had, after all, been one of the first of Massachusetts's leaders to recognize the constitutional implications of parliamentary attempts to raise revenue by placing duties on imports. In 1763, Americans had been aware that the British ministry would undertake to reform the customs service and replace the Sugar Act of 1733 with different legislation. The expectation had been that the rates set in the first Sugar Act would be lowered so that the duty would no longer be a prohibition on the trade, smuggling would end, and the Crown would receive revenue. The speaker of the Massachusetts House, the future whig Thomas Cushing, overlooked the constitutional aspects of the question and advised the London agent that a lower duty was desirable. It had been the future loyalist, Thomas Hutchinson, who realized that even amending the Sugar Act of 1733 could introduce a substantive change to the imperial constitution. "To reduce the duty to a penny a gallon," he wrote to the man who soon would be appointed Massachusetts's new agent, "I find would be generally agreeable to the people here and the merchant would readily pay it. But do they see the consequence? Will not this be introductory to taxes, duties and excises upon other articles, and would they consist with the so much esteemed privilege of English subjects—the being taxed by their own representatives?"[27]

The issue was obvious, too obvious to be missed. Thomas Hutchinson had stated it even before hearing there would be a wholly new Sugar Act. As soon as the statute was published, others also recognized the constitutional connection. It was not a matter of trade or costs; it was a matter of the constitutional right to be taxed only by consent. In Massachusetts, Oxenbridge Thacher, described by John Adams as "then at the head of the popular branch of our constitution," characterized the duties imposed by the Sugar Act as "a grievance inasmuch as the same are laid without the consent of the representatives of the colonists." In Virginia, Richard Henry Lee wrote of the "essential principles of the British constitution," wondering "how men, who have almost imbibed them in their mother's milk, whose very atmosphere is charged with them, should be of opinion that the people of America were to be taxed without consulting their representatives!" In North Carolina, the lower house of the Assembly protested being "Burthened with new Taxes and Impositions laid on us without our Privity and Consent," and asserted "our Inherent right, and Exclusive privilege of Imposing our own Taxes."[28]

There was confusion as to whether the Sugar Act was for revenue purposes or to regulate trade and to the extent that it was interpreted as a regulatory statute Americans objected to it on economic and commercial grounds. When it was understood to impose taxation upon the colonies for purposes of revenue, however, it was opposed for the same reasons that the Stamp Act and the Townshend duties would be opposed: it was taxation without consent and therefore contrary to British constitutional rights. As early as June 1764, after realizing that their failure to have raised constitutional objections had been interpreted as conceding authority to Parliament to tax the colonies for purposes of revenue, members of the Massachusetts House of Representatives made clear what they thought was the issue: "[T]he Silence of the Province should have been imputed to any Cause, even to Despair, rather than be construed into a tacit Cession of their Rights, or an Acknowledgment of a Right in the Parliament of *Great-Britain* to impose Duties and Taxes upon a People, who are not represented in the House of Commons." It was understood by officials in London as well as by fellow Americans in the colonies that they were claiming the "sole Right" of Taxation, the right to be taxed only by consent.[29] That was the objection. The perception on which the objection was based gained clarity as the British determination to tax became more discernible. By the late date of 1774 the first Continental Congress could say with confidence that the Sugar Act had been "for the purpose of raising a revenue in America" and cite it as a grievance. The constitutional issue was summed up a month before the Battle of Lexington by the New York Assembly when it drew a distinction between the constitutional regulatory aspects of the Sugar Act and its unconstitutional character as taxation.

> [T]hat the aforesaid act . . . so far as it imposes duties for the purpose of raising a revenue in America,— extends the admiralty courts beyond their ancient limits,— deprives his Majesty's American subjects of trial by jury . . . and holds up an injurious discrimination between the subjects in Great Britain and those in America; is a grievance.[30]

CHAPTER EIGHTEEN

ISSUE OF THE STAMP ACT

In 1774, one of America's most persistent and outspoken tories wrote that a decade earlier nearly everyone in the colonies had felt that the Stamp Act was "contrary to all our ideas of American rights."[1] Few historical studies have quarreled with that statement. The matter on which historians have disagreed has not been whether the colonists were opposed to the stamp tax but why they opposed it.

The Stamp Act was perceived more uniformly than was the Sugar Act. From the moment of the first rumor, it alarmed just about every American, not only those destined to be whigs. Benjamin Franklin may be the one significant exception. Although he would later contend that passage of the Stamp Act marked the beginning of the revolutionary controversy, in 1764 he was so unaware of the constitutional issues that he nominated a friend to be stamp distributor for Pennsylvania. It did not take him long, however, to realize the principle at stake. Franklin then sought a compromise no lawyer would have pursued. He urged the British government to suspend the Stamp Act "for a Term of Years, till the Colonies should be more clear of Debt, & better able to bear it," but his strategy was constitutional, not political or economic. He wanted the British to use American poverty as an excuse for suspending the Stamp Act and later, when politically feasible, to "drop it on some other decent Pretence, without ever bringing the Question of Right to a Decision." In that way, the constitutional conflict would not have been resolved, but it might have been avoided.[2]

An even better piece of evidence that some American whigs first missed the constitutional issue implicit in the Stamp Act legislation, previously mentioned in the discussion of the Sugar Act's issue, is Thomas Hutchinson's success in persuading the Massachusetts General Court to protest parliamentary taxation on grounds of indulgence rather than constitutional right. Several petitions to Parliament had been drafted, Hutchinson explained, "which expressed in strong terms an exclusive right in the assembly to impose taxes." He successfully urged that a constitutional argument would be "ill policy," especially as Parliament had passed a resolution asserting that it possessed authority to tax the colonies. "[A]fter a fortnight spent, at the desire of the committee, I drew an address, which considered the sole Power of taxation as an indulgence which we prayed the continuance of, and this was unanimously agreed to."[3]

This evidence could be read as indicating that the legislators thought the constitutional issue of secondary importance. To do so, however, it is necessary to disregard much other evidence. One piece of such evidence would be the letter that the Massachusetts Council and House sent to the colony's agent in London. "[W]e have endeavored to avoid giving offence," it said, "and have touched upon our rights in such a manner, as that no inference can be drawn, that we have given them up, on the one hand, nor that we set up in opposition to the Parliament, nor deny that we are bound to the observance of acts of Parliament, on the other." The agent was to understand that the right they were not conceding was the right "the people of the colonies have . . . to tax themselves."[4] Although they had not made their claim to that right the main thrust of their petition and in that sense had adopted Hutchinson's political strategy, they had not adopted his constitutional principle.

The hope that political strategy need not imply constitutional principle was more fully explained by a joint committee of the Georgia legislature when advising the colony's agent how best to oppose the Stamp Act. The committee instructed him to avoid "any expressions that might tend to call in question the Authority of parliament or give Motives for an Objection to your having a hearing." The fear was that if the petition or argument were directed to the "right," the House of Commons would refuse to hear the agent or council on behalf of the colony. The agent was told that at the hearing he should lay "before the Hon[ora]ble House the real hardships it would be upon America, should such a Bill pass into a law." The Georgia committee was apprehensive that "it may prove of fatal Consequence to some of the Colonys should, [sic] they go too [sic] great lengths in denying the Authority of parliament for we believe more may be gained by humbly and dutifully remonstrating than by any other Method."[5]

In point of law, these instructions could have been interpreted by Parliament as giving up the constitutional right. As historical evidence, however, they should not be read as proving that the Georgia legislators thought the right unimportant. They would soon dismiss the agent because he disagreed with them about the principle and publicly stated that the Stamp Act was constitutional. Rather, what the Georgians had intended was much the same as Franklin had had in mind when urging the ministry to suspend operation of the Stamp Act. They hoped to avoid the very difficult constitutional question by obtaining their objective with a less controversial argument.[6]

This cautious and seemingly sensible strategy did not please everyone. There is reason to believe that there were many members of the Massachusetts legislature, if not of Georgia's, who considered the constitutional issue so important they were willing to risk offending Parliament by taking an immediate stand on the right. The Massachusetts House, it will be recalled, attempted to reserve the issue by explaining to the agent why they had agreed to a petition that did not insist upon the constitutional principle. They had been "clearly for making an ample and full declaration of the exclusive Right of the People of the Colonies to tax themselves and that they ought not to be deprived of a right they had so long enjoyed and which they held by Birth and by Charter; but they cou[l]d not prevail with the Councill." The agent was to understand that "they have expressly asserted their exclusive right of Taxing themselves and have endeavored to prove that the Subjects here ought not to be taxed without their Consent either in person or by their Representative."[7]

The hope of the Massachusetts House that the arguments in the petition "will have success . . . from the dutiful manner in which they are formed" was not realized. Hutchinson's strategy failed on all counts. His tame petition fared no better than those that boldly asserted the constitutional right. No matter how carefully an address was worded, the leaders of Great Britain realized what was meant and no member of Parliament would introduce into either house any petition that denied Great Britain's right to tax the colonies. "With us there is not a difference of opinion," Thomas Whately explained. "The House of Commons would not receive any petitions, however expressed, that implied a doubt of the right of Parliament to lay taxes. To receive the petitions would have been an acknowledgment that the right was questionable, which we cannot admit."[8]

The evidence from Massachusetts, Georgia, Barbados, and Thomas Whately is offered to support an argument made early in this book: long before passage of the Stamp Act, people on both sides of the Atlantic, members of Parliament as well as members of colonial assemblies, were aware that serious constitutional objections would be raised against the tax. The question that this chapter asks is: what were the constitutional issues posed by the Stamp Act?

NONCONSTITUTIONAL OBJECTIONS

There were constitutional objections to the Stamp Act besides the question of consent to taxation. The jurisdiction of the court of vice-admiralty and trial by jury were serious issues. There were also a few nonconstitutional legal grievances concerning powers conferred on imperial officials by the Act and political complaints that the revenue raised by the stamps was intended to support the British army in North America. The most numerous and perhaps the most serious nonconstitutional arguments against the Stamp Act were economic. There have even been historians who have attributed colonial opposition to the tax wholly to the costs of the stamps. There is, of course, some evidence supporting the idea that the colonists were unhappy for economic reasons. The Americans did complain about the expense. If enforced, they said, the stamp tax would be "excessively grievous and burthensome," detrimental to trade, destructive of the press, and could drain the colonies of specie.[9]

Another nonconstitutional grievance concerned class. John Dickinson argued that the Stamp Act bore hardest on "our *merchants* and the *lower ranks of people*," on "the lower ranks" because they were "frequently engaged in law suits." Benjamin Franklin was more explicit. "The greatest part of the money," he told the House of Commons, referring to revenue raised by the stamp tax, "must arise from law-suits for the recovery of debts, and be paid by the lower sort of people, who were too poor easily to pay their debts. It is therefore a heavy tax on the poor, and a tax on them for being poor." Proimperialist writers thought this argument easily disproven. Colonial riots against the Stamp Act were "peculiarly remarkable," one of them told a London newspaper, because the tax could not possibly be a class grievance; although mob action against a tariff on beer could be understood, "the tax to be levied affects none of the necessaries of life; will never fall upon many of the poor; and will touch very gently and very seldom such of them as it may light upon."[10]

Most Britons professed to believe that the Americans had no economic complaint. The Stamp Act, its author Thomas Whately wrote, "is the easiest, the most equal and the most certain that can be chosen." It was "unexceptionable," costing the average American in a year no more than one-third of the day's wages of a common laborer. Whately thought the colonists could not complain of the tax as a grievance and *Pacificus* agreed, telling a London newspaper that "The Idea of a Rebellion in America, in Consequence of such an unimportant Subject of Dispute, is merely Chimerical." One logical conclusion was that objections could not be economic; they had to be constitutional.

> There might be some cause to complain (though it would even *then* be ungrateful) if the tax was either in itself, or in the mode of collecting it, burthensome and oppressive; if it impeded trade, if it fell upon the common necessaries of life, or was imposed on the poor and labouring part of the people. But the very reverse of this is manifest in every particular; and therefore it cannot be the tax itself that they object to, but to the *power of taxation*, which the Mother Country assumes over the Colonies.[11]

The argument had come half circle. From the realization that the stamp tax was not, after all, an economic grievance, imperialists reached the conclusion that the Americans were complaining about taxes imposed "by the authority of a p[arliamen]t in which they do not conceive themselves to be properly and constitutionally *represented*." Even Thomas Whately came around to this view. "I am sure a little reflexion would convince the people that there is not the least foundation for their discontent," he wrote on hearing of the Stamp Act riots in Boston. "I do not find that the tax itself is complain'd of, but the opposition to it arises from a dispute of the right." Anyone reading the dispatches from the leading British officials in North America would have understood what Whately meant. "The Taxability & not the Tax is what pinches," the governor of Massachusetts wrote a member of Parliament. "The Stamp Act is become in itself a matter of indifference; it is swallowed up in the importance of the effects of which it has been the cause. The taxing the *Americans* by the Parliament, had brought their very subjection to the Crown of *Great Britain* in question." The commander-in-chief of the king's troops in North America sent the same explanation to another general, the man who would move repeal of the tax in the House of Commons. "The Question is not of the inexpediency of the Stamp Act, or of the inability of the Colonys to pay the Tax, but that it is unconstitutional, and contrary to their Rights. . . ."[12]

PARLIAMENTARY PERCEPTIONS

Evidence has previously been summarized delineating the attitudes of members of Parliament. Both before passage of the Stamp Act and during repeal, they left no doubt that they appreciated that a constitutional issue was involved. The situation was never better stated than in a letter from London to New York reporting that "it is as unpopular here to deny the Authority of the British Senate, as it is unsafe in America to defend it."[13] Despite efforts by the ministry to avoid discussion of the right to tax, the constitutional issue permeated every aspect of the debate over repeal.[14] The general impression of imperialists and of members of the British government seems to have been the same that had prevailed at the time that the Stamp Act had been passed, when it had been said that "the Addresses from the Colonies were wrote with such warm and unbecoming Expressions, that it would have been dangerous to have presented them to the Parliament." The purpose was not to stop American protests but to persuade Americans to protest on other grounds. "[M]any people thought it had been imprudent to touch upon the subject, and declared their wishes that the repeal had been solicited upon the principle, that the law was inexpedient and oppressive, without insinuating the incompetency of Parliament to enact it."

> Had they only objected to the stamp-act, as being productive of much inconvenience in the transaction of their public and private business, still allowing the power, but modestly complaining of the mode in which it was exercised, they would have had a just demand on the attention of the British legislature, and would doubtless have obtained relief in a way most honorable both to themselves and us: but the method which they chose to adopt was to seek for redress in a way not to be justified on any principles of government whatsoever.[15]

It was well understood in London that colonial assemblies, although advised by their agents to avoid raising the question of right, had deliberately thrust the issue to the forefront of the debate. The Privy Council criticized the votes of Massachusetts as indecent and disrespectful and reported that the Virginia resolves contained "an absolute disavowal of the right of the Parliament of Great Britain to impose taxes upon the colonies, and a daring attack upon the constitution of this country." The Crown's law officers made certain that the House of Commons, at least, appreciated that repeal amounted to a vote on the constitution. "The experiment of the stamps has not yet been fully tried," the lawyer who had been solicitor general at the time of passage said. "We are no judge of the inconvenience attending it, we are only judge of the resistance, the strongest argument for supporting it." The attorney general also reminded the House of American resistance. "If you agree the Bill and the resistance arises which you find cannot be overcome without too great an expense," he warned, "how will it then be possible to retreat without giving up any authority over them? We must not pass up the defects of political wisdom with the right of sovereign authority."[16]

Because it was so well understood that "there is a great difference between a complaint and a claim," Blackstone urged restricting repeal to those colonies whose assemblies expunged resolutions questioning Parliament's right to tax. Whatever chance that proposal might have had was probably destroyed by Americans in London who insisted that the colonists would neither accept a token tax nor rescind their constitutional claims. Benjamin Franklin, asked several times in his examination by the House of Commons if the Americans would eliminate the issue of right from the debate, stated unequivocally that he did not believe the colonial assemblies could be persuaded to request repeal on the grounds that the stamp tax was an economic grievance. They would insist on the constitutional right, he said, implying that the principle was more important than was repeal.

"If the parliament should repeal the stamp act," Franklin was asked, "will the assembly of Pennsylvania rescind their resolutions?"

"I think not," he replied.

The question was restated three times. "Q. If the stamp-act should be repealed, would it induce the assemblies of America to acknowledge the rights of parliament to tax them, and would they erase their resolutions?"

"A. No, never."

"Q. Is there no means of obliging them to erase those resolutions?"

"A. None that I know of; they will never do it unless compelled by force of arms."

"Q. Is there a power on earth that can force them to erase them?"

"A. No power, how great soever, can force men to change their opinion."[17]

These answers were so clear that members of Parliament had to understand that Franklin meant that Americans were protesting the Stamp Act on one ground only, that they most likely would not accommodate the ministry by asking for repeal on grounds of economic grievance, and that the constitutional issue could not be avoided. Surely that was the perception of Robert Nugent, formerly a member of the treasury board and now both a privy councillor and first lord of trade and plantations, who told the Commons that "the honour of the kingdom was concerned to compel the execution of the Stamp-Act, until the right was acknowledged, and the Repeal solicited as a favor." A "pepper corn, in acknowledgment of the right," he insisted, "was of more value than millions without it."[18]

The peppercorn generally suggested was a token tax, a sum so small it would not have raised revenue but would have reminded colonists of Parliament's sovereignty. Again, it may be Franklin who discouraged the Commons from resorting to this face-saving formula. "Don't you think they would submit to the stamp-act, if it was modified, the obnoxious parts taken out, and the duty reduced to some particulars, of small moment?," he was asked during his testimony at the bar of the House. Franklin's answer was as emphatic as it had been when he was asked if the colonies would rescind their resolutions. "No," he answered, "they will never submit to it."[19]

STAMP ACT GRIEVANCES

The final question is: what were the constitutional objections that Americans raised against the Stamp Act? There are two answers. One, as with the Sugar Act, was that they were deprived of trial of jury. The other, the one that interests us as it concerns taxation, has been thoroughly discussed previously, particularly in chapter 11. It was that "no tax could constitutionally be imposed on them without their own consent." "Resolved," the assembly of Pennsylvania voted, "That the taxation of the people of this province, by any other persons whatsoever than such their representatives in assembly, is UNCONSTITUTIONAL, and subversive of their most valuable rights."[20] There is no need to repeat the similar resolutions of other American whig bodies. Rather, this survey can best be brought to a close by considering the words of two American loyalists. The first were written for publication by Brigadier Timothy Ruggles stating the reasons why he had refused to sign the resolutions of the Stamp Act Congress to which he had been sent as a delegate from Massachusetts. He had had no choice but to dissent, Ruggles explained, because the Congress had so openly insisted on colonial constitutional rights rather than praying for repeal on the expedient ground of economic or commercial hardships. "A Matter of so great Importance to the Colonies," Ruggles wrote, "and of so delicate a Nature as the open and avowed Claim of an exclusive Right of Taxation (however true) to be asserted in Addresses to the King and Parliament, for Relief from an Act made by this very Parliament, was a Measure I could not bring myself to adopt."[21]

The second loyalist is a New Yorker, writing in the privacy of his diary eleven years after Ruggles, a month before the Declaration of Independence, at a time when American and British armies faced one another on the battlefield, and when the writer had not decided which side to support. Chief justice of the colony and one of the most outstanding lawyers on the continent, William Smith no longer had the whig leanings that had characterized his younger days, yet in 1776 still recalled the stamp tax with constitutional abhorrence. "What a new and awful Idea of the Constitution did Great Britain hold up to her Colonies at the passing of the Stamp Act!" he wrote. "This was her Language."

> You Americans are absolutely ours—We may dispose of you, your Commerce, your Lands and Acquisitions as we please—You have no Rights—The Patents of our Kings to your Ancestors do not bind this Nation. The Privileges and Securities of English Men cannot be your's, unless you return to the old Realm.— Our antient Indulgences, were temporary Permissions, from which you can deduct the Title to permanent Injoyments—Your grand Plea that our Commons are not of your electing, & that we and they, are interested in the Increase of your Burdens, can come with Propriety only from the Mouth of a British Freeholder—All America is subject to our Taxations— Nor will we hear your Complaints, until you first own our Authority to deal with you as we please, and acknowledge that such Terms as you require are to be expected not of Right, but of Grace.[22]

There can be no more convincing evidence of the importance of the claim of right than the testimony of these two loyalists, one saying that Britain could not allow the Americans to claim the right, the second lamenting that Britain had dared to alter the constitution by asserting the right.

CHAPTER NINETEEN

ISSUE OF
THE TOWNSHEND DUTIES

American whig constitutional arguments must not be read too loosely. It is not enough to recognize that legal questions were raised; legal distinctions must also be taken into account. Although ideological arguments were blended with economic complaints in revolutionary pamphlets and petitions, it is incorrect to conclude that these two aspects of the controversy were inseparable. As has been suggested previously, attention must be given not merely to the ideological and the economic, but also to the grounds upon which objections were stated. Objections to the Townshend duties were often a blend of constitutional, political, and economic complaints. An example is provided by a Virginia nonimportation agreement whose preamble stated the grievance "that the late unconstitutional [Townshend] Act, imposing Duties on Tea, Paper, Glass, &c. for the sole Purpose of raising a Revenue in *America* is injurious to Property, and destructive to Liberty, hath a necessary Tendency to prevent the Payment of the Debt due from this Colony to *Great Britain*, and is, of Consequence, ruinous to Trade."[1] If this statement were the only instance of its type available from the revolutionary era, and if we were not familiar with the way that common lawyers had always blended constitutional and political objections in single documents, it might be concluded that the Virginians were saying that the Townshend act was "unconstitutional," not only because its purpose was to raise revenue, but also because it was ruinous to trade. But that was not what was meant. Rather, as was often stated, Americans had economic complaints against many of the acts of trade, but the real grievance was the constitutional one: that the Stamp Act and Townshend duties introduced the new principle of taxing the colonies for purposes of revenue.

Arguments against the Townshend Acts especially need to be distinguished on what they purported to say about the constitution. The legislation covered a wide variety of matters, including where ships were to sail and from what ports goods could be imported into the colonies, and these regulations produced some economic but not constitutional complaints. Colonial petitions, for example, acknowledged that Parliament had constitutional authority to impose duties on lemons, wine, raisins, and other products of Spain and Portugal, but said that to require that those goods pass through Great Britain before shipment to North America was unreasonable, expensive, and wasteful. The distinction that was drawn has been discussed above as an aspect of the trade-regulation criterion. To relate the argument to the Townshend controversy, we need only refer to Franklin's testimony at the bar of the House of Commons. A diary of a member reports that Franklin made three contentions: (1) "That the Americans in general never disputed the controlling power of this Kingdom to regulate their trade"; (2) "That regulation attended with an internal tax would be objected to"; and (3) "That they would not object to [a] duty laid upon importation as considering the sea as belonging to Great Britain, and anything passing that sea would be subject to Great Britain. They would object to duty upon exportation if it lay hard upon their commerce and prevent[ed] sale in foreign parts, but they might object by expediency without calling the right into question."[2]

Applying the distinction to the Townshend Acts means that only one part of that legislative package is relevant, the only part complained against as a constitutional rather than an economic grievance: the duties on paint, glass, paper, and tea. Some nonconstitutional objections also were raised against these taxes. One was that there were trade statutes in existence forbidding Americans to purchase these products anywhere except from British suppliers. Because those statutes had been passed by Parliament under its authority to regulate commerce, they were not challenged as unconstitutional; rather, it was said that the monoply conferred by them provided the British with all the profits they could reasonably expect and to tax the same products was unfair — whether or not the taxes were constitutional.[3] "If *Great-Britain* did not confine your trade to herself," John Mackenzie pointed out to the people of South Carolina, "all the duties she could have laid on . . . would not signify a rush: you could refuse them, and apply to those who would be more reasonable.—But, at present—there is but one alternative, take them burdened as they are, or refuse them."[4]

An alternative way to state the complaint was to say, as Lord North did, that the duties on paints, glass, and paper were "highly improper and anticommercial" as they were "imposed upon British Manufactures." Again, the objection was nonconstitutional. It was an economic grievance harmful both to the colonies and Great Britain because the duties appeared to be "a prohibition on our commerce with the mother country, which, for the mutual advantage of both, we conceive ought to be free and unrestrained."[5]

USE OF THE REVENUE

Although the preamble of the Townshend Tax Act was discussed above, one part bears repeating. It provided "that a revenue should be raised, in your Majesty's dominions in *America*, for making a more certain and adequate provision for defraying the charge of the administration of justice, and the support of civil government, in such provinces where it shall be found necessary. . . ." This provision introduced the constitutional issue unique to the Townshend duties: the purpose for which the revenue was to be spent. The intent of the statute had been clearly stated by Townshend when he introduced the legislation. "The salaries of governors and judges," he informed the Commons, "must be made independent of their [colonial] Assemblies."[6] From the imperial perspective, this reform meant that the governor of Massachusetts would now be supported in dignity "without the precarious Grant of the General Court." From the American perspective, by contrast, it appeared that the governor would now "be rendered independent of the people."[7] The proposed use of the revenue was immediately perceived in the colonies as an unconstitutional innovation[8] that threatened traditional legislative autonomy,[9] and, by departing from the ancient English concept of grants of support coming from the people as gifts, jeopardized the balanced government by eliminating the chief influence of the democratic element of society, thereby rendering Americans constitutionally unequal with their fellow subjects in Great Britain. Long after the Townshend duties had been repealed, this aspect of the constitutional case against them was summed up by the New York assembly.

> [R]aising a revenue for making provision for defraying the charge
> of the administration of justice, and the support of civil government,

is a grievance; as . . . it raises a revenue for the support of government, and the administration of justice in the colonies, independent
of the people; is contrary to, and a revocation of that system of rights
and privileges on which the government of the colonies hath been
established; as it deprives the legislatures of the colonies of the check
and control upon the servants of the public, which the parliament
hath in Great Britain, and deprives the subjects in the colonies of
the rights and privileges which they always, before the passing that
act, have been esteemed entitled to, and, of right, enjoy, equa[l] with
the people of Great Britain.[10]

"In the preamble, the assemblies thought they read their own annihila-
tion," Edmund Burke said of the Townshend statute. "The stamp act was
to go to the pay of the army; but this struck at the root of their assemblies." John Dickinson meant just that when he said that the Townshend
Act raised revenue "without our consent, for PURPOSES, that render it *if
possible*, more dreadful than the *Stamp-Act*."[11] After Townshend went
into operation and the salary of the Massachusetts governor was being
paid by the imperial treasury, the colony's House of Representatives wondered whether the colonial constitution was any longer worth defending. "For what purpose," it asked, "will it be to preserve the old forms
without the substance?"[12] One possibility, predicted by a Scottish publication, was that the colonial constitution would be replaced by the Irish
constitution in North America,[13] with imperially collected revenue used
to support "hungry Placemen and Pensioners," and "parasitical and novel
m[inisterial] officers."[14]

There is one last point to be made about the purpose for which the
revenue was to be spent. The Townshend duties, even though they initially appear to be peculiar to the American colonies and the revolutionary era (in that they were external levies specifically designed to satisfy
the colonists' objection to internal taxation), were not constitutionally
or historically unique. There were resemblances to the English constitutional past, most notably to the ship-money levy promulgated by Charles
I. Ship money also raised constitutional issues about the purpose for which
the revenue was to be spent. "Opposition," according to J. P. Kenyon, "was
not mobilised until the uses to which the 'ship money fleet' might be put
became more apparent." One did not have to live in the colonies to recognize the parallel. Americans objected to losing power to officials paid
with revenue they did not grant, a London pamphlet noted. "And can
we with any sense of justice censure them for contending against it; especially if we find the very same reasons, as was most certainly the case,
to have governed us in taking arms against the meditated tyranny of
Charles the first?"[15]

The Revenue Grievance

There would be little purpose spending paragraphs recounting the constitutional arguments raised against the revenue aspects of the Townshend duties. They were the same as those raised against the Stamp Act. Like the Stamp Act and unlike the sugar tax, the Townshend legislation did not contain "even the suggestion" of regulating trade. "[A] regulation of trade," a colonial whig noted, "is not pretended, *revenue* only is the confessed object. The power of regulating Trade is not then here exercised, but plainly *another power.*"[16] The constitutional point, as the Virginia Council and Burgesses told the Commons, was that because the Townshend duties had been enacted not "with a view to the general Interests of Commerce" but "for the sole Purpose of raising a Revenue," they were a tax "to all Intents and Purposes."[17]

Another familiar argument was that the Townshend duties were unprecedented. They were unprecedented both because they constituted a tax never before imposed and because of the manner in which the revenue raised was to be spent. In both respects, the law deprived Americans "of a privilege which the colonies have, till of late, uninterruptedly enjoyed."[18]

The chief constitutional complaint, stated over and over again, was that the Townshend duties had been imposed "by Parliament, for the sole and express Purposes of raising a Revenue."[19] The imposition of "duties on the colonies, with the sole view and for the express purpose of raising a revenue," the New York Assembly told George III, was regarded by Americans "as utterly subversive of their constitutional rights."[20] The New Hampshire House of Representatives spoke for almost all the legislatures on the continent when it protested that "taxes being imposed on us by way of Duties on any of the Necessaries of life or in any other measure whatsoever without our consent must necessarily terminate in the total loss of our Liberty and Distruction [*sic*] of our property."[21]

The evidence need not further be belabored. By now the issue must be obvious, just as it was obvious during the revolutionary era when the Massachusetts House of Representatives summed it up in the following resolution:

> As to imposing duties, so long as they are confined to the regulation of trade, and so conducted as to be of equal advantage to all parts of the empire, no great exception could be taken of it; but when duties are laid with a view of raising a revenue out of the Colonies, and this revenue also to be applied to establish a civil list in America, and by this means (as the report goes) the Governor, the Lieutenant Governor, Secretary, Judges, &c. &c., are to have their salaries fixed

from home and paid out of the monies that shall be from time to
time collected, by virtue of Act of Parliament already passed, or to
be passed; — this is looked upon to be unconstitutional.[22]

The issue was so obvious, in fact, that this resolution — anticipating all
the constitutional objections that American whigs would raise against
the Townshend duties — was drafted, debated, and voted before any of
Charles Townshend's legislation had been enacted by Parliament.

CHAPTER TWENTY

ISSUE OF THE TEA ACT

People on both sides of the prerevolutionary debate seem to have realized two facts more or less simultaneously. The first was that the Townshend duties were a failure and would have to be repealed. The second was that the imperial dispute about parliamentary taxation was now dominated by constitutional considerations to such an extent that a constitutional solution could soon become impossible.

Even before repeal became likely some important participants in the prerevolutionary debates seem to have apprehended that the Townshend duties might make the dispute too legal for a political solution. When the taxes were being considered by Parliament, Lord Mansfield had announced he was supporting them in the hope that they would become "the means of breathing a soul into the declaratory act." A few months later the other great lawyer in the House of Lords, Earl Camden, suggested that the very thing Mansfield spoke of — the need for a symbol proving Parliament's right to tax — would be the chief obstacle preventing repeal of the Townshend duties after it became generally realized that the tax produced imperial disunity, not royal revenue, and would have to be repealed. Parliament, Camden wrote, could not abolish the Townshend taxes "because that would admit the American principle to be right and their own doctrine erroneous."[1]

When it was generally appreciated that this situation had come to pass, that the Townshend argument had become too legal to permit repeal, some members of the British government blamed the Americans. After all, the colonial assemblies had refused to heed warnings that complaints against the Townshend duties should be limited to the commercial and economic aspects of the tax. They had instead defiantly insisted that their objections were to Parliament's right of taxation, leaving both houses little choice but to refuse to receive their petitions. Certainly, there were few if any on either side of the controversy who believed that the dispute was over the amount of the tax. "Charles Townshend's duties," William Dowdeswell observed, "are I believe not so heavy as to justify me in saying that they are grievous burdens on the colonies. The people there do not appear to make this stand against *these duties* on account of their purpose, but against the general principle of raising *any* revenue in America." The leading American whig critic of the Townshend duties also insisted that the amount was not the issue. "Some persons may think this act of no consequence, because the duties are so *small*," John Dickinson warned. "*That* is the very circumstance most alarming to me. For I am convinced, that the authors of this law would never have obtained an act to raise so trifling a sum as it must do, had they not intended by *it* to establish a *precedent* for future use. To console ourselves with the *smallness* of the duties, is to walk deliberately into the snare that is set for us." On the other side of the Atlantic, Edmund Burke agreed with Dickinson. He doubted that revenue had been the immediate purpose of Townshend's legislation. "The substance of the whole act was to draw from the Americans a recognition of our right," he told the Commons when repeal was being considered.[2] The ministry, Burke said of the Townshend statute, "laid a duty or tax upon America, not for the purpose of raising a revenue . . . but with the avowed design of asserting the right to raise a revenue." Burke's distinction is significant, as it explains what John Dickinson meant about the danger of Townshend becoming a precedent. The duties, Dickinson wrote, had been "designed to be a PRECEDENT, whereon the future vassalage of these colonies may be established," and when seen in that light they were less a tax than "an *experiment made of our disposition.*" American assemblies, appreciating what was at stake, refused to compromise. They persistently raised the question of right, making the Townshend debate so legal that, unlike the stamp tax, the Townshend tax could not be repealed on the excuse of expediency. "One might argue for the repeal of Charles Townshend's duties, as injudiciously laid," Dowdeswell explained. "But this would be avoiding the real question. . . . A repeated opposition from that side of the water, upon a principle directed against all duties for revenue, must be met. It must either be admitted which is timidity, weakness, irresolution, and inconsistency: or it must be resisted and the arms of this country must be exerted against her colonies."[3] Dowdeswell's words deserve close attention. They stated the imperial constitutional strategy that made civil war inevitable.

REPEAL OF THE TOWNSHEND DUTIES

Almost from the moment they had been enacted, the Townshend duties were perceived by British government officials to have been a mistake. Had it not been for the stand on constitutional right by American assemblies, they might have been repealed as early as 1768. One reason they were not was that Lord Hillsborough and the other shapers of the government's colonial policy realized that their options had narrowed since repeal of the Stamp Act. The constitutional controversy had become so legal it no longer could be solved by expediency. Calling in the colonial agents, Hillsborough sought a compromise, telling them that should the Americans concede the constitutional principle, the colonies could have the economic benefits of the political victory. "[I]f they would wa[i]ve the point of right, and petition for a repeal of the duties as *burdensome & grievous*," William Knox reported Hillsborough telling the agents, "Administration were disposed to come into it. The agents, however, declared they could not leave out the point of right, consistent with their present instructions, but should inform their respective colonies, and so it rests." The matter continued to rest that way for well over a year, the agents giving different advice to their assemblies, no assembly willing to concede the principle. "I wish," the agent for Massachusetts had written before meeting Hillsborough, "in all your applications, you had left the matter of right out of the question, and only applied for a repeal of the laws, as prejudicial to the colonies." "I wish," the agent for Georgia wrote of the chances for repeal of the Townshend legislation, "that this could be done at once, But 'tis perhaps too much to expect, considering the Pride Natural to a great Nation, the Prejudices that have so universally prevailed here [in London] with Regard to the Point of Right, and the Resentment at our disputing it." He believed that a majority of the Commons wished the duties had never been enacted, "but they think the national honour concern'd in supporting them, considering the manner in which the execution of them has been oppos'd. They cannot bear the denial of the right of Parliament to make them, tho' they acknowledge they ought not to have been made."[4]

There seemed no solution unless one side or the other conceded the

constitutional principle. Even after informing the agents that "the legislature and ministry, here, had laid aside every idea of raising a revenue
in America," Hillsborough insisted it would be constitutionally impossible to repeal Townshend without colonial concessions. What he expected
— not much politically, although it would also prove constitutionally
impossible — was reported by a contemporary pamphlet summing up a
letter that Hillsborough wrote the colonial governors: "a formal acquiescence was *all* that was desired; for it was the intention of Government, not only to *relax*, but to take the first opportunity to procure a
repeal of them [the Townshend duties], the mere unexercised right being
all that was actually insisted on."[5]

Colonial acquiescence never came and Hillsborough was out of office
when Lord North decided that repeal had been delayed long enough.
North's excuse was nonconstitutional, that the three Townshend duties
imposing taxes upon products of British manufacture were "highly improper and anticommercial." "[I]t must astonish any reasonable man,"
he told the Commons, "to think how so preposterous a law could originally obtain existence from a British legislature."[6] As this excuse did not
apply to the fourth Townshend duty, the tax on tea, Lord North did not
ask for its repeal. Because tea was not of British manufacture, North
could say the tax on it was not anticommercial as were the tariffs on paint,
glass, and paper, and he also could say it was worth retaining for revenue
purposes. No one was fooled: had revenue been sought, the old tax of
twelve pennies on its importation into Great Britain could have been retained. All tea sold in the colonies had to pass through the mother country, but on reshipment to North America, there would have been no tax
and no colonial constitutional objection. Instead, the tea tax was collected in the colonies. Although there may have been revenue reasons for
not repealing the tea duty, there is no doubt they were far outweighed
by constitutional reasons. As George III said, "there must always be one
tax to keep up the right." "America knew the real reason," a pamphleteer
wrote. "The duty upon tea was left, to shew that Parliament did not give
up the right"; it was "continued to preserve the sovereign authority in
actual exercise."[7] The tea tax had replaced the Townshend duties as the
symbol of Parliament's right to raise revenue from the colonies.

The duty upon tea had been kept, David Hartley was to lament, "only
as a pepper-corn rent, for the point of honour." When he wrote these words
the Revolution had begun and Great Britain was paying an extraordinary
price for a symbol of honor. The ministry had known there would be
risks. Even before Lord North had moved repeal of three of the Townshend
taxes, the Boston town meeting had voted that it would not be constitutionally acceptable for Parliament to repeal some but not all of the duties.

[T]he taking off of the dutys on Paper, Glass, and Painters colours, upon commercial principles only . . . will not give satisfaction: It will not even relieve the trade from the burdens it labours under; much less will it remove the grounds of discontent, which runs thro' the Continent, upon much higher principles. Their Rights are invaded by these Acts; therefore untill they are *all* repealed, the *cause* of their Just complaints cannot be removed: In short the Grievances which lie heavily upon us we shall never think redressed, till *every* Act passed by the British Parliament for the express purpose of raising a Revenue upon us without our consent is repealed; till the American Board of Commissioners of the Customs is dissolved; the Troops recalled, and things restored to the state they were in before the late extraordinary measures of Administration took place.

There were other grievances besides the Townshend duties to be redressed, and the tax on tea was one of them.[8]

Secondary Issues of the Tea Act

There were two statutory components of the tea tax. The first was the act that repealed the major parts of the Townshend duties but left importation taxes on many items in addition to tea. The second was the Tea Act of 1773, which not only retained the threepenny duty on tea landed in the colonies but also permitted the East India Company, if it chose, to ship tea directly to North America and to restrict its sale to agents or factors selected by the Company, that is, granting it a commercial monopoly. Both of these pieces of legislation raised secondary considerations of fact that clarify the constitutional issues.[9]

That colonial whigs continued to complain of the tea tax but not of the other taxes that had been retained provided grounds for their critics in Great Britain to charge hypocrisy. "It is of the Duty on Tea, the Americans principally complain," James Macpherson wrote, "yet they submitted to a Duty of 7 1. per Ton, laid on Wines, the Session which immediately preceded the passing of the Tea-Act." That the whigs "were not asking the repeal of the many Port-duties imposed by Mr. Grenville's first [Sugar] Act," John Dalrymple told them, "shewed that you insisted on this trifle as a matter of mere pride; as a mark of your exaltation and of our humiliation."[10] The evidence can, of course, be interpreted in this way. But in truth it is as much evidence of colonial constitutional sincerity as of colonial hypocrisy. American whigs did not protest the taxes on tobacco, wine, sugar, and molasses as unconstitutional because, unlike the tax on tea, they were not perceived as unconstitutional. They raised revenue only incidentally to their main purpose — regulation of trade — and, therefore, were not constitutionally challengeable.

A corresponding feature that critics professed to find puzzling was that American whigs were protesting a statute that benefited them economically. The Tea Act had lowered the price on a pound of tea to the colonial purchaser below what it cost the British consumer and even below what Americans had been paying to smugglers. "We could not complain of the three-penny duty on tea as burdensome," the loyalist lawyer Daniel Leonard asserted, "for a shilling which had been laid upon it, for the purpose of regulating trade, and therefore was allowed to be constitutional, was taken off; so that we were in fact gainers nine-pence in a pound by the new regulation." Another lawyer, John Dickinson, provided the answer, one we may be certain Leonard had understood but had chosen to ignore. "It is not the paltry Sum of Three-Pence which is now demanded, but the Principle upon which it is demanded, that we are contending against," Dickinson explained. *"Before we pay any Thing, let us see whether we have any Thing we call our own to pay."* Lord North would later claim that "it was impossible for any man to foresee that the Americans would refuse to pay three pence a-pound for tea, when a drawback of nine pence a-pound was taken off to encourage them to drink it." North knew that American objections to the tax were based on constitutional, not economic considerations, but he probably had not anticipated that the very economic attractiveness of the Tea Act, the low price, would be perceived in the colonies as a constitutional snare. Benjamin Franklin, foreseeing both the snare and that it would fail, had described the tea tax as a "scheme" by the British

> to take off so much duty here [in Great Britain], as will make tea cheaper in America than foreigners can supply us, and confine the duty there to keep up the exercise of the right. They have no idea that any people can act from any other principle but that of interest; and they believe, that 3d in a lb of tea, of which one does not perhaps drink 10 in a year, is sufficient to overcome all patriotism in America.[11]

Franklin exaggerated. Most members of Parliament understood the principle at stake. There were only a few voices remaining in Great Britain professing to believe that the quarrel was economic. One of those who did deserves to be quoted, as he raised a final secondary issue shedding light on the constitutional questions posed by the tea tax.

> Can the payment of three pence on the pound of tea, the use of which they may decline if they please, warrant a rebellion? . . . We say buy and sell and consume what you please, provided you have it of us.

If you do not chuse to have our tea, then you will not be charged any thing for it. What can be the reason of their being so spiteful against an act of a poor three-pence on the pound of tea, when they suffer duties upon other articles of trade, as wine, molasses, &c. except what they smuggle? Their opposition to the tea arose from a fear that we should prevent their smuggling that article.

The writer said that Americans could buy and not buy tea as they pleased, and that the only requirement laid down by Parliament was that whatever tea was purchased come from Great Britain. Colonial whigs admitted both points. The constitutional dispute was not over the restriction that only British tea could be purchased. At issue was the other argument: that Americans were otherwise free to buy or not to buy. Previously that fact had been true. Americans had paid the old tax of one shilling or they had avoided it by smuggling. The Tea Act of 1773 had introduced a new aspect. The tax was so low and so well hidden that there were many Americans besides Franklin who detected a plot to fool the colonists into paying a tax for purposes of revenue by lowering their constitutional guard. As New York merchants stated when thanking ship captains for not carrying tea to America, "The insidious purpose of levying the duty in America, and taking off a much greater in England, is equally manifest and detestable, being nothing less than to establish the odious precedent of raising a revenue in America." The theme was perhaps best stated by a correspondent to a Boston newspaper.

You cannot believe the Tea Act, with respect to its design and tendency, differs in one single point from the Stamp Act. If there be any difference, the Tea Act is the more dangerous. The Stamp Act was sensibly felt, by all ranks of people; and was therefore opposed by all; but the Tea Act, more insidious in its operation, required some pains to discover its malignity.— Under the first, no man could transfer his property; he could not even read a newspaper without seeing and feeling the detestable imposition; it was therefore, too glaring to pass unnoticed and unopposed.— But, under the Tea Law, the duty being paid on importation, is afterwards laid on the article, and becomes so blended with the price of it, that although every man who purchases tea, imported from Britain, must of course pay the duty; yet, every man does not know it, and may therefore not object to it.[12]

NONTAX CONSTITUTIONAL ISSUES

For purposes of evaluating American grievances against the tea tax, both Tea Acts — the one repealing the Townshend duties in 1770 and the

Tea Act of 1773 — may be considered together. The constitutional issues raised in the first were raised in the second. The act of 1773, however, posed two new constitutional questions, one not related to the taxation controversy, the other somewhat related, as it altered the procedures for collecting the tea duty.

The nontaxation constitutional issue belongs in a study dealing with Parliament's authority to legislate and can be accorded no more than passing mention in this volume. It was the monopoly granted to the East India Company to sell its tea in the colonies exclusively through consignees. Merchants of the colonies not only lost the trade in tea, but the Act provided a dangerous precedent.[13] "Will they not engross and monopolize every other article," a resident of New Hampshire asked?[14] The economic overtones to the monopoly issue need not concern us except to note how easily they were converted into constitutional grievances. One grievance was inequality; the tea monopoly meant that Americans were not being treated as constitutionally equal to their fellow subjects in Great Britain, where tea was sold on the free market. And, of course, any monopoly voted by Parliament and granted to "foreigners" could be depicted as a threat to American liberty.[15]

Another important cause for apprehension was the antimonopoly tradition in British constitutional law. The first substantial limitation put on the royal prerogative during the seventeenth century had been an act against monopolies passed by James I's last Parliament. The constitutional attack against monopolies extended back to Elizabeth's reign, had intensified under the Stuarts, and was even carried on during the Commonwealth. A commercial-law treatise published in 1765 stated that monopolies were contrary to common law, but that referrred to royal prerogativism, not statute law. Distinctions had been drawn between industrial and trade monopolies, and by the beginning of the eighteenth century, it was generally agreed that the Crown was forbidden to create either type. Parliament's authority, however, was unrestricted. By protesting that the Tea Act was unconstitutional, American whigs were claiming that a constitutional right the British people had won against the arbitrary actions of the Crown should provide them protection against the arbitrary actions of Parliament.

The second innovation arising from the Tea Act was more connected with the taxation issue. The tariff on tea was set so low that American whigs concluded that Parliament was less interested in raising revenue than in establishing a precedent. Actually, they feared three precedents — a precedent for other taxes, a precedent for the legality of parliamentary commercial monopolies in the colonies, and, because the duty was to be paid on entry at the customs house, not at sale, a precedent of the

tea tax having been paid. The possibility of the last becoming a precedent was especially alarming because the Tea Act continued the constitutional program started by the Townshend legislation. Money raised was
to be used, the Massachusetts committee of correspondence warned, "to
maintain the executive Powers of the several Governments of *America*
absolutely independent of their respective Legislatures; or rather absolutely dependent on the Crown, which will, if a little while persisted in,
end in absolute Despotism."[16]

The major American grievance against the Tea Act, then, was not the
grant of monopoly but the danger of creating precedents both for raising
revenue taxes and paying salaries. "This Act," the members of the Massachusetts Council resolved, "in a commercial view they think introductive
of Monopolies and tending to bring on them the extensive evils hence
arising. But their great objection to it is from its being manifestly intended
(tho' that intention is not expressed therein) more effectually to secure
the payment of a Duty upon Tea." John Adams elaborated.

> If it had been only a monopoly, (tho' in this light it would have been
> a very great grievance) it would not have excited, nor in the opinion
> of any one, justified the step [i.e., the Boston Tea Party] that was taken.
> It was an attack upon a fundamental principle of the Constitution,
> and upon that supposition was resisted, after multitudes of petitions
> to no purpose, and because there was no tribunal in the Constitu-
> tion, from whence redress could have been obtained.[17]

BRITISH APPREHENSIONS

Adams was explaining why the Tea Party had been unavoidable: the
ministry had made the Tea Act so much a symbol of Parliament's claim
of right to taxation that the colonists could not permit any precedent to
be established. In Scotland, the same premise — that the three pence duty
on tea had been enacted only to maintain the authority of Parliament —
was explained as the reason why the Tea Party had to be taken seriously.
When defying such a law, the Americans were rebels. That view would
prevail and lead directly to civil war. It is the opposite position, the contention that the issue was not worth the price the nation would have to
pay for American rebellion, that sheds light on contemporary British
thought. That notion was stated by the governor of North Carolina, who
thought the tea tax "will never yield any revenue to the state and must
be a perpetual source of division among the friends of government while
it exists." A member of the Commons said that "the tea tax was not wor-

thy the name of a tax; it seemed only meant to irritate the people, and to keep up a wrangle between Great-Britain and her colonies." Former Governor George Johnstone seems to have thought the Tea Party was proof that the tax should be repealed, not that it had to be enforced. "I would," he said during the debate on how Boston should be punished, "recommend the immediate repeal of the Tea Duty, which can be vindicated upon no principles, either of commerce or policy. Men may allege this would be giving up the point; but if we have no better points to dispute upon, I am ready to yield the argument. Raising taxes in *America* for the purpose of revenue, I maintain to be unnecessary and dangerous."[18]

Edmund Burke, who termed the tea tax "an exhaustless source of jealousy and animosity," gave the best summary of why some members of Parliament thought it had been a mistake to insist on even a symbol of the constitutional right. "I abhor the measure of taxation where it is only for a quarrel, and not for a revenue; a measure that is teazing and irritating without any good effect."

> Could anything be a subject of more just alarm to America than to see you go out of the plain highroad of finance, and give up your most certain revenues and your clearest interests, merely for the sake of insulting your colonies? No man ever doubted that the commodity of tea could bear an imposition of threepence. But no commodity will bear threepence, or will bear a penny, when the general feelings of men are irritated and two millions of people are resolved not to pay. . . . It is the weight of that preamble, of which you are so fond, and not the weight of the duty that the Americans are unable and unwilling to bear.[19]

AMERICAN OBJECTIONS

When the partial repeal of the Townshend duties was being rumored, Georgia's Commons House of Assembly expressed its partial pleasure "that some of the many Taxes lately imposed by Parliament are intended to be taken off and that no others of the like nature will be added, but deeply Concerned to observe that any unconstitutional Acts should remain." "A partial Suspension of Duties," Virginia's Burgesses warned the king, could not "remove the two [sic] well grounded Fears and Apprehension of your Majesty's loyal Subjects, whilst Impositions are continued on the same Articles of foreign Fabrick, and entirely retain'd upon Tea, for the avow'd Purpose of establishing a Precedent against us."[20]

Constitutional principle, not matters of revenue, was taking over the determination of events. On one side of the revolutionary controversy,

members of Parliament opposed repeal of the Townshend duties until the
colonial assemblies acknowledged the constitutional right of Great Britain to tax them. On the other side, American whigs, motivated by the
same constitutional principle, were dissatisfied that repeal had been accompanied by a claim of the right rather than a renunciation of it. "Far
are we," some New Yorkers protested, "from being relieved by this con-
descension, while the disgusting preamble and enacting words of the first
[Townshend] act are still in force, with an exception only of such of the
duties thereby imposed as by the subsequent act are repealed, merely because they are anti-commercial." "We cannot think the doctrine of the
right of Parliament to tax us is given up," the Massachusetts House of
Representatives agreed, "while an act remains in force for that purpose,
and is daily put in execution; and the longer it remains, the more danger
there is to the people's becoming so accustomed to arbitrary and unconstitutional taxes, as to pay them without discontent."[21]

Passage of the Tea Act of 1773 intensified but did not change the constitutional argument. The voters of Plymouth, Massachusetts, resolved
that it was "the same unconstitutional tax, or tribute, . . . we have upon
other occasions . . . opposed." On constitutional grounds, it was no
different from the stamp tax. "The Stamp and Tea Laws were both designed to raise a revenue, and to establish *parliamentary despotism* in
America."[22] Resolutions passed by the people of Philadelphia and adopted
by many other towns[23] summed up the issue by saying what had been
said many times before: "That the duty imposed by Parliament upon tea
landed in America, is a tax on the Americans, or levying contributions
on them without their consent."[24]

After the Boston Tea Party, when the British ministry was demanding compensation for the destroyed property and when many Americans
realized for the first time that they might be facing civil war, the committee of correspondence of Pennsylvania wrote a circular letter to other
colonies reminding them that a constitutional principle was at stake.

> If satisfying the *East India Company* for the damage they have sus-
> tained, would put an end to this unhappy Controversy, and leave
> us on the footing of constitutional Liberty of the future, it is pre-
> sumed, that neither you nor we, could continue a moment in Doubt
> what part to act; for it is not the Value of the Tax, but the indefeasible
> Right of giving and granting our own Money, from which we can
> never recede, that is the Matter now in Consideration.

It was the same issue as in 1765, an English constitutional principle, as
by now the British well understood.[25]

PROPOSED CONSTITUTIONAL SOLUTIONS

On the first day of October 1765, at the height of the Stamp Act crisis, a future loyalist wrote to the future governor of rebellious New Jersey wondering if there was a solution to the taxation question. "No man see[s] in a stronger light than I do," Jared Ingersoll insisted, "the dangerous tendency of admitting for a principle that the Parliament of Great Britain may tax us ad libitum. I view it as a gulph ready to devour, but when I look all round I am at a loss for a plan. I think there is all the reason in the world why we should be in a Situation Equally safe with the people in England; but how, and what, and when, I am almost weary in the Enquiry. . . . I spent the whole winter among Politicians, both English & American, and among Em all found no plan for America that did not appear to me full of the greatest difficulty & Embarassment."[1]

The plan that Ingersoll sought had to come not from the colonies but from Parliament. The American position all along was that they could not be taxed for purposes of revenue without consent of elected representatives. For nine years, until 1774, the ministry and the legislators of Great Britain let the situation drift as there had been no urgency to formulate a definitive constitutional solution. After the Boston Tea Party, passage of the Intolerable Acts, and defiance of Parliament's authority by the first Continental Congress, the question could no longer be avoided. Members of Parliament knew that if they were to prevent war, they had to devise a new constitutional relationship with the colonies. The problem was to agree on a way out of the impasse. As we have seen, and as the next two chapters will also show, there were many officials on all levels of the British government who felt the constitutional right to tax could not be abrogated or diluted. Those willing to abandon the principle viewed the matter in so many different ways that they could never have agreed on a single solution. By the end of 1774, for example, the British secretary-at-war was certain that no ministry would again levy an internal tax on the colonies. He was still persuaded of Parliament's right but doubted "at least the equity of such taxations." The word "equity" is worth attention; a solution based on equity would have been more legal and less political than one of expediency, as it would have taken into consideration such factors as that "Parliament is less acquainted with the state of the Colonies than of Great Britain" and "Members of neither House are to bear any part of the burthen they impose." But what was equitable? There was no agreement. One pamphlet writer even seems to have believed that to meet the requirements for fairness or equity it would not matter who levied a tax, Parliament or the local colonial assembly. "[I]f the parliament actually take no more than is just and reasonable, it cannot be materially different, whether we or they grant, provided it be really granted, and the sum be mutually agreed on." Another 1774 pamphleteer, however, thought that equity barred Parliament from any taxing function. "Upon the whole," he wrote, "I humbly think that a right to tax the colonies is neither founded on reason, the situation of things, the opinions of civilians, nor yet is expedient at this very time, and consequently the mode of laying taxes ought to be committed to the colonies themselves."[2]

Some proposed constitutional solutions to the problem of parliamentary taxation of the colonies may be passed over quickly, as they were too extreme to have attracted sufficient support. Among these were proposals that Americans be granted representation in the House of Commons so that they could be taxed constitutionally and that Great Britain, by statute, renounce its right of taxation. Although the latter would be the ultimate British solution, it would be adopted only after the revolutionary war had long been in progress.

A solution that could have succeeded had it obtained sufficient support while it was still possible for Americans to have accepted it was to do nothing: to maintain the status quo, and admit that the colonies paid their share of imperial defense through the commercial contract. "I would be very explicit in disclaiming any wish for a revenue . . . while we cramp their trade," the duke of Richmond explained. "We must be satisfied with

one or t'other and the advantages of commerce are far the more preferable." Edmund Pendleton even thought of having the Continental Congress offer London an "either-or" proposal based on the commercial contract: either the British be satisfied with the profits of trade or end the
commercial contract.

> [W]e consider & ever must consider the Monopoly of Our trade in
> Point of Profitt to Britain & [a] disadvantage to Us, as a full com-
> pensation for our proportion of the Expense of the Navy, so necessary
> for the Protect[io]n of the whole Empire; But if we are mistaken
> in this, and Parliament shall think proper to put us on a footing
> with Our fellow Subjects in Britain by as free a trade as they enjoy,
> we shall be ready, as in justice we ought, to pay a settled proportion
> of that expence.[3]

FLAWED PROPOSALS

Little attention has been given in histories of the Revolution to the solutions proposed to the problem of imperial taxation. That is surprising,
not only because a remarkable number of plans were suggested, but even
more because these proposals, as much as any other evidence, shed light
on how contemporary British citizens perceived the constitutional issues.
Even flawed plans, especially those based on misinterpretations of the
American constitutional argument, deserve consideration; nothing tells
us more about the difficulties of compromise than evidence that informed
members of the British public, including a few experts on colonial affairs,
offered suggestions for settling the revolutionary controversy that American whigs had already rejected as unconstitutional. Perhaps the most
startling example is the writers who as late as 1774 continued to cling
to the erroneous belief that Americans objected only to internal taxation
and did not object to customs duties imposed for purposes of revenue.[4]
The reason may be that Governor Thomas Pownall in his influential book
on colonial governance harped on the fact that Americans acknowledged
Parliament's customary right to impose duties for purposes of trade regulation but never mentioned the qualification that customs duties could
not constitutionally be used to raise revenue. John Lind is another who
got the issue confused or deliberately confused it. He would have based
the power to tax for revenue on the authority to regulate trade, an absurd solution that served no end other than to make American whigs appear inconsistent and unreasonable to the British public.[5]
Another flawed proposal would have had Parliament taxing the colo-

nies for a single purpose for which it was reasonable Americans pay, such as retirement of the national debt. The earl of Shelburne argued that Great Britain had to retain

> the right of judging not only of the *mode* of raising, but the *quantum*, and the appropriation of such aids as they shall grant.—To be more explicit; the debt of *England*, without entering into invidious distinctions how it came to be contracted, might be acknowledged the debt of every individual part of the whole Empire, Asia, as well as America, included.—Provided, that full security were held forth to them, that such free aids, together with the Sinking Fund (Great Britain contributing her superior share) should not be left as the privy purse of the minister, but be unalienably appropriated to the original intention of that fund, the discharge of the debt.[6]

Closely related to Lord Shelburne's plan and with the advantage of being more constitutionally acceptable to American whigs was a scheme suggested by Adam Ferguson, professor of moral philosophy at Edinburgh University. He felt the colonies should be obliged to contribute "some reasonable proportion" toward the support of "the state," not to be "augmented without their own consent," leaving to the local assemblies how the tax would be collected. A third suggestion, combining Shelburne's solution with Ferguson's, was to have the colonies tax themselves for a specific, limited purpose—support of the royal navy.[7]

Francis Maseres, Quebec's attorney general, erroneously thought that the problem was to keep Parliament from taxing America for Britain's benefit. He would have had taxes first proposed by the colony's governing body, and, if approved by the king in council, submitted to the House of Commons to be enacted into law. "With these precautions," he wrote, "the property of the inhabitants of this province would be as secure against a wanton, or injudicious, exercise of the power of taxation, as if the taxes were to be granted only by an assembly of their own chusing." As an alternative, Maseres would have inserted

> a clause in every act of parliament . . . by which it should be provided, that the revenue raised by the duties imposed by such act, whatever they might amount to, should not be disposed of by either the king alone, or the king and the British parliament conjointly, but be left to the disposal of the legislatures of the several provinces in which it should arise. By this means the parliament of Great-Britain could not be under any temptation to pass acts for raising a revenue on the inhabitants of America with a view to lessen their own burthens, under colour of regulating the American trade.[8]

Solutions of Equality

Several proposed constitutional solutions to the taxation controversy were based on the assumption that Americans would be satisfied if they were secured from taxes unequal to those paid in Great Britain.[9] It was possible to state that the constitutional right contended for was consent to taxation and yet suggest that the principle could be overlooked if some formula was found for guaranteeing that tax rates would be fair or equal. This approach was advanced in 1776 by an anonymous pamphlet, which remarkably recognized the constitutional principle but suggested that it could be ignored.

> While the Taxes imposed on us, are only extended to America, in a very small Proportion, their [colonists'] Complaints are groundless, their Fears chimerical, and the Opposition REBELLION, of the blackest Dye: If ever our Parliament should reach out its Hand to create one Tax in America which we did not pay in Common with them; this would be indeed *giving* and *granting* what they could have no Right to give: This would precisely constitute Tyranny on our Side, and Slavery on their's, if they submitted; but that is not likely to happen in your Time or mine, or that of our Children.[10]

William Knox seems to have been the most influential imperial official to agree with this theory of the controversy — to think that if the Americans could be assured of fair and equal treatment, they would not object to parliamentary taxation. His solution was to define the limits of imperial taxation in terms acceptable to both parties. "Parliament must," Knox contended, "endeavour to beget confidence by putting it out of its own power to deceive. The line by which the exercise of its authority in point of taxation over the Colonies is to be limited, must be clearly drawn and defined in an act of Parliament, and the conditions to which the Colonies are to submit fully expressed."[11] The question was where to draw the line.

One proposed line was that the colonists be guaranteed that they would not be taxed differently than their fellow British subjects. "The true and only constitutional principle upon which the Parliament of Great Britain can tax the people of America," one writer argued, "is to tax them in common with the people of England, where the nature of the tax will permit." This could be accomplished if the British legislature, in a statute, were "to grant the Americans a salutary secure Barrier . . . to effectually and for ever prevent them from being SEPARATELY taxed by Parliament, or otherwise, than in . . . the same Mode, and in the same Proposition, wherein the British subjects residing in Britain are also taxed." The difficulty with this scheme was that it conceded parliamentary supremacy, the very doctrine it was intended to eliminate. The colonies would have been asking Parliament to restrain itself, a tacit acknowledgment of parliamentary sovereignty. "Whatever the terms we may give them," Knox said of the Americans, "they can have no security for our adherence, but our own good faith. . . . They cannot, indeed, compel us to the performance of *any* terms when they have once submitted, but they may justly think, that to whatever terms the public faith shall be solemnly pledged in an act of Parliament . . . the honour and probity of the English nation will compel an adherence on the part of Government."[12]

Knox believed that Americans could depend on parliamentary good faith because it was in Britain's "interest" to adhere to the statutory pledge of no separate taxation. A second scheme to avoid separate American taxes also utilized the eighteenth-century doctrine of legal protection through interlocking constitutional "interests." It was the proposal to "let all future taxes be extended through the colonies,"[13] to

> let all our taxation laws, become general laws, and affect every part of the community alike; so that no tax may be paid, by our distant provinces, but what we shall be obliged to pay, in the same manner, and proportion, at home.
>
> By this equitable rule, no man, in the British Empire, can apprehend any injury, from any partial distribution of taxes; and every man . . . will have the satisfaction to know, that he pays no more than every other man, in the like circumstances, at home.[14]

Two aspects of this plan were specifically designed to meet American constitutional objections. One was that imperial taxation would be "an equal tax," "affecting the whole community alike." The second was the interlocking of "interests," "for we cannot take care of our own interest, withont [sic] taking the same care of theirs. Neither can we hurt them, without hurting ourselves; our interests, and welfare being mutual." In other words, American security would have rested on the same constitutional base as did the doctrine of virtual representation in Great Britain, for interlocking interests provided "the constitutional security that every man in England, receives, at present who is not an elector." The argument came directly from the virtual-representation doctrine and colonial whigs could no more accept it than they could accept virtual representation, and for the same reason: American and British interests were not similar. An act of Parliament would not operate in Boston as it did in Yorkshire, nor would Americans enjoy the security that came from sharing interests with members of Parliament — the assurance that abuses would be corrected because the consequence of abuse was felt equally by elected representatives, electors, and nonelectors.[15]

Some of those who worked to solve the revolutionary controversy sought a plan permitting Parliament both to tax the colonies and to disburse the revenue, even though acknowledging that American and British interests were different. As a result, they had to devise additional constitutional safeguards protecting the colonies' diverse interests. Some of these proposals were wildly farfetched. One attempted to provide "the Colonists a proper allowance for the superior commercial privileges of the mother-country" by working out a proportional share of taxation. "Supposing, for instance, that the privileges of British subjects are four times greater than the privileges of American subjects, the taxes of the American subjects might be four times lighter than ours." A somewhat sounder but no less constitutionally flawed alternative was suggested by the General Assembly of Nova Scotia. Acknowledging London's right to a "tax to be raised in the colonies, and which shall be at the disposal of the British parliament," the Nova Scotians thought whig apprehensions would be overcome if the tax were "of such a nature as should not depreciate, but should increase in the same ratio with the affluence of the inhabitants of this province."

> [T]he fittest tax for this purpose would be a duty of so much per cent. upon all commodities imported into this province, not being the produce of the British dominions in Europe and America. . . . This tax will include almost all the luxuries made use of, and will increase in an equal ratio with the affluence of the inhabitants; and if the rates of the several articles are fixed every ten years, for the future and subsequent ten years, it will not be liable to depreciate in value by the increase of the metals of gold and silver.[16]

The principle that the Nova Scotians sought to make constitutional might be called "equitable proportion." There were various ways in which it could have been implemented. The Nova Scotia Assembly would have limited proportional taxes to import duties on goods not manufactured in Great Britain. It would have been difficult, if not impossible, to agree on amounts because the formulation depended on relative factors, not on any absolute ratio between Americans and British based on a certain figure.[17] One writer suggested that the proportion be related to "the sum-total of whatever money we yearly raise at home among ourselves.— From this principle, it will undeniably follow, that the Americans can never be taxed for any thing, but what we shall first have taxed ourselves." In other words, the standard for setting the proportion would be the amount of taxes raised in Great Britain, the equation based on the British land tax.

> A certain proportion should have been fixed, so that when Great Britain raised any given sum by a land-tax, the colonies should raise each a proportionate sum: the mode of levying this tax to be left entirely to the provincial legislatures; the appropriation of it left to parliament.
>
> By this mode the same relation would have been created between the house of commons, and the colonies, as between the house of commons and the inhabitants of Great Britain. The house of commons could not tax *them* any more than they can *us*, without at the same time taxing themselves.[18]

It was thought that the rate could be proportioned to "the just value of the Lands, if possessed by the Proprietors," or on "the real value of the rents of the houses and land." The tax would have been *"upon all the lands possessed by British subjects in America, ad valorem of their rents, to be for ever rated by the imposition of the land-tax in Great-Britain; so that the same act which imposes the one, should impose the other, always in the same degree."* The tax would be fair because rents differed from place to place, and by measuring value in terms of rent an equitable ratio based on economic worth could be maintained.[19]

John Wilkes seems to have been America's most influential British supporter to see some merit in the solution of using the land tax to prorate colonial taxes. "The proportion of each Colony," he thought, "might be settled according to the Land Tax in England, at one, two, or more shillings in the pound." But unlike the other writers whose proposals have been quoted, Wilkes did not think the land-tax ratio a constitutional solution to the taxation dilemma. "I insist," he also said, "not a shilling should be taken without their consent." That was the rub. No matter how fair and equal the proportion might be, it did not convert unconstitutional taxation without consent into taxation by consent. One reviewer inadvertently conceded that fact when praising the equity of proportionate taxation. "If this contribution were to be regulated by the land-tax, parliament could not tax the colonies without taxing its own constituents, and they might be considered as virtually represented." That notion could hardly have appealed to American whigs who long ago had rejected the constitutionality of taxation by virtual representation.[20]

All of these proposals were ultimately flawed because they did not resolve the issue of Parliament's right to tax the colonies. The authors of these plans surely knew that the colonies were objecting not to taxation but to taxation without consent. As these proposals failed to resolve that issue, they may have been put forward more as political compromises than as constitutional solutions — not to settle the question but to avoid its constitutional implications. The hope most likely was that if a formula could be found that proscribed separate taxation and shared the burden in a fair and equal manner, American whigs would accept it for the sake of peace. Perhaps they would have, had the dispute been economic or political rather than constitutional. All of these plans would have had them pay but a small fraction of imperial defense and would have been far less costly than a war for independence. But the constitutional principle stood in the way. That fact was appreciated even by casual observers of the revolutionary controversy on both sides of the Atlantic. As early as 1769, a book reviewer for a London political journal analyzed a plan that attempted to guarantee equality for American taxpayers by proportioning forever their rates to the British land tax. The scheme might have had possibilities, the reviewer thought. "But we are not set right as to this means being constitutional, or likely to put an end to the disputes with the colonies. If therefore the Americans should not view our author's scheme of a tax on their lands in a constitutional light, I see no prospect of adjusting our differences on this plan."[21]

THE CUSTOMARY SOLUTION

One proposal for resolving the prerevolutionary crisis over parliamentary taxation did not have to be defended either as new or workable. It was believed to have been part of the customary imperial constitution, acceptable to American whigs and sanctioned by past British governments. Described by South Carolina's legislature as the "Constitutional Way" and by a member of Parliament as "the old-accustomed and safe way," it provided that London could raise money from the colonies by requesting grants or, as the New Jersey Assembly put it, by "the constitutional Requisitions of the Crown."[22] Endorsed by almost every colonial legislative body opposing the Stamp Act, it was frequently depicted as a constitutional pledge of good faith, or, in the words of Pennsylvania's House, as a constitutional duty American assemblies could be depended upon to perform.

> That whenever his Majesty's Service shall, for the future, require the Aids of the Inhabitants of this Province, and they shall be called upon for that Purpose in a constitutional Way, it will be their indispensable Duty most chearfully and liberally to grant to his Majesty their Proportion of Men and Money for the Defence, Security, and other public Services of the *British American* Colonies.[23]

It is quite possible that this pledge was sincerely meant. "I had it in instruction from the assembly," Pennsylvania's agent told the House of Commons a few months later, "to assure the ministry, that as they always had done, so they should always think it their duty to grant such aids to the Crown as were suitable to their circumstances and abilities, whenever called upon for the purpose, in the usual constitutional manner."[24]

As a general proposition, the requisitions solution encountered little constitutional opposition. Although George Grenville privately expressed doubts whether requisitions could ever be equally assessed, the only constitutional question raised publicly seems to have been whether they could be enforced. A dispute occurred during the revolutionary years that was more of fact than of law, imperialists saying that the colonies had not honored requisitions in the past, colonial assemblies saying that they not only had but could be counted on to do so in the future. As the revolutionary controversy heated up, the evidence shifted from past to present actions and the argument reached an impasse. To prove that Americans would not honor requisitions, supporters of Parliament's right to tax cited colonial resistance to the military requisitions mandated by the Mutiny Act — demands for money that the British government attempted to associate with requisitions previously paid in wartime, and that American whigs resisted on the theory they were not true requisitions but direct statutory taxation disguised as requisitions.

Following the Tea Party there were moderates in Great Britain still hopeful that requisitions might yet solve the constitutional impasse. The Lord Mayor, Aldermen, and Commons of London petitioned George III to grant the colonies "every opportunity of giving, as Freemen, what they seem resolutely determined to refuse under the injunction of laws made independent of their own consent."[25] Even persons professing to champion the doctrine of parliamentary supremacy urged Great Britain to return to asking for requisitions and to forget direct taxation.[26] British lawyers such as Lord Camden who asserted that Parliament could not constitutionally tax the colonies, as well as American whigs, claimed that this was the only constitutional means of acquiring money from the colonies. A subtle change had occurred, however. Although colonial assemblies continued to claim the privilege of voluntarily and freely granting gifts to the Crown on request and not on demand, the Townshend statutes had made them aware that the money, even if constitutionally raised, might be spent for constitutionally questionable purposes such as paying salaries of local officials. As a result, by 1775 there was substantial support for the argument that the colonies had to have some control over expenditures; they would "continue to grant supplies upon Constitutional requisitions by our Sovereign" but we must judge of the Occasion and quantum of the Aid as well [as the mode] of raising and application of it, and therefore to offer a sum of money without any Object to direct Us as to the Quantum, or any Satisfaction to our Judgements of the necessity of any grant, would be a step in the Dark we do not choose to make, more especially as 'tis to be disposable by Parliament and may be emploid for our distruction, as we think a great deal of the National Treasure has lately been.[27]

REQUISITIONS BY CONSENT

It is possible that the requisition scheme could never have worked successfully. There simply were too many divergent ideas about the constitutional relevancies. At one extreme was the concept of parliamentary sovereignty, incapable of delegation and dilution. At the other was the insistence that America owed the mother country nothing as long as the commercial contract was enforced; only if Great Britain repealed the Acts of Navigation and no longer profited from its monopoly of the trade should the colonies pay requisitions. Even then, Pennsylvania whigs insisted, the sum to be paid should be determined by Americans, not by Parliament.[28]

Few on the British side of the controversy could concede to Americans the power to set as well as to raise the requisition. Even people untroubled by the sovereignty question thought that London had to play a role. Governor Francis Bernard explained why to the representatives from Boston during the Stamp Act crisis.

That If every province was to be left to raise the Money in what manner they pleased, the particular sum expected from each province as their proportion must be first ascertained. That if a stamp Duty was to be imposed by provincial Acts as forming of itself a proportion of charge, The Duties themselves must be first settled, as they ought to be the same in every province; otherwise they will not be a proportional charge. That neither of these things can be done by the provinces themselves, they must be settled by some authority that can mediate between the Provinces and moderate their partialities for themselves.[29]

It was to solve this matter — who would determine the amount and equalize the proportions — that most of the plans supplementing the requisition scheme were directed.

The solution almost universally suggested was an American congress.

There were several plans put forward,[30] but only one received serious attention, mainly because it was sponsored by William Pitt, the earl of Chatham. Pitt was still trying to reconcile his dichotomy dividing taxation from legislation. On the one hand, he sought to "have duly recognized the supreme legislative authority, and superintending power of the parliament of Great-Britain over the colonies"; on the other hand, he wanted Parliament to promulgate the principle "that no tallage, tax, or other charge for his majesty's revenue, shall be commanded or levied, from British freemen in America, without *common consent*, by *act of provincial assembly there*, duly convened for that purpose." The "provincal assembly" in which Pitt would have vested the authority to make the decision was not the colonial legislatures but the Continental Congress then meeting in Philadelphia. The Congress would be authorized by the imperial government to vote "a free grant to the king, his heirs and successors, of a *certain perpetual revenue*, subject to the disposition of the British parliament." The respective colonies, for their part, would empower their representatives in Congress "to adjust and fix the proportions and *quotas* of the several charges to be borne by each province respectively, towards the general contributory supply; and this, in such fair and equitable measure, as may best suit the abilities and due convenience of all."[31]

Chatham's plan gave something to each side. Saving the sovereignty of Parliament to regulate trade, quarter troops, and enact general legislation, the plan surrendered to the colonies as a group the authority to levy taxes. Hence, it is not surprising that it obtained some token support in Parliament and was praised by Virginia's House of Burgesses as a ground on which to conduct negotiations. It had drawbacks, however. For American whigs, the proposal implied more than most dared to concede. Chatham wanted Parliament to empower the Continental Congress to raise taxes, a step Parliament could take only if it possessed the ultimate authority to tax. Should Parliament ever change its mind, there was no constitutional way it could be prevented from repealing Chatham's bill and then citing America's acquiescence of it as authority of Parliament's power to tax. Moreover, Chatham did not contemplate giving Congress discretion to pass on the merits of the requisitions; although the Congress would be empowered to determine the mode of collection, it would not be authorized to determine the amount of the tax or the purpose for which it would be raised, leaving the colonies still subject to a form of parliamentary taxation.

From the imperial perspective, Chatham gave away too much. Even some of those who agreed that the Americans should be permitted to tax themselves objected to putting control into a congress elected by the colonial assemblies. Better for Great Britain to grant the appearance of representation and consent but to keep the substance of control by appointing all or part of the congress.[32] Another objection was that an American congress just would not work. When William Knox was formulating a proposal for a continental assembly to receive requisitions from London and parcel the burden among the colonies, George Grenville told him that he would not even consider the idea. "[I]t will be extremely difficult, if not impracticable, for the Colonies to apportion a certain sum by a convention of deputies from each Colony," Grenville protested. "They would, therefore, never do it, and the convention of deputies would quarrel, which would probably be attended with very bad consequences, both to themselves and to us, besides the novelty of such an assembly." And, of course, the same constitutional question raised about every plan was raised to this one: how would it be enforced? It was widely assumed that left to themselves Americans would contribute nothing to the imperial treasury. They had to be compelled and only Parliament possessed the constitutional authority to compel them.[33]

CHAPTER TWENTY-TWO

THE ADMINISTRATION'S SOLUTION

From the American constitutional perspective, the solution of requisitions demanded by and paid to the Crown was supported—even demanded—by the logic of constitutional tradition. First, it avoided the implications of parliamentary taxation by giving Parliament no immediate role to perform. Requisitions that came from Parliament, after all, were not much different from direct parliamentary taxation, especially if the colonies were expected to pay and the expectation could be enforced. Second, royal requisitions, in theory, put the colonial assemblies on a constitutional parity with Parliament. They did so because taxes raised by Parliament in the mother country were not in constitutional theory a taking of the people's property for public purposes, but free gifts granted to the Crown in response to requests that were not much different from requisitions. In that one theoretical respect, therefore, Crown requisitions would have made the assemblies equal to Parliament in their constitutional relationship to the king. Finally, there was constitutional precedent in American history for Crown requisitions. Because requisitions in the past had always been made in the name of the king and not of Parliament, royal requisitions were more constitutionally defensible than were parliamentary requisitions. The difference was custom. Royal requisitions could be justified as a formalization of customary procedure.

Parliamentary requisitions could not, for they, in constitutional parlance, would have been an "innovation."

From the British perspective, opposite constitutional considerations were at work. British constitutional liberty was maintained and defined in parliamentary sovereignty. Royal requisitions threatened that sovereignty and, therefore, British liberty, not because they lessened Parliament's supremacy over the colonies, but because they jeopardized the cornerstone of eighteenth-century British constitutionalism: parliamentary supremacy over the Crown.

Parliament was supreme over the king partly because the Glorious Revolution had made the throne an office subject to Parliament's election and partly because Parliament controlled royal revenue. Contemporary constitutional theory explained the relative impotency of the British Crown almost entirely in terms of Parliament's monopoly of the authority to tax. One of the most influential constitutional treatises of the eighteenth century summed up the legal theory when it stated that

> if we consider the extent of the prerogative of the king of England, and especially the circumstance of his completely uniting in himself all the executive and active powers of the state, we shall find that it is no exaggeration to say, that he has power sufficient to be as arbitrary as the kings of France, were it not for the right of taxation, which, in England, is possessed by the people; and the only constitutional difference between the French and English nations is, that the former can neither confer benefits on their sovereign, nor obstruct his measures; while the latter, how extensive soever the prerogative of their king may be, can deny him the means of exerting it.

The American scheme for royal requisitions threatened to upset this carefully structured balance between monarchy and consent by increasing the influence of the Crown at the expense of Parliament. In 1776, when it was apparent there might be war with the colonies, a writer explained to Scottish readers the constitutional danger posed by the colonial solution.

> The Americans, formerly, declared themselves willing to contribute to the exigencies and expences of the state, provided the demand should come by requisition from the King, and not by an immediate exertion of parliamentary authority. This offer his Majesty declined. . . . Had his Majesty been actuated by those motives of ambition which are not uncommon among princes, he would have eagerly closed with the offers of the Americans. Instead of making himself dependent, for the maintenance of his dignity, upon the grants of one assembly, he might have extricated himself from even the fear

of pecuniary difficulties, by a proper management of many assemblies. The representatives of one province might be gratified into the views of the crown, from the revenue of another; British members might receive the wages of corruption in America; and American represenatives be sent for the price of their votes to this kingdom.[1]

The predicament was constitutional. American whigs, to protect themselves from what they regarded as unconstitutional parliamentary taxation, favored the constitutional alternative of requisitions paid directly to the Crown. Parliament could not accept that alternative as a solution to the revolutionary controversy because its adoption would jeopardize the current balance of government and the basic safeguard of British liberty.[2] The very constitutional premises that drove American whigs to the conclusion that only the king could make requisitions drove British lawyers to the conclusion that Parliament had to make them. Lord North invoked those constitutional premises when he told the House of Commons that "royal requisitions" were constitutionally objectionable: "he could not see the difference between such a requisition and the demand of Charles I. of ship-money, as it was the same thing, whether we ask for ships, or money to build ships." North was criticizing David Hartley's alternative requisitions plan, but his objections raised something of a red herring; Hartley appreciated the constitutional values at stake and had had no intention of restoring prerogative government. "[I]f," Hartley protested, "royal requisitions be, as it is argued, contrary to the spirit and principles of the Revolution, mine are not intended to be royal requisitions."

> If the power of making requisitions to the colonies, is not in the King; my motion is to give the authority and sanction of Parliament to this measure. It is so far from being my proposition, to enable the crown to raise what supply it can from America, independent of Parliament; that my motion is the very first which has ever had in contemplation, to lay a parliamentary controul upon that power; and to require that all answers from America shall be laid before this House for the very purpose of controuling that power in the crown.[3]

It is not relevant to consider Hartley's scheme. Containing the constitutionally dubious innovation of parliamentary supervision over the expenditure of money theoretically under the control of the Crown, there was no prospect it would have been adopted. What is important is Hartley's defense of the scheme. His words demonstrate that members of Parliament were aware that royal requisitions from the colonies might, in the words of Governor George Johnstone, "throw too much power into the hands of the Crown."[4]

What was needed was a solution that would assuage both the American fear of being deprived of the ancient English right of taxation by consent and the British fear of resurgent prerogativism. Considering the political realities of the day and the difficulties of the constitutional predicament, that solution had to come from the administration making some concessions to colonial apprehensions without strengthening the potentials of prerogativism.

LORD NORTH'S PROPOSAL

When the British cabinet met at the home of the earl of Sandwich on 21 January 1775, those present knew they were faced with a constitutional predicament, not a political problem. Their task was not to formulate some concession on the issue of taxation that could be offered Americans as grounds for reconciliation, but to strike a constitutional balance between two constitutional fears — the colonial fear of parliamentary power and the British fear of royal power. The solution they formulated stood squarely within the established traditions of English and British constitutional pragmatism: it was shrouded in vagueness and made palatable by imprecision. Americans were to be spared forever from parliamentary taxation, yet Parliament's constitutional authority to tax was to be preserved. Because that authority has sometimes been misunderstood, it should be reiterated that it was less the right of Great Britain to tax the colonies than the right of Parliament to originate taxes. Parliament had to reserve to itself the theoretical authority because of the potential power of the Crown, not because anyone still hoped for American revenue. "Agreed," the cabinet voted,

> that an address be proposed to the two Houses of Parliament to declare that if the Colonies shall make sufficient and permanent provision for the support of the civil government and administration of justice and for the defence and protection of the said Colonies, and in time of war contribute extraordinary supplies, in a reasonable proportion to what is raised by Great Britain, we will in that case desist from the exercise of the power of taxation, except for commercial purposes only.

In the meantime, the government was "to take the most effectual methods to enforce due obedience to the laws and authority of the supreme legislature of Great Britain."[5]

A month after the cabinet meeting, Lord North introduced the plan to the House of Commons. North was reported to explain that he was "for preserving the right of parliament to tax the colonies; but for transferring the exercise of that right to the colony assemblies. He was for leaving the colonies at liberty to contribute voluntarily to the alleviating the public burdens; and for reserving to parliament, a right of rejecting or increasing those voluntary aids at pleasure."

The administration's solution to the taxation controversy, the plan with which it hoped to avoid civil war, took the form of a motion introduced by Lord North. "That it is the opinion" of the House of Commons, North moved,

> that when the governor, council, and assembly, or general court, of any of his Majesty's provinces or colonies in America, shall propose to make provision, according to the condition, circumstances, and situation, of such province or colony, for contributing their proportion to the common defence (such proportion to be raised under the authority of the general court, or general assembly, of such province or colony, and disposable by parliament) and shall engage to make provision also for the support of the civil government, and the administration of justice, in such province or colony, it will be proper, if such proposal shall be approved by his Majesty and the two Houses of Parliament, and for so long as such provision shall be made accordingly, to forbear, in respect of such province or colony, to levy any duty, tax, or assessment, or to impose any farther duty, tax, or assessment, except only such duties as it may be expedient to continue to levy or to impose for the regulation of commerce; the nett produce of the duties last mentioned to be carried to the account of such province or colony respectively.

If each colony contributed its administration-determined share of the common defense, Parliament would waive all taxation, even relinquishing revenue collected incidentally to the regulation of trade. "Very often the best method of regulating commerce is by taxation," North explained. "But to remove every objection, that other taxes may be raised upon them under the colour of regulations on commerce, I mean, that the produce of such duties shall be applied to the particular use of that province where they are levied."[6]

The resolution is best understood by keeping the constitutional predicament in mind. Vague wording intentionally accommodated several interpretations. It seemed to contemporaries that it was as reasonable to claim that the resolution "gave up the important right of taxation" as it was to assert that "no power of taxing was actually retained by the British Legislature, but the laying of duties, for the regulation of Commerce" or to say, as Lord North did in a letter to the king, that the proposal "gives up no right." North told the Commons that they were voting for "the suspension of the exercise of our right." With uncharacteristic exaggeration, he even claimed that the plan was not vague.[7] "This resolution," North contended, "marks the ground on which negociation may take place. It is explicit, and defines the terms, and specifies the persons from whom the proposals must come, and to whom they must be made. It points out the end and purpose for which the contributions are to be given, and the persons from whom the grant of them is to originate."[8]

No matter what the prime minister might claim, the administration's proposal was vague, vague enough that when pressed to defend it, North was so reluctant to state what contributions he expected from the colonies that the reported version of his speech could have been read by American whigs as giving up the right to tax in principle as well as in fact.

> [H]e did not nor could, at present, pretend to specify the exact sum they ought to raise, as it would probably fluctuate by bearing a certain proportion to the sums raised in Great Britain. . . . In answer to the honourable gentleman, who asked whether the grant was to be an annual one, or for a term of years, he replied, he could not tell; but for his part he should wish it to be the latter, otherwise it would return to interrupt the public business every session, and consequently, be a perpetual subject of discussion and disagreement.

It would seem that North anticipated that the question would not be pressed in the future, no matter how the colonies might choose to honor requisitions. The governors of the colonies who told Americans that "[n]o specific Sum is demanded of you," that the amount was left to the "judgment" of local assemblies, were offering a reasonable interpretation of the plan.[9]

North may have been asking the Commons to overlook the reality that they were giving up all expectation of colonial taxation, perhaps even surrendering a part of Parliament's sovereignty. He was also asking American whigs to overlook the fact that Parliament was insisting on the theoretical right even if it was to remain constitutionally dormant. One colonial governor, New Jersey's William Franklin, realized that for American whigs the crucial aspect of the proposal was not whether revenue would be expected or how much, but rather Parliament's reservation of the right. He attempted to deemphasize its significance by arguing that although Parliament made the claim the colonies did not have to acknowledge it.

> It does not require from the People of this Country any formal Acknowledgment of the Right of Taxation in the Parliament. It waves all Dispute on that Head, and suspends the Exercise of it for ever, if so long the Colonists shall perform their Part of the Compact.

Franklin correctly pointed to what could have been the most sensitive constitutional issue. Had the colonists been required to acknowledge the right before Parliament pledged not to exercise it, the proposal would have been rejected at the start. The governor was wrong, however, to suggest that Lord North was not seeking at least an implied acknowledgment. North's plan went only so far, transferring the exercise of the right to colonial assemblies by permitting Americans to raise their proportions through local consent. But exercise of the right was not the right itself. By reserving to Parliament the decision whether to reject or increase the proportions offered, North was retaining in Parliament the right in practice as well as in theory. From a constitutional if not from a political perspective he was eliciting from the assemblies tacit recognition that ultimate sovereignty was vested in Parliament. "[W]hatever proportions they might make," North explained, referring to the colonies, "would be received in a legal way, from assemblies lawfully and properly constituted, in order to be laid before Parliament for their final apportion." This, to him, was "the legal way" because sanctioned by Parliament. Governor William Franklin recognized the implications and attempted to minimize them partly on grounds of necessity and partly by suggesting that Parliament's role was now more judicial than legislative.

> His Majesty and Parliament, 'tis true, are to judge whether the Aids which each Colony may offer are worth Acceptance, or adequate to their respective Abilities. . . . The Necessity of some such Supreme Judge is evident from the very Nature of the Case, as otherwise some Colonies might not contribute their due Proportion.[10]

THE PLAN SUPPORTED

When Governor William Franklin presented Lord North's plan to the New Jersey legislature, he complained that "a great Variety of Interpretations [had been] put upon it, mostly according to the different Views and Dispositions by which Men are actuated, and scarcely any having seen it in it's proper Light." It was the duty of Franklin and his fellow governors to explain the plan in "it's proper light," as it was their task to persuade the American legislatures to adopt the plan. John Penn of Pennsylvania was the first to make the attempt. Addressing the Assembly, he described the resolution of the Commons as "a Solemn Declaration" exempting the colonies from parliamentary taxation for purposes of revenue; by codifying "the Terms on which they think it just and reasonable a final Accommodation should be grounded," it removed "the Causes which have given rise to the discontents and Complaints of His

Majesty's Subjects in the Colonies." In Virginia, Lord Dunmore urged the Burgesses "to seize this opportunity . . . of establishing the freedom of your Country upon a fixed and known foundation, and of uniting yourselves with your fellow subjects of *Great Britain* in one common bond of interest, and mutual assistance."[11]

The governors wrote these speeches themselves. Their words were not prepared for them by an undersecretary in London. They were, however, guided by instructions from Lord Dartmouth. Aside from what was said in parliamentary debate, Dartmouth's explanation of North's proposal was the closest that eighteenth-century imperial government came to producing an authorized interpretation. Dartmouth's optimism was almost incredible. North's plan, he told the colonial governors, complied "with every just and reasonable wish of the King's subjects in America."

> The resolution neither points out what the civil establishment should be nor demands any specific sum in aid of the public burthens. In both these respects it leaves full scope for that justice and liberality which may be expected from colonies that, under all their prejudices, have never been wanting in expressions of an affectionate attachment to the mother country and a zealous regard for the general welfare of the British empire. . . . By such a mode of contribution the colonies will have full security that they can never be required to tax themselves without Parliament's taxing the subjects of this kingdom in a far greater proportion, and there can be no doubt that any proposition of this nature made by any of the colonies and accompanied with such a state of their faculties and abilities as may evince the equity of the proposal will be received with every possible indulgence, provided it be at the same time unaccompanied with any declarations and unmixed with any claims which will make it impossible for the King consistent with his own dignity, or for Parliament consistent with their constitutional rights, to receive it.

Dartmouth stressed three aspects of the administration's plan, two of which the governors emphasized in their messages to the colonial legislatures. The first was that the Parliament was offering security from taxation. It was doing so, of course, only to the extent that future parliaments felt bound to honor the commitment not to tax. Governor Penn appreciated that limitation. "I will not do you so much Injustice," he told his Assembly, "as to suppose you can desire a better Security for the inviolable performance of this Engagement, than the Resolve itself, and His Majesty's Approbation of it, gives you."[12]

Dartmouth's second emphasis was on the British supposition that the colonies would be assured by the plan that each would contribute what

Penn described as a "just proportion"; that, in the words of Lord Dunmore, "according to their Abilities and Situation," the colonies would, as the lieutenant governor of New York said, "make provision by such ways and means, as are best suited to their respective circumstances." Again, there was no assurance that the proportions would be "just" except for the promise of the Parliament and, as Governor Franklin added, the "gracious Assurance" of the king.[13]

Dartmouth's third point was the most significant because he conceded much more of the central constitutional issue than North had in his explanation of the plan to the Commons. The imperial government no longer would insist that Americans acknowledge Parliament's right to tax them, Dartmouth said, if in return the colonies would not deny the right. If not an implied acknowledgment, Dartmouth wanted at least tacit silence. This is what he meant when saying that payment of requisitions must not be accompanied by claims making "it impossible for the King consistent with his own dignity, or for Parliament consistent with their constitutional rights, to receive it." What he did not want was colonies claiming that their payments were free gifts unconnected with parliamentary requisitions. That was what had happened when, in providing British troops with supplies as required by the Mutiny Act, some assemblies had passed resolutions making it appear they were not obeying the command of Parliament.[14]

The governors generally avoided mentioning Dartmouth's third point. New Hampshire's John Wentworth was somewhat of an exception. He referred to the matter of right much in Dartmouth's terms, although a bit elliptically, praising Lord North's plan as "consistent with the just Rights and Dignity of the Parent State and the Priviledges of the Colonies."[15]

British Opposition

Lord North might have been less optimistic about the success of his plan had he anticipated the reaction of American loyalists. Thomas Hutchinson described it as "a poor performance" that "dishonours [the] Administration," and complained of the ambiguity of the word "proportion." William Smith, another leading loyalist, supported the plan in the hope that if Parliament renounced the taxing power "Harmony would have instantly been restored." He may, however, have been troubled by North's insistence that the right to tax be maintained even if not exercised, saying it would have been better had the resolutions declared "that the right of approving the Aid afforded, was founded on the Principle, that every Part of the Empire was bound to promote the Common Interest," a claim that would have been less constitutionally irritating to American whigs than parliamentary supremacy.[16]

The first objections raised to North's plan, however, came not from colonists, but from the British opposition. Some of these were of course political: it was charged that the administration's resolutions were "a mere pretext calculated to amuse the public"; and Isaac Barré asserted that North's purpose was to divide and conquer, that the plan "is meant only to propose something specious, which he knows the Americans will refuse; and, therefore, offers to call down tenfold more vengeance on their devoted heads." The chief grounds of criticism, though, were constitutional. General Conway most concisely summed up the legal objection when he argued that the plan was "but the old claim of taxing, dressed in another garb." As was so often the case, the member of Parliament who best stated the opposition's constitutional theory was Edmund Burke. "It is oppressive," Burke said of North's plan, "because it was never the complaint of the Americans that the mode of taxation was not left to themselves; but that neither the amount and *quantum* of the grant, nor the application, was in their free choice." The entire plan, he said, "is delusion from one end to the other."[17]

David Hartley, agreeing with Burke, called North's plan a "compulsory" requisition. "What is this less than raising a revenue by a tax?" he asked. Burke had an answer of sorts: requisitions would be worse than a tax. The Americans, he told the Commons, "complain that they are taxed without their consent; you answer that you will fix the sum at which they shall be taxed. That is you give them the very grievance for the remedy." The same idea occurred to Richard Price. "It will be scarcely believed," he wrote, "that such a proposal could be thought conciliatory. It was only telling them: 'if you will tax yourselves BY OUR ORDER, we will save ourselves the trouble of taxing you'."[18]

Members of the opposition in the House of Commons raised two significant constitutional objections to North's plan. One pertained to the British constitution, the other to the imperial constitution. The first was stated best by Burke. The proposal, he argued, did not solve the constitutional danger posed by royal requisitions to the colonies; although Lord North would have the amount set by Parliament and the request made in Parliament's name, eliminating the role that the king previously had played, the change was one of form only, not of substance. Because of the practicalities of parliamentary operation, the executive branch of government would be making all decisions and determining all expenditures, a result that would be as "fatal in the end to our constitution" as requisitions set by and paid to the Crown alone.[19]

David Hartley stated the objection pertaining to the imperial constitution: because Lord North's plan insisted upon the right to tax the colonies, it changed nothing. The constitution remained the same. Hartley wanted the requisitions to be voluntary, not based on any claim of right. He insisted that, at the very least, even if the right was not renounced, it should not have been asserted. If it was part of the constitution, it was something better left unmentioned. "[M]ake a free requisition; and be contented to keep to yourselves the satisfaction of thinking, that you have something in reserve, in case of non-compliance. Keep that *sub silentio;* at least till you find that it becomes necessary."[20]

AMERICAN REACTION

American whigs might have been satisfied with silence on the matter of right, if what was unsaid was also unenforced. It was precisely because the right was implied that the plan was unacceptable. "Does the noble lord really think," North was asked by a member of the Commons who thought the plan gave up too much to the colonists, "that a people who deny all right of taxation will be satisfied with having the *mode of taxation* left to them?" Determination of the mode, the one authority that Lord North's resolutions conceded to the colonial assemblies, was not enough. In fact, the Continental Congress professed to believe that North's error had been to assume "that there was nothing in dispute between us but the *mode* of levying taxes; and that the parliament having now been so good as to give up this, the colonies are unreasonable if not perfectly satisfied." In truth, there was much more in dispute. As Virginia's House of Burgesses reminded Governor Lord Dunmore, "[I]t is not merely the mode of raising, but the freedom of granting our money for which we have contended."[21]

The Burgesses stated a second reason American whigs could not accept a plan that gave them control only of the mode of collection: the colonial assemblies "alone are the judges of the condition, circumstances and situation of our people, as the Parliament are of theirs." "We cannot consent," New Jersey's legislators explained, "to subject the Property of our Constituents to be taken away for service and Uses, of the Propriety of which we have no right to judge, while to us are only left the Ways and Means of raising the Money." The assemblies insisted that they had to be judges of two matters besides the mode of collection. One was the amount of the tax. As the North Carolina House had told the king in 1768, America's elected representatives "can alone be the proper Judges" of "what sum they are able to pay." Indeed, Lord North's plan was "so indeterminate" that New Jersey's legislators complained they were unable to "form any Judgment" about how extensive that sum might be or whether the people would be in a position to pay it when Parliament made its demand.[22] The second matter requiring their judgment had been stated as early as the Stamp Act crisis by Charles Carroll of Carrollton. Americans could not be taxed unless their assemblies were "constituted Judges of the necessity or even of the expediency of such levies." Ten years later, the Continental Congress applied that rule to Lord North's plan, found that only Parliament was made the judge, and argued:

> [A]s the colonies possess a right of appropriating their gifts, so are they entitled at all times to enquire into their application, to see that they be not wasted among the venal and corrupt for the purpose of undermining the civil rights of the givers, nor yet be diverted to the support of standing armies, inconsistent with their freedom and subversive of their quiet. To propose therefore, as this resolution does, that the monies given by the colonies shall be subject to the disposal of parliament alone, is to propose that they shall relinquish this right of enquiry, and put it in the power of others to render their gifts, ruinous in proportion as they are liberal.[23]

This argument must be seen in its proper context. An objection might be made that it was new, that American whigs were changing their argument, that they previously had not insisted on, in fact had seldom mentioned the right of judging the amount to be raised or its expenditure. The point is correct historically, but not constitutionally. Again, it was not the Americans but the British who introduced novel issues. Although the question of who was to judge had always been implicitly present in the revolutionary debate, Lord North's plan made it explicit. It became an issue because Parliament asserted its authority not only to demand requisitions but to determine the need and set the amount. For Americans, in the words of Edmund Pendleton, "to offer a sum of money without any Object to direct Us as to the Quantum, or any Satisfaction to Our Judgements of the necessity of any grant, would be a Step in the Dark." More precisely, acceptance of these terms would have been a step into the constitutional dark for Americans, as it would have altered the imperial and colonial constitutions by providing Parliament for the first time with the means of obtaining an American revenue.[24]

That last point reiterated the familiar argument of taxation without consent. Lord North's plan attempted to skirt that issue — an attempt that failed as every American assembly able to vote rejected it. Colonial whigs knew that no matter how carefully phrased, Lord North's plan was still taxation without representation and it was principally upon that ground that the proposal was spurned. The statement of the New Jersey House is representative of what was said. At stake, they claimed, was "the Freedom of Granting, as well as the Mode of raising Monies which this House cannot voluntarily part with without betraying the just Rights of the Constitution." The representatives had "always thought and contended that we had a right to dispose of our Property ourselves." North's plan meant "submitting the Disposal of all our Property to others in whom we have no Choice," with the result that "we shall be to all Intents and Purposes as fully and effectually taxed by our Fellow Subjects in *Great-Britain*, where we have not any Representation, as by any of the late Acts of the *British* Parliament, under which we have been aggrieved." North's solution, therefore, was not really a solution because it "seems to require us to raise a Proportion which a Parliament of *Great-Britain* may at any Time think fit to grant."[25]

It is most likely that this was the first issue on which the Continental Congress spoke on behalf of all the colonies. Some assemblies had deferred to the Congress by refusing to consider Lord North's plan; those that did comment said they were only making preliminary remarks, that Congress would speak for them whatever it might decide. For that reason alone the resolutions of the Continental Congress deserve close scrutiny. The first fact that strikes our attention is that they were blunt. The Congress did not hesitate to state that it saw no merit to Lord North's plan: the proposal was "altogether unsatisfactory, because it imports only a suspension of the mode, not a renunciation of the pretended right to tax us." Speaking for all the colonies, the Congress rejected the plan by summing up the objections that had been made against it.

> That the colonies of America are entitled to the sole and exclusive privilege of *giving* and *granting their own money;* that this involves a right of deliberating whether they will make any gift, for what purposes it shall be made, and what shall be its amount; and that it is a high breach of this privilege for any body of men, extraneous to their constitutions, to prescribe the purposes for which money shall be levied on them, to take to themselves the authority of judging of their conditions, circumstances, and situations; and of determining the amount of the contribution to be levied.[26]

Subsequent Proposals

From a historical perspective it might be said that Lord North's plan never had a chance of solving the controversy about Parliament's authority to tax because it was published in Boston newspapers during the very week General Thomas Gage dispatched his troops to the town of Concord. Yet it could not be abandoned. The British government was caught in the constitutional dilemma of having to insist on the right or grant the colonies independence. If the constitutional balance between Parliament and Crown was to be maintained at home, parliamentary supremacy over North America also had to be maintained, even if only in theory. Thus, a year later, in 1776, the plan was revived during Lord Drummond's peace attempt. One item was added to the proposal. The colonies now would tax themselves, making a perpetual grant to the Crown of Great Britain. To establish "a security against the apprehended invasion of property by parliament," Drummond explained, "a formal relinquishment shall be made, on the part of G. Britain, of all future claim to taxation over these her colonies." The colonies could not permit the mother country even this much of theoretical constitutional face-saving. They would not agree "to give away in perpetuum their essential right of judging whether they should give or with[h]old their money, for what purposes they should make the gift, and what should be it's continuance."[27]

The task may have been impossible. As desperately as the British government might search for a solution, the constitutional barrier remained to prevent the last step from being taken. The reality had been illustrated shortly before Lord Drummond's peace proposal was made public when General Conway urged the House of Commons to face political reality and renounce the constitutional right. "Will you give up taxation entirely?" he asked. "One noble lord in the cabinet says, yes; another no. Is this House agreed upon it? If you are, specify it fairly and openly; if not, in God's name, how can Lord Howe treat upon that essential point . . . ?" Lord North replied that "taxation was not to be given up: it was to be enforced: but whether at present, or hereafter, was a point of policy which the [peace] commissioners would learn, by sounding the people upon the spot."[28]

North's answer was deliberately vague, hinting that there could be a political solution despite the constitutional barrier. Lord George Germain, who as secretary of state for the colonies was directing the war effort against the Americans, knew better. Disagreeing with his prime minister, Germain warned the Commons that the constitutional barrier might be impregnable. "The act of parliament does not give up the sovereignty of the supreme legislature," he pointed out. "The legislature itself cannot give up the right of taxation. No instruction can authorise any one ever to treat about these subjects; and unless we give up all these, a revenue must be had from America, as from a part in common with the whole."[29]

Two years later, Parliament realized that the constitutionally impossible had to be attempted. The two houses enacted and George III signed into law a statute declaring "that the King and Parliament of *Great Britain* will not impose any Duty, Tax, or Assessment, for the Purpose of raising a Revenue in any of the Colonies, Provinces, or Plantations." For American loyalists, this statute resolved all constitutional questions. "The King and Parliament of Great Britain," Georgia's royalist assembly voted, "having by Law relinquished the Claim of Taxation over America, ought to remove every discontent and doubt of the most bigoted Zealots for American Independency; and establish confidence in the Breast of every Individual." As a practical matter the argument had substance. Surely Americans could rely on the political certainty that Parliament would never again attempt to tax them. In terms of constitutional law, however, nothing had changed. Parliament not only lacked the constitutional authority to renounce the right, the very act of renunciation was an assertion of the right. "[A] declaration not to impose taxation on America," it was pointed out by a protest in the House of Lords, "is, in the very suspension of the exercise, a confirmation of the right: for, without the right, the declaration is void; whereas America denies the right, and upon that ground resists the exercise. If the right, then, be reserved, the object of resistance remains." As a matter of political expediency the statute of 1778 could have solved the taxation controversy by ignoring the constitutional barrier. As a matter of constitutional law the statute was meaningless.[30]

CHAPTER TWENTY-THREE

THE BRITISH PERSPECTIVE

The predicament Lord North had to solve with his plan to end the taxation controversy was constitutional. He no longer had to be concerned with members of Parliament who wanted to obtain revenue from the Americans. That hope was no longer seriously entertained. The people about whom he had to be concerned were those who, fearful of resurgent monarchy, insisted that parliamentary sovereignty must not be diluted by the slightest iota. Even after North learned that the colonies had rejected his plan and it was apparent he would have to make further concessions, he assured the House of Commons that he would go no further than suspending the right of taxation; he would not renounce it.[1]

The constitutional barrier that kept North from offering the colonies greater concessions consisted of more than the demand that the right be retained even if only in theory. There was also an extreme faction in and out of the British government that would not give even that much, that insisted that the reality of revenue did not matter, that the right to tax had to be exercised, not suspended, even if no income were obtained. These people, claiming there was no middle ground between American independence and parliamentary exercise of the right to tax the colonies, may have been the first on either side of the Atlantic to realize that the constitutional predicament could not be compromised. "[T]he colonies would be quite *emancipated*," it was said with more constitutional than political logic, "*if neither the* MODE *of raising taxes nor the* QUANTUM is to be left in the power of Parliament."[2]

Largely to reassure those who saw the constitutional predicament in such absolute terms, North insisted that his plan to suspend the exercise of the power was more a matter of form than of substance; sovereignty and parliamentary supremacy would remain unimpaired. One reason for including requisitions in his proposal was not to obtain revenue but to maintain the sovereign power. "[I]f the dispute in which the Americans have engaged goes to the whole of our authority, we can enter into no negociation, we can meet no compromise," North explained. "If it be only as to the suspension of the exercise of our right, or as to the mode of laying and raising taxes for a contribution towards the common defence, I think it would be just, it would be wise to meet any fair proposition, which may come in an authentic way from any province or colony."[3]

To avoid the constitutional barrier, the prime minister, walking an intellectual tightrope, postulated a theoretical concept in defiance of the dominant constitutional theory of the eighteenth century. It was then legal dogma that sovereignty was so absolute a principle that it could not be diluted or compromised without being destroyed. North claimed that his plan could suspend the exercise of sovereign power yet leave sovereignty intact, that he "was for preserving the right of Parliament to tax the Colonies, but for transferring the exercise of that right to the Colony Assemblies." For many members of Parliament, North's sleight of hand was too transparent, he was asking them to accept as theory what was constitutionally impossible. A former attorney general of England had stated the orthodox legal principle during the Stamp Act crisis when he warned that "[Y]ou cannot put a case for the dissolution of Governments by law."[4]

The logic of constitutional sovereignty explains both why Lord North's proposal did not go further and why some constitutional theorists felt it went too far. If sovereignty was the element of government that could not be diminished without being lost, it followed, at least in theory, that sovereign power had to be asserted to be retained. Suspension of power meant its surrender. More than any other consideration, this constitutional logic impelled those members of Parliament who insisted that the right must not only be asserted, as North asserted it, but it must also be exercised. Without exercise it did not exist, for, according to the earl of Suffolk, "[t]he right implied . . . the necessity of the exercise of it."[5]

THE DANGER OF CONCESSION

The constitutional logic impelling a minority of imperialist members of Parliament to insist that the right of taxation had to be exercised or it was no right impelled a much greater number of them, perhaps a majority of the Commons, to prevent outright repeal of the tea tax at a time when repeal might have averted American rebellion. From the imperial constitutional perspective, repeal was seen not as a political concession, but as a surrender of the right. When Rose Fuller, former chief justice of Jamaica, moved repeal of the Tea Act in April 1774, some leaders of Great Britain confronted for the first time the naked question of sovereignty over the North American colonies. "What," Lord Clare asked, "would they have us surrender the right of Great-Britain?" "The proposition which we are now called upon to decide," Charles Cornwall, a barrister, asserted, "is simply this: Whether the whole of our authority over the Americans shall be taken away?" "It is said," General John Burgoyne pointed out, "if you remove this duty, you will remove all grievances in America; but I am apprehensive that it is the right of taxation they contend about, and not the tax; it is the independent state of that country upon the legislature of this, which is contended for." "[T]he Americans are not contending for the mode of taxation, but the right," Lord Beauchamp agreed. "Had this repeal been proposed some sessions ago, I should most probably have adopted it; but the present disturbances in America totally prevent my giving my consent to it. I think it impracticable to repeal it, because we give up our right. . . . I would exert our authority now by a practicable claim of right, which I hope will not hereafter be disputed."[6]

These arguments had been made before, especially when the Stamp Act and the Townshend duties were being repealed, and were of course implicit in the decision by Parliament to retain the tea tax as a symbol of its right to tax. Indeed, the perception did not change from 1766 to 1775. During the first debate on repeal, Lord Halifax asserted "that it is not the Stamp Act that is opposed but the Authority of this Legislature"; during the second, Lord North said that "he was glad he did not, at that time, propose the repeal of that [tea] tax, when all the resolutions of the town-meetings denied the authority of this country."[7] Many members of Parliament drew a constitutional lesson from these repeals. Colonial whigs, they thought, believed that these repeals were constitutional surrenders of the right, a lessening of British supremacy. This perception was error; Americans generally regarded repeal as a return to the constitutional *status quo* as it had existed for a century and a half before passage of the Stamp Act, more the correction of a constitutional mistake than a constitutional surrender. Error or reality, the perception made it politically impossible for Lord North to repeal the Townshend duties without keeping the tea tax as a symbol, or to repeal the Tea Act without asking the colonies to adopt his requisitions proposals.

What has just been said should not be misunderstood. Imperialists did not believe that repeal of the Stamp and Townshend Acts had altered Parliament's constitutional authority to tax. What they feared was that Americans thought so: that repeal, perceived as an indication of political weakness to be exploited, had provided colonial whigs with the argument that the right was given up.[8]

One important consequence of the heightened imperialist perception of the constitutional implications of repeal was that the administration could not again use the excuse that it had used when it repealed the Stamp Act: the excuse of expediency. It will be recalled that the Townshend duties were repealed on grounds that they were anticommercial, not that they were inexpedient, a point supposedly proven by retainment of the levy on tea, a product not of British manufacture. What in the twentieth century looks like an expedient of political form was in the eighteenth century a matter of constitutional substance. The first Continental Congress cited as a grievance the excuse of expediency upon which the Stamp Act had been repealed. The delegates to the Congress were not given to raising minor objections in order to irritate. They thought the grounds upon which a tax was repealed almost as important as the tax itself, as both bore upon the matter of right. So too did the arch defender of imperial constitutionalism, Lord Chief Justice Mansfield. He admitted that the tea tax — in fact, any parliamentary tax on the colonies — might be inexpedient, "but said it was utterly impossible to say a syllable on the matter of expediency, till the right was first as fully asserted on one side, as acknowledged on the other." From the British perspective, therefore, the American refusal to acknowlege the right, not Parliament's assertion of it, had created the constitutional impasse. Colonial whigs had made repeal impossible. Had they conceded Parliament's authority to tax them, the tea tax could have been repealed and the matter of obtaining an American revenue could have been given up. From that perspective, the revolutionary controversy over parliamentary taxation was reduced to a legal abstraction — the abstraction of constitutional right.[9]

THE IMPERIALIST MEAN

The perceived need to defend the abstract legal concept of right led imperialists, even those who can be described as political and constitutional moderates, to insist that Parliament maintain three positions: that Americans not be allowed to claim the right, that Great Britain never concede the right, and that Great Britain declare that it possessed the right.

The first position has been documented in earlier chapters. It was implicit in the refusal of Parliament to receive petitions questioning the Stamp Act's constitutionality and in the advice of colonial agents to assemblies that when they protested against the Townshend duties "the question of right must be kept out of sight."[10] It was more explicit in Lord Dartmouth's warning to the governors that colonial acceptance of North's requisitions plan be "unaccompanied with any declarations, and unmixed with any claims, which will make it impossible for the King, consistent with his own dignity, or for parliament consistent with their constitutional rights, to receive it."[11]

The second position, that Great Britain could not concede the right of taxation, has also been referred to in earlier chapters. It was impelled by the realization that the right could not "be given up, without annihilating the British Constitution in British America." The position was evinced when the ministry reversed its decision to repeal the Townshend duties after receiving colonial petitions "claiming the Sole Right of Taxation." The administration "were then obliged to depart from their Plan or must appear to the World to adopt the Principle of the Colony Claims, which were inadmissible." By 1776, it was evident that this position had the support of a majority of the members of Parliament — a majority willing to risk the possibility of civil war to defend it. "On the point of taxation," Lord George Germain told the Commons in a statement of principle typical of what was being said by members of Parliament, "although he should never concede the right, he should never object to the withholding the exercise of it, if other modes could be adopted. But if we are to have no peace unless we give up the right, the contest is brought to its fair issue."[12]

The third position, that Great Britain had to declare that it had the right to tax the colonies, was evident throughout the entire revolutionary controversy. It was the reason repeal of the stamp tax had been accompanied by the Declaratory Act. "If you repeal the Act," William Dowdeswell explained during the Commons debate, "you will do it more safely after declaring the right." It is also the reason why the tea tax was retained as a "symbol" following repeal of the other Townshend duties and why, even after it was generally realized that Parliament could not tax the colonies, most proposals for ending the controversy contained a symbolic duty designed to maintain the constitutional principle.[13]

THE IMPERIAL EXTREME

A related constitutional position impelled by the same constitutional considerations motivated members of Parliament to demand that the authority to tax the colonies be explicitly declared whenever a tax was repealed. Simply stated, the colonies had to be made to admit the right. It was the most extreme position taken by imperialists during the taxation controversy, derived both from the perceived imperatives of parliamentary supremacy and the fear that the principle upon which taxes were repealed would be mistaken in America. Starkly delineated by Lord North and Lord George Germain when declaring that they would favor repeal of the tea duty "if the Americans humbly applied" for repeal, it was stated in its most rigid form by Robert Nugent, Lord Clare, during the Stamp Act debates. "[T]he HONOR and dignity of the kingdom," he insisted, "obliged us to compel the execution of the Stamp Act, except the right was acknowledged, and the repeal solicited as a favour."[14]

Although this position may not seem extreme in terms of constitutional theory, it was very extreme in practical reality. The American assemblies would never expressly acknowledge Parliament's right, and imperialists knew it. For that reason, by 1775, even Nugent had given up demanding colonial acknowledgment. Nonetheless, the position commanded wide respect as a matter of constitutional theory, and so adds a vital dimension to the explanation of why the British government found it so difficult to resolve the taxation controversy. Indeed, the story is more complicated because the other side was just as adamant. Colonial whigs made compromise almost impossible; not only would they not acknowledge the right, they were constantly on guard against saying anything from which acknowledgment might be implied. This constitutional defensiveness was demonstrated during the campaign to repeal the Townshend duties. The agent for South Carolina reported to his principals that he had agreed to join with agents from other colonies in a petition to Parliament that made no mention of the question of right. "But the Agents of some of the Colonies to the Northward," he complained, "doubting what Constriction [sic] might be put upon it in Great Britain and America, thought it not right to afford any Handle for an undue Construction of Concession or otherwise on our parts, and . . . as the Matter of right was so much an Object with their Constituents, that they would not even apply by Petition to the House of Commons." The agent was told that the agents to "the Northward" had been correct. His principals in South Carolina did not want to be associated with a petition that might imply acknowledgment of Parliament's right to tax the colonies. He was informed that they did not approve of his decision to support the abortive petition that had not mentioned right, and was instructed to join in only those petitions in which the right was "expressly asserted."[15]

It cannot be said that all American whigs insisted on so rigid a position. But as is apparent from the evidence presented in previous chapters, enough did to insure that the British extreme was the colonial mean. Impelled by the same constitutional imperatives that persuaded a few members of Parliament to demand that America acknowledge the right, members of colonial assemblies not only refused to ignore the matter of right, they also insisted that it be asserted. The legal abstraction, expressed by the words "right," "authority," "supremacy," and "sovereignty," both determined the premises of the debate and limited the grounds for resolution.

THE OPPOSITION PERCEPTION

Some participants in the revolutionary debates tried to find a constitutional position between the extremes of imperialist insistence on the right to taxation even when unexercised and militant American whig insistence that the right be denied even when seeking merely repeal of its exercise. Those participants were the parliamentary opposition. They concentrated their criticism not on the futility of pursuing an abstraction but on the futility of exercising it for no other purpose than asserting its existence. "A tax can only be laid for three purposes," Charles James Fox warned the Commons: "the *first* for a commercial regulation; the *second* for a revenue; and the *third* for asserting your right. As to the two first, it has been denied it [the tea tax] is for either; as to the latter, it is only done with a view to irritate and declare war there, which, if you persist, I am clearly of opinion you will effect, or force the Americans into open rebellion."[16]

Everyone knew what Fox meant. The imperialists themselves were divided as to whether taxation for the sake of asserting the right served a constructive constitutional purpose. During the Stamp Act debate, the attorney general had warned against keeping part of the tax as a symbol of the right. "A modification will leave only a shadow of the Bill," he told the Commons, "but that shadow by heightened imagination becomes the substance. Treat the Americans like children, like persons in a dream. Remove the idea which affects their imagination, take away the immediate cause, and the madness ceases at the same instant."[17] The warning was not heeded. The Townshend duties, some people thought, were enacted as a symbol of Parliament's right to tax and the levy on tea certainly was. The tea duty was described by a New York whig committee as "a badge of their [Parliament's] taxative power"; among British opposition figures, it was described by David Hartley as "a quit-rent for the point of honour" and by Burke as "the opprobrium of an empty, absurd, and false recital."[18]

To members of the opposition, the symbol had become too legal. The very people who insisted on keeping up the right, they complained, also asserted that they intended never again to tax the Americans. The question of taxation, one writer asserted after the defeat of Burgoyne at Saratoga, came down to "a mere punctilio, whether the exercise of a right, in itself evidently of little value, should be dropt entirely or be maintained at an enormous expence." Eight years earlier, *Junius* made the same point when he wondered whether the tax on tea had been transmuted from being a symbol of minimal worth to one of actual detriment. He contended that Parliament, by repealing the "most offensive" of the Townshend duties yet keeping the tea tax as a symbol, had "done everything but remove the offence. They have relinquished the revenue, but judiciously taken care to preserve the contention. It is not pretended that the continuance of the tea duty is to produce any direct benefit whatsoever to the mother country. What is it, then, but an odious, unprofitable exertion of a speculative right, and fixing a badge of slavery upon the Americans, without service to their masters?" The tea tax, *Junius* thought, "preserves the contention between the mother-country and the colonies, when every thing worth contending for, is, in reality, given up." The duke of Richmond, one of the lords most consistently in opposition to the administration, agreed that the symbol had too high a cost for so little a return. The American calamity, he charged, was due to the stubbornness of ministers who, "after the idea of taxation had been formally given up by the repeal of various acts of parliament, were obstinately determined to keep up the semblance of taxation, by the obnoxious and pitiful threepenny duty on tea." What was pitiful was not the small amount but that the small amount made the symbol foolhardy. "No man ever doubted," Burke told the Commons, "that the commodity of tea could bear an imposition of threepence. But no commodity will bear threepence, or will bear a penny, when the general feelings of men are irritated, and two millions of people are resolved not to pay." Pennsylvania's Hugh Williamson, thinking this a whiggish argument, developed it in a pamphlet written to persuade British whigs that Americans were not seditious. "You say the tax was trifling," he wrote, ostensibly addressing Lord Mansfield, and that "your chief object was to establish the authority to Parliament.

The Americans have no confidence in such declarations; if the tax was too small for them to resist, it was also too small for you to claim at so great an expence. . . ."[19]

Edmund Burke deserves the last word, not because he spoke for the British opposition — few in Parliament were willing to follow his lead — but because he best decribed the constitutional corner into which the imperialists had painted Great Britain and recognized the limitations of law in solving a controversy that should have been left to the politicians. More than any other spokesman of the day, Burke realized how legal the controversy had become; too legal for solution unless the law of books was separated from the law of affairs. "I am resolved," Burke told the Commons in his famed speech on reconciliation, "to have nothing at all to do with the question of the right of taxation." For too long that question had been left to the lawyers who had theorized themselves into irreconcilable constitutional positions. Others could quarrel whether taxation was an inherent power of government or whether it required the consent of the governed. "These are deep questions, where great names militate against each other, where reason is perplexed, and an appeal to authorities only thickens the confusion. For high and reverend authorities lift up their heads on both sides, and there is no sure footing in the middle." Burke wanted to stand on firmer ground, the ground of practicality and expediency, not on the ground of principle, right, or law. Eschewing formalistic legalism, Burke would have asked about reality and would have governed the Empire by the actual, not the theoretical, by the political, not the constitutional. "[I]f I were sure the colonists had at their leaving this country sealed a regular compact of servitude, that they had solemnly abjured all the rights of citizens, that they had made a vow to renounce all ideas of liberty for them and their posterity to all generations, yet I should hold myself obliged to conform to the temper I found universally prevalent in my own day, and to govern two millions of men, impatient of servitude, on the principles of freedom. I am not determining a point of law; I am restoring tranquillity."

Burke spoke from a tradition of pragmatic politics that has always ruled British government except on those rare occasions when the governors of Britain have decided that they must stand upon a right. They came to that decision in the 1770s and the revolutionary controversy was reduced to a point of constitutional principle too legal to be solved by a political system in which there was no supreme judicial tribunal to render a binding final judgment.[20]

CHAPTER TWENTY-FOUR

THE AMERICAN PERSPECTIVE

The American whig perspective on the constitutional issues was much less complicated than the British perspective; there were fewer differences between extremes and more general agreement on the solution. About the only area of uncertainty concerned the commercial contract. A few spokesmen, among them Arthur Lee, suggested that the colonies should be expected to contribute nothing to the imperial government as long as Great Britain was reaping the benefits of the commercial contract, and that there could be no talk of requisitions until Parliament gave up control of colonial trade. That position, although often expressed, commanded little support. The general American whig attitude was that matters should return to the constitutional status that had existed before the Sugar Act of 1764. Great Britain should continue to exercise total control over the trade of the Empire; the colonies should be free of all parliamentary taxation and asked only to honor traditional military requisitions submitted in the name of the king.[1]

A collateral principle was also sometimes stated: that revenue levied incidentally to the regulation of trade should be paid (as Lord North had proposed as part of his plan to resolve the taxation controversy) not into the imperial treasury but to the colony in which it was raised. This constitutional formula — acceptance of British taxation of trade for purposes

of regulation with the requirement that the revenue be kept in America —
was officially offered as a solution to the prerevolutionary controversy by
the New York Assembly less than a month before the Battle of Lexington.[2]

On one constitutional strategy all colonial assemblies agreed. It was
that they had to assert their right to be taxed only by consent. It was
noted in the last chapter that some agents had hoped to submit to Parliament petitions that did not mention the issue of right and that their principals had instructed them not to do so. The point must now be made
that American assemblies went further than merely refusing to ask for
relief without relying on the right of being taxed only by consent. Throughout the revolutionary controversy they refused to keep their claim to the
right under cover; they would not even state it cautiously or by implication, but required instead that it be asserted expressly and without reservation. During the early stages of the Stamp Act crisis, for example, one
of Connecticut's representatives in London reported that other colonial
agents hoped to avoid mentioning the doctrine of right. Their reason,
he explained, was "that the matter of the Parliaments right to tax us was
a thing so thoroughly Determined that there was no hopes of Relief."
The representative, by contrast, wanted the constitutional principle stated
and was supported by the Assembly. "[W]e can by no means," another
Connecticut agent was instructed, "be content that you should give up
the matter of right, but must beg you would on all proper occasions
claim and firmly insist upon the exclusive right of the Colonies to tax
themselves, and the priviledge of tryal by jury, and to maintain these
principles in the most effectual manner possible, as what we can never
recede from." For political reasons, the Connecticut legislators made
one concession. They allowed the agent to mention inexpediency when
pleading the right. "The arguments from inconvenience and the fatal
consequences," he was told, "which must flow from this exercise of parliamentary power, are obvious, and will no doubt be also fully insisted
upon by you."[3]

During the Townshend dispute, some colonial assemblies hesitated even
mentioning inexpediency or inconvenience lest the constitutional argument be misconstrued and their stand on right weakened. "You will perceive," a Pennsylvania committee explained, sending three petitions to
the colony's agent to be presented to the king, Lords, and Commons, "that
the Reasons, offered to induce a Repeal [of the Townshend duties], are
very much confined to the Right of the Colony in being exempted from
Parliamentary Taxation; — little is said on the Inexpediency of the Regulation adopted by the Act, lest seeming to rely on the latter should weaken
the Arguments in Support of the former." For the same reasons, some
Americans felt it would be unsafe to express any gratitude for repeal. As

Parliament had not possessed the right to enact the tax of which they had complained, repeal of that tax corrected a constitutional wrong; it did not bestow a favor.[4]

THE AMERICAN RIGHT

At this stage of our discussion, it may be superfluous to define the right that Americans asserted and Parliament resisted. For purpose of summary, however, it would be useful to recall that the American claim of right was divided into three parts. Colonial whigs asserted (1) a right to what the New York House of Representatives called "that great Badge of English Liberty, of being taxed only with our own Consent," that is, as the inhabitants of Boston voted; (2) a right of not being taxed "without our consent, by an authority in the constitution of which we have no share, and over which we have no kind of influence or controul;" and (3) a right also, in the words of the North Carolina House of Assembly, not to be taxed without consent "for the sole and express purpose of raising a Revenue."[5]

Two subsidiaries of the right help to explain how Americans perceived it: the ancient English doctrine that property had to be absolutely secured or it was not, in any real sense, property and the consideration, introduced by the preamble of the Townshend duties, of the purpose for which the revenue was to be expended.

The first subsidiary was summed up by the Briton Joseph Priestley when he contended that for his fellow citizens, through their elected representatives, to have the theoretical right of taxing Americans was "to establish a *principle*, which will at once give us all the property they have." "It is not," William Samuel Johnson said of the Townshend tax, "the amount of the duties . . . that is the chief ground of the dispute, but the nature and purpose of them. The principle on which they are founded, alone, is worth contesting. A tax of a penny is equally a tax as one of a pound; if they have a constitutional right to impose the first, they may the last; and if they continue the one, with the acquiescence of the Colonies . . . upon the ground of that precedent once admitted and established, they will impose the other also."[6]

It would be wrong to think this argument too extreme to have been seriously argued. It came directly from seventeenth-century English constitutional theory, was central to the definition of property as understood by eighteenth-century lawyers as well as nonlawyers, and was part and parcel of the cultural education of eighteenth-century British subjects. Moreover, with the example of Ireland in front of them, Americans could not have thought the argument farfetched. The property—or what was left of it—of the Catholic natives of Ireland was held at the will and pleasure of the British Parliament.

This shared, taught way of defining "property" explains much of the rhetoric of American whigs. It gave substance to their talk of liberty and enabled them to say without hypocrisy that the revolutionary controversy was not about taxes but about constitutional freedom. "It is not property only we contend for," Philadelphia's Charles Thomson insisted. "Our liberty and most essential privileges are struck at."[7]

It is remarkable how firmly American whigs agreed with Thomson's thesis. It was one for which they were prepared to fight. Just as remarkable was the uniformity with which they perceived the constitutional question for which they would fight. Although a few were concerned about the amount of future taxes if the "trifling" tea duty was not resisted, almost everyone drew a distinction between the grievance against the purpose for which American taxes were to be spent and the grievance against the purpose for which they were to be raised. Both were alarming but one clearly was more serious than the other. "[I]f," the inhabitants of Newburyport, Massachusetts, explained, "the money thus unconstitutionally taken from us, was to be expended for our real benefit and advantage, it would still be grievous, as the method of obtaining it is of a dangerous nature and most fatal tendency." Americans did not object on constitutional ground to parliamentary taxes for the purposes of regulating trade, unifying the Empire, or enforcing national policy directed toward a foreign nation; their grievance was against taxation without consent for the purpose of raising revenue. The colonial whig objection may never have been stated more forcefully than by the inhabitants of a New Jersey township two weeks after the Battle of Lexington: "[W]e consider the unnatural civil war, which we are about to be forced into, with anxiety and distress," they resolved, "but . . . we are determined to oppose the novel claim of the Parliament of Great Britain, to raise a revenue in America, and risk every possible consequence rather than submit to it."[8]

CHAPTER TWENTY-FIVE

THE SHARED PERSPECTIVE

There was a third constitutional perspective in addition to the British and American perspectives. It is the perspective that has been the emphasis of this book and might be called the "shared," or "common," or even "Atlantic" perspective. It was a way of looking at government and law from a taught or received cultural heritage. This heritage has almost invariably been depicted as a British political or social culture that the American colonists received from and shared with their mother country. More accurately, it should be recognized as a common English constitutional and legal culture. To sum up the shared perspective in this chapter is to sum up one of the prime intellectual origins of the American Revolution.

The shared constitution was the dominant intellectual fact of the revolutionary controversy. A speaker mentioning "the constitution" might mean the British constitution, the imperial constitution, the colonial constitution, two of them, all three, or only one. Even if three were meant, it would have been understood that all had identical foundations in a single English constitutional culture. The same shared doctrines or principles, although they might be phrased in different legal terminology, were recognized on both sides of the Atlantic. Americans, for example, spoke of the constitutional right of taxation by consent; contemporary

British constitutional treatises expressed the same maxim in terms of restraint upon the Crown. The emphasis was different, but the substance was the same.

An important product of this shared understanding was ease of communication. The earl of Chatham was able to appeal to British constitutional values when he pleaded for American constitutional rights during the January 1775 debate on his motion to recall the British troops garrisoned in Massachusetts Bay. "The Bostonians," he said of the Tea Party, "did not then complain upon a slight, or temporary evil; but on an evil which sapped the very vitals of their constitution, and reduced all the great blessings of life to chance, equivocation, and insecurity." By insisting on the taught, shared principles of the common constitution, Chatham pointed out, "America means only to have safety in property; and personal liberty." The felt need for such safety was so strongly thrust upon eighteenth-century Britons by the common constitutional heritage, Chatham believed, that not only were American whigs compelled to claim it, whigs in the mother country should feel compelled to support them: "The cause of America is allied to every true Whig. They will not bear the enslaving America. Some Whigs may love their fortunes better than their principles; but the body of Whigs will join; they will not enslave America."

Chatham's historical principle was not as well understood as he assumed. Even after the Revolution had begun and people were asking how the fighting could be stopped, many had to be reminded that the constitutional principles claimed by colonial whigs were derived from their own cultural heritage and that the Americans were asking to share rights the English had won in earlier constitutional struggles. The issue of the war, one writer told the British, was whether the right of Americans to share in their common liberty "is annihilated if they are not to have the disposal of their property like Englishmen, and if the supreme legislature of Great Britain is to enact laws for them." That issue could be amicably settled only by invoking the taught, common constitutional culture. "The whole Dispute, about which so much Altercation has passed, resolves itself into this simple Question: — Are the Inhabitants of the Colonies Subjects of this free Kingdom, or are they not? If they are, we have no Right to demand Taxes from them, but by the Consent of their Representatives; if they are not we have no Right to tax them at all."[1]

THE SHARED LANGUAGE AND HISTORY

Part and parcel of the constitutional heritage that the colonists shared with the British was a common constitutional language. Constitutional principles were expressed in formulas that belonged to a taught legal tradition, using language that could have originated on either side of the Atlantic. For purposes of this summary, it is necessary to refer to only one instance, the British tax on cider and perry enacted in 1763. In the colonies the cry against the Stamp Act would be "Liberty, Property, and no Stamps." Two years earlier in Great Britain the cry had been "liberty and property and no excise."[2]

The excise on cider and perry affected only a few arboricultural counties in England and Wales, but it was opposed in all parts of the kingdom, especially in whiggish, urban London. Although some objections were monetary, most were appeals to legal principle. British protests against the cider excise relied on the same constitutional culture that Americans shared and were, in fact, forerunners of colonial protests against the stamp and Townshend taxes. Similar words were employed on both sides of the Atlantic: "hateful," "arbitrary," "power," "oppressive," "unconstitutional," and "preservation of liberty." The lord mayor of London condemned the excise laws as "contrary to the spirit and letter of our free constitution" and the commons of the city called them "[a]n attack upon the liberty of the subject." "The EXCISE," it was contended, "is the most abhorred monster, which ever sprung from arbitrary power;" excise taxes "strike at the fundamentals of our constitution, and have ever been looked upon as most grievous and oppressive."[3]

Opponents of the cider excise not only used the same language as American opponents of the Stamp Act, they also used it to call for similar measures of constitutional resistance.

> Let us then, before it be too late, unite as one man in defence of our liberties; and as *Englishmen*, exert that power of saving ourselves, which (as *Locke* observes) we still retain, and is inherent in us. Let the people of the several counties, in the first place, immediately instruct their *representatives* strictly to attend their *duty* in parliament, and use their utmost efforts to obtain a repeal of this very unconstitutional, and most oppressive act: That they do . . . not consent to any tax for levying money on the people, till this 'Badge of slavery be taken from us,' and we have obtained the full possession of these two great privileges, *Tryals per Pares* and THE FREEDOM OF OUR OWN HOUSES.

Inevitably the two causes became linked. By 1771 the Bill of Rights Society in London, stretching definitions a bit by labeling the tea tax an excise, associated the British struggle against the cider excise with American taxation. The Society drafted a list of pledges for its members to present to candidates for the House of Commons during the next general election. "You shall endeavour," one pledge provided, "to restore to America the essential right of Taxation by Representatives of their own free election; repealing the Acts passed in Violation of that Right, since the Year 1763; and the universal Excise, so notoriously incompatible with every Principle of British Liberty, which has been lately substituted, in the Colonies, for the Laws of Customs."[4]

Finally, it must be obvious that when American whigs stated their case against parliamentary taxation they were appealing to a constitutional history that they claimed as a common heritage with the British. That history was well known throughout contemporary Britain, not only in England but in Scotland and Ireland, A writer for *The Scots Magazine* commenting on *Campbell* v. *Hall*, the lawsuit challenging the constitutionality of taxes levied on the ceded islands by royal decree without consent of Parliament, observed that "a more important cause than this has not been litigated since that of Hampden." A future lord chief baron of the Exchequer Court, arguing on behalf of the party who had refused to pay the tax, made an even more sweeping connection between prerogative taxation of the colonies and English constitutional history. "I take it," he said, "that laying on imposts without consent of parliament was one of the great points on which the Revolution turned; and another revolution much earlier; and Magna Charta, and almost innumerable statutes."[5]

The constitutional doctrine that some taxes could be unconstitutional gave rise to a second legal question: under what circumstances was it lawful to resist unconstitutional taxation? During the late seventeenth and early eighteenth centuries, some commonwealthmen took the question a step further, asking whether there was a constitutional duty to resist such taxation. David Hartley charged that Lord North's administration had forced the colonists to seek answers to those questions, answers they would find in the precedents of the shared constitutional history. "I shall always think that our American fellow subjects have been driven to resistance in their own defence, and in support of those very claims which we ourselves have successfully taken up arms in former times, to rescue us from the violence and tyrannical pretensions of the House of Stuart," Hartley told the Commons. "These rights are the giving and granting freely their own property, and the security of charters. Let us do to them what we have done for ourselves." Hartley's analogy was so much a part of the shared constitutional culture that it needed no elaboration. Nor did the precedent most frequently cited during the revolutionary debate on parliamentary taxation: John Hampden's refusal to pay ship money. Richard Pennant thought the precedent almost controlling: the tea tax, he told the Commons, "changed the nature of their [the colonists'] constitution, and took away the power which had always been held sacred to an Englishman, that of *levying their own money;* that it was similar to raising the *ship-money* in King Charles's time; that those who condemned that measure [ship money] must of course condemn this, the one being as arbitrary and unconstitutional as the other." Even after the fighting had begun, John Wilkes found the connection self-evident. "I call the war with our brethren in America," he said in a widely publicized speech, "an unjust, felonious war, because the primary cause and confessed origin of it is, the attempt to take their money from them without their consent, contrary to the common rights of all mankind, and those great fundamental principles of the English constitution, for which Hampden bled."

William Pitt, although finding the precedents less controlling as authority than persuasive as a lesson, made perhaps the best summary of the historical connection.

> This resistance to your arbitrary system of taxation might have been foreseen: it was obvious from the nature of things, and of mankind; and above all, from the Whiggish spirit flourishing in that country. The spirit which now resists your taxation in America, is the same which formerly opposed loans, benevolences, and ship-money, in England: the same spirit which called all England *on its legs,* and by the Bill of Rights vindicated the English constitution: the same spirit which established the great fundamental essential maxim of your liberties, *that no subject of England shall be taxed but by his own consent.*[6]

CONCLUSION

"The arguments on both sides of this important question on the right of taxation, must by this time be nearly exhausted," a writer remarked in the April 1774 issue of London's *Monthly Review*. He was almost correct. Except for the final pruning of the "right" issue and the determination of the line beyond which neither side would go, everything had been understood. There were observers in Great Britain who, even after the fighting began, ignored the claims made by American whigs and continued to maintain that the only issue in contention was sovereignty. According to this, the simplest yet most fateful British constitutional theory, the colonies and the mother country formed one nation, Empire, or community, and Parliament was supreme within it. Americans, as members of that single political community, were obliged to contribute their fair proportion to the defense of the whole. This constitutional theory was by no means new. It had played a crucial role at the start of the revolutionary controversy when a majority of Parliament had accepted it as constitutional justification for passage of the Stamp Act.

As an attempt to define participation in the national state, the "community" thesis was in part political. To the extent that it rested on a dogmatic concept of sovereignty, it was also constitutional. The argument did not take into account any of the constitutional defenses raised by

American whigs. There was, of course, no need for any one to do so who thought the defenses without legal merit or that there was no constitutional answer to Parliament's claim of absolute sovereign supremacy. As late as 1776, respectable British writers continued to premise the authority to tax the colonies for purposes of revenue on the imperial contract. Adam Smith, in *The Wealth of Nations*, a study of political economy that surveyed imperial trade, insisted that Americans "owed" a debt to Great Britain, and gave no consideration to — in fact did not mention — the commercial contract. Even Lord North, explaining his requisitions compromise to the Commons in 1775, claimed that one of his goals was to enforce the imperial contract. "Our army and navy establishment, we all know, are necessarily increased on their account, and for their protection; they ought therefore to contribute their just proportion to that expence, subject to the disposal of parliament."

It would be wrong to think North inconsistent. American whigs might think so, and claim that his plan impicitly adopted their constitutional argument that they were not to be taxed without consent. North and his parliamentary colleagues disagreed. When they reserved the right of taxation, they had intended to reserve all aspects of the right including the claim of a debt owed. North made that fact clear in the sentence immediately following his assertion that his plan enforced the imperial contract. "I will never," he promised, "depart from the proper exercise of that right, when they refuse to contribute voluntarily; which if they do, I shall think it right to suspend the exercise of our power to tax them, except for the regulation of commerce."[1]

We will never know if North believed his own argument. Despite Parliament's reservation of the right, American whigs may have been correct. One did not have to be a lawyer to make the case that their constitutional arguments had been accepted by the British government. All one had to do was recount the retreats of Parliament: from exercising the right to demanding that the colonial assemblies acknowledge the right, to reserving the right, to suspending the right, and finally, in 1778, to surrendering the right. The dispute was about a legal abstraction and, to the extent that the Revolution was caused by the taxation issue, the war was fought because the surrender came too late. The struggle began with passage of the Stamp Act, but it was the Townshend duties that made fighting inevitable. American whigs learned from the Townshend duties the constitutional lesson that it was not sufficient to demand repeal of parliamentary taxes. They had to insist that the colonial assemblies alone possessed the right of taxation: they had to assert the right to taxation by consent as well as deny Parliament's right. In other words, the lesson of the Townshend duties left colonial whigs no choice but to take a constitutional stand on a principle that lay just beyond the limits at which constitutional settlement was possible. What America was constitutionally compelled to defend, the British could not constitutionally concede. The difference might be a mere abstraction of law, but once stated, civil war was inescapable.

One cannot make too much of the abstraction: it prevented compromise. As noted earlier, many political observers in Great Britain held the mistaken belief that taxation was the only matter in dispute and that had it been settled, there would have been no war. It is true that there were other questions of right, power, authority, and supremacy much more difficult than taxation and even if the taxation issue had been compromised, resolved, or ignored these questions still would have divided the colonies from the mother country. But the taxation issue was not settled and the legal abstraction of sovereign right created a constitutional gulf neither side could bridge with constitutional safety. Because of it, war could not be avoided. To that extent, contemporaries were correct to think of taxation as the " original cause of dispute," "the immediate cause of all our present disputes," or "the sole cause of the present war."[2] It was a matter of perception and what people believed. "[A]ll America," the Massachusetts dissenting clergyman Isaac Backus observed, "are in arms against being taxed where they are not represented." Individuals supporting both sides of the question in Great Britain agreed.[3] No matter where the discussion was carried, it always returned to the principle of "right." If the British opposition "admit that Parliament *has* a Constitutional right to tax the Colonies," an anonymous pamphlet asked in 1778, "how is the rebellion to be defended?" The question had been answered by Baron Rokeby two years earlier. "[T]here is no crime of rebellion in America, if there is no right of taxation in Great-Britain."[4]

People knew that the fight was about a right, even those who wished it were not. New York–born Henry Cruger and Charles Manners, marquis of Granby and future duke of Rutland, both believed the dispute too legal and pleaded in vain to the Commons to ignore law and consider practicalities. "Will the bare acknowledgment of a right in Parliament to tax them," Cruger asked, "compensate for the millions expended, the dangers incurred, the miseries entailed, the destruction of human happiness and life?" Lord Granby was more extreme; he not only would have ignored the right, he would have renounced it. "From the fullest conviction," Granby declared, "I disclaim every idea both of policy and right internally to tax America. I disavow the whole system. It is commenced in iniquity; it is pursued with resentment; and it can terminate in nothing but blood."[5]

Cruger and Granby were in the minority. They understood the legal abstraction for which blood would be shed and did not think the constitutional right worth the cost. Most contemporaries thought the price had to be paid, either by Britons in defense of Parliament's authority to tax or by Americans in defense of their right not to be taxed without consent. Colonial loyalists were caught in the middle. Although they would fight for the imperial side, on the issue of taxation most may have been reluctantly supporting a right they felt constitutionally untenable. That was the suggestion of two of the most knowledgeable of Britain's royal governors, who warned London that the administration had entrapped itself by insisting on a right that the other side could never concede. "Oceans of blood may be spilt," New York's William Tryon wrote the earl of Dartmouth, "but in my opinion Americans will never receive Parliamentary taxation. I do not meet with any of the inhabitants who show the smallest inclination to draw the sword in support of that principle, a principle, I apprehend, the extremity of calamity which threatens America will not induce her to accept." William Franklin concurred; there was a principle for which American whigs would fight and which American loyalists would not contest despite constitutional constraints making it constitutionally impossible for Parliament to yield.

> It is true that there are many friends of government still remaining in the several provinces but they are too scattered to venture forming themselves into a body especially as they have no places of strength or security to resort to. Not that I believe there are any of the gentlemen of the country who would draw their swords in support of taxation by Parliament, but there are many who would fight to preserve the supremacy of Parliament in other respects and their connexion with Great Britain, until some constitution should be formed for America consistent with that idea of just and equitable principles.

Franklin misstated the situation. American loyalists were not being asked to "draw their swords in support of taxation by Parliament"; they were being asked to draw their swords for a right Parliament was constitutionally compelled to claim in theory but would never again exercise in practice — a legal principle that the lawyers of Great Britain in 1776 felt they had no choice but to defend, even at the cost of an empire.[6]

Almost forty years after that empire had been lost, Parliament again debated its authority to legislate for the colonies. The bill before the Commons concerned slavery in the West Indies, but Joseph Marryatt pointed out that, because of its provisions, it was also a tax measure. That fact had to be taken into consideration, he reminded the House, since in 1778 they had "renounced the right of raising money in any of his Majesty's colonies, without the consent of the assemblies of these colonies." Ed-

ward Protheroe knew that the 1778 statute was constitutionally nuga-
tory, that legislation by one Parliament could not bind a subsequent Parliament. He also realized, however, that the constitutionally valid could
be politically perilous. "[T]he Legislature of the parent country had a
paramount right to legislate for the colonies," Protheroe contended, "but
the exercise of the right ought to be determined by the combined consideration of the importance of the subject, and the possibility of its
being effected." Marryatt knew better. History had taught him that the
mere claim to a right could be as perilous as its exercise. "We ought to
recollect," he warned, "that by persisting in the question of right we lost
America."[7]

ACKNOWLEDGMENTS
SHORT TITLES
NOTES
INDEX

ACKNOWLEDGMENTS

Research for this study was supported by a fellowship grant from the John Simon Guggenheim Memorial Foundation and by a Huntington Library–National Endowment for the Humanities Fellowship. Leave from teaching duties at New York University School of Law was provided by the Filomen D'Agostino Greenberg and Max E. Greenberg Faculty Research Fund at the School of Law and by Norman Redlich, dean of the School of Law. The final version of this work has benefited to an immeasurable extent from the dedicated and professional expertise of Cornelia Dayton. The progress of the manuscript also profited in inexplicable ways from the labyrinthian and incognizant criticisms of an unusual group of legal historians: Norman Cantor, William E. Nelson, and the student members of the New York University School of Law Colloquium in Legal History. Their contributions could easily be exaggerated. More difficult to exaggerate, however, are the invaluable comments of one for whom legal history was once made fun, Hendrick H. Hartog of the University of Wisconsin Law School, and another to whom dedicating a book is fun as well as a duty, Martin Ridge, of the humanities faculty of the California Institute of Technology. A special debt of gratitude is owed to Robert Middlekauff and the marvelous staff of the Huntington Library in San Marino, California. If you can avoid the coyotes, there is no finer institution at which to pursue the elusive study of eighteenth-century Anglo-American constitutionalism. Finally, there is the scholarly contribution of Sharon Elizabeth Reid. It was she who reminded me of Franklin Pierce's important but unpublished paper on the Revolution, in which he revealed that it was a Dover, New Hampshire, physician who coined the slogan, "Pay Tax and Die."

New York University School of Law

SHORT TITLES

In citing works in the notes, short titles have generally been used. Works frequently cited have been identified by the following short titles:

Abingdon, *Thoughts on Burke's Letter*
Willoughby Bertie, earl of Abingdon, *Thoughts on the Letter of Edmund Burke, Esq; to the Sheriffs of Bristol, on the Affairs of America.* 6th ed. Oxford, [1777].

Account of Stamp Act Congress
Authentic Account of the Proceedings of the Congress held at New-York, in MDCCLXV, On the Subject of the American Stamp Act. N.i., 1767.

Acts of the Privy Council
Acts of the Privy Council of England. Colonial Series. Vol. IV. A.D. *1745–1766. Vol. V.* A.D. *1766–1783.* Edited by James Munro. 1911, 1912.

Acts & Resolves
The Acts and Resolves, Public and Private, of the Province of the Massachusetts-Bay. Vol. 1. Boston, 1869.

Adams, *Braintree Instructions*
"Instructions of the Town of Braintree to their Representative", 1765, *Massachusetts Gazette and Boston News-Letter* (10 October 1765): 2–3.

Adams, "Novanglus"
> John Adams, "Novanglus," reprinted in *The American Colonial Crisis: The Daniel Leonard-John Adams Letters to the Press 1774–1775.* Edited by Bernard Mason. New York, 1972, pp. 99–266.

Adams, *Writings*
> *The Writings of Samuel Adams.* Edited by Harry Alonzo Cushing. 4 vols. New York, 1904–8.

Allen, *American Crisis*
> William Allen, *The American Crisis: A Letter, Addressed by Permission to the Earl Gower, Lord President of the Council, &c. &c. &c. On the present alarming Disturbances in the Colonies.* London, 1774.

Allen, *English Political Thought*
> J. W. Allen, *English Political Thought 1603–1660.* Vol. 1. London, 1938.

Allen, *In English Ways*
> David Grayson Allen, *In English Ways: The Movement of Societies and the Transferal of English Local Law and Custom to Massachusetts Bay in the Seventeenth Century.* Chapel Hill, N.C., 1981.

American Archives
> *American Archives, Fourth Series. Containing a Documentary History of the English Colonies in North America From the King's Message to Parliament, of March 7, 1774, to the Declaration of Independence by the United States.* Vols. 1 and 2. Washington, D.C., 1837.

American Gazette
> *The American Gazette. Being a Collection of all the Authentic Addresses, Memorials, Letters, &c. Which relate to the Present Disputes Between Great Britain and her Colonies. Containing also Many Original Papers Never Before Published.* London, 1768.

Ammerman, *Common Cause*
> David Ammerman, *In the Common Cause: American Response to the Coercive Acts of 1774.* Charlottesville, Va., 1974.

Andrews, "Acts of Trade"
> Charles M. Andrews, "The Acts of Trade," in *The Cambridge History of the British Empire: Volume I, The Old Empire From the Beginnings to 1783.* Edited by J. Holland Rose, A. P. Newton, and E. A. Benians. Cambridge, England, 1929, pp. 268–99.

Andrews, "Western Phase"
> Charles M. Andrews, "Anglo-French Commercial Rivalry, 1700–1750: The Western Phase, II." *American Historical Review* 20 (1915): 761–80.

Anecdotes of Pitt
> *Anecdotes of the Life of the Right Hon. William Pitt, Earl of Chatham, and of the Principal Events of his Time.* Two volumes. Dublin, 1792.

Annual Register 1765
  The Annual Register, or a View of the History, Politics, and Literature
  For the Year 1765. 4th ed. London, 1784.

Annual Register 1766
  The Annual Register, or a View of the History, Politics, and Literature,
  For the Year 1766. 3d ed. London, 1802.

Annual Register 1768
  The Annual Register, or a View of the History, Politics, and Literature,
  For the Year 1768. 6th ed. London, 1803.

Anon., America Vindicated
  Anonymous, America Vindicated From the High Charge of Ingratitude
  and Rebellion: With a Plan of Legislation, Proposed to the Consideration
  of Both Houses, For Establishing a Permanent and Solid Foundation, For
  a just constitutional Union, Between Great Britain and her Colonies. Devizes, England, 1774.

Anon., American Resistance Indefensible
  Anonymous, American Resistance Indefensible. A Sermon, Preached on
  Friday, December 13, 1776, Being a Day appointed for a General Fast.
  London, [1776].

Anon., Americanus Examined
  Anon., Americanus Examined, and his Principles Compared with those
  of the Approved Advocates for America, by a Pennsylvanian. Philadelphia,
  1774.

Anon., Answer to Pitt's Speech
  Anonymous, The Answer at Large to Mr. P[i]tt's Speech. London, 1766.

Anon., Answer to Taxation no Tyranny
  Anonymous, An Answer to a Pamphlet, Entitled Taxation no Tyranny. Addressed to the Author, and to Persons in Power. London, 1775.

Anon., Appeal to Reason and Justice
  Anonymous, An Appeal to Reason and Justice in Behalf of the British Con-
  stitution, and the Subjects of the British Empire. In which the present Im-
  portant Contest with the Revolted Colonies is impartially considered, the
  Inconsistency of Modern Patriotism is demonstrated, the Supremacy of
  Parliament is asserted on Revolution Principles, and American Indepen-
  dence is proved to be a manifest Violation of the Rights of British Subjects.
  London, 1778.

Anon., Argument in Defence
  Anonymous, An Argument in Defence of the Exclusive Right Claimed by
  the Colonies to Tax Themselves, with a Review of the Laws of England,
  Relative to Representation and Taxation. To Which is Added, An Account
  of the Rise of the Colonies, and the Manner in which the rights of the sub-

jects within the realm were communicated to those that went to America, with the exercise of those rights from their first settlement to the present time. London, 1774.

Anon., *Arguments in Support of Supremacy*
Anonymous, *A Brief Extract or Summary of Important Arguments Advanced by Some Late Distinguished Writers in Support of the Supremacy of the British Legislature, and their Right to Tax the Americans, Addressed to the Freemen and Liverymen of London, And Recommended to the serious Perusal of every Candid and Dispassionate Man.* London, 1775.

Anon., *Budget Inscribed*
Anonymous, *The Budget. Inscribed to the Man, Who Thinks Himself Minister.* London, 1764.

Anon., *Case of Great Britain*
[Gervase Parker Bushe or George B. Butler,] *Case of Great Britain and America, Addressed to the King, and Both Houses of Parliament.* 3d ed. Boston, [1769].

Anon., *Celebrated Speech*
Anonymous, *The Celebrated Speech of a Celebrated Commoner.* New ed. corrected. London, 1766.

Anon., *Characters*
Anonymous, *Characters. Containing an Impartial Review of the Public Conduct and Abilities of the Most Eminent Personages in the Parliament of Great-Britain: Considered as Statesmen, Senators, and Public Speakers.* London, 1777.

Anon., *Conciliatory Address to People*
Anonymous, *Conciliatory Address to the People of Great Britain and of the Colonies, on the Present Important Crisis.* London, 1775.

Anon., *Conciliatory Bills Considered*
Anonymous, *The Conciliatory Bills Considered.* London, 1778.

Anon., *Considerations upon Rights of Colonists*
Anonymous, *Considerations Upon the Rights of the Colonists to the Privileges of British Subjects, Introduc'd by a brief Review of the Rise and Progress of English Liberty, and concluded with some Remarks upon our present Alarming Situation.* New York, 1766.

Anon., *Considerations on Stamp Act*
Anonymous, *Considerations on the American Stamp Act, and on the Conduct of the Minister Who planned it.* London, 1766.

Anon., *Constitutional Advocate*
Anonymous [Richard Goodenough], *The Constitutional Advocate: By which, From the Evidence of History, and of Records, and from The Principles of the British Government, Every Reader may form his own Judge-*

ment concerning the Justice and Policy of the present War with America. Addressed to the People at Large, And humbly submitted to the Consideration of their Representatives. London, 1776.

Anon., *Constitutional Answer to Wesley*
Anonymous, *A Constitutional Answer to the Rev. Mr. John Wesley's Calm Address to the American Colonies*. London, 1775.

Anon., *Constitutional Considerations*
Anonymous, *Constitutional Considerations on the Power of Parliament to Levy Taxes on the North American Colonies*. London, 1766.

Anon., *Constitutional Criterion*
Anonymous [William Jones], *The Constitutional Criterion: By a Member of the University of Cambridge*. London, 1768.

Anon., *Constitutional Right*
Anonymous, *The Constitutional Right of the Legislature of Great Britain, to Tax the British Colonies in America, Impartially Stated*. London, 1768.

Anon., *Crisis*
Anonymous, *The Crisis. Or, a Full Defence of the Colonies. In which it is incontestibly proven that the British Constitution has been flagrantly violated in the late Stamp Act, and rendered indisputably evident, that the Mother Country cannot lay any arbitrary Tax upon the Americans, without destroying the essence of her own Liberties*. London, 1766.

Anon., *Cursory Remarks on Price*
Anonymous [Jonathan Watson], *Cursory Remarks on Dr. Price's Observations on the Nature of Civil Liberty in a Letter to a Friend*. London, 1776.

Anon., *Dialogue on Constitution*
Anonymous, *A Dialogue on the Principles of the Constitution and Legal Liberty, Compared with Despotism; Applied to the American Question; and the Probable Events of the War, with Observations on some important Law Authorities*. London, 1776.

Anon., *Englands Safety in Laws Supremacy*
Anonymous, *Englands Safety in Laws the Supremacy*. London, 1659.

Anon., *Essays Commercial and Political*
Anonymous, *Essays Commercial and Political, on the Real and Relative Interests of Imperial and Dependent States, Particularly those of Great Britain and Her Dependencies: Displaying the Probable Causes of, and a Mode of Compromising the present Disputes Between this Country and her American Colonies*. Newcastle, England, 1777.

Anon., *Examination of the Legality*
Anonymous, *A Candid Examination of the Legality of the Warrant Issued by the Secretaries of State For Apprehending the Printers, Publishers, &c. of a late Interesting Paper*. London, 1764.

Anon., *Examination of Rights of Colonies*
Anonymous, *An Examination of the Rights of the Colonies, Upon Principles of Law*. London, 1766.

Anon., *Experience preferable to Theory*
Anonymous, *Experience preferable to Theory. An Answer to Dr. Price's Observations on the Nature of Civil Liberty, and the Justice and Policy of the War with America*. London, 1776.

Anon., *General Opposition*
Anonymous, *The General Opposition of the Colonies to the Payment of the Stamp Duty; and the Consequence of Enforcing Obedience by Military Measures; Impartially Considered. Also a Plan for uniting them to this Kingdom, in such a manner as to make their Interest inseparable from ours, for the future. In a Letter to a Member of Parliament*. London, 1766.

Anon., *History of Lord North*
Anonymous, *The History of Lord North's Administration, to the Dissolution of the Thirteenth Parliament of Great-Britain*. London, 1781.

Anon., *Independency the Object*
Anonymous, *Independency the Object of the Congress in America. Or, an Appeal to Facts*. London, 1776.

Anon., *Inquiry into Nature*
Anonymous, *An Inquiry into the Nature and Causes of the Present Disputes Between the British Colonies in America and their Mother-Country; and their reciprocal Claims and just Rights impartially examined, and fairly stated*. London, 1769.

Anon., *Knowledge of Laws*
Anonymous, *An Introduction to the Knowledge of the Laws and Constitution of England*. Dublin, 1764.

Anon., *Letter to Cooper*
Anonymous, *A Letter to the Rev. Dr. Cooper, on the Origin of Civil Government; in Answer to his Sermon, Preached before the University of Oxford, on the Day appointed by Proclamation for a General Fast*. London, 1777.

Anon., *Letter to Ladies*
Anonymous, *A Letter to those Ladies whose Husbands Possess a Seat in either House of Parliament*. London, 1775.

Anon., *Letter to Lord Camden*
Anonymous, *A Letter to the Right Honourable Lord Camden, on the Bill for Restraining the Trade and Fishery of the Four Provinces of New England*. London, 1775.

Anon., *Letter to Mansfield*
Anonymous, *A Letter to the Right Honourable Lord M[ansfield], on the Affairs of America: From a Member of Parliament*. London, 1775.

Anon., *Letter to Member*
Anonymous, *A Letter to a Member of Parliament on the Present Unhappy Dispute between Great-Britain and her Colonies. Wherein the Supremacy of the Former is Asserted and Proved; and the Necessity of Compelling the Latter to Pay Due Obedience to the Sovereign State, is Enforced, upon Principles of Sound Policy, Reason, and Justice.* London, 1774.

Anon., *Licentiousness Unmask'd*
Anonymous, *Licentiousness Unmask'd; or Liberty Explained.* London, n.d.

Anon., *Middle Line*
Anonymous, *The Middle Line: Or, An Attempt to Furnish Some Hints for Ending the Differences Subsisting between Great-Britain and the Colonies.* Philadelphia, 1775.

Anon., *Plain Question*
Anonymous, *The Plain Question Upon the Present Dispute with our American Colonies.* 4th ed. London, 1776.

Anon., *Plain and Seasonable Address*
Anonymous, *A Plain and Seasonable Address to the Freeholders of Great-Britain on the Present Posture of Affairs in America.* London, 1766.

Anon., *Plain State*
Anonymous, *A Plain State of the Argument Between Great-Britain and Her Colonies.* London, 1775.

Anon., *Plan for Conciliating*
Anonymous, *A Plan for Conciliating the Jarring Political Interests of Great Britain and her North American Colonies, and for promoting a general Re-union throughout the Whole British Empire.* London, 1775.

Anon., *Plan to Reconcile*
Anonymous, *A Plan to Reconcile Great Britain & her Colonies, and Preserve the Dependency of America.* London, 1774.

Anon., *Plan of Re-Union*
Anonymous, *Plan of Re-Union Between Great Britain and Her Colonies.* London, 1778.

Anon., *Political Mirror or Summary Review*
Anonymous, *A Political Mirror; or, a Summary Review of the Present Reign. With Notes, Explanatory and Historical, and an Authentic List of the Ships and Vessels of War, Taken and Destroyed, Since the Commencement of Hostilities.* London, 1779.

Anon., *Present State of Constitution*
Anonymous, *The Present State of the British Constitution, Deduced from Facts. By an Old Whig.* London, 1793.

Anon., *Priviledges of Parliament*
Anonymous, *The Priviledges and Practice of Parliaments in England.* Col-

lected out of the Common Lawes of this Land. Seene and allowed by the Learned in the Lawes. Commenced to the High Court of Parliament now Assembled. n.i., 1628.

Anon., *Prospect of Consequences*
Anonymous, *A Prospect of the Consequences of the Present Conduct of Great Britain Towards America.* London, 1776.

Anon., *Reflections on Contest*
Anonymous, *Reflections on the American Contest: In which the Consequence of a Formal Submission, and the Means of a Lasting Reconciliation are pointed out, Communicated by Letter to a Member of Parliament, Some Time Since, and now Addressed to Edmund Burke, Esq. By A. M.* London, 1776.

Anon., *Remarks on Price's Observations*
Anonymous, *Remarks on Dr. Price's Observations on the Nature of Civil Liberty, &c.* London, 1776.

Anon., *Right of British Legislature*
Anonymous, *The Right of the British Legislature to Tax the Colonies Considered, In a Letter to the Right Hon. Frederick Lord North.* London, [1774].

Anon., *Rights of Parliament*
Anonymous, *The Rights of Parliament Vindicated, On Occasion of the late Stamp-Act. In which is exposed the Conduct of the American Colonists. Addressed to all the People of Great Britain.* London, 1766.

Anon., *Short Appeal to People*
Anonymous, *A Short Appeal to the People of Great-Britain; Upon the Unavoidable Necessity of the Present War With our Disaffected Colonies.* 2d ed. London, 1776.

Anon., *Short and Friendly Caution*
Anonymous, *A Short and Friendly Caution to the Good People of England.* London, 1766.

Anon., *Some Candid Suggestions*
Anonymous, *Some Candid Suggestions Towards Accommodation of Differences with America. Offered to Consideration of the Public.* London, 1775.

Anon., *Speech Never Intended*
Anonymous, *Speech Never Intended to be Spoken, In Answer to a Speech Intended to Have Been Spoken on the Bill for Altering the Charter of the Colony of Massachuset's Bay.* London, 1774.

Anon., *Supremacy of Legislature*
Anonymous, *The Supremacy of the British Legislature over Colonies, Candidly Discussed.* London, 1775.

Anon., *"Taxation no Tyranny" Considered*
Anonymous, *The Pamphlet Entitled, "Taxation no Tyranny," Candidly Considered, and It's Arguments, and Pernicious Doctrines, Exposed and Refuted.* London, [1775].

Anon., *Taxation, Tryanny*
Anonymous, *Taxation, Tyranny. Addressed to Samuel Johnson, L.L.D.* London, 1775.

Anon., *Thoughts on Constitution*
Anonymous, *Some Thoughts on the Constitution; Particularly with respect to the Power of making Peace and War: The Use of Prerogative: The Rights of the People, &c.* London, 1748.

Anon., *Three Letters*
Anonymous, *Three Letters to a Member of Parliament, On the Subject of the Present Dispute With Our American Colonies.* London, 1775.

Anon., *To People of Britain in General*
Anonymous, *An Address to the People of Great-Britain in General, the Members of Parliament, and the Leading Gentlemen of Opposition in Particular, on the Present Crisis of American Politics.* Bristol, 1776.

Anon., *To Tax Themselves*
Anonymous, *An Argument in Defence of the Exclusive Right Claimed by the Colonies to Tax Themselves; With A Review of the Laws of England, Relative to Representation and Taxation. To which is Added, an Account of the Rise of the Colonies, and the Manner in which the Rights of the Subjects within the realm were communicated to those that went to America, with the Exercise of those Rights from the First Settlement to the Present Time.* London, 1774.

Anon., *True Constitutional Means*
Anonymous, *The True Constitutional Means For putting an End to the Disputes Between Great-Britain and the American Colonies.* London, 1769.

Anon., *True Interest of Great Britain*
Anonymous, *The True Interest of Great Britain, with Respect to her American Colonies, Stated and Impartially Considered. By a Merchant of London.* London, 1766.

Anon., *Tyranny Unmasked*
Anonymous, *Tyranny Unmasked. An Answer to a Late Pamphlet, Entitled Taxation no Tyranny.* London, 1775.

Anon., *Whigs and Tories*
Anonymous, *A Dissertation on the Rise, Progress, Views, Strength, Interests and Characters, of the Two Parties of the Whigs and Tories.* Boston, 1773.

Aptheker, *Revolution*
Herbert Aptheker, *The American Revolution 1763–1783. A History of the American People: An Interpretation.* New York, 1960.

Atwood, *Dependency of Ireland*
W[illiam] Atwood, *The History, and Reasons, of the Dependency of Ireland Upon the Imperial Crown of the Kingdom of England. Rectifying Mr. Molineux's State of the Case of Ireland's being bound by Acts of Parliament in England.* London, 1698.

Authority of Rights
John Phillip Reid, *Constitutional History of the American Revolution: The Authority of Rights.* Madison, Wis., 1986.

Backus, *Government and Liberty*
Isaac Backus, *Government and Liberty Described: and Ecclesiastical Tyranny Exposed.* Boston, [1778].

[Bacon,] *Short Address*
[Anthony Bacon,] *A Short Address to the Government, the Merchants, Manufacturers, and the Colonists in America, and the Sugar Islands, On the present State of Affairs.* London, 1775.

[Baillie,] *Appendix to Letter*
[Hugh Baillie,] *An Appendix to a Letter to Dr. Shebbeare. To which are added, Some Observations on a Pamphlet, Entitled, Taxation no Tyranny: In which the Sophistry of that Author's Reasoning is Detected.* London, 1775.

Bailyn, *Ideological Origins*
Bernard Bailyn, *The Ideological Origins of the American Revolution.* Cambridge, Mass., 1967.

Bailyn, *Ordeal*
Bernard Bailyn, *The Ordeal of Thomas Hutchinson.* Cambridge, Mass., 1974.

Bailyn, *Pamphlets*
Pamphlets of the American Revolution, 1750–1776. Vol. 1. Edited by Bernard Bailyn. Cambridge, Mass., 1965.

[Bancroft,] *Remarks*
[Edward Bancroft,] *Remarks on the Review of the Controversy Between Great Britain and her Colonies. In Which the Errors of its Author are exposed, and the Claims of the Colonies vindicated, Upon the Evidence of Historical Facts and authentic records.* London, 1769.

Banks, *York*
Charles Edward Banks, *History of York Maine.* Vol. 1. Boston, 1931.

Barnes, *Dominion of New England*
Viola Florence Barnes, *The Dominion of New England: A Study in British Colonial Policy*. New York, 1960.

Barrington, *Viscount Barrington*
Shute Barrington, *The Political Life of William Wildman Viscount Barrington, Compiled from Original Papers by his Brother, Shute, Bishop of Durham*. London, 1815.

Barrow, *Trade*
Thomas C. Barrow, *Trade and Empire: The British Customs Service in Colonial America 1660–1775*. Cambridge, Mass., 1967.

Bellot, *William Knox*
Leland J. Bellot, *William Knox: The Life & Thought of an Eighteenth-Century Imperialist*. Austin, Tex., 1977.

Beloff, *Debate*
Max Beloff, "Introduction," in *The Debate on the American Revolution 1761–1783*. Edited by Max Beloff. London, 1949.

Benton, *Whig-Loyalism*
William Allen Benton, *Whig-Loyalism: An Aspect of Political Ideology in the American Revolutionary Era*. Rutherford, N.J., 1969.

Bernard, *Select Letters*
Francis Bernard, *Select Letters on the Trade and Government of America; and the Principles of Law and Polity, Applied to the American Colonies. Written by Governor Bernard at Boston*. Boston, 1774.

Bernard & Barrington, *Correspondence*
The Barrington-Bernard Correspondence. Edited by Edward Channing and Archibald Cary Collidge. Cambridge, Mass., 1912.

Bernard & Gage, *Letters*
Letters to the Ministry From Governor Bernard, General Gage, and Commodore Hood. And Also Memorials to the Lords of the Treasury, From the Commissioners of the Customs. With Sundry Letters and Papers Annexed to the said Memorials. Boston, 1769.

Blackstone, *Commentaries*
William Blackstone, *Commentaries on the Laws of England*. 4 vols. Oxford, 1765–69.

Blackstone, *Tracts*
William Blackstone, *Tracts Chiefly Relating to the Antiquities and Laws of England*. 3d ed. Oxford, 1771.

Boorstin, *Lost World of Jefferson*
Daniel J. Boorstin, *The Lost World of Thomas Jefferson*. Boston, 1960.

Boorstin, *Mysterious Science of Law*
> Daniel J. Boorstin, *The Mysterious Science of the Law: An Essay on Black-stone's COMMENTARIES Showing how Blackstone, Employing Eighteenth-Century Ideas of Science, Religion, History, Aesthetics, and Philosophy, Made of the Law at Once a Conservative and a Mysterious Science.* Cambridge, Mass., 1941.

Boston Chronicle
> *The Boston Chronicle.* (Weekly newspaper.)

Boston Declaration
> *The Votes and Proceedings of the Freeholders and other Inhabitants of the Town of Boston, In Town Meeting assembled, According to Law.* Boston, [1772].

Boston Evening-Post
> *The Boston Evening-Post.* (Weekly newspaper.)

Boston Gazette
> *The Boston Gazette and Country Journal.* (Weekly newspaper.)

Boston Merchants, *Observations*
> *Observations on Several Acts of Parliament, Passed In the 4th, 6th, and 7th Years of his present Majesty's Reign: and also, on The Conduct of the Officers of the Customs, since Those Acts were passed, and The Board of Commissioners appointed to Reside in America. Published by the Merchants of Boston.* Boston, 1769.

Boston News-Letter
> *The Massachusetts Gazette and Boston News-Letter,* also sometimes *The Massachusetts Gazette and the Boston News-Letter,* or *The Boston News-Letter.* (Weekly newspaper.)

Boston Post-Boy
> *The Boston Post-Boy & Advertiser.* (Weekly newspaper.)

Boston Town Records
> *A Report of the Record Commissioners of the City of Boston, Containing the Boston Town Records, 1758 to 1769.* 16th Report. Boston, 1886. *A Report of the Record Commissioners of the City of Boston, Containing the Boston Town Records, 1770 Through 1777.* 18th Report. Boston, 1887.

[Boucher,] *Letter from a Virginian*
> [Jonathan Boucher,] *A Letter From a Virginian to the Members of the Congress to be held at Philadelphia, on the first of September, 1774.* Boston, 1774.

Bowdoin, "Notes"
> "Notes" to *The Bowdoin and Temple Papers: Collections of the Massachusetts Historical Society.* 6th series, Vol. 9. Boston, 1897.

Bowdoin Papers
> The Bowdoin and Temple Papers: Collections of the Massachusetts His-
> torical Society. 6th series, vol. 9. Boston, 1897.

Breen, *Good Ruler*
> T. H. Breen, *The Character of the Good Ruler: A Study of Puritan Politi-
> cal Ideas in New England, 1630–1730*. New Haven, Conn., 1970.

Breen, "Localism"
> T. H. Breen, "Persistent Localism: English Social Change and the Shaping
> of New England Institutions," *William and Mary Quarterly* 32 (1975): 3–28.

Brennan, "James Otis"
> Ellen Elizabeth Brennan, "James Otis: Recreant and Patriot," *New Eng-
> land Quarterly* 12 (1939): 691–725.

Briefs of American Revolution
> The Briefs of the American Revolution: Constitutional Arguments Between
> Thomas Hutchinson, Governor of Massachusetts Bay, and James Bowdoin
> for the Council and John Adams for the House of Representatives. Edited
> by John Phillip Reid. New York, 1981.

Brown, "Hulton"
> Wallace Brown, "An Englishman Views the American Revolution: The Let-
> ters of Henry Hulton, 1769–1776," *Huntington Library Quarterly* 36 (1972–
> 73): 1–26, 139–51.

Brown, *John Hancock*
> Abram English Brown, *John Hancock: His Book*. Boston, 1898.

Brown, *Middle-Class Democracy*
> Robert E. Brown, *Middle-Class Democracy and the Revolution in Massa-
> chusetts, 1691–1780*. Ithaca, N.Y., 1955.

Brown, *Revolutionary Politics*
> Richard D. Brown, *Revolutionary Politics in Massachusetts: The Boston
> Committee of Correspondence and the Towns, 1772–1774*. New York, 1976.

Burgh, *Political Disquisitions*
> J. Burgh, *Political Disquisitions; or, An Enquiry into public Errors, De-
> fects, and Abuses. Illustrated by, and established upon Facts and Remarks,
> extracted from a Variety of Authors, Ancient and Modern*. 3 vols. Phila-
> delphia, 1775.

Burgoyne, "Letter to Lee"
> "A Copy of General Burgoyne's Answer, (dated July 8, 1775) to General
> Lee's Letter of June 7, 1775," in *Letters of Major General Lee, to the Right
> Honourable Earl Percy, and Major General John Burgoyne. With the
> Answers*. New York, 1775.

Burke on American Revolution
  Edmund Burke on the American Revolution: Selected Speeches and Letters. Edited by Elliot Robert Barkan. New York, 1966.

Burke, "Speech on American Taxation"
  Edmund Burke, "Speech on American Taxation, House of Commons, 19 April 1774," in *The Debate on the American Revolution 1761–1783.* Edited by Max Beloff. London, 1949, pp. 135–50.

[Burnet,] *Submission to Supream Authority*
  [Gilbert Burnet,] *An Enquiry Into the Measures of Submission to the Supream Authority: And of the Grounds upon which it may be lawful or necessary for Subjects, to defend their Religion, Lives, and Liberties.* n.i., [1688].

Butler, *North Carolina*
  Lindley S. Butler, *North Carolina and the Coming of the Revolution, 1763–1776.* Raleigh, N.C., 1976.

[Butler,] *Standing Army*
  [John Butler,] *A Consultation On the Subject of a Standing Army, Held at the King's-Arms Tavern, On the Twenty-eighth Day of February 1763.* London, 1763.

Camden, "Speech on American Taxation"
  Lord Camden, "Speech on American taxation, House of Lords, 24 February 1766," reprinted in *The Debate on the American Revolution 1761–1783.* Edited by Max Beloff. London, 1949, pp. 119–24.

Campbell, *Lives of Chancellors*
  John Lord Campbell, *The Lives of the Lord Chancellors and Keepers of the Great Seal of England, From the Earliest Times till the Reign of King George IV.* 3d ed. Vol. 5. London, 1849.

Care, *English Liberties Boston Edition*
  Henry Care, *English Liberties, or the Free-Born Subject's Inheritance; Containing Magna Charta, Charta de Foresta, The Statute De Tallagio non concedendo, The Habeas Corpus Act, and several other Statutes; with Comments on each of them.* 5th ed. Boston, 1721.

[Care,] *English Liberties First Edition*
  [Henry Care,] *English Liberties; or, the Free-Born Subject's Inheritance, Containing I. MAGNA CHARTA, The Petition of Right, The Habeas Corpus Act; and divers other most Useful Statutes: With Large Comments upon each of them.* London, [ca. 1690].

Carroll, "First Citizen"
  Charles Carroll, "First Citizen," reprinted in *Maryland and the Empire, 1773: The Antilon – First Citizen Letters.* Edited by Peter S. Onuf. Baltimore, 1974.

[Cartwright,] *American Independence*
[John Cartwright,] *American Independence the Interest and Glory of Great Britain; Containing Arguments which prove, that not only in Taxation, but in Trade, Manufactures, and Government, the Colonies are entitled to an entire Independency on the British Legislature; and that it can only by a formal Declaration of these Rights, and forming thereupon a friendly League with them, that the true and lasting Welfare of both Countries can be promoted. In a Series of Letters to the Legislature.* Philadelphia, 1776.

Cartwright, *People's Barrier*
John Cartwright, *The People's Barrier Against Undue Influence and Corruption: Or the Commons' House of Parliament According to the Constitution.* London, 1780.

Cato's Letters
Cato's Letters: or, Essays on Liberty, Civil and Religious, And other Important Subjects. In Four Volumes. 6th ed. London, 1755.

Chaffin, "Declaratory Act"
Robert J. Chaffin, "The Declaratory Act of 1766: A Reappraisal," *The Historian* 37 (1974): 5–25.

[Chalmers,] *Answer from Bristol to Burke*
[George Chalmers,] *An Answer from the Electors of Bristol to the Letter of Edmund Burke, Esq. on teh [sic] Affairs of America.* London, 1777.

Chalmers, *Opinions*
George Chalmers, *Opinions of Eminent Lawyers on Various Points of English Jurisprudence, Chiefly Concerning the Colonies, Fisheries and Commerce of Great Britain.* Burlington, Vt., 1858.

[Chandler,] *Friendly Address*
[Thomas B. Chandler,] *The Friendly Address to all Reasonable Americans on the Subject of our Political Confusions: Carefully abridged from the Original.* New York, 1774.

Chatham, "Speech in Lords, 20 January 1775"
Earl of Chatham [William Pitt], "Speech in the House of Lords, 20 January 1775," reprinted in *The Debate on the American Revolution 1761–1783.* Edited by Max Beloff. London, 1949, pp. 189–94.

Christie, *Crisis*
I. R. Christie, *Crisis of Empire: Great Britain and the American Colonies 1754–1783.* New York, 1966.

Christie, "Pitt and Taxation"
Ian R. Christie, "William Pitt and American Taxation, 1766: A Problem of Parliamentary Reporting," *Studies in Burke and his Time* 17 (1976): 167–79.

Christie & Labaree, *Empire*
> Ian R. Christie and Benjamin W. Labaree, *Empire or Independence 1760–1776: A British-American Dialogue on the Coming of the American Revolution.* New York, 1977.

Clarke, *Representation and Consent*
> M. V. Clarke, *Medieval Representation and Consent: A Study of Early Parliaments in England and Ireland, with Special Reference to the Modus Tenendi Parliamentum.* New York, 1964.

Commons Debates 1628
> *Commons Debates 1628.* Edited by Robert C. Johnson, Mary Frear Keeler, Maija Jansson Cole, and William B. Bidwell. 6 vols. New Haven, Conn., 1977–1983.

Cook, *King Charl[e]s his Case*
> John Cook, *King Charl[e]s his Case: Or, an Appeal To all Rational Men, Concerning his Tryal at the High Court of Justice. Being for the most part that which was intended to have been delivered at the Bar, if the King had Pleaded to the Charge, and put himself upon a fair Tryal.* London, 1649.

Correspondence of Shirley
> *Correspondence of Willaim Shirley Governor of Massachusetts and Military Commander in America 1731–1760.* Edited by Charles Henry Lincoln. 2 vols. New York, 1912.

Courtney, *Montesquieu and Burke*
> C. P. Courtney, *Montesquieu and Burke.* Westport, Conn., 1975.

Cowell & Manley, *Interpreter*
> John Cowell & Thomas Manley, *The Interpreter of Words and Terms, Used either in the Common or Statute Laws of this Realm, and in Tenures and Jocular Customs.* London, 1701.

Crane, "Franklin and Stamp Act"
> Verner W. Crane, "Benjamin Franklin and the Stamp Act," *Publications of the Colonial Society of Massachusetts* 32 (1934): 56–77.

Creasy, *Imperial Constitutions*
> Sir Edward Creasy, *The Imperial and Colonial Constitutions of the Britannic Empire, Including Indian Institutions.* London, 1872.

Critical Review
> *The Critical Review: Or Annals of Literature by a Society of Gentlemen.* (Monthly magazine, London.)

[Crowley,] *Dissertations*
> [Thomas Crowley,] *Dissertations on the Grand Dispute Between Great-Britain and America.* n.i., [1774].

[Crowley,] *Letters*
[Thomas Crowley,] *Letters and Dissertations, by the Author of the Letter Analysis A. P. on the Disputes between Great Britain and America.* London, 1782.

Dale, *Constitutional History*
Lucy Dale, *The Principles of English Constitutional History.* London, 1902.

[Dalrymple,] *Address of the People*
[John Dalrymple,] *The Address of the People of Great-Britain to the Inhabitants of America.* London, 1775.

Dartmouth Manuscripts
The Manuscripts of the Earl of Dartmouth. Vol. I. Historical Manuscripts Commission, 11th report, appendix, part 5. London, 1887. *The Manuscripts of the Earl of Dartmouth.* Vol. 2. *American Papers.* Historical Manuscripts Commission, 14th report, appendix, part 10. London, 1895.

Davis, *Reports*
Sir John Davis [Davies], *Les Reports Des Cases & Matters en Ley, Resolves & Adjudges en les Courts del Roy en Ireland.* London, 1674.

Day, *Present State of England*
Thomas Day, *Reflections Upon the Present State of England, and the Independence of America.* 2d ed. London, 1782.

De Beer, "Locke and English Liberalism"
Esmond S. De Beer, "Locke and English Liberalism: the *Second Treatise of Government* in Its Contemporary Setting," in *John Locke: Problems and Perspectives: A Collection of New Essays.* Edited by John W. Yolton. Cambridge, England, 1969, pp. 34–44.

"Declaration of Gentlemen"
"The Declaration of the Gentlemen, Merchants and Inhabitants of Boston, and the Country Adjacent. April 18, 1689," reprinted in *Narratives of the Insurrections 1675–1690.* Edited by Charles M. Andrews. New York, 1915, pp. 175–82.

"Declaration of 1689"
"The Declaration of the Gentlemen, Merchants and Inhabitants of Boston, and the Country Adjacent. April 18, 1689," reprinted in *The Andros Tracts* 1. Prince Society Publications Vol. 5. Boston, 1868, pp. 11–20.

Delaware House Minutes (1765–70)
Votes and Proceedings House of Representatives of the Government of the Counties of New Castle, Kent and Sussex, upon Delaware. At Sessions held at New Castle in the Years 1765–1766–1767–1768–1769–1770. Dover, Del., 1931.

De Lolme, *Constitution*
J. L. De Lolme, *The Constitution of England, or an Account of the English Government.* Dublin, 1775.

De Lolme, *Constitution: New Edition*
> J. L. De Lolme, *The Constitution of England; or, an Account of the English Government; in which it is Compared Both with the Republican Form of Government, and the Other Monarchies in Europe.* New ed. London, 1807.

Denison, *Westerly*
> Frederic Denison, *Westerly and Its Witnesses.* Providence, R.I., 1878.

Derry, *Fox*
> John W. Derry, *Charles James Fox.* New York, 1972.

[Devotion,] *The Examiner*
> [Ebenezer Devotion,] *The Examiner Examined. A Letter From a Gentleman in Connecticut, To his Friend in London. In Answer to a Letter from a Gentleman in London to his Friend in America: Intitled, The Claim of the Colonies to an Exemption from Internal Taxes imposed by Authority of Parliament, examined.* New London, Conn., 1766.

Dickerson, *Acts*
> Oliver M. Dickerson, *The Navigation Acts and the American Revolution.* Philadelphia, 1951.

Dickerson, "Use of Revenue"
> O. M. Dickerson, "Use Made of the Revenue from the Tax on Tea," *New England Quarterly* 31 (1958): 232–43.

[Dickinson,] "Address . . ."
> [John Dickinson,] "An Address to the Committee of Correspondence in Barbados. Occasioned by a late letter from them to their Agent in London," Philadelphia pamphlet reprinted in *South-Carolina Gazette* (4 August 1766): 1–2.

Dickinson, *Late Regulations*
> John Dickinson, *The Late Regulations Respecting the British Colonies Considered* (1765), reprinted in Dickinson, *Writings,* pp. 207–45.

Dickinson, "Letter to Inhabitants"
> John Dickinson, "Letter to the Inhabitants of the British Colonies," reprinted from the *Pennsylvania Journal* of May and June 1774, in Dickinson, *Writings,* pp. 469–501.

Dickinson, *Letter to Merchants*
> John Dickinson, *Letter to the Philadelphia Merchants Concerning Non-Importation, July, 1768,* reprinted in Dickinson, *Writings,* pp. 439–45.

Dickinson, *Letters*
> John Dickinson, *Letters from a Farmer in Pennsylvania to the Inhabitants of the British Colonies* (1768), reprinted in Dickinson, *Writings,* pp. 305–406.

[Dickinson,] *New Essay*
[John Dickinson,] *A New Essay [By the Pennsylvania Farmer] on the Constitutional Power of Great-Britain over the Colonies in America; with the Resolves of the Committee For the Province of Pennsylvania, and their Instructions to their Representatives in Assembly.* London, 1774.

Dickinson, "Preface"
Johnson Dickinson, "Preface [to the 1801 Edition]," printed in Dickinson, *Writings*, pp. xiii–xx.

Dickinson, *Stamp Act*
John Dickinson, *An Address to "Friends and Countrymen" on the Stamp Act* (1765), reprinted in Dickinson, *Writings*, pp. 197–205.

Dickinson, "Tea Tax"
John Dickinson, "Letter on the Tea Tax," reprinted in Dickinson, *Writings*, pp. 459–63.

Dickinson, *To Barbados*
John Dickinson, *An Address to the Committee of Correspondence in Barbados* (1766), reprinted in Dickinson, *Writings*, pp. 247–76.

Dickinson, *Writings*
The Writings of John Dickinson: Political Writings 1764–1774. Edited by Paul Leicester Ford. Philadelphia, 1895.

D'Innocenzo & Turner, "New York Newspaper Part 2"
Michael D'Innocenzo and John J. Turner, Jr., "The Role of the New York Newspapers in the Stamp Act Crisis, 1764–66, Part 2," *New-York Historical Society Quarterly* 51 (1967): 345–65.

Documents of New Hampshire
Documents and Records Relating to the Province of New-Hampshire, From 1764 to 1776; Including the whole Administration of Gov. John Wentworth; the Events immediately preceding the Revolutionary War; the Losses at the Battle of Bunker Hill, and the Record of all Proceedings till the end of our Provincial History. Volume VII Provincial Papers. Edited by Nathaniel Bouton. Nashua, N.H., 1873.

Donoughue, *British Politics*
Bernard Donoughue, *British Politics and the American Revolution: The Path to War, 1773–75.* London, 1964.

Douglass, *Historical and Political*
William Douglass, *A Summary, Historical and Political, Of the first Planting, progressive Improvements, and present State of the British Settlements in North-America.* Boston, Vol. 1, 1749, Vol. 2, 1753.

Dowell, *Taxation and Taxes*
Stephen Dowell, *A History of Taxation and Taxes in England From the Earliest Times to the Present Day.* 4 vols. London, 1884.

[Downer,] *Discourse in Providence*
[Silas Downer,] *A Discourse Delivered in Providence, in the Colony of Rhode-Island, upon the 25th Day of July 1768. At the Dedication of the Tree of Liberty, From the Summer House in the Tree.* Providence, R.I., 1768.

Dulany, "Antilon"
Daniel Dulany, Junior, "Antilon," reprinted in *Maryland and the Empire, 1773: The Antilon-First Citizen Letters.* Edited by Peter S. Onuf. Baltimore, 1974.

[Dulany,] *Considerations*
[Daniel Dulany,] *Considerations on the Propriety of Imposing Taxes in the British Colonies, For the Purpose of raising a Revenue, by Act of Parliament* (1765), reprinted in Bailyn, *Pamphlets,* pp. 608–58.

[Dulany,] *Considerations on the Propriety*
[Daniel Dulany,] *Considerations on the Propriety of Imposing Taxes in the British Colonies, For the Purpose of raising a Revenue, by Act of Parliament.* 2d ed. Annapolis, Md., 1765.

Dunn, "Politics of Locke"
John Dunn, "The Politics of Locke in England and America in the Eighteenth Century," in *John Locke: Problems and Perspectives, a Collection of New Essays.* Edited by John W. Yolton. Cambridge, England, 1969, pp. 45–80.

Dunn, *Puritans and Yankees*
Richard S. Dunn, *Puritans and Yankees: The Winthrop Dynasty of New England 1630–1717.* Princeton, N.J., 1962.

Edgar, *Colonial Governor*
Lady Edgar, *A Colonial Governor in Maryland: Horatio Sharpe and His Times 1753–1773.* London, 1912.

Egnal & Ernst, "Economic Interpretation"
Marc Egnal and Joseph A. Ernst, "An Economic Interpretation of the American Revolution," *William and Mary Quarterly* 29 (1972): 3–32.

Ellys, *Tracts on Liberty*
Anthony Ellys, *Tracts on the Liberty, Spiritual and Temporal, of the Subjects in England. Addressed to J. N. Esq; at Aix-la-Chapelle. Part II. [Of the Temporal Liberty of Subjects in England.]* London, 1765.

English Historical Documents
English Historical Documents: American Colonial Documents to 1776. Edited by Merrill Jensen. Vol. 9. New York, 1955.

[Erskine,] *Reflections on the Rise*
[John Erskine,] *Reflections on the Rise, Progress, and Probable Conse-*

quences, of the Present Contentions with the Colonies. By a Freeholder. Edinburgh, 1776.

Estwick, *Letter to Tucker*
Samuel Estwick, *A Letter to the Reverend Josiah Tucker, D. D. Dean of Glocester, in Answer to His Humble Address and Earnest Appeal, &c. with a Postscript, in which the present War against America is shewn to be the Effect, not of the Causes assigned by Him and Others. But of a Fixed Plan of Administration Founded in System.* London, 1776.

Evans, "Antiquity of Parliaments"
E. Evans, "Of the Antiquity of Parliaments in England: Some Elizabethan and Early Stuart Opinions," *History: The Quarterly Journal of the Historical Association* 23 (1938): 206–21.

[Evans,] *Letter to John Wesley*
[Caleb Evans,] *A Letter to the Rev. Mr. John Wesley, Occasioned by his Calm Address to the American Colonies.* London, 1775.

Evans, *Political Sophistry detected*
Caleb Evans, *Political Sophistry detected, or, Brief Remarks on the Rev. Mr. Fletcher's late Tract, entitled "American Patriotism." In a Letter to a Friend.* Bristol, England, 1776.

Evans, *Reply to Fletcher*
Caleb Evans, *A Reply to the Rev. Mr. Fletcher's Vindication of Mr. Wesley's Calm Address to Our American Colonies.* Bristol, England, [1776].

Examination of Franklin
The Examination of Doctor Benjamin Franklin, before an August Assembly, relating to the Repeal of the Stamp-Act, &c. Philadelphia, [1776].

Extract of Letter to De Berdt
Extract of a Letter From the House of Representatives of the Massachusets-Bay to their Agent Dennys De Berdt, Esq; with some Remarks. London, 1770.

[Ferguson,] *Remarks on Dr. Price*
[Adam Ferguson,] *Remarks on a Pamphlet Lately Published by Dr. Price, Intitled, Observations on the Nature of Civil Liberty, the Principles of Government, and the Justice and Policy of the War with America, &c. in a Letter from a Gentleman in the Country to a Member of Parliament.* London, 1776.

Filmer, *Anarchy of Mixed Monarchy*
Robert Filmer, *The Anarchy of a Limited or Mixed Monarchy or A succinct Examination of the Fundamentals of Monarchy, both in this and other Kingdoms, as well about the Right of Power in Kings, as of the Originall or Naturall Liberty of the People* (1648), reprinted in Filmer, *Patriarcha*, pp. 275–313.

Filmer, *Patriarcha*
Patriarcha and Other Political Works of Sir Robert Filmer. Edited by Peter Laslett. Oxford, 1949.

Fisk, *English Public Finance*
Harvey E. Fisk, *English Public Finance from the Revolution of 1688 with Chapters on the Bank of England.* New York, 1920.

[Fitch et al.,] *Reasons Why*
[Thomas Fitch, Jared Ingersoll, Ebenezer Silliman, and George Wyllys,] *Reasons Why the British Colonies in America, Should not be Charged with Internal Taxes, by Authority of Parliament; Humbly offered, For Consideration, In Behalf of the Colony of Connecticut.* New Haven, Conn., 1764.

Fletcher, *American Patriotism*
J. Fletcher, *American Patriotism Farther confronted with Reason, Scripture, and the Constitution: Being Observations on the Dangerous Politicks Taught by the Rev. Mr. Evans, M.A. and the Rev. Dr. Price. With a Scriptual Plea for the Revolted Colonies.* Shrewsbury, England, 1777.

Forbes, *Artillery Company Sermon*
Eli Forbes, *The Dignity and Importance of the Military Character illustrated. A Sermon Preached to the Ancient and Honorable Artillery Company, in Boston, New-England, June 3d. 1771. Being the Anniversary of their Election of Officers.* Boston, 1771.

Forster, *Charles Townshend*
Cornelius P. Forster, *The Uncontrolled Chancellor Charles Townshend and His American Policy.* Providence, R.I., 1978.

Foss, *Judges of England*
Edward Foss, *The Judges of England.* 9 vols. London, 1848–64.

Foundations of Colonial America
Foundations of Colonial America: A Documentary History. Edited by W. Keith Kavenagh. 3 vols. New York, 1973.

Franklin, *Writings*
The Writings of Benjamin Franklin. Vols. 3, 5, and 6. Edited by Albert Henry Smyth. New York, 1906.

Franklin-Jackson Letters
Letters and Papers of Benjamin Franklin and Richard Jackson 1753–1785. Edited by Carl Van Doren. Memoirs of the American Philosophical Society. Vol. 24. Philadelphia, 1947.

Franklin's Letters to the Press
Benjamin Franklin's Letters to the Press, 1758–1775. Edited by Verner W. Crane. Chapel Hill, N.C., 1950.

Freeman Letters
> *The Letters of Freeman, Etc. Essays on the Nonimportation Movement in South Carolina Collected by William Henry Drayton.* Edited by Robert M. Weir. Columbia, S.C., 1977.

[French,] *Constitution of Ireland*
> [Richard French,] *The Constitution of Ireland, and Poyning's Laws Explained.* Dublin, 1770.

Frese, "Board"
> Joseph R. Frese, "Some Observations on the American Board of Customs Commissioners," *Proceedings of the Massachusetts Historical Society* 81 (1969): 3–30.

Frese, "Tax"
> Joseph R. Frese, "Henry Hulton and the Greenwich Hospital Tax," *American Neptune* 31 (1971): 192–216.

Gage, *Correspondence*
> *The Correspondence of General Thomas Gage With the Secretaries of State 1763–1775.* Vol. 1. Edited by Clarence Edwin Carter. New Haven, Conn., 1931. *The Correspondence of General Thomas Gage with the Secretaries of State, and with the War Office and the Treasury 1763–1775.* Vol. 2. Edited by Clarence Edwin Carter. New Haven, Conn., 1933.

Gage, *Papers*
> Military Papers of General Gage. Ann Arbor, Mich. Clements Library, University of Michigan.

[Galloway,] *Americanus*
> [Joseph Galloway,] A Letter signed Americanus, *New-York Gazette,* 15 August 1765, reprinted in Anon., *Americanus Examined.*

"Garth Correspondence"
> "Correspondence of Charles Garth," [Part 1] *South Carolina Historical and Genealogical Magazine* 28 (1927): 79–93; [Part 2] 28 (1927): 226–35; [Part 3] 29 (1928): 41–48; [Part 4] 29 (1928): 115–32; [Part 5] 29 (1928): 212–30; [Part 6] 29 (1928): 295–305; [Part 7] 30 (1929): 27–49; [Part 8] 30 (1929): 105–16; [Part 9] 30 (1929): 168–84; [Part 10] 30 (1929): 215–35; [Part 11] 31 (1930): 46–62; [Part 12] 31 (1930): 124–53; [Part 13] 31 (1930): 228–55; [Part 14] 31 (1930): 283–91; [Part 15] 33 (1932): 117–39; [Part 16] 33 (1932): 228–44; [Part 17] 33 (1932): 262–80.

Garth, "Letter"
> "Letter from Charles Garth to South Carolina, 19 January 1766," *The South Carolina Historical and Genealogical Magazine* 26 (1925): 68–92.

Garth, "Letter on Repeal"
> Letter from Charles Garth to Ringgold, Murdoch, and Tilghman, 5 March 1766, in Morgan, *Prologue,* pp. 148–54.

Gazette & News-Letter
>*The Massachusetts Gazette and Boston News-Letter.* (Weekly newspaper. An alternative title sometimes used for the *Boston News-Letter* and to be located with that newspaper on the same microfilm.)

Gazette & Post-Boy
>*The Massachusetts Gazette and Boston Post-Boy and the Advertiser.* (Weekly newspaper. An alternative title sometimes used for the *Boston Post-Boy* and to be located with that newspaper on the same set of microfilm.)

Gentleman's Magazine
>*The Gentleman's Magazine and Historical Chronicle.* (Monthly magazine, London.)

Georgia Commons House Journal
>*The Colonial Records of the State of Georgia. Volume XIV. Journal of the Commons House of Assembly January 17, 1763, to December 24, 1768, Inclusive. Volume XV. Journal of the Commons House of Assembly October 30, 1769, to June 16, 1782, Inclusive.* Atlanta, Ga., 1907.

Gerard, *Liberty Cloke of Maliciousness*
>Alexander Gerard, *Liberty the Cloke of Maliciousness, both in the American Rebellion, and in the Manners of the Times. A Sermon Preached at Old Aberdeen, February 26, 1778, Being the Fast-Day appointed by Proclamation on account of the Rebellion in America.* Aberdeen, Scotland, 1778.

Gibbes, *Documentary History*
>R. W. Gibbes, *Documentary History of the American Revolution: Consisting of Letters and Papers Relating to the Contest for Liberty, Chiefly in South Carolina 1764–1776.* New York, 1855.

Gipson, *British Empire*
>Lawrence Henry Gipson, *The British Empire Before the American Revolution.* 15 vols. Revised ed. New York, 1958–70.

Gipson, "Debate on Repeal"
>Lawrence Henry Gipson, "The Great Debate in the Committee of the Whole House of Commons on the Stamp Act, 1766, as Reported by Nathaniel Ryder," *Pennsylvania Magazine of History and Biography* 86 (1962): 10–41.

[Goodricke,] *Observations on Price's Theory*
>[Henry Goodricke,] *Observations on Dr. Price's Theory and Principles of Civil Liberty and Government, Preceded by a Letter to a Friend, on the Pretensions of the American Colonies, in respect of Right and Equity.* York, England, 1776.

Gordon, *History*
>William Gordon, *The History of the Rise, Progress, and Establishment of the Independence of the United States of America.* 3d American ed. Vol. 1. New York, 1801.

Gough, *Fundamental Law*
J. W. Gough, *Fundamental Law in English Constitutional History*. Oxford, 1955.

Gough, *Social Contract*
J. W. Gough, *The Social Contract: A Critical Study of Its Development*. Oxford, 1936.

[Gray,] *Right of the Legislature*
[John Gray,] *The Right of the British Legislature to Tax the American Colonies Vindicated; and the Means of Asserting that Right Proposed*. 2d ed. London, 1775.

Greene, *Quest*
Jack P. Greene, *The Quest for Power: The Lower Houses of Assembly in the Southern Royal Colonies, 1689–1776*. Norton Library ed. New York, 1972.

Greene, *Reappraisal*
Jack P. Greene, *The Reappraisal of the American Revolution in Recent Historical Literature*. American Historical Society, Service Center for Teachers of History. Washington, D.C., 1967.

Grenville Letterbooks
Letterbooks of George Grenville. ST 7, Huntington Library, San Marino, Calif.

Grenville Papers
The Grenville Papers: Being the Correspondence of Richard Grenville Earl Temple, K. G., and the Right Hon: George Grenville, their Friends and Contemporaries. 4 vols. Edited by William James Smith. London, 1852–53.

Grenville, "Present State"
[Knox,] *The Present State*, printed in *Boston Chronicle*.

"Grotius," *Pills for Delegates*
"Grotius," *Pills for the Delegates: or the Chairman Chastised, In a Series of Letters, Addressed to Peyton Randolph, Esq; On his Conduct, as President of the General Congress: Held at the City of Philadelphia, September 6, 1774*. New York, 1775.

Guttridge, *English Whiggism*
G. H. Guttridge, *English Whiggism and the American Revolution*. Berkeley, Calif., 1966.

Habersham Letters
The Letters of Hon. James Habersham. Collections of the Georgia Historical Society. Vol. 6. Savannah, Ga., 1904.

Hacker, "The First American Revolution"
Louis M. Hacker, "The First American Revolution," reprinted in *Causes*

and Consequences of the American Revolution. Edited by Esmond Wright. Chicago, 1966, pp. 114–42.

Hale, *History*
Sir Matthew Hale, *The History of the Common Law of England.* 2d ed. corrected. London, 1716.

Hale, "Reflections"
Matthew Hale, "Reflections by the Lrd. Chiefe Justice Hale on Mr. Hobbes His Dialogue of the Lawe," printed in W. S. Holdsworth, *A History of English Law.* London. 5 (1924): 500–13.

Hamilton, *Farmer Refuted*
Alexander Hamilton, *The Farmer Refuted: or A more impartial and comprehensive View of the Dispute between Great-Britain and the Colonies, Intended as a Further Vindication of the Congress* (1775), reprinted in *The Papers of Alexander Hamilton.* Vol. 1. Edited by Harold C. Syrett. New York, 1961, pp. 81–165.

Harlow, *Adams*
Ralph Volney Harlow, *Samuel Adams Promoter of the American Revolution: A Study in Psychology and Politics.* New York, 1923.

Harper, "Mercantilism and Revolution"
Lawrence A. Harper, "Mercantilism and the American Revolution," reprinted in *Causes and Consequences of the American Revolution.* Edited by Esmond Wright. Chicago, 1966, pp. 155–72.

Hartley, *Letters on the War*
David Hartley, *Letters on the American War. Addressed to the Right Worshipful the Mayor and Corporation, to the Worshipful the Wardens and Corporation of the Trinity-House, and to the Worthy Burgesses of the Town of Kingston-Upon-Hull.* 6th ed. London, 1779.

Hartley, *Speech and Motions*
David Hartley, *Speech and Motions Made in the House of Commons, on Monday, the 27th of March, 1775. Together with a Draught of a Letter of Requisition to the Colonies.* 2d ed. London, 1775.

Hawkins, *Life of Johnson*
Sir John Hawkins, *The Life of Samuel Johnson, LL.D.* 2d. ed. London, 1787.

Headlam, "Constitutional Struggle"
Cecil Headlam, "The Constitutional Struggle with the American Colonies, 1765–1775," in *The Cambridge History of the British Empire: Volume I, The Old Empire From the Beginnings to 1783.* Edited by J. Holland Rose, A. P. Newton, and E. A. Benians. Cambridge, England, 1929, pp. 646–84.

Headlam, "Imperial Reconstruction"
Cecil Headlam, "Imperial Reconstruction, 1763–1765," in *The Cambridge History of the British Empire: Volume I, The Old Empire from the Begin-*

nings to 1783. Edited by J. Holland Rose, A. P. Newton, and E. A. Benians. Cambridge, England, 1929, pp. 634–46.

Hibernian Magazine
The Hibernian Magazine or Compendium of Entertaining Knowledge Containing The greatest Variety of the most Curious & useful Subjects in every Branch of Polite Literature. (Monthly magazine, Dublin.)

[Hicks,] *Nature of Parliamentary Power*
[William Hicks,] *The Nature and Extent of Parliamentary Power Considered; In some Remarks upon Mr. Pitt's Speech in the House of Commons, previous to the Repeal of the Stamp-Act: With an Introduction, Applicable to the present Situation of the Colonies.* Philadelphia, 1768.

Higden, *View of Constitution*
William Higden, *A View of the English Constitution, With Respect to the Sovereign Authority of the Prince, and the Allegiance of the Subject. In Vindication of the Lawfulness of Taking the Oaths, To Her Majesty, by Law Required.* London, 1709.

Higginbotham, "James Iredell's Efforts"
Don Higginbotham, "James Iredell's Efforts to Preserve the First British Empire," *North Carolina Historical Review* 49 (1972): 127–45.

Hinkhouse, *Preliminaries*
Fred Junkin Hinkhouse, *The Preliminaries of the American Revolution as Seen in the English Press 1763–1775.* New York, 1926.

Hobbes, *Dialogue of Common Laws*
Thomas Hobbes, *A Dialogue Between a Philosopher and a Student of the Common Laws of England.* Edited by Joseph Cropsey. Chicago, 1971.

Holliday, *Life of Mansfield*
John Holliday, *The Life of William Late Earl of Mansfield,* London, 1797.

[Hopkins,] *Grievances of the Colonies*
[Stephen Hopkins,] *The Grievances of the American Colonies Candidly Examined.* London, 1766.

Hopkins, *Rights*
Stephen Hopkins, *The Rights of the Colonies Examined* (1765), reprinted in Bailyn, *Pamphlets* 1:507–22.

[Hopkins,] "Vindication of a Pamphlet"
[Stephen Hopkins,] "A Vindication of a Late Pamphlet, entitled, The Rights of Colonies examined, from the Censures and Remarks contained in a *Letter* from a Gentleman in Halifax, to his friend in Rhode Island, just published in Newport," in *The Providence Gazette and Country Journal,* 23 February, 2 March, and 9 March 1765.

Hosmer, *Adams*
James K. Hosmer, *Samuel Adams.* Boston, 1899.

[Howard,] *Defence of Letter*
[Martin Howard,] *A Defence of the Letter from a Gentleman at Halifax, to His Friend in Rhode-Island.* Newport, R.I., 1765.

[Howard,] *Halifax Letter*
[Martin Howard, Jr.,] *A Letter from a Gentleman at Halifax, to his Friend in Rhode-Island, Containing Remarks Upon a Pamphlet, Entitled, The Rights of the Colonies Examined* (1765), reprinted in Bailyn, *Pamphlets* 1:532–44.

Howe, *Readings in Legal History*
Mark DeWolfe Howe, *Readings in American Legal History.* Cambridge, Mass., 1949.

Hurstfield, *Freedom, Corruption & Government*
Joel Hurstfield, *Freedom, Corruption and Government in Elizabethan England.* Cambridge, Mass., 1973.

Hutchinson, *Diary*
The Diary and Letters of His Excellency Thomas Hutchinson, Esq. Edited by Peter Orlando Hutchinson. 2 vols. London, 1883–86.

Hutchinson, *History* (1828)
Thomas Hutchinson, *The History of the Province of Massachusetts Bay, From 1749 to 1774, Comprising a Detailed Narrative of the Origin and Early Stages of the American Revolution.* London, 1828.

[Hutchinson,] *Strictures Upon the Declaration*
[Thomas Hutchinson,] *Strictures Upon the Declaration of Congress at Philadelphia; In a Letter to a Noble Lord, &c.* London, 1776.

"In Accordance with Usage"
John Phillip Reid, "In Accordance with Usage: The Authority of Custom, the Stamp Act Debate, and the Coming of the American Revolution," *Fordham Law Review* 45 (1976): 335–68.

"In a Constitutional Void"
John Phillip Reid, "In a Constitutional Void: The Enforcement of Imperial Law, the Role of the British Army, and the Coming of the American Revolution," *Wayne Law Review* 22 (1975): 1–37.

"In a Defensive Rage"
John Phillip Reid, "In a Defensive Rage: The Uses of the Mob, the Justification in Law, and the Coming of the American Revolution," *New York University Law Review* 49 (1974): 1043–91.

In Defiance of the Law
John Phillip Reid, *In Defiance of the Law: The Standing-Army Controversy, the Two Constitutions, and the Coming of the American Revolution.* Chapel Hill, N.C., 1981.

In a Defiant Stance
John Phillip Reid, *In a Defiant Stance: The Conditions of the Law in Massachusetts Bay, the Irish Comparison, and the Coming of the American Revolution.* University Park, Pa., 1977.

"In the First Line of Defense"
John Phillip Reid, "In the First Line of Defense: The Colonial Charters, the Stamp Act Debate and the Coming of the American Revolution," *New York University Law Review* 51 (1976): 177–215.

"In Our Contracted Sphere"
John Phillip Reid, "'In Our Contracted Sphere:' The Constitutional Contract, the Stamp Act Crisis, and the Coming of the American Revolution," *Columbia Law Review* 76 (1976): 21–47.

In a Rebellious Spirit
John Phillip Reid, *In a Rebellious Spirit: The Argument of Facts, the Liberty Riot, and the Coming of the American Revolution.* University Park, Pa., 1979.

Independent Reflector
The Independent Reflector or Weekly Essays on Sundry Important Subjects More Particularly adapted to the Province of New-York By William Livingston and Others. Edited by Milton M. Klein. Cambridge, Mass., 1963.

"Ingersoll Correspondence"
"A Selection from the Correspondence and Miscellaneous Papers of Jared Ingersoll" [Edited by Franklin B. Dexter], *Papers of the New Haven Colony Historical Society* 9 (1918): 201–472.

Interesting Letters
A New and Impartial Collection of Interesting Letters from the Public Papers; Many of them Written by Persons of Eminence. Vol. 2. London, 1767.

"In the Taught Tradition"
John Phillip Reid, "In the Taught Tradition: The Meaning of Law in Massachusetts-Bay Two Hundred Years Ago," *Suffolk University Law Review* 14 (1980): 931–74.

"Irrelevance of the Declaration"
John Phillip Reid, "The Irrelevance of the Declaration," in *Law in the American Revolution and the Revolution in the Law: A Collection of Review Essays on American Legal History.* Edited by Hendrik Hartog. New York, 1981, pp. 46–89.

[Jacob,] *Laws of Liberty*
[Giles Jacob,] *The Laws of Liberty and Property: Or, A Concise Treatise of all the Laws, Statutes and Ordinances, made for the Benefit and Protection of the Subjects of England.* 2d ed. London, 1734.

Jacob, *New Law Dictionary*
Giles Jacob, *A New Law-Dictionary: Containing the Interpretation and Definition of Words and Terms used in the Law.* 8th ed. London, 1762.

Jarrett, *Pitt the Younger*
Derek Jarrett, *Pitt the Younger.* New York, 1974.

Jefferson, *Summary View*
Thomas Jefferson, *A Summary View of the Rights of British America Set Forth in some Resolutions Intended For the Inspection of the Present Delegates of the People of Virginia Now in Convention* (1774), reprinted in *Papers of Jefferson* 1:121–35.

[Jenings,] *Plan for Settling Dispute*
[Edmund Jenings,] *A Plan for Settling the Unhappy Dispute Between Great Britain and her Colonies.* n.i., 1775.

Jenkins, *Lex Terrae*
David Jenkins, *Lex Terrae; or, Laws of the Land* (1647), in *Somers' Tracts* 5:98–114.

Jenkins, *Works*
David Jenkins, *The Works of the Eminent and Learned Judge Jenkins Upon Divers Statutes Concerning the King's Prerogative and the Liberty of the Subject: Now Reprinted from the Original Authentick Copy, Written and Published by Himself, when Prisoner in Newgate.* London, 1681.

Jenkinson Papers
The Jenkinson Papers 1760–1766. Edited by Ninetta S. Jucker. London, 1949.

[Johnson,] *Important Observations*
[Stephen Johnson,] *Some Important Observations, Occasioned by, and adapted to, The Publick Fast, Ordered by Authority, December 18th, A.D. 1765. On Account of the peculiar Circumstances of the present Day.* Newport, R.I., 1766.

[Johnson,] *Political Tracts*
[Samuel Johnson,] *Political Tracts. Containing, The False Alarm. Falkland's Islands. The Patriot; and Taxation no Tyranny.* London, 1776.

Johnstone, *Speech on Question*
George Johnstone, *Governor Johnstone's Speech on the Question of Recommitting the address declaring the Colony of Massachuset[t]s Bay in Rebellion: To which is added the two Most Masterly Letters of Junius to the people of England in favour of the Americans.* London, [1776].

Johnstone, "Speech of November, 1775"
"Governor Johnstone's Speech to the House of Commons, November, 1775," in *The American Revolution: The Anglo-American Relation, 1763–1794.* Edited by Charles R. Ritcheson. Reading, Mass., 1969, pp. 85–91.

Jones, "Clegate Case"
> J. R. Jones, "The Clegate Case," *English Historical Review* 90 (1975): 262–86.

Journal of Burgesses
> *Journals of the House of Burgesses of Virginia [Vol. 8] 1752–1755, 1756–1758, [Vol. 10] 1761–1765, [Vol. 11] 1766–1769, [Vol. 12] 1770–1772, [Vol. 13] 1773–1776 Including the records of the Committee of Correspondence.* Edited by John Pendleton Kennedy. Richmond, Va., 1905, 1906, 1907.

Journal of the First Congress
> *Journal of the Proceedings of the Congress, Held at Philadelphia, September 5, 1774.* Philadelphia, 1774.

Journal of New York Assembly
> *Journal of the Votes and Proceedings of the General Assembly of the Colony of New-York. Began the 8th Day of November, 1743; and Ended the 23d of December, 1765.* Vol. 2. New York, 1766.

Journal of New York Assembly (1766–76)
> *Journal of the Votes and Proceedings of the General Assembly of the Colony of New-York, From 1766 to 1776 Inclusive. Reprinted in pursuance of a joint resolution of the Legislature of the State of New-York, passed 30 April, 1820.* Albany, N.Y., 1820.

Journal of the Times
> *Boston Under Military Rule 1768–1769 as Revealed in a Journal of the Times.* Compiled by Oliver Morton Dickerson. Boston, 1936.

Judson, *Crisis*
> Margaret Atwood Judson, *The Crisis of the Constitution: An Essay in Constitutional and Political Thought in England 1603–1645.* New Brunswick, N.J., 1949.

"Junius," *Junius*
> ["Junius,"] *Junius.* 2 vols. London, [1772].

[Kames,] *History of Man*
> [Henry Home, Lord Kames,] *Sketches of the History of Man. Considerably Improved in a Third Edition.* 2 vols. Dublin, 1779.

Kammen, *Rope*
> Michael G. Kammen, *A Rope of Sand: The Colonial Agents, British Politics, and the American Revolution.* New York, 1974.

Keir, *Constitutional History*
> Sir David Lindsay Keir, *The Constitutional History of Modern Britain Since 1845.* 8th ed. Princeton, N.J., 1966.

Kenyon, *Stuarts*
> J. P. Kenyon, *The Stuarts: A Study in English Kingship.* London, 1966.

Knollenberg, *Origin*
> Bernhard Knollenberg, *Origin of the American Revolution: 1759–1766.*
> Revised ed. New York, 1965.

[Knox,] *Claim of the Colonies*
> [William Knox,] *The Claim of the Colonies to an Exemption from Internal Taxes Imposed By Authority of Parliament, Examined: In a Letter from a Gentleman in London, to his Friend in America.* London, 1765.

[Knox,] *Controversy*
> [William Knox,] *The Controversy Between Great Britain and her Colonies Reviewed; The Several Pleas of the Colonies, In Support of their Rights to all the Liberties and Privileges of British Subjects, and to Exemption from the Legislative Authority of Parliament, Stated and Considered; and the Nature of their Connection with, and Dependence on, Great Britain, Shewn, Upon the Evidence of Historical Facts and Authentic Records.* London, 1769.

[Knox,] *Controversy* (Dublin Edition)
> [William Knox,] *The Controversy Between Great Britain and her Colonies Reviewed; The Several Pleas of the Colonies, In Support of their Right to all the Liberties and Privileges of British Subjects, and to Exemption from the Legislative Authority of Parliament, Stated and Considered, and The Nature of their Connection with, and Dependence on, Great Britain, Shewn, Upon the Evidence of Historical Facts and Authentic Records.* Dublin, 1769.

[Knox,] *Extra Official Papers*
> [William Knox,] *Extra Official State Papers. Addressed to the Right Hon. Lord Rawdon, and the Other Members of the Two Houses of Parliament, Associated for the Preservation of the Constitution and Promoting the Prosperity of the British Empire. Volume the Second.* London, 1789.

[Knox,] *Interest of Merchants*
> [William Knox,] *The Interest of the Merchants and Manufacturers of Great Britain, in the Present Contest with the Colonies Stated and Considered.* London, 1774.

[Knox,] *Present State*
> [William Knox,] *The Present State of the Nation: Particularly with respect to its Trade, Finances, &c. &c. Addressed to the King and both Houses of Parliament.* 4th ed. London, 1769.

Konig, *Puritan Massachusetts*
> David Thomas Konig, *Law and Society in Puritan Massachusetts: Essex County, 1629–1692.* Chapel Hill, N.C., 1979.

"L.," *Letter to G[renville]*
> "L.," *A Letter to G. G. Stiff in Opinions, always in the wrong.* London, 1767.

Larkin, *Property in Eighteenth Century*
Paschal Larkin, *Property in the Eighteenth Century with Special Reference to England and Locke.* Dublin and Cork, Ireland, 1930.

Laslett, "Social Contract"
Peter Laslett, "Social Contract," in *The Encyclopedia of Philosophy.* Vol. 7, 1967, pp. 465–67.

Leder, *Liberty*
Lawrence H. Leder, *Liberty and Authority: Early American Political Ideology 1689–1763.* Chicago, 1968.

Lee, *Answer*
Arthur Lee, *Answer to Considerations on Certain Political Transactions of the Province of South Carolina* (1774), reprinted in *the Nature of Colony Considerations: Two Pamphlets on the Wilkes Fund Controversy in South Carolina by Sir Egerton Leigh and Arthur Lee.* Edited by Jack P. Greene. Columbia, S.C., 1970, pp. 131–205.

Lee, *Appeal to Justice*
[Arthur] Lee, *An Appeal to the Justice and Interests of the People of Great Britain, in the Present Dispute with America.* 4th ed. New York, 1775.

Lee, *Election Sermon*
Jonathan Lee, *A Sermon Delivered before the General Assembly of the Colony of Connecticut, at Hartford; On the Day of the Anniversary Election, May 8th, 1766.* New London, Conn., 1766.

Lee Letters
The Letters of Richard Henry Lee, 1762–1778. Edited by James Curtis Ballagh. 2 vols. New York, 1911–14.

Lee, *Richard Henry Lee*
Richard Henry Lee, *Memoir of the Life of Richard Henry Lee, and His Correspondence with the Most Distinguished Men in America and Europe, Illustrative of their Characters, and of the Events of the American Revolution.* 2 vols. Philadelphia, 1825.

[Lee,] *Second Appeal*
[Arthur Lee,] *A Second Appeal to the Justice and Interests of the People, on the Measures Respecting America. By the Author of the First.* London, 1775.

[Lee,] *Speech Intended*
[Arthur Lee,] *A Speech, Intended to have been Delivered in the House of Commons, in Support of the Petition from the General Congress at Philadelphia.* London, 1775.

[Lee,] *True State of the Proceedings*
[Arthur Lee,] *A True State of the Proceedings in the Parliament of Great Britain, and in the Province of Massachusetts Bay, Relative to the Giving*

and Granting the Money of the People of that Province, and of all America, in the House of Commons, in which they are not represented. Philadelphia, 1774.

Leonard, "Massachusettensis"
Daniel Leonard, "Massachusettensis Letters," reprinted in *The American Colonial Crisis: The Daniel Leonard–John Adams Letters to the Press 1774–1775.* Edited by Bernard Mason. New York, 1972, pp. 1–97.

[Leslie,] *Constitution, Laws and Government*
[Charles Leslie,] *The Constitution, Laws and Government of England, Vindicated in a Letter to the Reverend Mr. William Higden. On Account of his View of the English Constitution, with Respect to the Soveraign Authority of the Prince, &c. In Vindication of the Lawfulness of Taking the Oaths, &c. By a Natural Born Subject.* London, 1709.

Letters of Charles Carroll
Unpublished Letters of Charles Carroll of Carrollton, and of his Father, Charles Carroll of Doughoregan. Edited by Thomas Meagher Field. New York, 1902.

Letters of Delegates to Congress
Letters of Delegates to Congress: 1774–1789. 8 vols. Edited by Paul H. Smith. Washington, D.C., 1976–81.

"Letters of Dennys De Berdt"
"Letters of Dennys De Berdt, 1757–1770," *Publications of the Colonial Society of Massachusetts* 13 (1911): 293–461.

Letters and Papers of Pendleton
The Letters and Papers of Edmund Pendleton 1773–1803 — Volume One. Edited by D. J. Mays. Charlottesville, Va., 1967.

[Lind,] *Answer to Declaration*
[John Lind,] *An Answer to the Declaration of the American Congress.* London, 1776.

[Lind,] *Englishman's Answer*
[John Lind,] *An Englishman's Answer, To the Address From the Delegates, To the People of Great-Britain, In a Letter to the Several Colonies which were Represented in the Late Continental Congress.* New York, 1775.

[Lind,] *Letter to Willoughby Bertie*
[John Lind,] *A Letter to the Right Honourable Willoughby Bertie, By Descent Earl of Abingdon, By Descent Lord Norreys; High Steward of Abingdon and Wallingford. In Which His Lordship's Candid and Liberal Treatment of the Now Earl of Mansfield Is full vindicated.* London, 1778.

[Lind,] *Thirteenth Parliament*
[John Lind,] *Remarks on the Principal Acts of the Thirteenth Parliament*

of Great Britain. Vol. I. Containing Remarks on the Acts relating to the Colonies. With a Plan of Reconciliation. London, 1775.

Livingston, *Address to House*
The Address of Mr. Justice Livingston, to the House of Assembly, In Support of his Right to a Seat. New York, [1769].

London Magazine
The London Magazine or Gentleman's Monthly Intelligencer. (Monthly magazine, London.)

"Lords Debate on Declaratory Act"
"Debate on the Conway Resolutions. House of Lords, 10 February 1766," in *The Debate on the American Revolution.* Edited by Max Beloff. London, 1949, pp. 106–18.

Lovejoy, *Glorious Revolution*
David S. Lovejoy, *The Glorious Revolution in America.* New York, 1972.

Macaulay, *Address to People*
Catharine Macaulay, *An Address to the People of England, Scotland, and Ireland, on the Present Important Crisis of Affairs.* Bath, England, 1775.

MacKay, "Coke"
R. A. MacKay, "Coke—Parliamentary Sovereignty or the Supremacy of the Law?", *Michigan Law Review* 22 (1924): 215–47.

[Macpherson,] *Retrospective View*
[James Macpherson,] *A Retrospective View of the Causes of the Difference Between Great Britain and her Colonies in America: And a Consideration of Some Probable Consequences of the Dismemberment of the Empire.* n.i., [1782].

[Macpherson,] *Rights of Great Britain*
[James Macpherson,] *The Rights of Great Britain Asserted against the Claims of America: Being an Answer to the Declaration of the General Congress.* 6th ed. London, 1776.

Maitland, *Constitutional History*
F. W. Maitland, *The Constitutional History of England: A Course of Lectures Delivered.* Cambridge, England, 1908.

Mantell, *Short Treatise of Lawes*
Walter Mantell, *A Short Treatise of the Lawes of England: With the jurisdiction of the High Court of Parliament, With the Liberties and Freedomes of the Subjects.* London, 1644.

Marcham, *Constitutional History*
Frederick George Marcham, *A Constitutional History of Modern England, 1485 to the Present.* New York, 1960.

Marshall, *History of Colonies*
>John Marshall, *A History of the Colonies Planted by the English on the Continent of North America, from their Settlement, to the Commencement of that War Which Terminated in their Independence.* Philadelphia, 1824.

[Marvell,] *Account*
>[Andrew Marvell,] *An Account of the Growth of Popery and Arbitrary Government in England.* Amsterdam, 1677.

Maryland Votes and Proceedings (September 1765)
>*Votes and Proceedings of the Lower House of Assembly of the Province of Maryland. September Session, 1765. Being the First Session of this Assembly.* Annapolis, Md., n.d.

Maryland Votes and Proceedings (November 1765)
>*Votes and Proceedings of the Lower House of Assembly of the Province of Maryland. November Session, 1765. Being the Second Session of this Assembly.* Annapolis, Md., n.d.

Maryland Votes and Proceedings (1766)
>*Votes and Proceedings of the Lower House of Assembly of the Province of Maryland. November Session, 1766. Being the Fourth Session of this Assembly.* Annapolis, Md., n.d.

Maryland Votes and Proceedings (1768)
>*Votes and Proceedings of the Lower House of Assembly of the Province of Maryland. May Session, 1768. Being the First Session of this Assembly.* Annapolis, Md., 1768.

Maryland Votes and Proceedings (1769)
>*Votes and Proceedings of the Lower House of Assembly of the Province of Maryland. November Session, 1769. Being the Second Session of this Assembly.* Annapolis, Md., [1770].

Maryland Votes and Proceedings (1771)
>*Votes and Proceedings of the Lower House of Assembly of the Province of Maryland. October Session, 1771. Being the First Session of this Assembly.* Annapolis, Md., [1772].

[Maseres,] *Canadian Freeholder*
>[Francis Maseres,] *The Canadian Freeholder: In Two Dialogues Between an Englishman and a Frenchman, Settled in Canada.* 3 vols. London, 1777, 1779.

[Maseres,] *Considerations on Admitting Representatives*
>[Francis Maseres,] *Considerations on the Expediency of Admitting Representatives From the American Colonies into the British House of Commons.* London, 1770.

[Maseres,] *To Obtain an Assembly*
> [Francis Maseres,] *An Account of the Proceedings of the British, And other Protestant Inhabitants, of the Province of Quebeck, In North America, In order to obtain An House of Assembly In that Province.* London, 1775.

Massachusetts Gazette
> *The Massachusetts Gazette.* (Weekly newspaper, Boston; printed with, and generally collected with, *Boston News-Letter.*)

Massachusetts House Journal (1764)
> *Journal of the Honourable House of Representatives Of His Majesty's Province of the Massachusetts-Bay, in New-England, Begun and held at Concord, in the County of Middlesex, on Wednesday the Thirtieth Day of May, Annoque Domni, 1764.* Boston, 1764–65.

Massacre Orations
> *Orations Delivered at the Request of the Inhabitants of the Town of Boston, to Commemorate the Evening of the Fifth of March, 1770; When a Number of Citizens were Killed by a Party of British Troops, Quartered Among them, in a Time of Peace.* Boston, 1785.

[Mather,] *America's Appeal*
> [Moses Mather,] *America's Appeal to the Impartial World. Wherein the Rights of the Americans, as Men, British Subjects, and as Colonists; the Equity of the Demand, and of the Manner in which it is made upon them by Great-Britain, are stated and considered. And, the Opposition made by the Colonies to Acts of Parliament, their resorting to Arms in their necessary Defence, against the Military Armaments, employed to enforce them, Vindicated.* Hartford, Conn., 1775.

Mather, *Vindication*
> Increase Mather, *A Vindication of New-England* (1690), reprinted in 2 *The Andros Tracts.* Prince Society Publications. Vol. 6, 1869, pp. 19–79.

Mauduit, *Legislative Authority*
> Jasper Mauduit, *The Legislative Authority of the British Parliament, with respect to North America, and the Privileges of the Assemblies there, briefly Considered.* London, 1766.

Mauduit Letters
> *Jasper Mauduit: Agent in London for the Province of the Massachusetts Bay 1762–1765.* Boston, 1918.

[Mauduit,] *Letters of Hutchinson*
> [Israel Mauduit,] *The Letters of Governor Hutchinson, and Lieut. Governor Oliver, &c. Printed at Boston. And Remarks thereon. With the Assembly's Address, and the Proceedings Of the Lords Committee of Council. Together with the Substance of Mr. Wedderburn's Speech relating to those Letters. And the Report of the Lords Committee to his Majesty in Council.* 2d ed. London, 1774.

[Mauduit,] *Northern Colonies*
 [Israel Mauduit,] *Some Thoughts on the Method of Improving and Securing the Advantages which Accrue to Great-Britain from the Northern Colonies.* London, 1765.

Mauduit, *Short View*
 Israel Mauduit, *A Short View of the History of the Colony of Massachusetts Bay, With Respect to their Charters and Constitution.* 3d ed. London, 1774.

May, *Constitutional History*
 Thomas Erskine May, *The Constitutional History of England Since the Accession of George Third 1760–1860.* 2 vols. Boston, 1863–64.

May, *Parliamentary Practice*
 Sir Thomas Erskine May, *A Treatise on the Law, Privileges, Proceedings and Usage of Parliament.* 14th ed. Edited by Sir Gilbert Campion. London, 1946.

McAdam, *Johnson and Law*
 E. L. McAdam, Jr., *Dr. Johnson and the English Law.* Syracuse, N. Y., 1951.

McCormac, *Colonial Opposition*
 Eugene Irving McCormac, *Colonial Opposition to Imperial Authority During the French and Indian War.* Berkeley, Calif., 1911.

McCulloh, *General Thoughts*
 Henry McCulloh, *General Thoughts, endeavouring to demonstrate that the Legislature here, in all Cases of a public and General Concern, have a Right to Tax the British Colonies; But that, with respect to the late American Stamp Duty Bill, there are several Clauses inserted therein which are very Exceptionable, and have, as humbly Conceived, passed upon wrong Information.* HM 1480, Huntington Library, San Marino, Calif.

McIlwain, *Constitutionalism*
 Charles Howard McIlwain, *Constitutionalism: Ancient and Modern.* Ithaca, N.Y., 1940.

McIlwain, *Revolution*
 Charles Howard McIlwain, *The American Revolution: A Constitutional Interpretation.* Ithaca, N.Y., 1958.

Memoirs of William Smith
 Historical Memoirs from 16 March 1763 to 9 July 1776 of William Smith Historian of the Province of New York Member of the Governor's Council and Last Chief Justice of that Province Under the Crown. Chief Justice of Quebec. Edited by William H. W. Sabine. Vol. 1. New York, 1956.

Miller, *Sam Adams*
 John C. Miller, *Sam Adams: Pioneer in Propaganda.* Boston, 1936.

Miller, "Stamp Act in Georgia"
Randall M. Miller, "The Stamp Act in Colonial Georgia," *Georgia Historical Quarterly* 56 (1972): 318–31.

[Mitchell,] *Present State*
[John Mitchell,] *The Present State of Great Britain and North America, with Regard to Agriculture, Population, Trade, and Manufactures, impartially considered.* London, 1767.

Monthly Review
The Monthly Review; or, Literary Journal: by Several Hands. (Monthly magazine, London.)

Moore, *Taxing Colonies*
Maurice Moore, *The Justice and Policy of Taxing the American Colonies, in Great-Britain, considered* (1765), reprinted in *Not a Conquered People: Two Carolinians View Parliamentary Taxation.* Edited by William S. Price, Jr. Raleigh, N.C., 1975, pp. 37–48.

Morgan, *Birth*
Edmund S. Morgan, *The Birth of the Republic, 1763–89.* Chicago, 1956.

Morgan, "Colonial Ideas"
Edmund S. Morgan, "Colonial Ideas of Parliamentary Power 1764–1766," *William and Mary Quarterly* 5 (1948): 311–41.

Morgan, *Gentle Puritan*
Edmund S. Morgan, *The Gentle Puritan: A Life of Ezra Stiles, 1727–1795.* Chapel Hill, N.C., 1962.

Morgan, "Parliamentary Power"
Edmund S. Morgan, "Colonial Ideas of Parliamentary Power, 1764–1766," in *Pivotal Interpretations of American History* 1. Edited by Carl N. Degler. New York. 1966, pp. 43–72.

Morgan, "Postponement of Stamp Act"
Edmund S. Morgan, "The Postponement of the Stamp Act," *William and Mary Quarterly* 7 (1950): 353–92.

Morgan, *Prologue*
Prologue to Revolution: Sources and Documents on the Stamp Act Crisis, 1764–1766. Edited by Edmund S. Morgan. Chapel Hill, N.C., 1959.

Morgan, "Thomas Hutchinson"
Edmund S. Morgan, "Thomas Hutchinson and the Stamp Act," *New England Quarterly* 21 (1948): 459–92.

Mullet, *Fundamental Law*
Charles F. Mullet, *Fundamental Law and the American Revolution 1760–1776.* New York, 1933.

Murdoch, *Rebellion in America*
    Rebellion in America: A Contemporary British Viewpoint, 1765–1783.
    Edited by David H. Murdoch. Santa Barbara, Calif., 1979.

Murrin, "Great Inversion"
    John M. Murrin, "The Great Inversion, or Court Versus Country: A Comparison of the Revolution Settlements in England (1688–1721) and America (1776–1816)," in *Three British Revolutions, 1641, 1688, 1776.* Edited by J. G. A. Pocock. Princeton, N.J., pp. 368–453.

Namier, *Age of Revolution*
    L. B. Namier, *England in the Age of the American Revolution.* London, 1930.

Namier, "Charles Garth"
    L. B. Namier, "Charles Garth and his Connexions," *English Historical Review* 54 (1939): 443–70, 632–52.

Namier & Brooke, *Charles Townshend*
    Sir Lewis Namier and John Brooke, *Charles Townshend.* New York, 1964.

New Jersey Votes and Proceedings (November 1765)
    Votes and Proceedings of the General Assembly of the Province of New-Jersey. At a Session of General Assembly, began at Burlington, November 26, 1765, and continued till the 30th following. Burlington, N.J., 1765.

New Jersey Votes and Proceedings (1768)
    Votes and Proceedings of the General Assembly of the Province of New-Jersey. At a Session of the General Assembly, began at Perth-Amboy, April 12, 1768, and continued till the 10th of May following. Woodbridge, N.J., 1768.

New Jersey Votes and Proceedings (January 1775)
    Votes and Proceedings of the General Assembly of the Colony of New-Jersey. At a Session began at Perth-Amboy, Wednesday January 11, 1775, and continued until the 12th Day of February following. Burlington, N.J., 1775.

New Jersey Votes and Proceedings (May 1775)
    Votes and Proceedings of the General Assembly of the Colony of New-Jersey. At a Sitting began at Burlington, Monday, May 15, 1775, and continued until the 20th Day of the same Month. Burlington, N.J., 1775.

New York Journal of Votes
    Journal of the Votes and Proceedings of the General Assembly of the Colony of New-York. Began the 8th Day of November, 1743; and Ended the 23th of December, 1765. Vol. II. Published by Order of the General Assembly. New York, 1766.

Nicholas, *Present State of Virginia*
    Robert Carter Nicholas, *Considerations on the Present State of Virginia Examined* (1774), reprinted in *Revolutionary Virginia* 1:259–85.

North Briton
    The North Briton. Revised and Corrected by the Author. Illustrated with Explanatory Notes, and A Copious Index of Names and Characters. Dublin, 1764.

North Carolina Colonial Records
    The Colonial Records of North Carolina, Published Under the Supervision of the Trustees of the Public Libraries, By Order of the General Assembly. Vols. 6, 7, 8, 9, and 10. Edited by William L. Saunders, Raleigh, N.C., 1888, 1890.

Onuf, "Introduction"
    Peter S. Onuf, "Introduction" to *Maryland and the Empire, 1773: The Antilon-First Citizen Letters.* Edited by Peter S. Onuf. Baltimore, 1974, pp. 3–39.

Osgood, "American Revolution"
    Herbert L. Osgood, "The American Revolution," reprinted in *Causes and Consequences of the American Revolution.* Edited by Esmond Wright. Chicago, 1966, pp. 65–77.

O'Sullivan, "Philosophy of Common Law"
    Richard O'Sullivan, "The Philosophy of the Common Law," *Current Legal Problems* 2 (1949): 116–38.

[Otis,] *Considerations*
    [James Otis,] *Considerations On Behalf of the Colonists in a Letter to a Noble Lord.* London, 1765.

Otis, *Rights*
    James Otis, *The Rights of the British Colonies Asserted and Proved* (1764), reprinted in Bailyn, *Pamphlets* 1:419–82.

Paley, *Essay upon the Constitution*
    W. Paley, *An Essay Upon the British Constitution: Being the Seventh Chapter of the Sixth Book of the Principles of Moral and Political Philosophy.* London, 1792.

Papers of Iredell
    The Papers of James Iredell: Volume I. 1767–1777. Edited by Don Higginbotham. Raleigh, N.C., 1976.

Papers of Jefferson
    The Papers of Thomas Jefferson. Edited by Julian P. Boyd. 20 vols. Princeton, N.J., 1950–82.

[Parker,] *Case of Shipmoney*
    [Henry Parker,] *The Case of Shipmoney briefly discoursed, according to the Grounds of Law, Policy, and Conscience. And Most Humbly Presented to the Censure and Correction of the High Court of Parliament.* N.i., 1640.

Parliament Register
> The Parliamentary Register; or, History of the Proceedings and Debates of the House of Commons. 17 vols. London, 1775–80.

Parliamentary History
> The Parliamentary History of England, From the Earliest Period to the Year 1803. 36 vols. London, 1806–20.

Pennsylvania Archives
> Pennsylvania Archives: Eighth Series [Votes and Proceedings of the House of Representatives.] 8 vols. [Harrisburg, Pa.,] 1931–35.

Pennsylvania Council
> Minutes of the Provincial Council of Pennsylvania, From the Organization to the Termination of the Proprietary Government. Vol. IX. Containing the Proceedings of Council From October 15th, 1762, to 17th of October, 1771, Both Days Included. Vol. X. Containing the Proceedings of Council From October 18th, 1771, to 27th of September, 1775, Both Days Included; Together with Minutes of the Council of Safety From June 30th, 1775, to November 12th, 1776, Both Days Included. Harrisburg, Pa., 1852.

Phillips, *Salem*
> James Duncan Phillips, Salem in the Eighteenth Century. Boston, 1937.

Pitkin, *Civil History*
> Timothy Pitkin, A Political and Civil History of the United States of America From the Year 1763. Vol. 1. New Haven, Conn., 1828.

Pocock, *Machiavellian Moment*
> J. G. A. Pocock, The Machiavellian Moment: Florentine Political Thought and the Atlantic Republican Tradition. Princeton, N.J., 1975.

Pole, *Political Representation*
> J. R. Pole, Political Representation in England and the Origins of the American Republic. New York, 1966.

Political Debates
> Political Debates. Paris [Philadelphia?], 1766.

Political Register
> The Political Register; and Impartial Review of New Books. (Monthly magazine, London.)

Political Writings of James Otis
> Some Political Writings of James Otis: Collected with an Introduction by Charles F. Mullett. The University of Missouri Studies: A Quarterly of Research. Vol. 4, July–October 1929.

Pollock, "Politics"
> Sir Frederick Pollock, "The History of English Law as a Branch of Politics," in Sir Frederick Pollock, Jurisprudence and Legal Essays. New York, 1961, pp. 185–211.

Pownall, *Administration*
> Thomas Pownall, *The Administration of the Colonies. Wherein their Rights and Constitution are Discussed and Stated.* 4th ed. London, 1768.

Pownall, *Administration Fifth Edition*
> Thomas Pownall, *The Administration of the British Colonies. The Fifth Edition. Wherein their Rights and Constitution are discussed and stated.* 2 vols. London, 1774.

[Pownall,] *Considerations*
> [Thomas Pownall,] *Considerations on the Points lately brought into Question as to the Parliament's Right of Taxing the Colonies, And of the Measures necessary to be taken at this Crisis. Being an Appendix, Section III, to the Administration of the Colonies.* London, 1766.

Pownall, *Pownall*
> Charles A. W. Pownall, *Thomas Pownall M.P., F.R.S., Governor of Massachusetts Bay.* London, 1908.

Pownall, *Right, Interest, and Duty*
> Thomas Pownall, *The Right, Interest, and Duty of the State, as concerned in the Affairs of the East Indies.* London, 1773.

Prall, *Agitation*
> Stuart E. Prall, *The Agitation for the Law Reform During the Puritan Revolution 1640–1660.* The Hague, 1966.

[Prescott,] *Calm Consideration*
> [Benjamin Prescott,] *A Free and Calm Consideration of the Unhappy Misunderstandings and Debates, which have of late Years arisen, and yet subsist, Between the Parliament of Great-Britain, and these American Colonies. Contained in Eight Letters, Six whereof, Directed to a Gentleman of Distinction in England, Formerly printed in the Essex Gazette. The other Two, directed to a Friend.* Salem, Mass., 1774.

Price, *Nature of Civil Liberty*
> Richard Price, *Observations on the Nature of Civil Liberty, the Principles of Government, and the Justice and Policy of the War with America.* London, 1776.

[Priestly,] *Address to Dissenters*
> [Joseph Priestly,] *An Address to Protestant Dissenters of all Denominations, on the Approaching Election of Members of Parliament, With Respect to the State of Public Liberty in General, and of American Affairs in Particular.* Philadelphia, 1774.

Prior Documents
> *A Collection of Interesting, Authentic Papers, Relative to the Dispute Between Great Britain and America; Shewing the Causes and Progress of that Misunderstanding, From 1764 to 1775.* London, 1777.

Proceedings against Manwaring
    The Proceedings of the Lords and Commons In the Year 1628. Against Roger Manwaring Doctor in Divinity, [The Sacheverell of those Days] For Two Seditious High-flying Sermons, intitled, Religion and Allegiance. London, 1709.

"Proceedings Committee of Correspondence"
    "Proceedings of the Virginia Committee of Correspondence," 12 *Virginia Magazine of History and Biography* (1904–5): 1–14, 157–69, 225–40, 353–64.

Proceedings and Debates of Parliaments
    Proceedings and Debates of the British Parliaments respecting North America. Edited by Leo Francis Stock. 5 vols. Washington, D.C., 1924–41.

Protests of Lords
    A Complete Collection of the Protests of the Lords With Historical Introductions. Edited by James E. Thorold Rogers. 3 vols. Oxford, 1875.

Providence Gazette
    The Providence Gazette and Country Journal. (Weekly newspaper, Providence, R.I.)

Public Records of Connecticut
    The Public Records of the Colony of Connecticut. Edited by Charles J. Hoadley and J. H. Trumbull. Vols. 12–15. Hartford, Conn., 1881–90.

Pudsey, *Constitution and Laws*
    William P[udse]y, *The Constitution and Laws of England Consider'd.* London, 1701.

Pulteney, *Thoughts on Present State*
    William Pulteney, *Thoughts on the Present State of Affairs with America, and the Means of Conciliation.* 4th ed. London, 1778.

Pym, *Declaration of Grievances*
    John Pym, *A Declaration of the Grievances of the Kingdome (1642),* reprinted in *Somers' Tracts,* 4:390–404.

Pym, *Speech of Summing Up*
    John Pym, *The Speech or Declaration of John Pym, Esquire: After the Recapitulation or summing up of the Charge of High-Treason, Against Thomas, Earle of Strafford, 12 April, 1641.* London, 1641.

[Ramsay,] *Historical Essay*
    [Allan Ramsay,] *An Historical Essay on the English Constitution: Or, An impartial Inquiry into the Elective Power of the People, from the first Establishment of the Saxons in this Kingdom. Wherein the Right of Parliament, to Tax our distant Provinces, is explained, and justified, upon such constitutional Principles as will afford an equal Security to the Colonists, as to their Brethren at Home.* London, 1771.

Ramsay, *History*
> David Ramsay, *The History of the American Revolution*. New edition. 2 vols. London, 1793.

[Randolph,] *Present State of Virginia*
> [John Randolph,] *Considerations on the Present State of Virginia* (1774), reprinted in *Revolutionary Virginia* 1:206–18.

[Rawson,] *Revolution in New England*
> [Edward Rawson,] *The Revolution in New England Justified, And the People there Vindicated From the Aspersions cast upon them by Mr. John Palmer, In his Pretended Answer to the Declaration, Published by the Inhabitants of Boston, and the Country adjacent, on the Day when they secured their late Oppressors, who acted by an Illegal and Arbitrary Commission from the Late King JAMES.* Boston, 1691.

Ray, *Importance of Colonies*
> Nicholas Ray, *The Importance of the Colonies of North America, and the Interest of Great Britain with regard to them, Considered. Together with Remarks on the Stamp-Duty.* London, 1766.

Reid, "Economic Burden"
> Joseph D. Reid, Jr., "Economic Burden: Spark to the American Revolution?," *Journal of Economic History* 38 (1978): 81–100.

"Remarks" on Letter to De Berdt
> "Remarks" on the Letter in *Extract of a Letter From the House of Representatives of the Massachusetts-Bay to their Agent Dennys De Berdt, Esq; with some Remarks.* London, 1770, pp. 15–28.

Remembrancer for 1775
> *The Remembrancer, or Impartial Repository of Public Events, for the Year MDCCLXXV.* London, [1776].

Remembrancer for 1776: Part III
> *The Remembrancer; or, Impartial Repository of Public Events. Part III. For the Year 1776.* London, 1777.

Report of Lords on Massachusetts
> *The Report of the Lords Committees, Appointed by the House of Lords to Enquire into the several Proceedings in the Colony of Massachuset's Bay, in Opposition to the Sovereignty of His Majesty, in His Parliament of Great Britain, over that Province; and also what hath passed in this House relative thereto, from the First Day of January, 1764.* London, 1774.

Revolution Documents
> *Documents of the American Revolution 1770–1783.* Edited by K. G. Davies. Vols. 1–16. Dublin, 1972–81.

Revolution Justified
> [Edward Rawson and Samuel Sewall,] *The Revolution in New England Justified, And the People there Vindicated From the Aspersions cast upon*

them By Mr. John Palmer . . . (1691), reprinted in *The Andros Tracts* 1:
Prince Society Publications, Vol. 5., 1868, pp. 65–131.

Revolutionary Virginia
*Revolutionary Virginia The Road to Independence – Volume I: Forming
Thunderclouds and the First Convention, 1763–1774. A Documentary Record.* Compiled by William J. Van Schreeven, edited by Robert L. Scribner.
*Volume II: The Committees and the Second Convention, 1773–1775. A
Documentary Record.* Compiled by William J. Van Schreeven and Robert L. Scribner. *Volume III: The Breaking Storm and the Third Convention, 1775. A Documentary Record.* Compiled and edited by Robert L.
Scribner. *Volume IV: The Committee of Safety and the Balance of Forces,
1775. A Documentary Record.* Compiled and edited by Robert L. Scribner and Brent Tarter. *Volume V: The Clash of Arms and the Fourth Convention, 1775–1776. A Documentary Record.* Compiled and edited by
Robert L. Scribner and Brent Tarter. [Charlottesville, Va.,] 1973–79.

Rhode Island Colony Records
*Records of the Colony of Rhode Island and Providence Plantations in New
England.* Edited by John R. Bartlett 10 vols. Providence, R.I., 1856–65.

Rhode Island Correspondence
*The Correspondence of the Colonial Governors of Rhode Island, 1723–
1775.* Edited by Gertrude Selwyn Kimball. 2 vols. Boston, 1902–3.

Ritcheson, "Introduction"
Charles R. Ritcheson, "Introduction," to *The American Revolution: The
Anglo-American Relation, 1763–1794.* Edited by Charles R. Ritcheson.
Reading, Mass., 1969, pp. 1–9.

Robertson, *Chatham*
Sir Charles Grant Robertson, *Chatham and the British Empire.* New York,
1962.

Robson, *American Revolution*
Eric Robson, *The American Revolution in Its Political and Military Aspects 1763–1783.* New York, 1966.

Roebuck, *Enquiry whether the Guilt*
John Roebuck, *An Enquiry Whether the Guilt of the Present Civil War
in America, Ought to be Imputed to Great Britain or America.* New ed.
London, 1776.

[Rokeby,] *Considerations on the Measures*
[Matthew Robinson-Morris, Second Baron Rokeby,] *Considerations on the
Measures Carrying on with Respect to the British Colonies in North Amer-
ica.* 2d ed. London, [1774].

[Rokeby,] *Further Examination*
[Matthew Robinson-Morris, Second Baron Rokeby,] *A Further Examina-*

tion of our Present American Measures and of the Reasons and the Principles on which they are founded. Bath, England, 1776.

Rossiter, *Political Thought*
Clinton Rossiter, *The Political Thought of the American Revolution.* New York, 1963.

Rossiter, *Six Characters*
Clinton Rossiter, *Six Characters in Search of a Republic: Studies in the Political Thought of the American Colonies.* New York, 1964.

[Ruffhead,] *Considerations*
[Owen Ruffhead,] *Considerations on the Present Dangerous Crisis.* Edinburgh, 1763.

[Ruffhead,] *Reasons Why Treaty*
[Owen Ruffhead,] *Reasons Why the Approaching Treaty of Peace Should be Debated in Parliament: As a Method most Expedient and Constitutional.* London, 1760.

Ruggles, "Reasons"
"Brigadier Ruggles's Reasons for his Dissent from the Resolutions of the Congress at *New York,* as given into the House, February 19, 1766," in *Boston Gazette* (Supplement), 5 May 1766, p. 1.

Ryder, "Parliamentary Diaries"
"Parliamentary Diaries of Nathaniel Ryder, 1764–7," edited by P. D. G. Thomas. *Camden Miscellany Vol. XXIII.* Camden Society, 4th ser., Vol. 7. London, [1969].

Sainsbury, "Pro-Americans"
John Sainsbury, "The Pro-Americans of London, 1769 to 1782," *William and Mary Quarterly* 35 (1978): 423–54.

St. Amand, *Legislative Power*
George St. Amand, *An Historical Essay on the Legislative Power of England. Wherein the Origin of Both Houses of Parliament, Their Antient Constitution, and the Changes that have happen'd in the Persons that compos'd them, with the Occasions thereof, are related in Chronological Order.* London, 1725.

St. John, *Speech or Declaration*
[Oliver St. John,] *The Speech or Declaration of Mr. St. John, His Majesties Solicitor-Generall. Delivered at a Conference of both Houses of Parliament, held 16. Caroli, 1640. Concerning Ship-Money. As it is revised, and allowed according to order.* London, 1641.

[Sayre,] *Englishman Deceived*
[Stephen Sayre,] *The Englishman Deceived; A Political Piece: Wherein Some very Important Secrets of State are briefly recited, And offered to the Consideration of the Public.* London, 1768.

Schlesinger, "Uprising Against Company"
Arthur Meier Schlesinger, "The Uprising Against the East India Company," *Political Science Quarterly* 32 (1917): 60–79.

Schuyler, *Empire*
Robert Livingston Schuyler, *Parliament and the British Empire: Some Constitutional Controversies Concerning Imperial Legislative Jurisdiction*. New York, 1929.

Scots Magazine
The Scots Magazine. (Monthly magazine, Edinburgh.)

[Scott,] *Remarks on the Patriot*
[John Scott,] *Remarks on the Patriot. Including some Hints Respecting the Americans: with an Address to the Electors of Great Britain*. London, 1775.

[Seabury,] *Congress Canvassed*
[Samuel Seabury,] *The Congress Canvassed: or, an Examination into the Conduct of the Delegates, at their Grand Convention, Held in Philadelphia, Sept. 1, 1774. Addressed, to the Merchants of New-York*. [New York,] 1774.

[Seabury,] *View of Controversy*
[Samuel Seabury,] *A View of the Controversy Between Great-Britain and her Colonies: Including a Mode of Determining their present Disputes, Finally and Effectually; and of Preventing all Future Contentions. In a Letter, to the Author of a Full Vindication of the Measures of the Congress, from the Calumnies of their Enemies*. New York, 1774.

Select Collection of Letters
A Select Collection of the Most Interesting Letters on the Government, Liberty, and Constitution of England; Which have appeared in the different News-papers from the elevation of Lord Bute, to the death of the Earl of Egremont. 3 vols. 2d ed. London, 1763–64.

[Serle,] *Americans against Liberty*
[Ambrose Serle,] *Americans against Liberty: or, an Essay on the Nature and Principles of True Freedom, Shewing that the Design and Conduct of the Americans tend only to Tyranny and Slavery*. 3d ed. London, 1776.

[Shebbeare,] *Answer to Edmund Burke*
[John Shebbeare,] *An Answer to the Printed Speech of Edmund Burke, Esq; Spoken in the House of Commons, April 19, 1774. In Which his Knowledge in Polity, Legislature, Humankind, History, Commerce and Finance, is candidly examined; his Arguments are fairly refuted; the Conduct of Administration is fully defended; and his Oratoric Talents are clearly exposed to view*. London, 1775.

Shebbeare, *Essay on National Society*
J. Shebbeare, *An Essay on the Origin, Progress and Establishment of National Society; in which the Principles of Government, the Definitions of*

physical, moral, civil, and religious Liberty, contained in Dr. Price's Observations, &c. are fairly examined and fully refuted: Together with a Justification of the Legislature, in reducing America to Obedience by Force. London, 1776.

[Shebbeare,] *Fifth Letter*
[John Shebbeare,] A *Fifth Letter to the People of England, on the Subversion of the Constitution: And, The Necessity of it's being restored.* 2d ed. London, 1757.

[Shebbeare,] *Seventh Letter*
[John Shebbeare,] A *Seventh Letter to the People of England. A Defence of the Prerogative Royal, As it was exerted in His Majesty's Proclamation For the Prohibiting the Exportation of Corn. In which it is Proved That this Authority ever has been, is, and must be essential to the constitution, and inseperable from the Rights and Liberties of the Subject.* London, 1767.

Simmons, "Massachusetts Revolution of 1689"
Richard C. Simmons, "The Massachusetts Revolution of 1689: Three Early American Political Broadsides," *Journal of American Studies* 2 (1968): 1–12.

Sinclair, *Public Revenue*
Sir John Sinclair, *The History of the Public Revenue of the British Empire. Containing An Account of the public Income and Expenditure from the remotest Periods recorded in History, to Michaelmas 1802. With a Review of the Financial Administration of the Right Honorable William Pitt.* 3 vols. 3d ed. London, 1803–4.

Smith, *The Wealth of Nations*
Adam Smith, *An Inquiry into the Nature and Causes of the Wealth of Nations.* Edited by Edwin Cannan. New York, 1937.

Somers' Tracts
A *Collection of Scarce and Valuable Tracts, on the Most Interesting and Entertaining Subjects: But Chiefly such as Relate to the History and Constitution of these Kingdoms. Selected from an Infinite Number in Print and Manuscript, in the Royal, Cotton, Sion, and other Public, as well as Private, Libraries; Particularly that of the Late Lord Somers.* Edited by Walter Scott. Vols. 4–6. London, 1809–15.

South-Carolina Gazette
(Weekly newspaper, Charles Town, S.C.)

Southwick, "Molasses Act"
Albert B. Southwick, "The Molasses Act — Source of Precedents," *William and Mary Quarterly* 8 (1951): 389–405.

Speeches
Speeches of the Governors of Massachusetts From 1765 to 1775; And the

Answers of the House of Representatives to the Same; with their Resolutions and Addresses for that Period. Boston, 1818.

Speeches of John Wilkes in Parliament
  The Speeches of John Wilkes, One of the Knights of the Shire for the County of Middlesex, In the Parliament appointed to meet at Westminster the 29th day of November 1774, to the Prorogation the 6th Day of June 1777. 2 vols. London, 1777.

Speeches in Last Session
  The Speeches in the Last Session of the present Parliament, Delivered by several of the Principal Advocates in the House of Commons, in Favour of the Rights of America. New York, 1775.

"Stamp Act Debates"
  "Debates on the Declaratory Act and the Repeal of the Stamp Act, 1766," *American Historical Review* 17 (1912): 563–86.

Stanlis, "British Views"
  Peter J. Stanlis, "British Views of the American Revolution: A Conflict over Rights of Sovereignty," *Early American Literature* 11 (1976): 191–201.

State Trials
  A Complete Collection of State Trials and Proceedings for High Treason and Other Crimes and Misdemeanors From the Earliest Period to the Year 1783, With Notes and Other Illustrations. Compiled by T. B. Howell. 34 vols. London, 1816–28.

[Stewart,] *Letter to Price*
  [James Stewart,] *A Letter to the Rev. Dr. Price, F. R. S. Wherein his Observations on the Nature of Civil Liberty, the Principles of Government, &c. Are Candidly Examined; His Fundamental Principles refuted, and the Fallacy of his Reasoning from these Principles detected. Also the True Principles of Liberty, Explained and Demonstrated; the Constitutional Authority of the Supreme Legislature of Great Britain, Over every Part of the British Dominions, Both in the Matter of Legislation and Taxation, and in every Act of Legal Authority, Asserted and Fully Vindicated.* London, 1776.

Stewart, *Total Refutation*
  James Stewart, *The Total Refutation and Political Overthrow of Doctor Price; or, Great Britain Successfully vindicated against all American Rebels, and their Advocates. In a Second Letter to that Gentleman.* London, 1776.

Stille, *John Dickinson*
  Charles J. Stille, *The Life and Times of John Dickinson 1732–1808.* Memoirs of the Pennsylvania Historical Society 13. Philadelphia, 1891.

Stout, "Goals and Enforcement of Policy"
Neil R. Stout, "Goals and Enforcement of British Colonial Policy, 1763–1775," *American Neptune* 27 (1967): 211–20.

Stout, *Royal Navy*
Neil R. Stout, *The Royal Navy in America, 1760–1775: A Study of Enforcement of British Colonial Policy in the Era of the American Revolution.* Annapolis, Md., 1973.

[Strafford,] *Briefe and Perfect Relation*
[Thomas Wentworth, earl of Strafford,] *A Briefe and Perfect Relation, of the Answeres and Replies of Thomas Earle of Strafford; To the Articles exhibited against him, by the House of Commons on the thirteenth of April, An. Dom. 1641.* London, 1647.

Sullivan, *Lectures on the Constitution*
Francis Stoughton Sullivan, *Lectures on the Constitution and Laws of England: With a Commentary on Magna Carta, and Illustrations of Many of the English Statutes. To which Authorities are added, and a Discourse is prefixed, concerning the Laws and Government of England by Gilbert Stuart, LL.D.* 2d ed. London, 1776.

"Surrender of Virginia"
"The Surrender of Virginia in 1651," *Virginia Historical Register, and Literary Advertiser* 2 (1849): 181–87.

Thacher, *Sentiments*
Oxenbridge Thacher, *The Sentiments of a British American* (1764), reprinted in Bailyn *Pamphlets* 1:490–98.

Thomas, *British Politics*
P. D. G. Thomas, *British Politics and the Stamp Act Crisis: The First Phase of the American Revolution, 1763–1767.* Oxford, 1975.

Thomas, "Townshend and Taxation"
P. D. G. Thomas, "Charles Townshend and American Taxation in 1767," *English Historical Review* 83 (1968): 33–51.

Thomson, *Constitutional History*
Mark A. Thomson, *A Constitutional History of England 1642 to 1801.* London, 1938.

Toulmin, *American War Lamented*
Joshua Toulmin, *The American War lamented. A Sermon Preached at Taunton, February the 18th and 25th, 1776.* London, 1776.

Town and Country Magazine
The Town and Country Magazine; or Universal Repository of Knowledge, Instruction, and Entertainment. (Monthly magazine, London.)

True Briton, *American Independency*
> T. True Briton, *Observations on American Independency.* N.i., 1779.

Tucker, *Letter to Burke*
> Josiah Tucker, *A Letter to Edmund Burke, Esq; Member of Parliament for the City of Bristol, and Agent for the Colony of New York, &c. In Answer to His Printed Speech, Said to be Spoken in the House of Commons on the Twenty-Second of March, 1775.* 2d ed. Gloucester, England, 1775.

[Tucker,] *Series of Answers*
> [Josiah Tucker,] *A Series of Answers to Certain Popular Objections, Against Separating from the Rebellious Colonies, and Discarding them Entirely: Being the Concluding Tract of the Dean of Glocester on the Subject of American Affairs.* Gloucester, England, 1776.

Tucker, *Tract Five*
> Josiah Tucker, *Tract V. The Respective Pleas and Arguments of the Mother Country, and of the Colonies, Distinctly Set Forth; and the Impossibility of a Compromise of Differences, or a Mutual Concession of Rights, Plainly Demonstrated. With a Prefatory Epistle to the Plenipotentiaries of the late Congress at Philadelphia.* London, 1775.

[Tyrrell,] *Brief Enquiry*
> [James Tyrrell,] *A Brief Enquiry into the Ancient Constitution and Government of England.* London, 1695.

Van Alstyne, "Bursts"
> Richard W. Van Alstyne, "The Revolution Bursts," in *The American Revolution: The Anglo-American Relation, 1763–1794.* Edited by Charles R. Ritcheson. Reading, Mass., 1969, pp. 59–74.

Wade, *Junius*
> John Wade, *Junius: Including Letters by the Same Writer Under Other Signatures; to Which are Added his Confidential Correspondence with Mr. Wilkes, and his Private Letters to Mr. H. S. Woodfall.* 2 vols. London, 1850.

Walpole, *Memoirs*
> Horace Walpole, *Memoirs of the Reign of King George the Third.* Edited by Sir Denis Le Marchant Bart. 2 vols. Philadelphia, 1845.

Washburn, "Preface"
> Charles G. Washburn, "Preface and Notes," in *Jasper Mauduit: Agent in London for the Province of the Massachusetts-Bay 1762–1765.* Boston, 1918.

Waters, *Ipswich in Massachusetts Bay Colony*
> Thomas Franklin Waters, *Ipswich in the Massachusetts Bay Colony. Volume II. A History of the Town from 1700 to 1917.* Ipswich, Mass., 1917.

Watson, *Principles of Revolution*
> Richard Watson, *The Principles of the Revolution vindicated in a Sermon*

Preached Before the University of Cambridge, on Wednesday, May 29, 1776. Cambridge, England, 1776.

Webb, "Trials of Andros"
Stephen Saunders Webb, "The Trials of Sir Edmund Andros," in *The Human Dimensions of Nation Making: Essays on Colonial and Revolutionary America.* Edited by James Kirby Martin. Madison, Wis., 1976, pp. 23–53.

Weir, *Most Important Epocha*
Robert M. Weir, *"A Most Important Epocha": The Coming of the Revolution in South Carolina.* Columbia, S.C., 1970.

Wells, *Samuel Adams*
Williams V. Wells, *The Life and Public Services of Samuel Adams, being A Narrative of His Acts and Opinions, and of his Agency in Producing and Forwarding the American Revolution.* 3 vols. Boston, 1865.

Wendell, *Cotton Mather*
Barrett Wendell, *Cotton Mather: The Puritan Priest.* New York, 1891.

Wesley, *Calm Address*
John Wesley, *A Calm Address to our American Colonies.* London, [1775.]

"Weston Papers"
"The Manuscripts of Charles Fleetwood Weston Underwood, Esq., of Somerby Hall, Lincolnshire," *Historical Manuscripts Commission: Reports on the Manuscripts of the Earl of Eglinton, Sir J. Stirling Maxwell, Bart., C. S. H. Drummond Moray, Esq., C. F. Weston Underwood, Esq., and G. Wingfield Digby, Esq.* (Report no. 10). London, 1885.

[Whately,] *Considerations on Trade*
[Thomas Whately,] *Considerations on the Trade and Finances of this Kingdom, and on the Measures of Administration, with Respect to those great National Objects since the Conclusion of the Peace.* 3d ed. London, 1769.

[Whately,] *Regulations Lately Made*
[Thomas Whately,] *The Regulations Lately Made Concerning the Colonies, and the Taxes imposed Upon Them, Considered.* London, 1765.

[Whitelocke,] *Concerning Impositions*
[Sir James Whitelocke,] *The Rights of the People Concerning Impositions, Stated in a learned Argument; With a Remonstrance presented to the Kings most excellent Majesty, by the Honorable House of Commons, in the Parliament, An. Dom. 1610. Annoq; Regis Jac. 7.* London, 1658.

Wilkes, *English Liberty*
John Wilkes, *English Liberty: Being a Collection of Interesting Tracts, From the Year 1762 to 1769. Containing the Private Correspondence, Public Letters, Speeches, and Addresses, of John Wilkes, Esq. Humbly Dedicated to the King.* London, [1770].

Williamson, "Imperial Policy"
J. A. Williamson, "The Beginnings of an Imperial Policy, 1649–1660," in *The Cambridge History of the British Empire: Volume I, The Old Empire From the Beginnings to 1783*. Edited by J. Holland Rose, A. P. Newton, and E. A. Benians. Cambridge, England, 1929, pp. 207–38.

[Williamson,] *Plea of the Colonies*
[Hugh Williamson,] *The Plea of the Colonies On the Charges brought against them by Lord Mansfield, and Others in a letter to His Lordship*. Philadelphia, 1777.

Wiltse, *Jeffersonian Tradition*
Charles Maurice Wiltse, *The Jeffersonian Tradition in American Democracy*. New York, 1960.

Wood, *Creation*
Gordon S. Wood, *The Creation of the American Republic 1776–1787*. Chapel Hill, N.C., 1969.

[Wood,] *Institute of the Laws*
[Thomas Wood,] *A New Institute of the Imperial or Civil Law*. London, 1704.

Wright, *American Interpretation*
Esmond Wright, *The American Revolution: Its Interpretations and Its Significance. Sir George Watson Lecture delivered in the University of Leicester, 21 February 1967*. Leicester, England, 1967.

Wright, *Fabric of Freedom*
Esmond Wright, *Fabric of Freedom, 1763–1800*. New York, 1961.

Writings of Edmund Burke
The Writings and Speeches of Edmund Burke in Twelve Volumes. New York, 1901.

Wynne, *Eunomus*
Edward Wynne, *Eunomus: or, Dialogues Concerning the Law and Constitution of England. With an Essay on Dialogue*. 2d ed. 4 vols. London, 1785.

[Young,] *Political Essays*
[Arthur Young,] *Political Essays Concerning the Present State of the British Empire*. London, 1772.

[Zubly,] *Right to Tax*
[John Joachim Zubly,] *Great Britain's Right to Tax her Colonies. Placed in the Clearest Light, By a Swiss*. [London, 1774].

NOTES

Introduction

1 Classic age: Wood, *Creation*, pp. 10–11; writer: [Shebbeare,] *Fifth Letter*, p. 77; Mythologists: Thomson, *Constitutional History*, 353; Tautology: Pole, *Political Representation*, p. 388.

2 *Monthly Review* 32 (1765): 59; Abingdon, *Thoughts on Burke's Letter*, p. 22; "A Constitutional and Political English Catechism," *London Magazine* 35 (1766): 266; "An Analysis of the British Constitution, in Its Genuine Purity," *Political Register* 5 (1769): 70–71; book reviewer: *Monthly Review* 28 (1763): 490.

3 Too often the distinction is not even considered. A recent reviewer, for example, insisted that this book should not be written because the American Revolution had little to do with constitutionalism (and, besides, the story had been fully told). J. M. Sosin, "Historian's History or Lawyer's History?," *Reviews in American History* 10 (1982): 38–43. Unfortunately, not only was the topic beyond the reviewer's competence, but the book being reviewed dealt with *legal*, not *constitutional* history.

A constitutional question was stated in the title of the book, but that constitutional question was of only minor significance to the coming of the Revolution. It was discussed to explain what was the main lesson of the book, the application of positive *legal* principles, not *constitutional* principles.

4 [Butler,] *Standing Army*, p. 27; Anon., *Budget Inscribed*, p. 4n.

5 William S. Price, Jr., "Introductory Essay," *Not a Conquered People: Two Carolinians View Parliamentary Taxation* (Raleigh, N.C., 1975), p. 10.

6 Lawfulness of Crowd: "In a Defensive Rage"; Criminal-law sanction: *In a Defiant Stance*, pp. 27–40; Army: "In a Constitutional Void"; Facts: *In a Rebellious Spirit;* Tea tax: *In a Defiant Stance*, pp. 98–99; Standing armies: *In Defiance of the Law.*

7 For such foolishness, see Sosin, "History" *supra* note 3, pp. 41–42.

CHAPTER ONE: THE CONSTITUTIONAL IMPERATIVE

1 Speech of Mr. W--ll--e, December 1770, "Debates in a Newly Established Society," *Gentleman's Magazine* 41 (1771): 294.

2 *Annual Register 1766*, p. [39]; Courtney, *Montesquieu and Burke*, pp. 87–89; *Works of Edmund Burke* 4:101; Stanlis, "British Views," p. 198; *Writings of Edmund Burke* 2:77; [Mauduit,] *Letters of Hutchinson*, p. 116.

3 "To ascertain the Constitutions of the Colonies has employed the Thoughts and the Pens of our ablest Politicians. But no System which has hitherto been published is solid or satisfactory." "James Duane's Speech to the Committee on Rights," 8 September 1774, *Letters of Delegates to Congress* 1:51.

4 Letter from Richard Jackson to Benjamin Franklin, 27 December 1763, *Franklin-Jackson Letters*, pp. 123–24; Instructions of Marblehead, 24 September 1765, *Boston Evening-Post*, 14 October 1765, p. 3, col. 1.

5 Connecticut Resolves, 25 October 1765, Morgan, *Prologue*, p. 56.

6 "Richard Henry Lee's Draft Address to the People of Great Britain," 27(?) June 1775, *Letters of Delegates to Congress* 1:548.

7 *Boston News-Letter*, 10 May 1764, p. 2, col. 3.

8 Letter from Agent Edward Montagu to the Committee of Correspondence, 11 April 1764, *Virginia Gazette* (Purdie & Dixon), 3 October 1766, p. 2, col. 1; Speech of George Grenville, Commons Debates, 9 March 1764, Ryder, "Parliamentary Diaries," pp. 234–35 (hereafter cited as Speech of Grenville).

9 Speech of William Baker, Commons Debates, 9 March 1764, Ryder, "Parliamentary Diaries," p. 236.

10 Speech of Charles Jenkinson, Commons Debates, 9 March 1764, ibid., p. 236.

11 Speech of John Huske, Commons Debates, 9 March 1764, ibid., p. 237.

12 *Boston Evening-Post*, 7 May 1764, p. 3, col. 1; "Instructions of the Town of Boston to its Representatives in the General Court. May, 1764," Adams, *Writings* 1:5; Pitkin, *Civil History* 1:165; Letter to Agent Mauduit, 13 June 1764, *Massachusetts House Journal* (1764), p. 75.

13 Petition and Representation of the New York House of General Assembly to the King, 18 October 1764, *New York Journal of Votes*, pp. 770, 771; Morgan, *Prologue*, p. 9.

14 Message from the House of Assembly to Governor Arthur Dobbs, 30 October 1764, *North Carolina Colonial Records* 6:1261; Letter from the South Carolina Commons House Committee of Correspondence to Agent Charles Garth, 4 September 1764, Gibbes, *Documentary History*, pp. 2–3.

15 Knox, *Claim of the Colonies*, reprinted in Morgan, *Prologue*, pp. 96–97; Greene, *Quest*, p. 365.

16 Thomas, *British Politics*, p. 87; Minutes and Order of 19 December 1764, *Acts of the Privy Council* 4:692; Letter from Edward Sedgwick to Edward Weston, 14 February 1765, "Weston Papers," p. 382; Letter from Jared Ingersoll to Governor Thomas Fitch, 11 February 1765, reprinted in Morgan, *Prologue*, pp. 29–30.

17 Speech of George Grenville, Commons Debates, 6 February 1765, Ryder, "Parliamentary Diaries," p. 254 [hereafter cited as Grenville Speech]; *Boston Post-Boy*, 6 May 1765, p. 3, col. 3.

18 Charters: "In the First Line of Defense," pp. 184–89; Grenville Speech (*supra*, n. 17), p. 255.

19 Theory of Precedent: "[I]f we reject this proposition [stamp tax] now, we shall declare that we ought not to tax the colonies. And we need not declare after a year's time we ought not, for then we cannot." Grenville Speech (*supra*, n. 17), p. 256; imperial perspective: "All colonies are subject to the dominion of the mother country, whether they are a colony of the freest or the most absolute government." Ibid., p. 254; reciprocity: "If they are not subject to this burden of tax, they are not entitled to the privilege[s] of Englishmen." Ibid., 256.

20 Speech of William Beckford, Commons Debates, 6 February 1765, Ryder, "Parliamentary Diaries," pp. 256–57.

21 Speech of William Pitt, Commons Debates, 16 January 1766, *Political Debates*, p. 4; for Pratt's opinion, see "L.," *Letter to G[renville]*, pp. 88–89; "Lord C[amde]n's Speech on the declaratory Bill of the Sovereignty of *Great Britain* over the Colonies," *Gentleman's Magazine* 37 (1767): 491.

22 Speech of Isaac Barré, Commons Debates, 6 February 1765, Ryder, "Parliamentary Diaries," p. 257 [hereafter cited as Barré, Speech]. For the legal distinction between "right and "power," see "In the Taught Tradition," pp. 947–61.

23 Letter from Jasper Mauduit to unknown, 11 January 1765, *Mauduit Letters*, p. 168, n. 1; Jackson's arguments on American Taxation (1765), *Franklin-Jackson Letters*, p. 194; Speech of Richard Jackson, Commons Debates, 6 February 1765, Ryder, "Parliamentary Diaries," p. 258.

24 Letter from Jared Ingersoll to Governor Thomas Fitch, 11 February 1766, "Ingersoll Correspondence," p. 309.

25 Speech of Lord North, Commons Debates, 6 February 1765, Ryder, "Parliamentary Diaries," p. 258; Barré, Speech (*supra*, n. 22), p. 258; Speech of Sir William Meredith, Commons Debates, 6 February 1765, Ryder, "Parliamentary Diaries," p. 259.

26 Speech of Rose Fuller, Commons Debates, 6 February 1765, Ryder, "Parliamentary Diaries," p. 259; Letter from Jared Ingersoll to the Connecticut General Assembly, 18 September 1765, "Ingersoll Correspondence," p. 336.

27 Hinkhouse, *Preliminaries*, 53–55; "Extract of a Letter from London, dated February 16, 1765," *South-Carolina Gazette*, 20 July 1765, p. 2, col. 2; *Boston Post-Boy*, 8 April 1765, p. 3, col. 2; *Boston News-Letter*, 4 April 1765,

p. 3, col. 2; Letter from Jared Ingersoll to the Connecticut General Assembly, 18 September 1765, "Ingersoll Correspondence," pp. 336–37.

28 [Lee,] *Speech Intended*, p. 22; Letter from Thomas Whately to John Temple, 9 February 1765, Thomas, *British Politics*, p. 86; [Sayre,] *Englishman Deceived*, p. 12.

29 Speech of Edmund Burke, Commons Debates, 22 March 1775, *Burke on American Revolution*, p. 83; Anon., "Some Account of a Pamphlet . . . ," *Providence Gazette*, 23 February 1765, p. 3, col. 1; Speech of Edmund Burke, Commons Debates, 19 April 1774, *Writings of Edmund Burke* 2: 17–18.

30 Argument of Mr. Macdonald for the plaintiff, *Campbell* v. *Hall*, 20 *State Trials* 239 (King's Bench, 1777), p. 290; [Hopkins,] "Vindication of a Pamphlet," 9 March 1765, p. 1, col. 1; Speech of Edmund Burke, Commons Debates, 16 November 1775, *Burke on American Revolution*, 130–31.

31 Creasy, *Imperial Constitutions*, p. 8; Anon., *Constitutional Advocates*, p. 34.

32 [Lee,] *Speech Intended*, p. 2. For an extended discussion of the "Englishness" of American rights, see *Authority of Rights*, pp. 9–28.

33 Walpole, *Memoirs* 3:91.

34 Petition of the Stamp Act Congress to the House of Commons, 23 October 1765, *Account of Stamp Act Congress*, p. 20; Town Meeting of 8 May 1770, *Boston Town Records* 18:22.

CHAPTER TWO: THE OTHER TAXES

1 *Political Debates*, p. 5; Anon., *Celebrated Speech*, p. 6.

2 St. John, *Speech or Declaration*, pp. 1–3, 26; [Parker,] *Case of Shipmony*, pp. 30, 5, 2, 24; Letter from the *North Briton*, no. CXXXV, *London Magazine* 34 (1765): 102.

3 St. John, *Speech or Declaration*, p. 20; [Parker,] *Case of Shipmony*, 22; [Fitch et al.,] *Reasons Why*, p. 4.

4 6 George II, cap. 13; Knollenberg, *Origin*, p. 131.

5 Namier, *Age of Revolution*, p. 277; Hinkhouse, *Preliminaries*, p. 43; *Boston News-Letter*, 26 April 1764, p. 2, col. 1.

6 Speech of John Huske, Commons Debates, 9 March 1764, Ryder, "Parliamentary Diaries," pp. 236, 237.

7 Resolution of 20 April 1764, *Journal of New-York Assembly* (1743–65), pp. 740–42; Letter from Thomas Cushing to Jasper Mauduit, 28 October 1763, *Mauduit Letters*, pp. 132–33; Headlam, "Imperial Reconstruction," p. 644; Robson, *American Revolution*, p. 55; Ritcheson, "Introduction," pp. 3–4; Brown, *Middle-Class Democracy*, p. 200; Forster, *Charles Townshend*, p. 29; *Political Register* 1 (1767): 27.

8 4 George III, cap. 15; Harlow, *Adams*, p. 31; Christie, *Crisis*, p. 46; Knollenberg, *Origin*, p. 140; Keir, *Constitutional History*, p. 358.

9 Robson, *American Revolution*, p. 54. Grenville explained the statute somewhat differently. "First object would be to permit West Indian trade, at the same time to regulate the other. To allow certain commodities from

the French islands which are absolutely necessary, but to give a preference of our own colonies' manufacturers by paying duty upon the others." He was not certain, but thought the revenue would be between £40,000 and £60,000. Speech of George Grenville, Commons Debates, 9 March 1764, Ryder, "Parliamentary Diaries," p. 234.

10 *Gentleman's Magazine* 34 (1764): 194.

11 7 George III, cap. 46; Speech of Edmund Burke, Commons Debates, 18 November 1768, *Burke on American Revolution,* pp. 2–3; Thomas, "Townshend and Taxation," p. 33; Thomas, *British Politics,* pp. 337, 347; Christie, *Crisis,* pp. 69–70; Brown, *Middle-Class Democracy,* p. 234; Speech of Charles Townshend, Commons Debates, 7 February 1766, Ryder, "Parliamentary Diaries," p. 283.

12 Letter from Edward Sedgwick to Edward Weston, 3 February 1767, "Weston Papers," p. 402; Extract of a Letter from London to Philadelphia, 2 February 1767, *South-Carolina Gazette,* 15 June 1767, p. 2, col. 2; Speech of Charles Townshend, Commons Debates, 13 May 1767, Ryder, "Parliamentary Diaries," p. 344.

13 The distinction between internal and external taxation is the topic of the next chapter.

14 Speech of Charles Townshend, 18 February 1767, Ryder, "Parliamentary Diaries," p. 331; Letter from William Johnson to Governor William Pitkin, quoted in Thomas, *British Politics,* p. 350.

15 7 George III, cap. 46; Keir, *Constitutional History,* p. 359.

16 *South-Carolina Gazette,* 25 April 1768, p. 1, col. 3.

17 Speech of Lord North, Commons Debates, 10 April 1771, *Gentleman's Magazine* 42 (1772): 102.

18 Letter from Benjamin Franklin to Joseph Galloway, 2 December 1772, Franklin, *Writings* 5:459–60; 13 George III, cap. 44; Hacker, "The First American Revolution," pp. 139–40; Thomas, *British Politics,* pp. 353–54.

19 Quoted in *Gazette & Post-Boy,* 20 December 1773, p. 2, col. 2.

CHAPTER THREE: THE INTERNAL-EXTERNAL CRITERION

1 Miller, *Adams,* 115; Morgan, "Colonial Ideas," p. 311; Thomas, "Townshend and Taxation," pp. 37–38; Thomas, *British Politics,* pp. 340, 351–52.

2 Thomas, *British Politics,* p. 356; Namier & Brooke, *Charles Townshend,* p. 173; [Whately,] *Considerations on Trade;* Letter from John Huske to Charles Townshend, 9 April 1767, Namier & Brooke, *Charles Townshend,* p. 187.

3 Speech of Lord North, Commons Debates, 14 March 1774, *Gentleman's Magazine* 44 (1774): 500. The assumption was made not only in government but also in the popular press and pamphlets written by lawyers. For example: Anon., *Examination of Rights of Colonies,* pp. 29–36. For the best and most detailed discussion, see Morgan, "Colonial Ideas." It has been suggested that American failure to protest continuation of the Sugar Act after repeal of the Stamp Act supported the notion that the colonies did not object to external taxation. Greene, *Quest,* p. 373.

4 It should be noted that at least three other Americans testifying at the same time also said the objection was to "internal" taxes. Thomas, *British Politics,* pp. 219–20.

5 Testimony of Benjamin Franklin before the Commons, 13 February 1766, Gipson, "Great Debate," p. 34; *Examination of Franklin,* pp. 4–5.

6 Bailyn, *Pamphlets,* p. 599; Morgan, "Parliamentary Power," p. 65.

7 Gipson, *British Empire* 10:185, 285.

8 *Examination of Franklin,* pp. 6, 15, 8, 11.

9 Crane, "Franklin and Stamp Act," pp. 68–69.

10 Providence Resolves, 13 August 1765, *Providence Gazette* (Extraordinary), 24 August 1765, p. 2, col. 2; Resolves of the Rhode Island Assembly, September 1765, *Rhode Island Colony Records* 6:452; Morgan, *Prologue,* pp. 50–51. See also Instructions of Marblehead, 24 September 1765, *Gazette & News-Letter,* 10 October 1765, p. 2, col. 2.

11 Anon., *Essays Commercial and Political,* p. 57 (for discussion, see Bailyn, *Pamphlets,* pp. 124–26, 298; Bailyn, *Ideological Origins,* pp. 210–12, 216); Maryland Resolves, 28 September 1765, Morgan, *Prologue,* p. 53. For other uses of the word "internal" to describe federal relationships, see Speech of Henry Seymour Conway, Commons Debates, 3 February 1766, Ryder, "Parliamentary Diaries," p. 261; Gipson, "Debate on Repeal," p. 15, n. 11; Representation and Remonstrance of the New York General Assembly to House of Commons, 1775, *Hibernian Magazine* 5 (1775): 359.

12 *Examination of Franklin,* p. 5; [Lind,] *Thirteenth Parliament,* p. 229. Lind also knew how to answer the complaint of innovation. To the charge by the earl of Abingdon that Parliament, by innovations, was the aggressor against the Americans, Lind replied: ". . . so long as Great Britain asked nothing of America, nothing was refused her: that so long as Great Britain expended much in, and for, America, no remonstrance was made against, no attempts to put a stop to that expenditure." [Lind,] *Letter to Willoughby Bertie,* p. 33.

13 Report of the Committee of the House of Representatives, *Gazette & Post-Boy,* 13 July 1772, p. 2, col. 2; [Ruffhead,] *Reasons Why the Treaty,* pp. 21–22. "Oh! Innovation is dangerous: It may be so; and therefore I am not at this time contending to introduce new Constitutions, but to revive and restore old ones." Pudsey, *Constitution and Laws,* p. 201.

14 *Extract of a Letter to De Berdt,* p. 12; Sir John Sucking, "A Letter written to the Lower House of Parliament (1628)," *Somers' Tracts* 4:111; Remonstrance to Charles I, 14 June 1628, *Commons Debates 1628* 4:314; *Boston Evening-Post,* 19 August 1765, p. 2, col. 2; Book Review, *Monthly Review* 50 (1774): 273.

15 Agreement of the Sons of Liberty, New London, Connecticut, 25 December 1765, Morgan, *Prologue,* p. 118; *Amicus Publico* to the *New York Gazette,* 7 November 1765, reprinted in *Boston Post-Boy,* 18 November 1765, p. 2, col. 1.

16 Letter from the Massachusetts House of Representatives to the earl of Shelburne, 15 January 1768, *Speeches,* p. 140; Adams, *Writings* 1:158; Brown,

Revolutionary Politics, p. 20; Jefferson: Boorstin, *Lost World of Jefferson*, p. 179; Burke: Wood, *Creation*, p. 5.

17 "Remarks" on Letter to De Berdt, pp. 16–17. See also Moore, *Taxing Colonies*, p. 46.

18 Connecticut Resolves, 25 October 1765, Morgan, *Prologue*, p. 55; Knollenberg, *Origin*, p. 149; Speech of Governor Thomas Pownall, Commons Debates, 15 May 1767, *Parliamentary History* 16:341; Instructions of Weymouth, n.d., *Boston Evening-Post*, 21 October 1765, p. 2, col. 2; Meeting of 21 April 1766, *Boston Town Records* 16:175.

19 Letter of 23 November 1765, Bernard, *Select Letters*, p. 30; Speech of Edmund Burke, Commons Debates, 19 April 1774, *Burke on American Revolution*, p. 41. Bernard often emphasized that whig actions were innovations in order to question their constitutionality as, for example, the Council's new policy of acting without his presence which he described as "a transaction never known or implied before, and wholly illegal and unconstitutional." Letter from Governor Francis Bernard to the earl of Hillsborough, 26 September 1768, Bernard & Gage, *Letters*, p. 64.

20 Instructions of Newburyport, 21 October 1765, *Boston Post-Boy*, 4 November 1765, p. 1, col. 3. Or "arbitrary and unconstitutional Innovations." Instructions of Boston, 18 September 1765, *Boston News-Letter*, 19 September 1765, p. 2, col. 1; Adams, *Writings* 1:7–8.

21 For example: Pulteney, *Thoughts on Present State*, p. 30.

22 Perhaps the best was contained in "Address to the Inhabitants of Philadelphia" (1768), *American Gazette*, pp. 83–84.

23 One of the few if not the only one was by William Knox, who was not a lawyer and may not have understood that although the test of constitutional innovation had once been a major foundation of the English constitution, it was not an absolute principle.

> If the novelty of a tax was to be admitted as an argument to prove a defect of jurisdiction in those who were about to impose it, we should probably have never seen either an excise or a land-tax in England; for there certainly was a time when neither of these modes of taxation were used. When the land-tax was first proposed, after the Revolution, every country-gentleman might then have said with the same degree of propriety as the American now makes the distinction between internal and external taxes. Tax the products of my lands, tax the commodities I consume, but don't tax my lands themselves, for that you have never done before, and therefore you have no authority to do it now!

[Knox,] *Claim of the Colonies*, pp. 15–16.

CHAPTER FOUR: THE TRADE REGULATION CRITERION

1 Anon., *General Opposition*, p. 5. But that same year another London pamphlet contended that the colonies did not oppose internal taxes, only

bad taxes such as the Stamp Act. Anon., *Considerations on the Stamp Act*, pp. 2–3.

2 Morgan, "Colonial Ideal," pp. 315, 325; Green, *Reappraisal*, pp. 34–35; Morgan, "Thomas Hutchinson," pp. 476–77.

3 Morgan, "Thomas Hutchinson," p. 477; Letter from Thomas Hutchinson to Richard Jackson, 23 July 1764, Knollenberg, *Origin*, p. 175.

4 Letter from Samuel Adams to Christopher Gadsden, 11 December 1766, Adams, *Writings* 1:110; [Hicks,] *Nature of Parliamentary Power*, p. 12; "Written and printed in Philadelphia in the Year 1768," *Political Register* 3 (1768): 287–88. At the time of the Sugar Act of 1764, a New York petition contended that "all Impositions, whether they be internal Taxes, or Duties paid for what we consume, equally diminish the Estates upon which they are charged." Knollenberg, *Origin*, p. 190.

5 Letter Two from a Pennsylvania Farmer, *Boston Evening-Post*, 28 December 1767, p. 1, col. 2; Dickinson, *Letters*, p. 328.

6 [Dulany,] *Considerations on the Propriety*, p. 34; Bailyn, *Pamphlets*, p. 638. Dulany referred to the income derived from trade duties as *"incidental Revenue."* Benjamin Franklin termed it "secondary taxes." Franklin, *Writings* 3:235–36.

7 Morgan, "Parliamentary Power," p. 64; Rossiter, *Political Thought*, p. 27.

8 Dickinson, *Letters*, p. 332; James Iredell, "Principles of an American Whig," [1775–76?], *Papers of Iredell* 1:333.

9 Letter from Governor Francis Bernard to Secretary at War Lord Barrington, 28 January 1768, Bernard & Barrington, *Correspondence*, p. 248. See also Speech of Lord Mansfield, Lords Debates, 3 February 1766, Holliday, *Life of Mansfield*, p. 247; Letter III in "Answer to the Farmer's," *Boston Evening-Post*, 20 February 1769, p. 4, col. 2.

10 Rossiter, *Political Thought*, p. 27.

11 [Dulany,] *Considerations on the Propriety*, p. 35. An imperialist looking at the same years from which Dulany drew his conclusion argued that the early customs duties had been taxes even though they had been imposed "in so moderate a degree as rather to have the appearance of being laid on with a view to regulate the commerce and assert the right of taxation, than for the purpose of a revenue." Roebuck, *Enquiry whether the Guilt*, p. 28.

12 This is a topic that must be deferred until authority to legislate is discussed. In summary, it can be said that although many American whigs concurred with Dickinson and said Parliament had a constitutional right to regulate trade, most felt that authority was not of right but of American acquiescence.

13 Bates's Case, 2 *State Trials* (1606): 371, 389–90; Marcham, *Constitutional History*, p. 91.

14 Letter from Governor Josiah Lyndon to the King, 16 September 1768, *Rhode Island Colony Records* 6:560; 7 George III, cap. 46.

15 Letter from the New Hampshire House of Representatives to the Virginia House of Burgesses (1768), *Documents of New Hampshire*, p. 190; Address from the Commons House of Assembly to the King, 24 December 1768, *Georgia*

Commons House Journal 14:644. See also Letter from the House of Burgesses to the Pennsylvania House of Representatives, 9 May 1768, *Pennsylvania Archives* 7:6191; Instructions of Boston, 22 December 1767, *Boston Post-Boy*, 28 December 1767, p. 1, col. 2.

16 [Knox,] *Controversy* (Dublin Edition), p. 40; "Pelopidas," *Boston Gazette*, 26 October 1767, p. 1, col. 1.

17 Speech of Charles Cornwall, Commons Debates, 19 April 1774, *Gentleman's Magazine* 44 (1774): 549; Burgoyne, "Letter to Lee," p. 2; Letter from *Junius* to John Wilkes, 7 September 1771, *Gentleman's Magazine* 41 (1771): 587; [Dalrymple,] *Address of the People*, p. 30. Even as late as 1781 a writer was insisting that Americans had changed their position. Anon., *History of Lord North*, p. 122. And some twentieth-century students of the Revolution have repeated the charge. E.g., Headlam, "Constitutional Struggle," p. 657.

18 Derry, *Fox*, p. 64; Minutes of 24 March 1775, *Journal of New York Assembly* (1766–76), pp. 92–93; Minutes of 3 March 1775, ibid., pp. 53, 56.

19 Declarations of the Stamp Act Congress, 19 October 1765, *English Historical Documents* 9:672; [Knox,] *Controversy*, pp. appendix lii.

20 Circular Letter from the earl of Hillsborough to Governor William Tryon, 13 May 1769, *North Carolina Colonial Records* 8:39; 18 George III, cap. 12 (1778); Speech of Governor James Wright to the royalist Assembly, 9 May 1780, *Georgia Commons House Journal* 15:549–50.

CHAPTER FIVE: THE SECOND ORIGINAL CONTRACT

1 Lee, *Election Sermon*, p. 14; Hopkins, *Rights*, pp. 510, 507.

2 *Gentleman's Magazine* 44 (1774): 310; Burke, "Debates in a Newly Established Society," *Gentleman's Magazine* 41 (1771): 53.

3 "A British American," *Gentleman's Magazine* 36 (1766): 612; Message from Governor William Franklin to the Council and Assembly, 16 May 1775, *New Jersey Votes and Proceedings* (May 1775), p. 10.

4 For the original-contract theory as it bore on the issue of American constitutional rights, see *Authority of Rights*, pp. 132–58. For a preliminary discussion of the contract and the American Revolution controversy in general, see "In Our Contracted Sphere," pp. 21–34, 42–47.

5 Laslett, "Social Contract," p. 466; Gough, *Social Contract*, p. 2.

6 *Boston Declaration*, pp. 2–3; Resolves of Abingdon, 19 March 1770, *Political Register* 7 (1770): 37–38; *Boston Gazette*, 2 April 1770, p. 3, col. 1.

7 But see [Johnson,] *Important Observations*, p. 18 n.

8 Letter from S. F. V. to the Printer, 20 February 1764, *Providence Gazette*, 5 May 1764, p. 2, col. 2; [Dulany,] *Considerations on the Propriety*, p. 30; Speech of William Pitt, Commons Debates, 27 January 1766, Walpole, *Memoirs* 1:378–79.

9 Hopkins, *Rights*, p. 510; *Gentleman's Magazine* 35 (1765): 561.

10 "A British American," *Gentleman's Magazine* 36 (1766): 613; Demophoon, "A Dissertation on the original Dispute between Great-Britain and her Colo-

nies," *Political Register* 7 (1770): 152; Instructions of Boston, 5 May 1773, *Boston Evening-Post*, 10 May 1773, p. 1, col. 1 [hereafter cited as Instructions].

11 Doctrine of ancient constitution: *Authority of Rights*, pp. 132–38; "In Our Contracted Sphere," pp. 22–25; Revolution of 1688: [Rawson,] *Revolution in New England*, p. 43; common lawyer: St. Amand, *Legislative Power*, pp. 37–38.

12 Letter from Boston, 5 August 1765, *Prior Documents*, p. 9; Instructions (*supra*, n. 10), p. 1, col. 1; Letter from the Massachusetts House of Representatives to Agent Dennys de Berdt, 12 January 1768, Adams, *Writings* 1:139–40; Petition from the Council and House of Burgesses of Virginia to the King, 18 December 1764, *Burgesses Journals* 10:302; *Gazette & News-Letter*, 21 March 1765, p. 2, col. 1.

13 "If a state receives all the advantages that law, protection, and assistance of another can afford, surely she ought to acknowledge herself indebted in the most grateful manner, independent of all natural subordination." Anon., *Remarks on Price's Observations*, p. 10.

14 "[C]an there be a more proper time for this mother country to leave off feeding out of her own vitals these children whom she has nursed up, than when they are arrived at such strength and maturity as to be well able to provide of themselves, and ought rather with filial duty to give some assistance to her distress?" Creasy, *Imperial Constitutions*, p. 150, n. 2 (quoting a 1765 pamphlet by Soame Jenyns).

15 "That Great Britain should acquire an extension of territory on the continent of North America, and not gain from it, would be something surprising. That the British state should afford an occasion to her own subjects of acquiring wealth, and of multiplying and increasing, and yet be no gainer from such an increase of subjects, would be a system of misgovernment not to be parallelled." [Gray,] *Right of the Legislature*, p. 61.

16 "The people of England cannot but think themselves aggrieved to see colonists, whom they protect in the cultivation of a fertile country, which they have bestowed upon them, refusing to bear a share in the public burdens, and calling out for an exemption from the authority of the supreme legislature." Ibid, p. 70.

17 Roebuck, *Enquiry whether the Guilt*, p. 28; owe: Book Review, *Critical Review* 21 (1766): 80; [Knox,] *Interest of the Merchants*, p. 7; [Steward,] *Letter to Price*, pp. 25–26.

18 "The King's Speech on Opening the Session," 26 October 1775, *Parliamentary History* 18:696; "Refutation of the Argument that the Colonies Were Established at the Expense of the British Nation," *Papers of Jefferson* 1: 277–84 [hereafter cited as Refutation]; "Jefferson's 'Original Rough draught' of the Declaration of Independence," *Papers of Jefferson* 1:426. Two years earlier Jefferson had written: "No shilling was ever issued from the public treasures of his majesty or his ancestors for their assistance, till of very late times, after the colonies had become established on a firm and permanent footing." Jefferson, *Summary View*, p. 122.

19 Refutation (*supra*, n. 18), p. 283. It was a contention Americans had long

made (Lovejoy, *Glorious Revolution*, p. 142), that loyalists such as Hutchinson supported (Bailyn, *Ordeal*, p. 63), and which is today sustained by historical scholarship. Dunn, *Puritans & Yankees*, pp. 26–27.

20 Instructions of the Town of Ipswich, 21 October 1765, in Waters, *Ipswich in Massachusetts Bay Colony* 2:294; Petition from the Pennsylvania House of Representatives to the House of Commons, 22 September 1768, *Pennsylvania Archives* 7:6275. Similarly, Petition from the Pennsylvania General Assembly to the King, 22 September 1768, *Pennsylvania Archives* 7: 6271; Resolves of Fairfax County, 18 July 1774, *Revolutionary Virginia* 1: 127; A New-Englandman, "Mother Country," *Providence Gazette*, 18 August 1764, p. 1, col. 2; "Samuel Ward's Notes for a Speech in Congress," 12 October 1774, *Letters of Delegates to Congress* 1:186.

21 [Lee,] *Speech Intended*, p. 54; *Boston Gazette*, 9 January 1769, reprinted in Adams, *Writings* 1:283.

22 "Benjamin Franklin's Vindication" (June–July ? 1775), *Letters of Delegates to Congress* 1:562–63 [hereafter cited as "Franklin's Vindication"]; Douglass, *Historical and Political* 1:222.

23 *Proceedings and Debates of Parliaments* 4: Preface, p. xvii; Miller, "Stamp Act in Georgia," p. 318.

24 "Franklin's Vindication" (*supra*, n. 22), p. 563.

25 Speech of David Hartley, Commons Debates, 27 March 1775, *Gentleman's Magazine* 45 (1775): 624; Hartley, *Speech and Motions*, p. 8.

26 "Written and printed at Philadelphia in the Year 1768," *Political Register* 3 (1768): 291; *Annual Register 1765*, p. [35]; Anon., *Reflections on the Contest*, p. 40; Anon., *To the People of Britain in General*, p. 55.

27 [Johnson,] *Important Observations*, p. 17; New York Resolves, 18 December 1765, Morgan, *Prologue*, p. 61.

28 Instructions of the House of Representatives to Richard Jackson, 22 September 1764, *Pennsylvania Archives* 7:5643–44; *Franklin-Jackson Letters*, pp. 183–84; Anon., *Right of British Legislature*, pp. 12–13; Letter from Jared Ingersoll to Thomas Whately, 6 July 1764, "Ingersoll Correspondence," p. 299.

CHAPTER SIX: THE IMPERIAL CONTRACT

1 [Stewart,] *Letter to Price*, p. 40. See also [Howard,] *Defence of Letter*, pp. 3–4; "William Pym," *London Evening-Post*, 20 August 1765, reprinted in *Boston Evening-Post*, 25 November 1765, p. 1, col. 2.

2 [Goodricke,] *Observations on Price's Theory*, p. 31; Book Review, *Gentleman's Magazine* 36 (1766): 627; *Anecdotes of Pitt* 1:331–32; Speech of George Grenville, Commons Debates, 14 January 1766, Anon., *Celebrated Speech*, p. 10.

3 Address of Lieutenant Governor Cadwallader Colden to the Assembly, 17 September 1764, *New York Journal of Votes*, p. 752; [Crowley,] *Dissertations*, pp. 6–7. See also [Gray,] *Right of the Legislature*, pp. 60–61; Fletcher, *American Patriotism*, p. iii.

4 Shebbeare, *Essay on National Society*, pp. 106–7.
5 Anon., *Independency the Object*, p. 26; Message from Governor William Franklin to the Council and Assembly, 16 May 1775, *New Jersey Votes and Proceedings* (May 1775), p. 6. The same equitable contract could be implied from the general imperial relationship and not just defense.

> If we reap emoluments from the existence of the colonies, the colonies owe every thing to our encouragement and protection. As therefore we share in the same prosperity, we ought to participate in the same distress; and nothing can be more inequitable, than the least disinclination to bear a regular portion of those disbursement[s], which were applied to support the general interest both of the mother-country and themselves.

"William Pym," *London Evening-Post*, 20 August 1765, reprinted in *Boston Evening-Post*, 25 November 1765, p. 1, col. 2.
6 Anon., *Inquiry into the Nature*, pp. 30–31; Shebbeare, *Essay on National Society*, p. 104. For arguments that were closely related but based on equitable fairness rather than equality, see [Young,] *Political Essays*, pp. 37–38; Anon., *Letter to Lord Camden*, pp. 34–35.
7 Anon., *To the People of Britain in General*, p. 54; *Critical Review* 22 (1766): 349; Anon., *To the People of Britain in General*, p. 26.
8 McAdam, *Johnson and Law*, p. 105; implied contract: Anon., *Remarks on Price's Observations*, pp. 13–14. There were of course some people who thought the imperial claim so strong they stated it less as a contract than as a matter of right. Anon., *Independency the Object*, p. 10.
9 Letter to Agent Mauduit, 13 June 1764, *Massachusetts House Journal* (1764), p. 73. The next year the House wrote and published a detailed defense, explaining its purpose in the opening sentence:

> One great reason alledged for imposing taxes on the colonies, being this; that they ought to contribute to defray the charges of a war undertaken for their defence; to which those who alledge this reason, suppose they have never yet sufficiently contributed: the province of the Massachusett's Bay, deem it proper briefly to set forth their several services, and expences in the common cause, from their first incorporation to the present time.

A Brief State of the Services and Expenses of the Province of the Massachusett's Bay, In the Common Cause (London, 1765), p. 3; "Benjamin Franklin's Vindication" (June–July 1775), *Letters of Delegates to Congress* 1:561–62 [hereafter cited as "Franklin's Vindication"].
10 Petition of the Virginia General Assembly to the House of Lords, 16 April 1768, *Revolutionary Virginia* 1:57; Letter from the Virginia House of Burgesses to the North Carolina House of Assembly, 9 May 1768, *North Carolina Colonial Records* 7:747; Pennsylvania Resolves, 21 September 1765, and South Carolina Resolves, 29 November 1765 [hereafter cited as South Carolina Resolves], Morgan, *Prologue*, pp. 51, 58.

11 New York Petition to the House of Commons, 18 October 1764, Morgan, *Prologue*, p. 9. See also *Examination of Franklin*, p. 3; James Iredell, "To his Majesty George The Third," February 1777, *Papers of Iredell* 1:437.

12 Petition of the House of Representatives to the King, 13 February 1775, *New Jersey Votes and Proceedings* (January 1775), p. 61; Resolves of the Delaware House of Assembly, 3 June 1766, *Delaware House Minutes* (1765–70), p. 54.

13 South Carolina Resolves (*supra*, n. 10), p. 59; Address to the People of Great Britain, 5 September 1774, *Journal of the First Congress*, p. 82; "Hutchinson's Essay on Colonial Rights," in Morgan, "Thomas Hutchinson," p. 489; New York Petition to the House of Commons, 18 October 1764, Morgan, *Prologue*, p. 9; [Dulany,] *Considerations on the Propriety*, p. 24. William Pitt, the minister who had directed the war effort from which the American debt was said to arise, apparently thought there was no debt. Giving the facts still a further legal twist, Pitt is said to have urged repeal of the Stamp Act "in gratitude to their having supported England through three wars." Walpole, *Memoirs* 1:392.

14 Rhode Island: Petition of the Governor and Company of Rhode Island to the King, 29 November 1764, *Rhode Island Colony Records* 6:414; Hopkins, *Rights*, p. 508. See also *Boston Evening-Post*, 1 July 1765, p. 1, col. 2.

15 A *New Englander*, "Mother Country," *Providence Gazette*, 18 August 1764, p. 1, col. 2; *Boston Evening-Post*, 17 September 1764, p. 1, col. 1; "Franklin's Vindication," (*supra*, n. 9), p. 564.

16 Anon., *America Vindicated*, p. 19; Thacher, *Sentiments*, p. 492.

17 Burgh, *Political Disquisitions* 2:313; Anon., *Case of Great Britain*, pp. 10–11. The legal conclusion was made stronger when Britain's self-interest was considered. Speech of Temple Luttrell, Commons Debates, 27 February 1775, *Gentleman's Magazine* 45 (1775): 610; *Speeches in Last Session*, p. 36; Jefferson, *Summary View*, p. 122.

18 Extracts from an Oration by Samuel Adams, 1 August 1776, *Hibernian Magazine* 6 (1776): 756; Letter from Governor William Pitkin to the earl of Hillsborough, 10 June 1768, *Public Records of Connecticut* 13:85. Similarly, Letter from the Virginia Committee to the Agent, 28 July 1764, "Proceedings Committee of Correspondence" 12:10; New York Petition to the House of Commons, 18 October 1764, Morgan, *Prologue*, p. 9.

19 "De Berdt's Remarks" (1770?), "Letters of Dennys De Berdt," p. 458. An additional but minor argument at law was to contend that the imperial contract provided for payment in a manner other than by parliamentary taxation of the colonies. For example, America paid for Britain's protection by aiding in the protection of Britain. "It is on this aid of the colonies, which is daily growing more powerful, that the safety of this nation depends; the people we have in *North America*, are the only balance to that great superiority, in numbers, which our enemies have over us in *Europe*." [Mitchell,] *The Present State*, p. 345.

20 [Dulany,] *Considerations on the Propriety*, p. 23.

21 Instructions of 24 May 1764, *Boston Town Records* 16:121; Instructions of 18

September 1765, ibid., pp. 155–56; "To the Inhabitants of the Colonies," 21 October 1774, *Journal of First Congress,* p. 101; Letter to Agent Mauduit, 13 June 1764, *Massachusetts House Journal* (1764), p. 73. Even Thomas Hutchinson thought the last fact probative in an argument about rights. "Hutchinson's Essay on Colonial Rights," in Morgan, "Thomas Hutchinson," p. 489.

22 [Mitchell,] *The Present State,* p. 345. See also the long, important argument in Petition of Virginia to the House of Lords, 16 April 1768, *Revolutionary Virginia* 1:57; Hopkins, *Rights,* pp. 519–20.

23 Resolves of the Bristol Town Meeting, 28 February 1774, *Rhode Island Colony Records* 7:275. A related question was whether the colonies had needed the support of the British army. Anon., *Independency the Object,* pp. 32–33; Forbes, *Artillery Company Sermon,* pp. 15–16; [Rokeby,] *Considerations on the Measures,* p. 49; Letter to Agent Mauduit, 13 June 1764, *Massachusetts House Journal* (1764), p. 73.

24 *Monthly Review* 49 (1773): 371; "Project of a Permanent Union and Settlement with the Colonies," [Knox,] *Extra Official Papers,* Appendix p. 33; Anon., *Plain and Seasonable Address,* p. 13; [Steward,] *Letter to Price,* p. 46. See, similarly, "A Summary of the Argument against repealing the Stamp-Act," *Gentleman's Magazine* 36 (1766): 107; "Considerations on the Trade," *Gentleman's Magazine* 36 (1766): 607; Anon., *Short and Friendly Caution,* p. 9; Anon., *Cursory Remarks on Price,* pp. 12–13.

25 *Political Debates,* p. 16; [Lee,] *Speech Intended,* pp. 48.

26 Anon., *Answer to Taxation no Tyranny,* p. 38. Similarly, it was contended that the war began in America because it was a maritime struggle, fought for the fisheries and mastery of the seas. [Mitchell,] *The Present State,* pp. 344–45.

27 *Examination of Franklin,* p. 12; Extracts from an oration by Samuel Adams, 1 August 1776, *Hibernian Magazine* 6 (1776): 756.

28 *Examination of Franklin,* p. 12; "Examination of Franklin," *Prior Documents,* p. 77. See also [Mitchell,] *The Present State,* p. 343; [Hicks,] *Nature of Parliamentary Power,* pp. 17–18.

29 [Knox,] *Controversy,* pp. 113–36; Knox, *Controversy* (Dublin Edition), pp. 106–37; Anon., *Inquiry into the Nature,* p. 63–64; Stewart, *Total Refutation,* p. 7; Anon., *Appeal to Reason and Justice,* p. 130.

30 Letter to Agent Mauduit, 13 June 1764, *Massachusetts House Journal* (1764), p. 74; [Mitchell,] *The Present State,* pp. 327–39; "Letter from a Gentleman at Boston, to his Correspondent in this City," 11 July 1768, *American Gazette,* p. 59.

31 Even future loyalists doubted the gains. Thomas Hutchinson questioned whether the fishery would mean much and, if it did, he said Great Britain would reap the profits. "Hutchinson's Essay on Colonial Rights," in Morgan, "Thomas Hutchinson," p. 489. Conquest of the Indians did not matter to some colonies. Governor Thomas Fitch, an ardent supporter of the war effort and the man largely responsible for the fact Connecticut more than once exceeded its quota of troops, claimed his colony "gains Nothing

by the conquests." [Fitch, et al.,] *Reasons Why,* pp. 28–32. The governor of Rhode Island, speaking for the Assembly, agreed with Massachusetts and Connecticut that the colonies "reaped no sort of advantage by these conquests." Hopkins, *Rights,* p. 520. See also the strong argument of Arthur Lee. [Lee,] *Speech Intended,* pp. 47, 51.

32 [Mitchell,] *The Present State,* p. 350; Letter to Agent Mauduit, 13 June 1764, *Massachusetts House Journal* (1764), p. 74; [Dulany,] *Considerations on the Propriety,* p. 24; Hopkins, *Rights,* p. 520.

CHAPTER SEVEN: THE COMMERCIAL CONTRACT

1 Anon., *Constitutional Answer to Wesley,* p. 18; Hartley, *Speech and Motions,* p. 11; Anon., *Constitutional Answer to Wesley,* p. 18. See also Petition from the General Assembly of New-York to the House of Lords, 18 October 1764, *New York Journal of Votes,* p. 775; [Dulany,] *Considerations on the Propriety,* pp. 19–20. See, similarly, [Lee,] *Speech Intended,* p. 50.

2 Letter from the Virginia House of Burgesses to the Pennsylvania House of Representatives, 9 May 1768, *Pennsylvania Archives* 7:6191; South Carolina Resolves, 29 November 1765, Morgan, *Prologue,* p. 58; [Mitchell,] *The Present State,* p. 319.

3 Estwick, *Letter to Tucker,* p. 92; Anon., *History of Lord North,* p. 146; Declaration of Congress setting forth the Causes and Necessity of taking up Arms, 6 July 1775, *Papers of Jefferson* 1:214; Anon., *"Taxation no Tyranny" Considered,* pp. 98–99; Speech of Sir William Meredith, Commons Debates, 5 February 1766, Ryder, "Parliamentary Diaries," p. 277. See also New York Assembly Resolves, 18 December 1765, *New York Journal of Votes,* p. 808; Pownall, *Administration,* p. 299. For a detailed discussion of the mathematics of the contract, see [Dulany,] *Considerations on the Propriety,* pp. 49–55. For the benefit conferred on Britons, see Anon., *Tyranny Unmasked,* p. 14.

4 Letter from the Massachusetts House of Representatives to Dennys de Berdt, 12 January 1768, and Letter from the Massachusetts House of Representatives to the earl of Shelburne, 15 January 1768, Adams, *Writings* 1:142, 159–60. See also "Considerations on the Trade," *Gentleman's Magazine* 36 (1766): 606; Hopkins, *Rights,* p. 521; [Hopkins,] "Vindication of a Pamphlet," 23 February 1765, p. 1, col. 1; [Dulany,] *Considerations on the Propriety,* p. 27.

5 Letter from Governor William Pitkin to the Earl of Hillsborough, 10 June 1768, *Public Records of Connecticut* 13:86; [Mauduit,] *Northern Colonies,* pp. 10–11; Address to the People of Great Britain, 5 September 1774, *Journal of First Congress,* p. 82; Petition of the Stamp Act Congress to the House of Commons, 23 October 1765, *Account of Stamp Act Congress,* p. 24; Petition of the New-York General Assembly to the House of Commons, 18 October 1764, *New York Journal of Votes,* p. 778 [hereafter cited as Petition].

6 Resolutions of 19 October 1765, *Account of Stamp Act Congress,* p. 7. "That the Profits of Trade arising form [*sic*] this Colony, centering in *Great-*

Britain, eventually contributes to the Supplies granted there to the Crown."
New Jersey Resolves, 30 November 1765, *New Jersey Votes and Proceedings*
(November 1765), p. 8; Morgan, *Prologue*, p. 60.

7 Nicholas, *Present State of Virginia*, p. 279; Hartley, *Letters on the War*, p.
77; Hartley, *Speech and Motions*, p. 12; Letter from Richard Jackson to
Benjamin Franklin, 27 December 1763, *Franklin-Jackson Letters*, p. 124.
"You protected them in their infant state, and they returned it, by confining to you the benefits of their trade." Speech of Henry Cruger, Commons
Debates, 16 December 1774, *Gentleman's Magazine* 45 (1775): 6; *Speeches
in Last Session*, p. 8.

8 Pitt's Speech on Repeal of the Stamp Act, in Morgan, *Prologue*, p. 140. The
Massachusetts House said that the colonies took "annually from Great Britain, manufacturers of the value of two million sterling," which meant they
paid "an annual tax of four hundred thousand pounds." Letter from the
Massachusetts House of Representatives to Dennys de Berdt, 12 January
1768, Adams, *Writings* 1:142. Another estimate was that America purchased
"one-third at least of all British manufactures" and "the colonies by that
purchase, paid a full third of all British taxes." *Americus*, "To the Printer
of the Public Ledger, London, Nov. 22, 1765," in *Massachusetts Gazette*,
6 February 1766, p. 1, col. 1. "The profits Britain derives from us every
year exceed two millions and a half sterling." Erskine, *Reflections on the
Rise*, p. 18.

9 E.g., Resolutions offered by Edmund Pendleton to the Continental Congress,
May 1775, *Letters & Papers of Pendleton* 1:106; Answer of the Continental
Congress, 31 July 1775, *Gentleman's Magazine* 45 (1775): 427.

10 Burgh, *Political Disquisitions*, 2:275, 280; "Indirect tax": Letter from the
Massachusetts House of Representatives to the Earl of Shelburne, 15 January 1768, Adams, *Writings* 1:159 [hereafter cited as Letter]; "Secondary
taxation": Letter from Benjamin Franklin to Governor William Shirley,
18 December 1754, Franklin, *Writings* 3:236 [hereafter cited as Letter from
Franklin].

11 Price, *Nature of Civil Liberty*, p. 99. "By purchasing our goods they [the col-
onies] paid our taxes; and, by allowing us to regulate their trade in any
manner we thought most for our advantage, they enriched our merchants,
and helped us to bear our growing burdens." Richard Price, "On the Nature of Civil Liberty," *Hibernian Magazine* 6 (1776): 190–91.

12 Pulteney, *Thoughts on Present State*, 22. "This gives the advantage to Great
Britain of raising the price of her commodities, and is equal to a tax. . . .
The loss, therefore, to the colonists, is equal to the gain which is made
in Britain. This in reality is a tax, though not a direct one." Letter from
the Massachusetts House of Representatives to Dennys de Berdt, 12 January 1768, Adams, *Writings* 1:142.

13 Letter from Franklin (*supra* n. 10), 236; Anon., *"Taxation no Tyranny" Considered*, p. 19; Anon., *Answer to Taxation no Tyranny*, p. 38.

14 Speech of the Duke of Grafton, Lords Debates, 11 March 1766, "Stamp Act
Debates," p. 581 ("The Duke of Grafton very ingeniously confessed, that

the Americans were sufficiently taxed, *by buying our taxed articles from Britain.*" Anon., *"Taxation no Tyranny" Considered,* 20); Letter (*supra* n. 10), p. 159 (see also Letter from the Virginia House of Burgesses to the Massachusetts House of Representatives, 8 May 1768, *Boston Chronicle,* 4 July 1768, p. 267, col. 3); Speech of Lord Rockingham, Lords Debates, 26 October 1775, *Gentleman's Magazine* 46 (1776): 536. "[B]y the Regulations to which the Trade of the Colonies is Subject, they greatly contribute to the Support of your Majesty's Government, and adding to this, what they are obliged to pay towards the Support of this civil Government here, they will appear in Effect as heartily taxed as your Subjects in *Britain.*" Petition from the New York House of General Assembly to the King, 11 December 1765, *New York Journal of Votes,* p. 796. See also [Dulany,] *Considerations on the Propriety,* p. 49; Letter from Benjamin Franklin to Governor William Shirley, 4 December 1754, *Correspondence of Shirley* 2:106. See also Letter from Franklin (*supra* n. 10), pp. 235–36; Burgh, *Political Disquisitions* 2:278–79, 295–96; [Mitchell,] *Present State,* pp. 290–91, 318–19.

15 [Knox,] *Controversy* (Dublin Edition), pp. 54–55.

16 Anon., *Essays Commercial and Political,* p. 9; Letter from Jared Ingersoll to the Connecticut General Assembly, 18 September 1765, "Ingersoll Correspondence," p. 340; "The Interest of the Merchants and Manufacturers of Great Britain," *Hibernian Magazine* 5 (1775): 44–45.

17 "Considerations on the Trade," *Gentleman's Magazine* 36 (1766): 608; Roebuck, *Enquiry whether the Guilt,* p. 38. See also Anon., *Short Appeal to the People,* p. 18.

18 Speech of Thomas Townshend, Commons Debates, 12 March 1776, *Hibernian Magazine* 6 (1776): 700. Similarly, see [Knox,] *Controversy,* p. 98; Roebuck, *Enquiry whether the Guilt,* p. 41; Anon., *Essays Commercial and Political,* p. 10.

19 It is relevant that spokesmen for Scotland made this same argument to prove Scotland paid more taxes than the English credited her and the argument was also rejected. Speeches of Sir Adam Fergusson and Sir Gilbert Elliot, Commons Debates, 12 March 1776, *Hibernian Magazine* 6 (1776): 700.

20 Thomas, *British Politics,* p. 240; Speech of George Grenville, Commons Debates, 14 January 1766, Anon., *Celebrated Speech,* p. 10.

21 For a list of those granted during Grenville's administration, see *Critical Review* 22 (1766): 349.

22 "Though the penalty for planting tobacco in England or Ireland, imposed by the last act [15 Charles II, cap. 7], was no less than ten pounds a rod, still the profits arising from it were so great, that this provision was insufficient to prevent the planting of it; and therefore, by another act [22 & 23 Charles II, cap. 26], power is given to the justices of the peace to '*pluck* up and utterly destroy' all tobacco planted in England or Ireland." [Lind,] *Thirteenth Parliament,* p. 202. See also "The Interests of the Merchants and Manufacturers of Great Britain," *Hibernian Magazine* 5 (1775): 44.

23 Roebuck, *Enquiry whether the Guilt*, p. 34; Anon., *Cursory Remarks on Price*, pp. 14–15.

24 Speech of William Pitt, Commons Debates, 14 January 1766, Anon., *Celebrated Speech*, pp. 13–14; Anon., *Three Letters*, p. 64; Price, *Nature of Civil Liberty*, p. 38 n.(a); Book Review, *Critical Review* 38 (1774): 424; Anon., *Three Letters*, p. 63; Estwick, *Letter to Tucker*, pp. 37–41; "The State of Europe," *Town and Country Magazine* 4 (1772): 175 [hereafter cited as "State of Europe"].

25 Anon., *Three Letters*, pp. 54–57. "Tobacco imported into England yearly about 75,000 hogsheads, pays a duty of £300,000 a year. Part of this is exported to France, and . . . pays another duty. . . . If you had laid a duty upon tobacco in America, you would have destroyed all that trade." Speech of Edmund Burke, Commons Debates, 21 February 1766, Ryder, "Parliamentary Diaries," p. 307. It was estimated that two-thirds of this tobacco was "re-exported from Great Britain, to Germany, France, and Holland." "State of Europe" (*supra* n. 24), p. 228.

26 Book Review, *Monthly Review* 51 (1774): 476.

27 See especially the argument that Britain was better off paying £200,000 a year in bounties than not paying. Estwick, *Letter to Tucker*, p. 37. See also the contention that Britain benefited when *reducing* the duty the British treasury collected on certain products. Memorial from South Carolina's Agent to the Lords Commissioners of the Treasury, 1769, "Garth Correspondence" [part 12], p. 143.

28 "Proceedings in . . . parliament 1763–4," *Scots Magazine* 27 (1765): 16.

29 Message from the Burgesses to Governor Lord Dunmore, 12 June 1775, *Journal of Burgesses* 13:220.

CHAPTER EIGHT: THE TAXATION-LEGISLATION DICHOTOMY

1 Letter from Charles Townshend to the Duke of Newcastle, 27 March 1764, Forster, *Charles Townshend*, p. 54; Speech of the Earl of Chatham to the Lords, 1774, quoted in Dickinson, "Preface," p. xiv.

2 Speech of Lord Chatham, Lords Debates, 20 January 1775, *American Archives* 1:1497.

3 Speech of William Pitt on Repeal, Commons Debates, 14 January 1766, Morgan, *Prologue*, p. 136. Pitt would repeat this theory to the end of the pre-revolutionary controversy. See, e.g., Speech (*supra* n. 2), p. 1502.

4 Anon., *Answer to Pitt's Speech*, pp. 8–9; Robertson, *Chatham*, p. 99; Jarrett, *Pitt the Younger*, p. 51; Beloff, *Debate*, p. 36; Christie, *Crisis*, p. 63; May, *Constitutional History* 1:444; Keir, *Constitutional History*, p. 362. Of course, many historians have stated Pitt's division correctly, the most valuable analyses having been made by those who associated the principle with the two constitutions. E.g., Guttridge, *English Whiggism*, pp. 34, 64. For the two constitutions, see *In Defiance of the Law*, pp. 32–49, 112–29.

5 For contemporary doubts about the constitutionality of the dichotomy, see, e.g., Anon., *Plan to Reconcile*, p. 27; Grenville quoted in Morgan, *Pro-*

logue, p. 137; the attorney general and other law officers summarized in Garth, "Letter on Repeal," p. 150; Speech of Lord Mansfield, Lords Debates, 6 February 1775, *Gentleman's Magazine* 45 (1775): 108; Letter from Charles Carroll of Carrollton to Edmund Jennings, 9 March 1767, *Letters of Charles Carroll,* pp. 116, 138.

6 Anon., *Plain Question,* p. 6; Foss, *Judges of England* 8:357.

7 Campbell, *Lives of the Chancellors* 5:253; *Boston Evening-Post,* 18 January 1768, p. 2, cols. 1–2; Camden, "Speech on American Taxation," p. 121; Gough, *Fundamental Law,* p. 194; *South-Carolina Gazette,* 7 December 1767, p. 2, col. 4; *Boston Chronicle,* 18 January 1768, p. 46, cols. 1–3.

8 Speech of William Pitt, Commons Debates, 1766, "Stamp Act Debates," p. 573; Norton: Thomas, *British Politics,* p. 198.

9 Speech of Lord Camden, Lords Debates, 1766, *Parliamentary History* 16:179; Speech of Lord Camden, Lords Debates, 20 January 1775, *Parliamentary History* 18:164.

10 Anon., *Letter to a Member,* p. 23; Anon., *Plan to Reconcile,* p. 27; Book Review, *Critical Review* 28 (1769): 153. Grenville described Camden's speech as "the slightest most ignorant & contemptible Performance that ever came from a man in high Station of the Law." Letter from George Grenville to William Knox, 15 August 1768, *Grenville Letterbooks.* See also [Knox,] *Claim of the Colonies,* p. 15; "Junius," *Junius* 2:268–69; Johnson, *Political Tracts,* p. 202; Anon., *To the People of Britain in General,* p. 5; [Stewart,] *Letter to Price,* pp. 34–38; Anon., *Plain State,* pp. 12–13. For criticism by lawyers, see Speech of William Blackstone, Commons Debates, 3 February 1766, Ryder, "Parliamentary Diaries," p. 269; Gipson, "Debate on Repeal," p. 17, n. 17; Speech of Sir Fletcher Norton, Commons Debates, 1766, "Stamp Act Debates," p. 573

11 Anonymous, *A Short History of the Conduct of the Present Ministry, With Regard to the American Stamp Act* (London, 1766), p. 18 (see also Anon., *Constitutional Right,* p. 42; Bailyn, *Pamphlets* 1:118–19); Petition of the General Assembly of New-York to the House of Lords, 18 October 1764, *New York Journal of Votes,* p. 774.

12 "It was observed, that in many parts of Germany, even in the electorate of Hanover, tho' the council of states made laws, it was the diet which granted supplies: Hence it was inferred, . . . that the notion which I fear obtains still with the majority of both houses, viz. of the supremacy of Parliament, comprehending taxation, had arisen merely from the accidental union of two distinct powers in the same hands." Anon., *Letter to Mansfield,* pp. 17–18.

13 Speech of George Johnstone, Commons Debates, 16 December 1774, *American Archives* 1:1482; *Speeches in Last Session,* p. 6; *Gazette & Post-Boy,* 27 March 1775, p. 2, col. 3; Chatham, "Speech in Lords, 20 January 1775," p. 193; Garth, "Letter," p. 72; Garth, "Letter on Repeal," p. 154.

14 *Hibernian Magazine* 5 (1775): 768; Anon., *Three Letters,* pp. 14–15; Anon., *To Tax Themselves,* p. 115; Petition of the New York General Assembly to the House of Lords, 11 December 1765, *New York Journal of Votes,* p. 799.

15 Anon., *Constitutional Advocate*, pp. 31–32. Distinction was always part of constitution: Anon., *Letter to Mansfield*, pp. 16–17.

16 *London Magazine* 35 (1766): pp. 609, 611; [Dulany,] *Considerations on the Propriety*, p. 5. See also [Leslie,] *Constitution, Laws and Government*, p. 113.

17 Petition from the Stamp Act Congress to the King, Morgan, *Prologue*, p. 65; Petition of the New-York General Assembly to the House of Commons, 11 December 1765, *New York Journal of Votes*, p. 800; Speech of William Pitt, Common Debates, 1766, "Stamp Act Debates," p. 573.

18 Hampden, "A full Vindication of the Livery of London's Petition to his Majesty as to the Charge upon the Ministry of raising a Revenue in our Colonies by Prerogative," *Political Register* 5 (1769): 186. See also Memorial of the Council and Burgesses of Virginia to the House of Commons, 16 April 1768, *Revolutionary Virginia*, 1:60; *London Magazine* 35 (1766): 610.

19 Speech (*supra* n. 17), p. 573; *Political Register* 7 (1770): 153; *London Magazine* 39 (1770): 417; Book Review, *Monthly Review* 52 (1775): 254.

20 *London Magazine* 35 (1766): 612. Similarly, [Hopkins,] "Vindication of a Pamphlet," 9 March 1765, p. 1, col. 1.

21 Quoted from the *Public Advertiser*, 12 February 1770, *Franklin's Letters to Press*, pp. 202–3. For Pitt's explanation, see Garth, "Letter," p. 69.

22 Speech of Hans Stanley, Commons Debates, 3 February 1766, Ryder, "Parliamentary Diaries," p. 262.

23 Speech of Sir William Blackstone, Commons Debates, 3 February 1766, ibid., 267; "Stamp Act Debates," p. 568; Anon., *Answer to Pitt's Speech*, pp. 11–12; [Seabury,] *Congress Canvassed*, p. 18.

24 Speech of William Pitt, Commons Debates, 14 January 1766, *Prior Documents*, p. 59; Morgan, *Prologue*, p. 136; "Extract of a Letter from London, dated February 16, 1765," *South-Carolina Gazette*, 20 July 1765, p. 2, col. 1.

25 Anon., *Constitutional Right*, p. 5.

26 Address of Governor James Wright to the Georgia Commons House of Assembly, 24 December 1768, *Massachusetts Gazette*, 9 February 1769, p. 2, cols. 1–2; [Stewart,] *Letter to Price*, pp. 37–38. See also Phil-Patriae, *Public Advertiser* (London), 23 September 1768, reprinted in *Boston Post-Boy*, 19 December 1768, p. 2, col. 1; Anon., *Plan of Re-Union*, pp. viii, 65; Allen, *English Political Thought*, p. 27.

27 "Extract of a Letter from a Gentleman in London to his Friend in America, dated Jan. 30, 1766," *Massachusetts Gazette*, 8 May 1766, p. 2, col. 3 (quoting Grenville); *Anecdotes of Pitt* 1:331. For Grenville's theory, see Letter from George Grenville to William Knox, 15 September 1768, [Knox,] *Extra Official Papers*, Appendix, p. 21; Headlam, "Constitutional Struggle," p. 659; Thomas, *British Politics*, p. 195.

28 Anon., *Letter to a Member*, p. 24; Letter from George Grenville to William Knox, 27 June 1768, *Grenville Letterbooks*; Anon., *Characters*, p. 2 (also Speech of Lord Mansfield, 10 February 1766, "Lords Debates on Declaratory Act," p. 118); Letter from George Grenville to William Knox, 15 July 1768, *Grenville Letterbooks*.

29 [Hicks,] *Nature of Parliamentary Power*, p. 28; *Boston Evening-Post*, 7 March 1768, p. 4, col. 1.

CHAPTER NINE: THE DEFENSE OF CHARTER

1 Instructions of the Town of Weymouth, n.d., *Boston Evening-Post*, 21 October 1765, p. 2, col. 2.

2 "Resolutions of the House of Representatives, expressive of their sense of the rights of the colonies, October 25, 1765," *Speeches*, p. 51; critic: Mauduit, *Short View*, p. 6; "Declaration of 1689," p. 12; "Declaration of Gentlemen," p. 176; *The New England Weekly Journal*, 18 March 1728, p. 1, col. 1; "a constitution:" "Æquus," *Massachusetts Gazette*, 6 March 1766, p. 2, col. 1; Instructions of the Town of Rowley, 10 October 1765, *Boston Evening-Post*, 21 October 1765, p. 1, col. 3.

3 Letter from Governor Horatio Sharpe to Proprietor Cecilius Calvert, 22 August 1764, quoted in Knollenberg, *Origin*, p. 154.

4 For an argument against the constitutionality of parliamentary taxation that relies primarily on the charter defense and inadvertently reveals the weakness of the defense, see [Devotion,] *The Examiner*. For the deficiencies of charter in the defense of American rights, see *Authority of Rights*, pp. 159–68.

5 "In the First Line of Defense," pp. 184, 209–10.

6 *Examination of Franklin*, p. 15.

7 Instructions of the Pennsylvania Assembly to Richard Jackson, 22 September 1764, *Franklin-Jackson Letters*, p. 183; "Observations on the Review of the Controversy between Great Britain and her Colonies," *Monthly Review* 40 (1769): 436.

8 [Goodricke,] *Observations on Price's Theory*, p. 6; Wesley, *Calm Address*, pp. 10–11 (Samuel Johnson made the same argument in almost the same words. Johnson, *Political Tracts*, p. 216); "An Answer to Mr. Wesley's Address," *Hibernian Magazine* 5 (1775): 788.

9 Johnson, *Political Tracts*, p. 217; [Lind,] *Thirteenth Parliament*, p. 165.

10 Anon., *Answer to Taxation no Tyranny*, p. 59. A second tactic was to treat the Pennsylvania proviso as an aberration, as Franklin did in his testimony. See also Hamilton, *Farmer Refuted*, pp. 119–20.

11 [Knox,] *Controversy* (Dublin Edition), p. 141, 123 (see also [Maseres,] *Canadian Freeholder* 1:93–120); Anon., *Case of Great Britain*, p. 2.

12 Not probative: "In the First Line of Defense," pp. 208–11; the London *Public Advertiser*, 11 January 1770, *Franklin's Letters to Press*, p. 176; Dickinson: "In the First Line of Defense," pp. 209–10; Original contract: Higginbotham, "James Iredell's Efforts," p. 139; [Goodricke,] *Observations on Price's Theory*, p. 22.

13 Of course, one of the rights that was deduced by the evidence of charter was the right that no British subject could be taxed without consent. Anon., *Taxation, Tyranny*, pp. 42–43. Even so, charter was not a significant factor in the constitutional case for American rights against parliamentary supremacy. *Authority of Rights*, pp. 164–68.

14 Resolves of the Connecticut House of Representatives, May 1774, *Public Records of Connecticut* 14:348; Answer from the Massachusetts House of Representatives to Governor Francis Bernard, 23 October 1765, *Speeches*, p. 45.

15 Anon., *Appeal to Reason and Justice*, p. 58.

16 Maryland Resolves, 28 September 1765, *Maryland Votes and Proceedings* (September 1765), p. 10; Address of the Lower House of Assembly to Governor Robert Eden, 22 November 1771, *Maryland Votes and Proceedings* (1771), p. 65. For the revocability of charter, see "In the First Line of Defense," pp. 199–204.

CHAPTER TEN: THE DOCTRINE OF CONSENT TO TAXATION

1 Hutchinson, *History* (1828), p. 164 (but see [Hutchinson,] *Strictures Upon the Declaration*, pp. 22–23); Book Review, *Critical Review* 42 (1776): 333; [Lind,] *Answer to the Declaration*, p. 64.

2 [Hopkins,] "Vindication of a Pamphlet," 23 January 1765, p. 1, col. 1; Letter from Thomas Cushing to Jasper Mauduit, January 1764, *Mauduit Letters*, pp. 145–46; denial: Wells, *Samuel Adams* 1:48–49; Letter from the Massachusetts House of Representatives to the Commons House of Assembly, 25 June 1764, *Georgia Commons House Journal*, 14:142 (see also [Lee,] *True State of the Proceedings*, p. 5); Petition from the Council and Burgesses of Virginia to the King and Parliament, 18 December 1764, Morgan, *Prologue*, p. 14; Remonstrance from the Council and Burgesses to the House of Commons, 18 December 1764, Morgan, *Prologue*, p. 16; Memorial of the Council and Burgesses to the House of Lords, 18 December 1764, *Journal of Burgesses* 10:302.

3 Letter to Agent Jasper Mauduit, 13 June 1764, *Massachusetts House Journal* (1764), p. 74; Pennsylvania Resolves, 21 September 1765, *Prior Documents*, p. 21.

4 Connecticut Resolves, 25 October 1765, Morgan, *Prologue*, p. 55; South Carolina Resolves, 29 November 1765, ibid., p. 58; Pennsylvania Resolves, 21 September 1765, *Prior Documents*, p. 21; Morgan, *Prologue*, pp. 51–52.

5 The emigration theory was one of the principal props upon which the colonists based their claim to possess rights independently of parliamentary grant. Briefly stated, it was "[t]hat their Ancestors brought over with them intire, and transmited to their Descendants, the natural and constitutional Rights they had enjoyed in their native Country; and the first Principles of the British Constitution were early engrafted into the Constitution of the Colonies." Message from the Virginia House of Burgesses to the Massachusetts House of Representatives, 9 May 1768, *American Gazette*, p. 20. For extended discussion, see *Authority of Rights*, pp. 114–31.

6 Resolves of the Lower House of Assembly, 22 June 1768, *Maryland Votes and Proceedings* (1768), pp. 204–5; Instructions of Boston, 28 December 1767, *Boston Gazette*, 28 December 1767, p. 4, col. 1; Resolution of the Boston Town Meeting, 13 September 1768, *Boston News-Letter*, 15 September 1768, p. 2, col. 2. Another New England town said the privilege was a "natural right" and attributed its source to constitutional law. "[E]very Tax imposed upon English Subjects without Consent, is against the natural Rights and

the Bounds prescribed by the English Constitution." New London Resolves, 10 December 1765, *Boston Post-Boy*, 16 December 1765, p. 3, col. 2.

7 For a discussion of the "positiveness" of natural law as a source of eighteenth-century British rights, see *Authority of Rights*, pp. 87–95.

8 Pennsylvania Resolves, 21 September 1765, *Prior Documents*, p. 21; Petition from New Jersey to the King, *Boston Chronicle*, 25 July 1768, p. 293, col. 2.

9 Marblehead Resolves, 8 December 1772, *Boston Evening-Post*, 14 December 1772, p. 2, col. 1; Instructions of the Pennsylvania Assembly to Richard Jackson, 22 September 1764, *Franklin-Jackson Letters*, p. 183; Representation of the New York General Assembly to the House of Commons, 31 December 1768 (entered in the Journal 7 April 1769), *Journal of New York Assembly* (1766–76), p. 16; Petition from the Town of Boston to Governor Francis Bernard, 14 June 1768, *Boston Town Records* 16:254.

10 Anon., *Crisis*, p. 3; Memorial of the Stamp Act Congress to the House of Lords, Morgan, *Prologue*, p. 65; Resolves of the First North Carolina Provincial Congress, 27 August 1774, *North Carolina Colonial Records*, 9:1044.

11 Instructions of 18 September 1765, *Boston Town Records* 16:155; "Freeman," *New York Gazette*, reprinted in *Boston Post-Boy*, 2 December 1765, p. 2, col. 1; Ray, *Importance of the Colonies*, pp. 2–3; *Gentleman's Magazine* 35 (1765): 569–70; Ellys, *Tracts on Liberty*, p. 50. For the authority of the right to taxation by consent, see *Authority of Rights*, pp. 110–13, 148–49.

12 Instructions of Providence, 13 August 1765, *Boston Evening-Post*, 19 August 1765, p. 2, col. 2; [Mauduit,] *Northern Colonies*, p. 16; *South-Carolina Gazette*, 10 November 1766, p. 1, col. 1; Anon., "A Letter from a Plain Yeoman," *Providence Gazette*, 11 May 1765, Morgan, *Prologue*, p. 76; [Zubly,] *Right to Tax*, p. 4.

13 [Otis,] *Considerations*, p. 2; Petition from the General Assembly to the King, 7 May 1768, *New Jersey Votes and Proceedings* (1768), p. 37; *American Gazette*, p. 93. See also Higginbotham, "James Iredell's Efforts," p. 134.

14 Message from the Assembly of Rhode Island to the earl of Hillsborough, 17 September 1768, *Boston Post-Boy*, 22 May 1769, p. 1, col. 1.

15 Petition of the Council and Burgesses to the House of Commons, 14 April 1768, *Journal of Burgesses* 11:166; Letter from the Virginia House of Burgesses to the Pennsylvania House of Representatives, 9 May 1768, *Pennsylvania Archives* 7:6189–90; Petition of the Council and Burgesses to the House of Lords, 14 April 1768, *Journal of Burgesses* 11:166; *Revolutionary Virginia* 1:56.

16 Anon., *Considerations upon Rights of Colonists*, p. 13; Instructions of Providence, 13 August 1765, *Boston Evening-Post*, 19 August 1765, p. 2, col. 3; Annapolis, Maryland, newspaper, 5 September 1765, reprinted in *Boston Post-Boy*, 23 September 1765, p. 3, col. 1; *Boston News-Letter*, 26 September 1765, p. 3, col. 2.

CHAPTER ELEVEN: THE STATUS OF THE DOCTRINE

1 Connecticut Resolves, 25 October 1765, Morgan, *Prologue*, p. 55; Petition of the Virginia Council and Burgesses to the House of Lords, 14 April 1766,

Journal of Burgesses 11:166; Hinkhouse, *Preliminaries*, p. 86; Book Review, *Monthly Review* 54 (1776): 146; *Scots Magazine* 38 (1776): 27, n. 4. This book is not concerned with the topic of civil rights, but it should be mentioned that the civil right American whigs cited when asserting the constitutional privilege to be taxed only by consent was (primarily) the principle of equality. *Political Register* 1 (1767): 250–51; Extracts from the Votes of the New York House, 31 December 1768, *Scots Magazine* 31 (1769): 92; Resolution of Ipswich, 17 December 1772, *Boston Evening-Post*, 18 January 1773, p. 1, col. 3; Instructions of Boston, 22 December 1767, *Boston Town Records* 16:229; Instructions of Portsmouth, New Hampshire, 23 December 1765, *Boston Evening-Post*, 6 January 1766, p. 2, col. 3. For discussion, see *Authority of Rights*, pp. 148–49.

2 [French,] *Constitution of Ireland*, p. 5.

3 For example, 1793: Anon., *Present State of the Constitution*, p. 3; 1792: Paley, *Essay upon the Constitution*, pp. 17–18; Toulmin, *American War Lamented*, p. 15.

4 "According to the first formulation of this excellent constitution . . . we find that the people thus took care no laws should be enacted, no taxes levied but by their consent, expressed by their representatives in the great council of the nation." Speech of John Wilkes, Commons Debates, 21 March 1776, *Hibernian Magazine* 6 (1776): 780. Similarly, see Anon., *Constitutional Criterion*, pp. 19–20.

5 [Maseres,] *Considerations on Admitting Representatives*, pp. 3–5.

6 Price, *Nature of Civil Liberty*, p. 49; Price, "On the Nature of Civil Liberty," *Hibernian Magazine* 6 (1776): 185. Joseph Priestly also asserted the doctrine to be the highest right. [Priestly,] *Address to Dissenters*, p. 15.

7 Anon., *Characters*, p. 95; "Political Character of Lord Shelburne," *London Magazine* 45 (1775): 578; "Proceedings in the session," *Scots Magazine* 29 (1767): 144; Blackstone, *Commentaries* 1:135–36.

8 T.M., "An Essay on Liberty and Independency," *Political Register* 5 (1769): 248–49. See also [Crowley,] *Letters*, p. 30; Anon., *Constitutional Answer to Wesley*, p. 12; [Evans,] *Letter to John Wesley*, p. 4.

9 *Boston Evening-Post*, 18 January 1768, p. 2, col. 2. See also Speech of Lord Camden, Lords Debates, 14 March 1776, *London Magazine* 45 (1776): 457; Anon., "Life of Lord Camden," *The Law Magazine; or Quarterly Review of Jurisprudence* 9 (1833): 34, 46–47.

10 Pitt quoted in Cartwright, *People's Barrier*, p. 4; Anon., *To Tax Themselves*, p. 132; [Crowley,] *Dissertations*, p. 9. Similarly, see [Rokeby,] *Considerations on the Measures*, p. 28; [Shebbeare,] *Seventh Letter*, p. 25. For the argument applied to the colonies, see "Proceedings in the session," *Scots Magazine* 29 (1767): 144.

11 Proposed Rockinghamite Address to the King, January 1777, *Burke on American Revolution*, p. 151.

12 Bill of Rights, 1 William and Mary, sess. 2, cap. 2; De Lolme, *Constitution*, p. 36; Blackstone, *Commentaries* 1:135; Boorstin, *Mysterious Science of Law*, p. 173; positive: Ellys, *Tracts on Liberty*, pp. 65–66; negative: Anon., *Whigs and Tories*, p. 5.

13 "The North Briton, No. 135," *Scots Magazine* 27 (1765): 118; Letter from the *North Briton*, No. CXXXV, *London Magazine* 34 (1765): 102, 103. See also *Authority of Rights*, pp. 151–52, 156–58.

14 [Ramsay,] *Historical Essay*, p. 196; "Z.T.," *Boston Evening-Post*, 3 July 1769, p. 4, col. 1; Anon., *Constitutional Considerations*, p. 5; Anon., *Examination of Rights of Colonies*, p. 14; 1 William and Mary, sess. 2, cap 2.

15 Remonstrance and Petition of the Lord Mayor, Aldermen, and Livery of London to the King, 11 April 1775, *London Magazine* 44 (1775): 209; *Hibernian Magazine* 5 (1775): 286; Resolutions of the Bill of Rights Society, 23 August 1774, *Scots Magazine* 36 (1774): 440; Speech of George Grenville, Commons Debates, 6 February 1765, Ryder, "Parliamentary Diaries," p. 254.

16 That fact can be accepted almost without comment whenever a colonial whig body made the claim. Petition of the Virginia Council and Burgesses to the House of Commons, 14 April 1768, *Journal of Burgesses* 11:169; Petition of the Virginia Council and Burgesses to the House of Lords, 14 April 1768, *Journal of Burgesses* 11:166; "Articles of association, by the citizens of Westmoreland, for the purpose of opposing the stamp act," 27 July 1766, Lee, *Richard Henry Lee* 1:34; Leedstown Resolves, 27 February 1766, *Journal of Burgesses* 10:lxxii–lxxiii.

17 Letter to a Gentleman in London, 31 May 1764, *Lee Letters*, p. 6; Lee, *Richard Henry Lee* 1:28.

18 [Dulany,] *Considerations on the Propriety*, pp. 31, 32.

19 "The North Briton, No. 135," *Scots Magazine* 27 (1765): 118.

20 Watson, *Principles of the Revolution*, p. 12 (for this and similar contemporary quotations, see Guttridge, *English Whiggism*, p. 142); The *New London Gazette*, 20 September 1765, reprinted in *Boston Evening-Post*, 14 October 1765, p. 1, col. 3; *Public Advertiser*, 8 January 1770, reprinted in *Franklin's Letters to Press*, p. 172. See also Evans, *Political Sophistry detected*, pp. 8–9; Letter from Julian, 15 November 1776, *Remembrancer for 1776: Part III*, p. 46; Anon., *Letter to those Ladies*, pp. 9–10.

21 Anon., *To Tax Themselves*, pp. 90–91. See also Hampden, "A full Vindication of the Livery of London's Petition to his Majesty as to the Charge upon the Ministry of raising a Revenue in our Colonies by Prerogative," *Political Register* 5 (1769): 187.

22 Letter from Thomas Cushing and Samuel Adams to Reverend G.W., 11 November 1765, Adams, *Writings* 1:30.

23 Anon., *American Resistance Indefensible*, p. 17. "Taxation, and Government, are inseparable." [Boucher,] *Letter from a Virginian*, p. 24; "[W]as there ever any supreme authority in the world without the power of taxation?" [Bacon,] *Short Address*, p. 3. See also Tucker quoted in Pulteney, *Thoughts on Present State*, pp. 96–97; [Seabury,] *View of the Controversy*, p. 14.

24 [Gray,] *Right of the Legislature*, p. 24; [Knox,] *Controversy* (Dublin Edition), p. 90; Letter from George Grenville to William Knox, 16 August 1768, *Grenville Letterbooks* [hereinafter cited as Letter]; Grenville, "Present State," 23 January 1769, p. 25, col. 1; [Knox,] *The Present State*, p. 87. See also Grenville, quoted in Thomas, *British Politics*, pp. 90–91; Pownall, *Administration*, pp. 147–48; Book Review, *Critical Review* 38 (1774): 475;

Letter from Jared Ingersoll to Thomas Fitch, 11 February 1765, Morgan, *Prologue*, p. 30. Grenville and Knox, like many imperialists opposing American whig arguments, cited John Locke as their authority, especially Locke's theory of tacit consent. Americans, by continuing "to be part of our community," consented to parliamentary taxation. [Knox,] *Controversy*, pp. 68, 69–70.

25 [Gray,] *Right of the Legislature*, p. 11; [Lind,] *Thirteenth Parliament*, p. 59.
26 "General View of the British Constitution," *Scots Magazine* 38 (1776): 225–31; Anon., *Plan of Re-Union*, pp. 65–74; Gerard, *Liberty Cloke of Maliciousness*, p. 10.
27 Anon., *Experience preferable to Theory*, pp. 43–44.
28 "Sophism:" [Gray,] *Right of the Legislature*, pp. 29–30. Also see [Knox,] *Controversy*, pp. 60–61, 87; [Goodricke,] *Observations on Price's Theory*, p. 7; Anon., *Speech Never Intended*, pp. 13–16; Anon., *Rights of Parliament*, p. 13.
29 Speech of Attorney General Yorke, Commons Debates, 3 February 1766, Ryder, "Parliamentary Diaries," p. 266; Mansfield: "Lords Debate on Declaratory Act," p. 116.
30 Anon., *Celebrated Speech*, pp. 9–10; Speech of George Grenville, Commons Debates, 6 February 1765, Ryder, "Parliamentary Diaries," p. 254; Book Review, *Monthly Review* 51 (1774): 477; Book Review, *Monthly Review* 52 (1775): 522.

CHAPTER TWELVE: THEORY OF PRECEDENT

1 Letter from S.F.V. to the Printer, 20 February 1764, *Providence Gazette*, 5 May 1764, p. 2, col. 2; Knollenberg, *Origin*, p. 208.
2 D'Innocenzo & Turner, "New York Newspapers Part 2," p. 349; Instructions of 18 September 1765, *Boston Town Records* 16:156; *Boston Evening-Post*, 21 October 1765, p. 1, col. 2.
3 Dickinson, *Stamp Act*, pp. 203, 202; *Boston Post-Boy*, 9 December 1765, p. 1, col. 1; *Gazette & News-Letter*, 6 December 1765, p. 2, col. 1.
4 Dulany, "Antilon," p. 176.
5 Book Review, *Critical Review* 22 (1766): 362 (similarly, [Cartwright,] *American Independence*, pp. 29–30); Life: McIlwain, *Constitutionalism*, p. 14; Dulany, "Antilon," p. 176; *Providence Gazette*, 11 May 1765, reprinted in *Boston Post-Boy*, 15 July 1765, p. 2, col. 1; Morgan, *Prologue*, pp. 74–75; Pollock, "Politics," p. 197; Prall, *Agitation*, p. 6.
6 [Lind,] *Answer to the Declaration*, p. 69; [Knox,] *Controversy*, p. 191; Pownall, *Pownall*, p. 179.
7 "Junius on the Privilege of the House of Commons," *Hibernian Magazine* 1 (1771): 184; South Carolina: Weir, *Most Important Epocha*, p. 41; Speech of Lord Barrington, "Parliament," *Scots Magazine* 38 (1776): 15.
8 Dickinson, *Letters*, 319–20. The Hat Act (23 George II, cap. 29) was a statute enacted to suppress hat manufacturing in the colonies and to provide a monopoly for British hat makers. It was the only piece of parliamentary

legislation curtailing colonial manufacturing that was generally effective, and was one of the strongest precedents imperialists cited for establishing Parliament's legislative authority over the economic and internal affairs of the North American colonies. It was seldom cited as precedent for Parliament's authority to tax the colonies for purposes of revenue without consent, and even as precedent to legislate for them internally its force as precedent was as convincingly rejected as it was defended. For the fullest discussion in Great Britain of the Hat Act's validity as a precedent for both taxation and legislation, see Anonymous, *A Letter to the Gentlemen of the Committee of London Merchants, Trading to North America* (London, 1766), pp. 17–19.

9 Letter from Richard Henry Lee to John Dickinson, 26 November 1768, and Letter from John Dickinson to Richard Henry Lee, 16 July 1769, Lee, *Richard Henry Lee*, pp. 66–67, 68–69.

10 Message from the Lower House of Assembly to Governor Horatio Sharpe, 13 December 1765, *Maryland Votes and Proceedings* (November 1765), p. 61; Resolves of Providence, 19 January 1774, *Rhode Island Colony Records*, 7:272.

11 "Extract of a Letter from London, dated March 24," *Pennsylvania Gazette*, 7 June 1764, p. 2, col. 2; *Boston Post-Boy*, 11 June 1764, p. 3, col. 1; *Gazette and News-Letter*, 14 June 1764, p. 1, col. 3.

12 [Knox,] *Claim of the Colonies*, pp. 31–33 quoted in Morgan, "Postponement of Stamp Act," p. 362; Bellot, *William Knox*, p. 62; Letter from Charles Garth to the South Carolina Committee of Correspondence, 5 June 1764, Namier, "Charles Garth," p. 648.

13 Letter from the Virginia Committee to the Agent, 28 July 1764, "Proceedings Committee of Correspondence," 12:13; [Dulany,] *Considerations on the Propriety*, p. 38; *Boston Gazette*, 9 January 1769, reprinted in Adams, *Writings* 1:285–86.

14 Speech of George Grenville, Commons Debates, 6 February 1765, Ryder, "Parliamentary Diaries," p. 256; "Extract of a Letter from a considerable Merchant in *London*, to his friend in *Connecticut*, dated April 9, 1765," *Boston Post-Boy*, 8 July 1765, p. 3, col. 2.

15 Letter from George Grenville to Robert Nugent, 21 June 1766, *Grenville Papers* 3:250. See also "A Summary of the Argument against repealing the Stamp-Act," *Gentleman's Magazine* 36 (1766): 107. But contrary, see Protest of 11 May 1774, *Protests of Lords*, p. 145.

16 Letter from Thomas Cushing to Jasper Mauduit, 28 October 1763, *Mauduit Letters*, p. 135; Letter from the General Committee, Charles Town, to the Sons of Liberty in North Carolina, 25 April 1770, *North Carolina Colonial Records*, 8:197; Dickinson, *Letters*, pp. 395, 382–83. The statutes mentioned by Dickinson are discussed below.

17 Petition from the Virginia House of Burgesses to the King, 27 June 1770, *Revolution Documents* 2:129. It was "retained merely as a *Precedent.*" Nicholas, *Present State of Virginia*, p. 262.

18 Petition of the General Court of the East India Company, 24 May 1773,

Gentleman's Magazine 43 (1773): 252; "The Lords' Protest against Passing the East-India Regulation Bill," ibid., p. 264. See also the vote of the Court of Common Council of London. Ibid., p. 253.

19 Letter from Deputy Governor Robert Eden to the Earl of Hillsborough [ca. June 1770], *Revolution Documents* 2:130; Address of New York Citizens to Sea Captains who refused to Carry Tea, n.d., *Gazette & Post-Boy*, 1 November 1773, p. 2, col. 3.

20 [Boucher,] *Letter from a Virginian*, p. 21 (see also [Randolph,] *Present State of Virginia*, p. 213); Resolves of the First Provincial Congress, 27 August 1774, *North Carolina Colonial Records* 9:1044; Resolves of the Richmond Town Meeting, 28 February 1774, and Resolves of the Barrington Town Meeting, 21 March 1774, *Rhode Island Colony Records* 7:276, 279; Resolves of Westerly, Rhode Island, 2 February 1774, Denison, *Westerly*, p. 112.

21 "Scaevola," *Gazette & Post-Boy*, 25 October 1773, p. 2, col. 1. See also Anon., *Argument in Defence*, p. 3; Anon., *To Tax Themselves*, p. 3; Adams, "Novanglus," p. 178; "Consideration," *Gazette & Post-Boy*, 20 June 1774, p. 2, col. 1.

22 [Dickinson,] *New Essay*, p. 109; Letter from George Mason to the Committee of London Merchants, 6 June 1766, Morgan, *Prologue*, p. 160.

23 *Boston Post-Boy*, 27 January 1766, p. 2, col. 3; Address from a Committee of Gentlemen to Governor William Tryon, November 1765, ibid., p. 2, col. 3; from the *North Carolina Gazette*, 20 November 1765, *North Carolina Colonial Records* 7:129; "At a Conference of the Members of both Houses of Assembly," 19 November 1766, *Maryland Votes and Proceedings* (1766), p. 459.

CHAPTER THIRTEEN: HISTORICAL ASPECTS OF THE DOCTRINE

1 See, e.g., Larkin, *Property in Eighteenth Century*, p. 2, 145; Southwick, "Molasses Act," p. 402; Dunn, "Politics of Locke," p. 75; "Irrelevance of the Declaration," p. 69–89.

2 Kames, *History of Man*, 1:490–92; *Scots Magazine* 36 (1774): 81 (see also Hawkins, *Life of Johnson*, p. 503); Camden; "Speech on American Taxation," p. 123; Address of John Dickinson, 25 April 1769, *American Gazette*, p. 39; *Political Writings of James Otis*, p. 23; "Junius Americanus," *Boston Evening-Post*, 28 January 1771, p. 1, col. 1; Junius Americanus, "To Junius," *Political Register* 9 (1771): 325.

3 Maryland Resolves, 28 September 1765, *Maryland Votes and Proceedings* (September 1765), p. 9; Morgan, *Prologue*, p. 52; *Scots Magazine* 37 (1775): 63.

4 Care, *English Liberties Boston Edition*, pp. 58–62; Ellys, *Tracts on Liberty*, pp. 50–55; Junius Americanus (*supra*, n. 2), p. 325; *Providence Gazette* reprinted in *Boston Post-Boy*, 15 July 1765, p. 1, col. 3.

5 *Proceedings against Manwaring*. p. 10.

6 Anon., *Political Mirror or Summary Review*, p. 5; Johnstone, *Speech on Question*, p. 4.

7 Pym, *Declaration of Grievances*, p. 395; *Proceedings against Manwaring*,

pp. 10–11; Feudal era: Anon., *Constitutional Advocate*, p. 6. For recent authority on the history of the doctrine, see Keir, *Constitutional History*, p. 14; Dowell, *Taxation and Taxes* 1:229.

8 Clarke, *Representation and Consent*, p. 255; Knollenberg, *Origin*, p. 152.

9 Speech of William Pitt, Commons Debates, 4 March 1766, Ryder, "Parliamentary Diaries," p. 316; Letter from Æquus, 16 January 1766, *London Magazine* 35 (1766): 32; Speech of Sir William Blackstone, Commons Debates, 1766, "Stamp Act Debates," pp. 568–69.

10 Feudal aids: Anon., *To Tax Themselves*, p. 26 (see also Dale, *Constitutional History*, p. 123); David Hume, *The History of England from the Invasion of Julius Ceasar to the Accession of Henry VII* (London: A. Millar, 1762) 2:103; Hume paraphrased in Sinclair, *Public Revenue* 1:106.

11 Sullivan, *Lectures on Constitution*, p. 346; Care, *English Liberties Boston Edition*, p. 53; Care, *English Liberties First Edition*, pp. 36–37. See also De Lolme, *Constitution*, p. 21; "Junius Americanus to Junius," *Political Register* 9 (1771): 325; Anon., *To Tax Themselves*, pp. 27–28; Letter from Æquus (*supra*, n. 9), p. 32; Jacob, *New Law Dictionary*, "Tax."

12 Sinclair, *Public Revenue* 1:114. Recent legal scholarship attributes the development of representative government to the need for the Crown in the thirteenth century to obtain consent to taxation. May, *Parliamentary Practice*, p. 6; O'Sullivan, "Philosophy of Common Law," p. 122.

13 J. G. Edwards, "Confirmatio Cartarum and Baronial Grievances in 1297," *English Historical Review* 58 (1943): 273–300; Dowell, *Taxation and Taxes* 1:66–67; Blackstone, *Commentaries* 1:136; De Lolme, *Constitution: New Edition*, p. 35.

14 Maitland, *Constitutional History*, pp. 179–80; Mantell, *Short Treatise of Lawes*, pp. 15–16; Anon., *Three Letters*, p. 20; Anon., *To Tax Themselves*, pp. 27–28; [Dulany,] *Considerations on the Propriety*, p. 9; *De Laud. Leg. Ang.*, c. 36, p. 84, quoted in Cartwright, *People's Barrier*, p. 4. See also from 1628, Anon., *Priviledges of Parliaments*, pp. 40–41.

15 Hurstfield, *Freedom, Corruption and Government*, p. 43; Keir, *Constitutional History*, pp. 98–99; Evans, "Antiquity of Parliaments," p. 217. A contemporary who did discuss it was Sir Edward Coke. MacKay, "Coke," p. 245. For an advocate (a future Chief Baron of the Exchequer) relying on Coke's authority for the doctrine during the prerevolutionary era, see Argument for the plaintiff by Mr. Macdonald, *Campbell v. Hall*, 20 *State Trials* 239 (K.B., 1774), p. 290.

16 *Historicus*, "To the Printer," *Political Register* 11 (1772): 97.

17 Petition to King James from the Commons, 1610, [Whitelocke,] *Concerning Impositions*, pp. 115–16; "Petition of Grievances by the Commons in 1610," 2 *State Trials*, p. 521. For the address to James in which the Commons defined and asserted its right to consent, see [Whitelocke,] *Concerning Impositions*, pp. 114–15.

18 The *New London Gazette* quoted in *Boston Evening-Post*, 28 October 1765, p. 1, col. 2. See also Speech of Governor George Johnstone, Commons Debates, 6 February 1775, *Gentleman's Magazine* 45 (1775): 159–60; [Rokeby,]

Further Examination, p. 57; Price, *Nature of Civil Liberty*, p. 49; Anon., *Letter to Cooper*, pp. 39–40.

19 Anon., *Prospect of Consequences*, p. 16; Anon., *Letter to Cooper*, p. 32; Anon., *Political Mirror or Summary Review*, p. 3n.; Bill of Attainder passed against the earl of Strafford (1641), in *Somers' Tracts* 4:227; "The Declaration of the Commons Against Dr. Manwaring" (1628), *Proceedings against Manwaring*, p. 7. The Declaration also stated "That whereas by the Laws and Statutes of this Realm the free Subjects of *England* do undoubtedly inherit this Right and Liberty, not to be compel'd to contribute any Tax, Tallage, Aid, or to make any Loans not set or impos'd by common Consent, by Act of Parliament."

20 Session of 26 March 1628, *Commons Debates 1628* 2:125; *Gazette & News-Letter*, 13 February 1766, p. 2, col. 3; Letter from Æquus, 16 January 1766, *London Magazine* 35 (1766): 32; Petition of Right (1628) 3 Charles I, cap. 1. See also Speech of Sir Robert Phelips, 25 April 1628, *Commons Debates 1628*, 3:76; Jones, "Clegate Case," pp. 282–86; Pollock, "Politics," p. 204; Judson, *Crisis*, pp. 42–43; Pym, *Speech of Summing Up*, pp. 24–25; Mantell, *Short Treatise of Lawes*, p. 7; Cook, *King Charl[e]s his Case*, p. 7.

21 Parliament's Humble Petition and Advice presented to the Lord Protector, 25 May 1657, *Somers' Tracts* 6:406; Anon., *Englands Safety in Laws Supremacy*, p. 14; Thomson, *Constitutional History*, p. 44.

22 Of course, as previously noted, the doctrine was included in the settlement following the Glorious Revolution. The Bill of Rights declared "That levying money for or to the use of the crown, by pretence of prerogative, without grant of parliament, for longer time, or in other manner than the same is or shall be granted, is illegal." 1 William & Mary, sess. 2, cap. 2, sec. 4 (1688).

23 [Tyrrell,] *Brief Enquiry*, pp. 11, 62–63; [Leslie,] *Constitution, Laws and Government*, pp. 16, 119; vested in Parliament: 1734: [Jacob,] *Laws of Liberty*, p. 112; 1748: Anon., *Thoughts on the Constitution*, pp. 10–11; Marvell, *Account*, p. 4; Edward Chamberlayne, *Angliae Notitia* (9th ed., 1676), p. 71, quoted in De Beer, "Locke and English Liberalism," p. 39.

24 Massachusetts: Breen, "Localism," p. 26; North Carolina: Greene, *Quest*, pp. 149–51. For the controversy in Maryland on the eve of the Revolution, see Onuf, "Introduction."

25 Law of 5 March 1623/24, *Foundations of Colonial America* 3:2132; Adams, "Novanglus," 202–3; Lovejoy, *Glorious Revolution*, p. 39; "Articles at the Surrender of the Countrie," 12 March 1651, "Surrender of Virginia," p. 183. For citations and discussions of this agreement as precedent during the pre-revolutionary controversy, see Adams, "Novanglus," pp. 202–3; Richard Bland, *An Inquiry* (1766), reprinted in *Revolutionary Virginia* 1:38. For a similar agreement made with Barbadoes, see Williamson, "Imperial Policy," p. 219.

26 Richard Bland (*supra*, n. 25), p. 40.

27 *Giddings* v. *Brown*, Essex County (1657), Howe, *Readings in Legal History*,
     p. 233–34. See Konig, *Puritan Massachusetts*, pp. 93–96; Allen, *In English
     Ways*, p. 144.

28 Massachusetts General Court: Book Review, *Critical Review* 21 (1766): 38
     (for a similar Massachusetts stand in 1678, see Lovejoy, *Glorious Revolu-
     tion*, pp. 141–42); Mather, *Vindication*, p. 77; [Rawson,] *Revolution in New
     England*, p. 43.

29 Barnes, *Dominion of New England*, pp. 90, 118–19; Webb, "Trials of Andros,"
     p. 40; Wiltse, *Jeffersonian Tradition*, p. 27; contemporary evidence: *Revo-
     lution Justified*, p. 126. For discussion, see Wendell, *Cotton Mather*, p. 71.
     Not all historians have agreed. Barnes, *Dominion of New England*, pp.
     96–97.

30 *Revolution Justified*, p. 122; [Rawson,] *Revolution in New England*, p. 40;
     [Rawson,] *Revolution in New England*, p. 7. "[W]e are wholly without
     Law. . . . Besides, The essential part of *English* Laws is, That they are made
     by the *People* who must obey them, and neither Law *made* nor Tax rais'd
     without their own consent. . . ." *The Case of Massachusetts Colony Con-
     sidered, in a Letter to a Friend at Boston* (18 May 1689), reprinted in Sim-
     mons, "Massachusetts Revolution of 1689," pp. 8–9.

31 [Rawson,] *Revolution in New England*, pp. 7–8.

32 Barnes, *Dominion of New England*, pp. 86, n. 43, 87, 88; Mauduit, *Short
     View*, p. 46.

33 Act of 13 October 1692, *Acts and Resolves*, 1:40; summary of charges: Breen,
     Good Ruler, p. 164.

34 Leder, *Liberty*, pp. 122–25; McCormac, *Colonial Opposition*, pp. 94–95.

35 Leder, *Liberty*, p. 111; Rossiter, *Six Characters*, pp. 161–63; Resolves of the
     Lower House of Assembly, 2 November 1765, *Maryland Votes and Proceed-
     ings* (November 1765), p. 15; Carroll, "First Citizen," pp. 134–35.

36 Stillé, *John Dickinson*, p. 46.

37 *Boston Post-Boy*, 9 September 1765, p. 2, col. 1; Leder, *Liberty*, p. 122. In
     1753, Virginia's Burgesses in an address to the governor declared that "The
     Rights of the Subjects are so secured by Law, that they cannot be deprived
     of the least Part of their Property, but by their own consent." Address of
     28 November 1753, *Journal of Burgesses* 8:143.

38 *The Maryland Gazette*, 16 March 1748, p. 1, col. 2, and 10 February 1748,
     p. 1, col. 1. "We find in the Lower House Journal of *May* Session 1692,
     the following Entries: 'Voted by the House, *Nemine contradicente*, that
     it is the undoubted Right of the Freemen of this Province, not to have *any
     Fees* imposed upon them but by the Consent of the Freemen in a General
     Assembly." Address of the Lower House of Assembly to Governor Robert
     Eden, 22 November 1771, *Maryland Votes and Proceedings* (1771), p. 66.

39 Resolves of 13 September 1768, *Boston Town Records* 16:261–63.

40 Message from the Pennsylvania Assembly to Governor Richard Penn, 12 April
     1773, *Pennsylvania Council* 10:82.

41 It was also claimed in London that a plan for colonial union proposed by

the Albany Congress of 1754 had been rejected partly because of the doctrine of consent to taxation. *Gentlemen's Magazine* 36 (1766): 85.

42 Wood, *Creation*, pp. 183–84.

43 *Independent Reflector*, 7 December 1752, p. 62.

44 [Evans,] *Letter to John Wesley*, p. 4.

CHAPTER FOURTEEN: THE AUTHORITY OF ANALOGY

1 *Examination of Franklin*, p. 13.

2 Speech of Lord Mansfield, Lords Debates, 3 February 1766, Holliday, *Life of Mansfield*, p. 244; [Hicks,] *Nature of Parliamentary Power*, p. 27.

3 Burgh, *Political Disquisitions* 2:308.

4 Evans, *Political Sophistry detected*, p. 13; Burgh, *Political Disquisitions* 2:310.

5 Bracton, *De Legibus* f1(b), quoted in Rupert Cross, *Precedent in English Law*, 2d ed. Oxford: (Clarendon Press, 1977), p. 24. For the most authoritative translation, see *Bracton on the Laws and Customs of England* (Samuel E. Thorne, translator, Cambridge, Mass., 1968) 2:21.

6 Evans, *Reply to Fletcher*, pp. 45–46.

7 Letter to Agent Mauduit, 13 June 1764, *Massachusetts House Journal* (1764), p. 76; Petition to the King, 20 October 1765, Morgan, *Prologue*, p. 65; *Account of Stamp Act Congress*, p. 14; Lee, *Appeal to Justice*, p. 14. For many analogies between Ireland and the colonies applied to the principle of equality and the question of taxation, see [Evans,] *Letter to John Wesley*, pp. 15–16.

8 Anon., *to Tax Themselves*, pp. 115–16; Book Review, *Monthly Review* 52 (1775): 254–55.

9 *Annual Register 1766*, p. [40]; Anon., *Three Letters*, pp. 17–18; Fisk, *English Public Finance*, p. 84.

10 Speech of George Grenville, Commons Debates, 14 January 1766, *Parliamentary History* 16:101; Morgan, *Prologue*, p. 137; Speech of William Pitt, Commons Debates, 14 January 1766, *Parliamentary History* 16:104; Anon., *Celebrated Speech*, pp. 12–13; Morgan, *Prologue*, p. 139.

11 25 Charles II, cap. 9; Anon., *To Tax Themselves*, p. 119. For appraisals of recent constitutional historians, see Thomson, *Constitutional History*, p. 77; Marcham, *Constitutional History*, pp. 22–23. The Chester statute was more explicit than that of Durham, as it laid stress on the fact that Chester suffered a detriment as a result of not being represented: "by reason whereof the said inhabitants have hitherto sustained manifold disherisons, losses and damages, as well in their lands, goods and bodies, as in the good, civil and politick governance and maintenance of the commonwealth of their said country." 34 & 35 Henry VIII, cap. 13.

12 Law officers: Garth, "Letter on Repeal," pp. 150–52; American claims: "By these acts we see what was the sense of the nation in the years 1535 [Wales], 1542 [Chester], and 1672 [Durham]. The two first are eighty years before, and the last is fifty years after the first settlement of *New England*. The rights of *all the subjects* by the more ancient statutes, are so fully explained

and knit together in these as it is impossible ever to divide them." Anon., *To Tax Themselves*, p. 34; Third interpretation: Anon., *Plan of Re-union*, p. 81.

13 [Hopkins,] "Vindication of a Pamphlet," 9 March 1765, p. 1, col. 1; Schuyler, *Empire*, p. 17; Extract of a Letter from London, 1 December 1764, *Boston Evening-Post*, 18 March 1765, p. 2, col. 2.

14 *Demophoon*, "A Dissertation on the Original Dispute between Great-Britain and her Colonies," *Political Register* 7 (1770): 155; *London Magazine* 39 (1770): 418.

15 Anon., *Dialogue on the Constitution*, pp. 75–85; Dickinson, *Letters*, pp. 375–81; *Gazette & Post-Boy*, 25 October 1773, p. 2, col. 1.

16 "To his Majesty," February 1777, *Papers of Iredell* 1:436; Anon., *Three Letters*, pp. 44–46; Speech of Attorney General Yorke, Commons Debates, 3 February 1766, Ryder, "Parliamentary Debates," p. 264. In the last speech, Yorke criticized William Molyneux's 1698 treatise, *The Case of Ireland*. It is a constitutional study that has been discussed as a definitive work by at least one twentieth-century student of the American Revolution. Unfortunately, its thesis is irrelevant to the American issue. McIlwain, *Revolution*, pp. 45–80; Schuyler, *Empire*, pp. 81–91.

17 For example, nonexistent statutes were cited as authority. Hinkhouse, *Preliminaries*, p. 97. John Dickinson cited Blackstone for the doctrine that Ireland was not taxed because it was not represented. Blackstone did not say that and could be read as saying the opposite. Dickinson, "Letter to Inhabitants," p. 483 n.

18 See the evidence collected in Schuyler, *Empire*, pp. 27–34. What should not be confused with the problems of history as evidence is the use of forensic history. James Wilson, for example, has been criticized for selecting evidence from the history of Ireland supporting the American whig argument and ignoring facts that hurt his case. Mullett, *Fundamental Law*, p. 172. But Wilson was acting as an advocate not as a historian and should be criticized as an advocate not as a historian. *Briefs of Revolution*, pp. 50–53, 103–7.

19 Speech of Charles Jenkinson, Commons Debates, 22 March 1775, *Gentleman's Magazine* 45 (1775): 623–24; Anon., *Examination of Rights*, pp. 24–25; Letter from Governor William Pitkin to Agent William Samuel Johnson, 10 June 1768, *Public Records of Connecticut* 13:89.

20 Speech of Lord Mansfield, Lords Debates, 3 February 1766, Holliday, *Life of Mansfield*, p. 250; Letter from the Massachusetts House of Representatives to the earl of Shelburne, 15 January 1768, *Adams, Writings* 1:158; Speech of William Beckford, Commons Debates, 23 January 1765, Walpole, *Memoirs* 1:268; Anon., *Argument in Defence*, 113; [Baillie,] *Appendix to a Letter*, p. 54.

21 Evans, *Reply to Fletcher*, p. 44. The *Boston Gazette* used the analogy for similar sarcasm. "Behold the difference between free-born Americans and conquered Irishmen! the one cannot be saddled with taxes without their Parliament is managed, while the other are loaded with duties without

asking their parliament one question about it." Editorial comment on a Letter from Cork, Ireland, 7 July 1767, *Boston Gazette* (Supplement), 19 October 1767, p. 2, col. 1.

22 Gipson, "Debate on Repeal," p. 31, n. 45; *Franklin's Letters to Press*, p. 111.

CHAPTER FIFTEEN: PRECEDENTS FOR TAXATION

1 Petition from the Pennsylvania General Assembly to the King, 22 September 1768, *Pennsylvania Archives* 7:6272; *Boston Chronicle*, 13 February 1769, p. 51, col. 3; *Boston News-Letter*, 23 February 1769, p. 1, col. 1; [Lind,] *Englishman's Answer*, p. 18; Speech of Richard Hussey, Commons Debates, 3 February 1766, Ryder, "Parliamentary Diaries," p. 313; Speech of Alexander Wedderburn, Commons Debates, 1766, "Stamp Act Debates," pp. 570–71; Chaffin, "Declaratory Act," p. 14; Christie, *Crisis*, p. 51; Letter from Jared Ingersoll to Governor Thomas Fitch, 11 February 1765, "Ingersoll Correspondence," p. 307.

2 Dulany, *Considerations*, p. 637; Speech of Edmund Burke, Commons Debates, 19 April 1774, *Burke on American Revolution*, p. 41; Abingdon, *Thoughts on Burke's Letter*, p. 43; [Lind,] *Thirteenth Parliament*, pp. 249–50.

3 Johnson, *Political Tracts*, p. 161; Speech of William Blackstone, Commons Debates, 3 February 1766, Ryder, "Parliamentary Diaries," p. 269; "Stamp Act Debates," p. 569; [Knox,] *Claim of the Colonies*, quoted in *Critical Review* 19 (1765): 226–27. The statute was 5 George II, cap. 7.

4 [Macpherson,] *Rights of Great Britain*, pp. 30–40; Mauduit, *Legislative Authority*, p. 17.

5 Leonard, "Massachusettensis," p. 69; Anon., *Plain Question*, p. 9.

6 Marshall, *History of the Colonies*, p. 354. See also a discussion in which it is pointed out that Marshall's distinction was adopted by Parliament in 1778 when it pledged to impose no customs duties upon North America "except only such duties as it may be expedient to impose for the Regulation of Commerce." Knollenberg, *Origin*, p. 149.

7 *Gazetteer*, 23 January 1766, reprinted in *Franklin's Letters to Press*, p. 54.

8 Ramsay, *History* 1:49. For elaborations on Ramsay's theme, see *Burke on American Revolution*, pp. 40–41, 46; Burke, "Speech on American Taxation," pp. 136–37, 141–42.

9 For lists, see [Macpherson,] *Rights of Great Britain*, pp. 101–2; *Scots Magazine* 38 (1776): 182–83; [Sir John Dalrymple,] "The Address," *Scots Magazine* 37 (1775): 384; Book Review, *Gentleman's Magazine* 46 (1776): 224–25; "Grotius," *Pills for the Delegates*, pp. 28–29; Mauduit, *Legislative Authority*, p. 17. Again, the important fact should be reiterated that supporters of parliamentary taxation began compiling these lists at the very start of the controversy, with the Stamp Act debate. Extract of a letter from a gentleman in London to his friend in Charles-Town, 8 February 1765, *South-Carolina Gazette*, 20 April 1765, p. 3, col. 2.

10 E.g., Roebuck, *Enquiry whether the Guilt*, pp. 8–9; [Lind,] *Answer to the Declaration*, p. 65.

11 12 Charles II, cap. 4; "Rights of G. Britain asserted," *Scots Magazine* 38 (1776): 68; Roebuck, *Enquiry whether the Guilt*, p. 10.

12 "Rights of G. Britain" (*supra*, n. 11), pp. 68-69; Shebbeare, *Essay on National Society*, pp. 99-100.

13 [Knox,] *Controversy*, p. 167. See also Anon., *Supremacy of Legislature*, p. 19; Anon., *Plain Question*, p. 8; Anon., *Essays Commercial and Political*, pp. 42-43. The quote is from 25 Charles II, cap. 7, sec. 2.

14 Hamilton, *Farmer Refuted*, p. 121. See also [Mather,] *American's Appeal*, p. 41; Andrews, "Acts of Trade," p. 278; Stout, *Royal Navy*, p. 4.

15 25 Charles II, cap. 7, Sec. 2; [Lind,] *Thirteenth Parliament*, pp. 203, 206.

16 Leonard, "Massachusettensis," p. 69; Anon., *Letter to a Member*, p. 20; [Knox,] *Controversy*, p. 169-71. For similar reasoning reaching the same conclusion, see Anon., *Supremacy of Legislature*, p. 20; [Lind,] *Thirteenth Parliament*, pp. 205-6.

17 [Bancroft,] *Remarks*, p. 73; [Knox,] *Controversy*, p. 169.

18 [Lind,] *Answer to the Declaration*, pp. 65-66; Anon., *Supremacy of Legislature*, p. 20.

19 1 George I, stat. 2, cap. 12, sec. 4; [Lind,] *Thirteenth Parliament*, p. 210; Anon., *Supremacy of Legislature*, p. 21; Speech of Thomas Pownall, Commons Debates, 16 November 1775, *Gentleman's Magazine* 46 (1776): 54. The point was that although "the purposes in this act expressed" were not for "the particular services of the Colonies, but to the maintenance of the *household;* and to [British] public general *services*," "Yet the American did not complain of this Act; though it imposed a tax . . . for a particular establishment in England." [Lind,] *Answer to the Declaration*, p. 67.

20 7 & 8 William III, cap. 22; Speech of Thomas Pownall (*supra*, n. 19), 54; [Lind,] *Thirteenth Parliament*, pp. 206-7. "[A] fuller and more formal exemplification and assertion of the supremacy of parliament over the colonies, in all matters whatsoever, can hardly be imagined; and this a statute, one of the express purposes of which is the laying taxes for the purpose of a revenue." Ibid., p. 208. Similarly, see Anon., *Supremacy of Legislature*, p. 23.

21 Cited: Anon., *History of Lord North*, p. 122; Shebbeare, *Essay on National Society*, p. 100; Anon., *Supremacy of Legislature*, p. 29; *Boston News-Letter* (Supplement), 11 April 1765, p. 1, col. 2; Words: [Lind,] *Thirteenth Parliament*, p. 219. Similarly, see Anon., *Short Appeal to the People*, p. 12; Leonard, "Massachusettensis," pp. 70-71; [Lind,] *Answer to the Declaration*, p. 68.

22 6 George II, cap. 13 (preamble); [Lind,] *Thirteenth Parliament*, p. 219.

23 Price, *Nature of Civil Liberty*, p. 61; Richard Price, "On the Nature of Civil Liberty," *Hibernian Magazine* 6 (1776): 188; Evans, *Reply to Fletcher*, p. 46n.

24 Speech of Edmund Burke, Commons Debate, 19 April 1774, *Burke on American Revolution*, p. 41; Burke, "Speech on American Taxation," pp. 136-37; [Lind,] *Thirteenth Parliament*, pp. 220-21, 223.

25 Southwick, "Molasses Act," pp. 394-96; [Lind,] *Thirteenth Parliament*, p. 223; Agent: Christie, *Crisis*, p. 14; Fire: [Howard,] *Halifax Letter*, p. 540.

26 Speech of Sir William Yonge, Commons Debates, 8 March 1732/33, *London Magazine*, October 1733, quoted in *Gazette & News-Letter*, 14 February 1765, p. 2, col. 1; *Parliamentary History* 8:1261; *Proceedings and Debates of Parliaments* 4:190.

27 [Howard,] *Halifax Letter*, p. 540.

28 Speech of Thomas Winnington, Commons Debates, 8 March 1732/33, *Proceedings and Debates of Parliaments* 4:191; *Parliamentary History* 8:1261; *London Magazine* (*supra*, n. 26).

29 Speech of Sir John Bernard, Commons Debates, 8 March 1733, *Gentleman's Magazine* 3 (1733): 510; Speech of Sir John Bernard, Commons Debates, 8 March 1733, *Parliamentary History* 8:1263.

30 Dowell, *Taxation and Taxes* 2:146 (see also ibid., 4:25; Andrews, "Western Phase," p. 773; Southwick, "Molasses Act," p. 405); [Whately,] *Regulations Lately Made*, pp. 104–5.

31 [Lind,] *Englishman's Answer*, p. 11; [Whately,] *Considerations on Trade*, p. 155; Anon., *Supremacy of Legislature*, p. 22; [Lind,] *Answer to the Declaration*, pp. 66–67; [Lind,] *Thirteenth Parliament*, p. 224; Anon., *Plain Question*, pp. 8, 9 n.; Roebuck, *Enquiry whether the Guilt*, p. 14. For the Greenwich hospital tax see Frese "Board," p. 25; Frese, "Tax," p. 193; Brown, "Hulton," p. 9.

32 7 & 8 William III, cap. 21; 8 & 9 William III, cap. 23; 10 Anne, cap. 17; 2 George II, cap. 7. See also 2 George II, cap. 36; 18 George II. Although colonists disputed the fact, the first act surely was intended to apply to America, as it provided that the tax should be paid by "every seaman whatsoever, that shall serve his Majesty, his heirs, or successors, or any other person or persons whatsoever, in any of his Majesty's ships, or in any ship or vessel whatsoever, belonging or to belong to any of the subjects of *England*, or any other his Majesty's dominions." 7 & 8 William III, cap. 21, sec. 10; [Knox,] *Controversy*, pp. 171–72.

33 [Knox,] *Controversy*, p. 172 (similarly, Leonard, "Massachusettensis," p. 70); [Pownall,] *Considerations*, p. 10; Schuyler, *Empire*, pp. 15–16.

34 Otis, *Rights*, p. 467.

35 *Journal of Times*, 24 October 1768, p. 10, col. 2. The Greenwich hospital tax collector in North America claimed that owners of Massachusetts fishing vessels had deducted the tax from their crews' share of the catch but never paid it to the government. Frese, "Board," p. 25.

36 A historian found evidence the tax had been paid before 1767 but it is not certain if fishermen contributed. Frese, "Tax," p. 193.

37 Henry Hulton, one of the commissioners of the American customs created by Townshend, was also collector of the Greenwich hospital tax. He obtained an income from that post of over £200 a year over his £500 salary as a customs commissioner. Frese, "Tax," p. 216. In 1764 the hospital tax collected £1,931 in the colonies. Hulton, who assessed fisherman, raised a yearly average of £2,500 between 1768 and 1776. Ibid., p. 193; Frese, "Board," p. 29.

38 Letter from Charles Garth to the Committee of Correspondence of the South

Carolina Assembly, 5 June 1764, Morgan, *Prologue*, p. 28; [Boucher,] *Letter from a Virginian*, pp. 20–21; [Lind,] *Thirteenth Parliament*, p. 209.

39 Shebbeare, *Essay on National Society*, p. 100; [Maseres,] *Canadian Freeholder* 1:259; Roebuck, *Enquiry whether the Guilt*, p. 13. See also Letter from O.P., *Interesting Letters*, p. 124; Tucker, *Tract Five*, p. 23.

40 Shebbeare, *Essay on National Society*, p. 146.

41 [Knox,] *Controversy*, p. 176.

42 This topic is more logically treated in the volume on Parliament's authority to legislate. For arguments, see [Dulany,] *Considerations on the Propriety*, pp. 39–40; [Mather,] *America's Appeal*, pp. 42–43.

43 [Whately,] *Regulations Lately Made*, printed in *Boston News-Letter* (Supplement), 11 April 1765, p. 1, col. 2; Morgan, *Prologue*, pp. 19–20.

44 9 Anne, cap. 10, sec. 35. Its title was "An act for establishing a general post office for all her Majesty's dominions, and for settling a weekly sum of the revenues thereof, for the service of the war, and other her Majesty's occasions." These purposes were repeated in 9 Anne, cap. 23, sec. 54.

45 Leonard, "Massachusettensis," p. 70; [Knox,] *Controversy*, p. 176; Anon., *Plain Question*, p. 8; [Lind,] *Englishman's Answer*, p. 12; Anon., *Supremacy of Legislature*, pp. 26–27. "The Revenue of the Post Office was extended to America by the 9th of Queen Ann & in the Preamble of the act it is expressly recited to be in order to raise a Revenue to make good the Supplies & for carrying on the War against France." Letter from George Grenville to William Knox, 16 August 1768, *Grenville Letterbooks*.

46 "Proceedings in the session of parliament 1765," *Scots Magazine* 27 (1765): 677; Thomson, *Constitutional History*, p. 94, n. 2, 199, 202; [Whately,] *Regulations Lately Made* (*supra*, n. 43), p. 1, cols. 2–3; Morgan, *Prologue*, p. 20.

47 Blackstone, *Commentaries* 1:311; Petition of the Governor and Company of Rhode Island to the King, 29 November 1764, *Rhode Island Colony Records* 6:415.

48 Speech of Richard Hussey, Commons Debates, 3 February 1776, Ryder, "Parliamentary Diaries," p. 270 (the New Hampshire–born John Huske agreed that the American post office was in bad condition, but thought that with regulation it could be made to "yield a good revenue, perhaps an eighth of the present revenue of the Post Office here." Speech of John Huske, Commons Debates, 9 March 1764, ibid., p. 238); Fisk, *English Public Finance*, p. 68 (see also Dowell, *Taxation and Taxes* 2:146–47); Franklin: Thomas, *British Politics*, p. 37; Leonard, "Massachusettensis," p. 70.

49 [Prescott,] *Calm Consideration*, pp. 12–13; [Mather,] *America's Appeal*, p. 42; Dulany, *Considerations*, p. 643.

50 Thomas, *British Politics*, p. 91. Beckford was speaking to the Commons. For a similar argument, see Speech of Richard Hussey, Commons Debates, 1766, "Stamp Act Debates," p. 570.

51 Anon., *Three Letters*, p. 9; *Examination of Franklin*, p. 16; *Boston Evening-Post*, 4 April 1774, p. 1, col. 1 (interestingly, Thomas Hutchinson was making the same distinction in Boston less than a month after Franklin had

made it in London. "[T]he Post office was supposed to be established for publick convenience." Letter from Thomas Hutchinson to Thomas Pownall, 8 March 1766, Morgan, *Prologue*, p. 123); Otis, *Rights*, p. 467; Testimony of Benjamin Franklin, House of Commons, 13 February 1766, Ryder, "Parliamentary Diaries," p. 301; London, *Gazetteer*, 23 January 1766, reprinted in *Franklin's Letters to the Press*, p. 54 (similarly, see *Examination of Franklin*, p. 8; Morgan, *Prologue*, pp. 144–45. "Here there is no tax; I pay for a service performed, and am served cheaper by the king's messenger, than I could be by my own." "A.L.," *London Magazine* 35 (1766): 77); *Examination of Franklin*, p. 14; *Prior Documents*, p. 78.

52 Richard Jackson's Arguments on American Taxation, 1765, *Franklin-Jackson Letters*, pp. 195–96; Speech of Rose Fuller, Commons Debates, 6 February 1765, Ryder, "Parliamentary Diaries," p. 259; London *Public Advertiser*, 11 January 1770, reprinted in *Franklin's Letters to the Press*, p. 175.

53 Jefferson, *Summary View*, p. 125; [Downer,] *Discourse in Providence*, pp. 8–9.

54 *Providence Gazette*, 11 May 1765, reprinted in *Boston Post-Boy*, 15 July 1765; p. 1, col. 3; *Boston Evening-Post*, 29 July 1765, p. 3, col. 2; Morgan, *Prologue*, p. 74.

55 Boston committee of correspondence quoted in Brown, *Revolutionary Politics*, p. 181; *Scots Magazine* 36 (1774): 263; *Boston Evening-Post*, 4 April 1774, p. 1, col. 1. See also Letter from Governor John Wentworth to the earl of Dartmouth, 8 June 1775, *Revolution Documents* 7:345; *Gentleman's Magazine* 44 (1774): 285.

56 Boston Committee of Correspondence to the Committees of Salem, Marblehead, Newburyport, and Portsmouth, 24 March 1774, in Brown, *Revolutionary Politics*, p. 183; Committee of Correspondence at Boston to the Committee at Newport, 29 March 1774, *Rhode Island Correspondence*, pp. 434–35.

57 Brown, *Revolutionary Politics*, p. 184. Surely it is incorrect to dismiss the Post Office Act as "so innocuous a statute" as to be of no significance in the prerevolutionary controversy. Ammerman, *Common Cause*, p. 68.

58 Letter from Francis Lightfoot Lee to Landon Carter, 21 October 1775, *Letters of Delegates to Congress* 2:227; "Extract of a Letter from a Gentleman at New-York to his Friend in this Town, dated Feb. 28, 1774," *Gazette & Post-Boy*, 21 March 1774, p. 3, col. 1; *Boston Evening-Post*, 21 March 1774, p. 2, col. 3.

59 Letter from Chief Justice Thomas Hutchinson to Thomas Pownall, 8 March 1766, Morgan, *Prologue*, p. 123.

60 Shebbeare, *Essay on National Society*, p. 100 (similarly, [Bacon,] *Short Address*, p. 14); Adams "Novanglus," p. 141, 223; Dulany, *Considerations*, pp. 644–45.

61 Speech of Alexander Wedderburn, Commons Debates, 1766, "Stamp Act Debates," p. 571; Thomas, *British Politics*, p. 224; Burke: "Observations on Grenville's State," *Boston Chronicle*, 15 May 1769, p. 153, col. 3; Robert Carter Nicholas, *Considerations on the Present State of Virginia Exam-*

ined (1774), reprinted in *Revolutionary Virginia* 1:280; Book Review, *Gentleman's Magazine* 46 (1776): 129.

62 "Observations on the Conduct of the Present Ministry," *Remembrancer for 1776: Part III*, p. 342; *Boston Post-Boy*, 9 December 1765, p. 1, col. 1.

CHAPTER SIXTEEN: DOCTRINE OF CUSTOM

1 *Journal of Times*, 24 October 1768, p. 10, col. 2; Instructions of Providence, 13 August 1765, *Boston Post-Boy*, 19 August 1765, p. 3, cols. 1–2; *Boston Evening-Post*, 19 August 1765, p. 2, col. 3; Rhode Island Resolves, September 1765, in Morgan, *Prologue*, pp. 50–51.

2 George Louis Beer, *British Colonial Policy, 1754–1765*, p. 311 (New York, 1922); Harlow, *Adams*, p. 36.

3 *Political Register* 1 (1767): 250–51; basis of sanction: "In Accordance with Usage," pp. 335–38; "In the Taught Tradition," pp. 931–41; Lee, *Answer*, p. 155; Connecticut: [Fitch et al.,] *Reasons Why*, pp. 13–14.

4 For a discussion of the theory as it related to the right of taxation, see "In Accordance with Usage," pp. 351–58.

5 Lords: Donoughue, *British Politics*, p. 144; Guide: Petition of the Gentlemen, Clergy, and Freeholders of Cornwall to the King, 3 January 1770, *Political Register* 6 (1770): 117; Popular consent: Hale, "Reflections," p. 507 (see also Boorstin, *Lost World of Jefferson*, p. 209); [Burnet,] *Submission to Supream Authority*, p. 3; Davis, *Reports*, "Preface," p. 3 (similarly, see Case of Tanistry, id., pp. 29–42; 80 *Eng. Rep.* 516, 519 (1608); 1762 edition of Davis, *Reports*, p. 87).

6 Jenkins, *Lex Terrae*, p. 104 (Jenkins's fellow royalist, Wentworth, meant the same when he said in 1641, "That the use and custome of the Lawe, was the best Interpreter thereof." [Strafford,] *Briefe and Perfect Relation*, p. 29. See also Speech of James Cocks, Commons Debates, 1741, in *Parliamentary History* 11:1435); Decree of Henry VI, 8 March 1450 [?], *London Magazine* 45 (1776): 255.

7 Wood, *Institute of the Laws*, pp. 9–10; Anon., *Examination of Legality*, pp. 4–5.

8 Wynne, *Eunomus* 3:109. See, for colonial whigs, Proceedings of Bellingham, 19 May 1773; *Boston Evening-Post*, 18 October 1773, p. 1, col. 1. "[A]ll English law was common law, common law was custom." Pocock, *Machiavellian Moment*, p. 340.

9 *Monarchy asserted to be the best* . . . (1660), *Somers' Tracts*, 6:360. See also Jenkins, *Works*, p. 1; Filmer, *Anarchy of Mixed Monarchy*, p. 297.

10 Cowell & Manley, *Interpreter* (for a law dictionary saying the same at the start of the prerevolutionary era, see Jacob, *New Law Dictionary*. See also Anon., *Examination of Legality*, p. 4; Blackstone, *Tracts*, p. 15. Also, the law of dependencies such as Jersey were largely custom. Pownall, *Administration Fifth Edition* 1:62–63); *Black's Law Dictionary* (5th ed., St. Paul, Minn., 1979).

11 Judge: Jenkins, *Works*, p. 34 (see also McIlwain, *Constitutionalism*, pp. 115–

16); Pamphleteer: [Lind,] *Thirteenth Parliament*, p. 21n.; colonial constitutions: Opinion of Attorney General William Murray [later Lord Mans-
field] and Solicitor General Richard Lloyd, 29 April 1755, Chalmers, *Opinions*, pp. 352–53; Livingston, *Address to the House*, p. 2; Greene, *Quest*,
pp. 16, 403–5; 1767 writer: "L.," *Letter to G[renville]*, pp. 35–36.

12 For the most detailed discussion of tests, written the year of the Stamp Act's
passage, see Blackstone, *Commentaries* 1:76–78; *Millar v. Taylor*, [1558–
1774] *All Eng. Law Rep.* 119, 120, (K.B., 1770).

13 Anon., *Knowledge of the Laws*, pp. 7–8.

14 Petition of the New York Assembly to the House of Commons, 31 December
1768, *Boston Post-Boy*, 8 May 1769, p. 2, col. 1. What was meant was that,
"from the first Settlement of the Colonies, it has been the Sense of the Government at Home" that taxes upon the colonies "could not be constitutionally made" by Parliament, a rule proven by the fact that "Applications for
the Support of Government, and other publick Exigencies, have always
been made to the Representatives of the People in this Colony." New York
Assembly Resolves, 18 December 1765, *New York Journal of Votes*, p. 808.
For similar assertions that the right of taxation only by local consent had
been given imperial recognition by the Crown and Parliament, see Petition of the Pennsylvania House of Representatives to the House of Commons, 22 September 1768, *Pennsylvania Archives* 7:6276; Petition of the
Massachusetts General Court to the House of Commons, *Providence Gazette*, 16 March 1765, p. 2, col. 1. Thus, the Connecticut lower house claimed
rights by charter, as Englishmen, and also by custom, "which they have
enjoyed for more than a century past, and have neither forfeited nor surrendered, but the same have been constantly recognized by the King and
Parliament of *Great-Britain*." Connecticut Resolves, May 1774, *Boston
Evening-Post*, 20 June 1774, p. 4, col. 1.

15 *Millar v. Taylor* (*supra*, n. 12), p. 120; Time immemorial: Hale, *History*, p.
23; Higden, *View of the Constitution*, p. 1; [Wood,] *Institute of the Laws*,
p. 9; [French,] *Constitution of Ireland*, p. 23.

16 Atwood, *Dependency of Ireland*, p. 208; Camden: *Entick v. Carrington*, 19
State Trials 1029, 1067 (C.P., 1765); "too modern": *Entick v. Carrington*,
[1558–1774] *All Eng. Law Rep.* 41, 45–46 (C.P., 1765); "evidence": *Entick
v. Carrington*, 19 *State Trials*, p. 1068.

17 [Dickinson,] An Address to the Committee of Correspondence in Barbados,
South-Carolina Gazette, 4 August 1766, p. 1, col. 2; Dickinson, *To Barbados*, p. 255.

18 Memorial from the House of Burgesses to the House of Lords, 18 December
1764, Morgan, *Prologue*, p. 15; Petition from the Virginia House of Burgesses to the King, 18 December 1764, *Journal of Burgesses* 10:302; *Boston
Post-Boy*, 25 March 1765, p. 1, col. 1; Morgan, *Prologue*, p. 14.

19 Pennsylvania Resolves, 21 September 1765, Morgan, *Prologue*, p. 52. See,
similarly, Petition from the North Carolina Commons House to the King,
10 November 1768, *Boston Chronicle*, 20 March 1769, p. 91, col. 3. For
the claim stated by individuals, see Lee, *Appeal to Justice*, p. 16; Letter

from Richard Henry Lee to Lord Shelburne, 31 May 1769, *Lee Letters*, p. 37; [Priestly,] *Address to Dissenters*, p. 17.

20 Petition from the Pennsylvania Assembly to the King, *Boston Chronicle*, 13 February 1769, p. 51, col. 3.

21 Dickinson, *Letters*, p. 336; Anon., *To Tax Themselves*, p. 116.

22 Doubted: Hobbes, *Dialogue of Common Laws*, p. 96; Filmer, *Patriarcha*, pp. 106–7; Letter from Agent Mauduit to the Committee of the House, 19 February 1765, *Speeches*, p. 31.

23 Anon., *Rights of Parliament*, p. 42; Anon., *Dialogue on the Constitution*, p. 34.

24 Letter from George Grenville to William Knox, 16 August 1768, *Grenville Letterbooks*; [Lind,] *Englishman's Answer*, p. 15. Similarly, it was said that because the colonies were larger and more prosperous, they had to be governed with greater control and tighter regulation. [Seabury,] *View of the Controversy*, p. 19.

25 [Maseres,] *Canadian Freeholder* 1:129–32. Another argument of law that also accepted the American whig evidence and took it to a different conclusion of law would have decreased the legal consequence of Parliament "Nonusage" of taxation from a constitutional right not to be taxed by Parliament to "a kind of possessory Right, which might naturally induce" Americans "not thoroughly acquainted with the Nature and Constitution of our Parliament, to imagine the sole right of laying Taxes, belonged to themselves." Anon., *General Opposition*, pp. 25–26.

26 Resolves of the North Carolina House of Assembly, 2 November 1769, *North Carolina Colonial Records* 8:122; Resolves of the Virginia House of Burgesses, 16 May 1769, *Boston Post-Boy*, 12 June 1769, p. 1, col. 1; *Revolutionary Virginia* 1:70; Memorial from the House of Burgesses to the House of Lords, 18 December 1764, Morgan, *Prologue*, p. 15 [hereafter cited as Memorial].

27 Representation and Remonstrance of the New York General Assembly to the House of Commons, 1775, *Hibernian Magazine* 5 (1775): 358–59; Memorial (*supra*, n. 26), p. 15.

28 Resolves of the Virginia House of Burgesses, 16 May 1769, *Boston Gazette* (Supplement), 12 June 1769, p. 1, col. 1; *Boston Post-Boy*, 12 June 1769, p. 1, col. 1; *Revolutionary Virginia* 1:70; Virginia Resolves, 30 May 1765, Morgan, *Prologue*, p. 48; *Journal of Burgesses* 10:360; *Prior Documents*, p. 23. The essence of this resolve was adopted by three of the other colonial assemblies that protested the Stamp Act. Rhode Island Resolves, September 1765, Maryland Resolves, 28 September 1765, Connecticut Resolves, 25 October 1765, Morgan, *Prologue*, pp. 50–51, 53, 55.

29 Book Review, *Monthly Review* 50 (1774): 208; Estwick, *Letter to Tucker*, p. 78.

CHAPTER SEVENTEEN: ISSUE OF THE SUGAR ACT

1 Christie, *Crisis*, p. 14. See also id., p. 55; [Macpherson,] *Restrospective View*, p. 8.

2 Letter from Edward Sedgwick to Edward Weston, 28 February 1765, "Weston Papers," p. 384; [Fitch et al.,] *Reasons Why.*

3 Unhappy: Hopkins, *Rights,* p. 512; Agencies: *South-Carolina Gazette,* 19 November 1764, p. 3, col. 1; newspaper: *South-Carolina Gazette* (Supplement), 1 October 1764, p. 1, cols. 1–2; *Boston Evening-Post,* 25 June 1764, pp. 1–3 and 22 July 1764, p. 1 cols. 1–3; Georgia: Address from both houses of the Assembly to the King, 22 July 1766, and Address from the Commons House of Assembly to Governor James Wright, 17 July 1766, *Georgia Commons House Journal* 14:380–81, 374.

4 Message from the Council and House to Governor Francis Bernard, 3 November 1764, *Speeches,* p. 18.

5 Explanation: Christie, *Crisis,* p. 50; "Semblance": Robert Carter Nicholas, *Considerations on the Present State of Virginia Examined* (1774), reprinted in *Revolutionary Virginia* 1:263; Dickinson, "Letter to Inhabitants," p. 475; Speech of Edmund Burke, Commons Debates, 19 April 1774, *Burke on American Revolution,* pp. 46–47; *Gentleman's Magazine* 44 (1774): 605.

6 No innovation: Osgood, "American Revolution," p. 71; Dowell, *Taxation and Taxes* 2:149; Traditional: Wright, *Fabric of Freedom,* p. 51; Reid, "Economic Burden," p. 91; Morgan, *Birth,* p. 16; Revenue measure: Thomas, *British Politics,* pp. 47–49, 109, 271; Stout, *Royal Navy,* p. 166; Thomson, *Constitutional History,* p. 399; Knollenberg, *Origin,* pp. 142–43; Without implications: Christie, *Crisis,* p. 53; Harper, "Mercantilism and Revolution", p. 164; Introduced changes: Ritcheson, "Introduction," p. 4; Aptheker, *Revolution,* p. 36; Alter constitution: Brown, *Middle-Class Democracy,* p. 203, n. 22; Dickerson, *Acts,* pp. 172–86, 190.

7 Murrin, "Great Inversion," p. 392; Christie, "Pitt and Taxation," p. 177; Christie, *Crisis,* p. 65; Stout, "Goals and Enforcement of Policy," p. 217; Thomas, *British Politics,* 271; Headlam, "Constitutional Struggle," p. 660.

8 *Papers of Iredell* 1:lvii. An example of how historians can find what they need in the Sugar Act is provided by some seeking to prove that the prerevolutionary controversy involved economics. The 1764 and 1766 versions of the statute, they said, declared in the preambles the purpose of raising a revenue to support "English" placemen. Egnal & Ernst, "Economic Interpretation," p. 8. Several years earlier, it was said, "I do not see how the argument can stand against the wording of the Acts (which speak of 'defending, protecting and securing' the colonies, not, like the Townshend Act, of paying salaries), and against the fact . . . that money raised by parliament was not used for this purpose until later." Richard Pares, "Book Review," *English Historical Review* 72:122, 124–25 (1957) (reviewing Brown, *Middle-Class Democracy*).

9 Dickinson, *Letters,* pp. 314–15; Speech of Edmund Burke (*supra,* n. 5), pp. 46–47; Wright, *Fabric of Freedom,* p. 51; Christie, "Pitt & Taxation," p. 177; 4 George III, cap. 15.

10 Speech of Edmund Burke, Commons Debates, 19 April 1774, *Burke on American Revolution,* p. 46; Speech of Edmund Burke, Commons Debates, 19

April 1774, *Gentleman's Magazine* 44 (1774): 605; Burke, "Speech on American Taxation," p. 141.

11 Letter from Thomas Whately to Jared Ingersoll, [April 1764,] "Ingersoll Correspondence," p. 294. So did an American-born member of Parliament. Speech of John Huske, Commons Debates, 9 March 1764, Ryder, "Parliamentary Diaries," p. 238.

12 Anon., *True Interest of Great Britain*, p. 11.

13 Speech of Rose Fuller, Commons Debates, 6 February 1765, Ryder, "Parliamentary Diaries," p. 259. A member of Parliament who was also serving as a joint secretary in the treasury when the Sugar Act became law wrote in a private letter: "The intention of it is to prevent all commerce between our Colonies and any part of Europe except Great Britain, unless in cases specially allowed, and to permit under certain regulations the commerce of our Continental Colonies with Foreign Islands so as to leave a clear and undoubted proof [?profit] to our own Islands." Letter from Charles Jenkinson to R. Wolters, 18 January 1765, *Jenkinson Papers*, p. 348.

14 [Hopkins,] "Vindication of a Pamphlet," 9 March 1765, p. 1, col. 2; Boston Merchants, *Observations*, p. 5; Dickinson, *Letters*, p. 345n.; Dickinson, "Letter to Inhabitants," pp. 474–75.

15 [Hopkins,] *Grievances of the Colonies*, p. 26.

16 Instructions of the House of Representatives to Richard Jackson, 22 September 1764, *Pennsylvania Archives* 7:5644–45; *Franklin-Jackson Letters*, p. 185; Instructions of the House of Representatives to Richard Jackson, 20 October 1764, *Pennsylvania Archives* 7:5679, 5681; Petition of the Governor and Company of Rhode Island to the King, 29 November 1764, *Rhode Island Colony Records* 6:415; Petition of the New York General Assembly to the House of Lords, 11 December 1765, *New York Journal of Votes*, p. 798 (see, similarly, Petition of the Massachusetts Council and House to the House of Commons, *Providence Gazette*, 16 March 1765, p. 1, col. 1, p. 2, cols. 1–2); "burthensome": Resolutions 8th, 9th, 10th, Resolutions of 19 October 1765, *Account of Stamp Act Congress*, pp. 6–7; Memorial of the Stamp Act Congress to the House of Lords, 22 October 1765, Morgan, *Prologue*, pp. 65–66. Similarly, see Petition of the Stamp Act Congress to the House of Commons, 23 October 1765, *Account of Stamp Act Congress*, pp. 19–20.

17 [Lind,] *Thirteenth Parliament*, pp. 256–57; *Annual Register 1765*, p. [23]; Murdoch, *Rebellion in America*, p. 24. That same year, a London book reviewer discussed the Sugar Act entirely in economic terms—"an absolute prohibition"—and the Stamp Act in terms of constitutional issues. *Critical Review* 20 (1765): 474.

18 Rhode Island Petition to the King, 29 November 1764, quoted in Morgan, "Colonial Ideas," p. 317. For other constitutional objections to the Sugar Act based on the principle of equality, see Virginia Petition to the King, 18 December 1764, Morgan, *Prologue*, p. 14; Virginia Petition to the House of Lords, 18 December 1764, id., p. 15; New York Petition to the House

of Commons, 18 October 1764, id., pp. 8–12; Instructions of Boston, 28 May 1764, *Boston News-Letter*, 31 May 1764, p. 2, col. 2.

19 Resolutions of the Connecticut General Assembly, October 1765, *Public Records of Connecticut* 12:424. "The civil rights of the colonies are affected by it [the Sugar Act], by their being deprived, in all cases of seizures, of that inestimable privilege and characteristic of English liberty, a trial by jury." Message from the Massachusetts Council and House to Governor Francis Bernard, 3 November 1764, *Speeches*, p. 18.

20 *Authority of Rights*, pp. 47–59, 178–83.

21 Instructions to the Committee appointed to the Stamp Act Congress, 26 September 1765, *Maryland Votes and Proceedings* (September 1765), p. 7; Resolutions of 19 October 1765, *Account of Stamp Act Congress*, pp. 7–8; Declarations of the Stamp Act Congress, Morgan, *Prologue*, p. 63; Minutes of 3 March 1775, *Journal of New York Assembly* (1766–76), p. 54; Letter from the Massachusetts Council and House to Agent Mauduit, [1764,] *Speeches*, pp. 24–25; Thacher, *Sentiments*, p. 492.

22 New Jersey did not object to the Sugar Act, but to the stamp tax and vice-admiralty. New Jersey Resolves, 30 November 1765, *New Jersey Votes and Proceedings* (November 1765), p. 7. Similarly, Petition of the New York General Assembly to the House of Commons, 18 October 1764, *New York Journal of Votes*, p. 779; Petition of the Massachusetts Council and House to the House of Commons, *Boston News-Letter*, 14 March 1765, p. 1, cols. 1–2.

23 Letter from a Committee of the Massachusetts House to the Maryland House of Assembly, 13 June 1764, *Maryland Votes and Proceedings* (September 1765), p. 3; Instrument of Five Members of the House of Assembly for the Counties Upon Delaware, 21 September 1765, *Delaware House Minutes* (1765–70), p. 35.

24 Often, however, the Stamp Act was stated as the major grievance. Instructions of 18 September 1765, *Boston Town Records* 16:155; Adams, *Braintree Instructions*, p. 2, col. 3; *New-London Gazette*, 20 September 1765, reprinted in *Boston Evening-Post*, 14 October 1765, p. 1, col. 2.

25 Letters from Thomas Cushing to Jasper Mauduit, 11 November 1763, 9 April 1764, and January 1764, *Mauduit Letters*, pp. 139, 158–59, 145–46.

26 Morgan, *Birth*, p. 17; Letter from Thomas Cushing to Jasper Mauduit, 17 November 1764, *Mauduit Letters*, pp. 170–71; Morgan, "Thomas Hutchinson," p. 478.

27 [Hutchinson,] *Strictures Upon the Declaration*, p. 5; Letter from Thomas Hutchinson to Richard Jackson, August 1763, *Mauduit Letters*, p. 130, n. 1.

28 Thacher, *Sentiments*, p. 491; Adams, "Novanglus," pp. 223–24; Letter to a Gentleman in London, 31 May 1764, *Lee Letters*, p. 6; Greene, *Quest*, p. 364. See also Butler, *North Carolina*, pp. 10–11.

29 Letter to Agent Mauduit, 13 June 1764, *Massachusetts House Journal* (1764), p. 72; *Report of Lords on Massachusetts*, p. 2; [Lee,] *True State of the Proceedings*, p. 5. John Adams thought that was "the almost universal sense of this colony" in 1764. Adams, "Novanglus," p. 224.

30 Declaration of Rights, 14 October 1774, *Journal of First Congress*, p. 64; "To the Inhabitants of the Colonies," 21 October 1774, id., p. 95; Minutes of 3 March 1775, *Journal of New York Assembly* (1766–76), pp. 52–53.

CHAPTER EIGHTEEN: ISSUE OF THE STAMP ACT

1 [Chandler,] *Friendly Address*, p. 18.
2 Franklin, *Writings* 5:454; Letter from Benjamin Franklin to William Franklin, 9 November 1765, quoted in Crane, "Franklin and Stamp Act," p. 66. Franklin would even attribute the inability of himself and his fellow agents to prevent passage of the Stamp Act not to politics but to colonial insistence upon the constitutional principle. "The nation," he explained, "was provoked by American claims of independence, and all parties joined in resolving by this act to settle the point." "Extract of a letter from a North-American in London, to his friend in America, dated July 11, 1765," *Scots Magazine* 27 (1765): 609. For a lawyer's explanation of why suspension was not acceptable, see Letter from Charles Carroll of Carrollton to Daniel Barrington, 17 March 1766, *Letters of Charles Carroll*, pp. 109–10.
3 Letter from Thomas Hutchinson to Thomas Pownall, 8 March 1766, Morgan, *Prologue*, pp. 123–24. See also Letter from Thomas Hutchinson to William Bollan, 7 November 1764, quoted in Washburn, "Preface," p. 167, n. 2; Gordon, *History* 1:108; Bailyn, *Ordeal*, pp. 64–66; Knollenberg, *Origin*, p. 186.
4 Letter from the General Court Committee to Agent Jasper Mauduit, [3 November 1764,] *Speeches*, p. 24. John Adams would later assert that "there was not any member of either house who thought that parliament had such a right at that time." Hutchinson, "expressly said . . . that parliament had no right." Adams, "Novanglus," p. 140.
5 Letter from the Committee of Correspondence of the Georgia Council and Commons House to William Knox, 18 July 1765, *Habersham Letters*, pp. 40–41.
6 The committee of both houses of the Barbados legislature instructed the colony's agent not to be too bold. He was not to "give offence to those from whom only our redress can come, our appeal being to the very powers by whom we think ourselves oppressed; tho' we may remonstrate to them with justice, *we cannot reproach them without danger.*" Instructions quoted in [Dickinson,] "Address . . ." p. 1, col. 2.
7 Letters from Thomas Cushing to Jasper Mauduit, 17 November 1764 and 12 November 1764, *Mauduit Letters*, pp. 170, 167. Hutchinson asserted that the Massachusetts legislators took a more militant constitutional stand because of criticism after their economic protest was compared to Virginia's assertion of the constitutional right. It should be noted, however, that the letters to the agent now being discussed were sent eight months before Boston newspapers first attacked the Hutchinson-drafted petition as "a certain tame, pusillanimous, daub'd, insipid Thing, delicately touch'd up and call'd an address . . . to please the taste of the tools of corruption" in Lon-

don. *Boston Gazette*, 8 July 1765, reprinted in *South-Carolina Gazette* (Supplement), 26 August 1765, p. 1, col. 2. See also Morgan, "Parliamentary Power," p. 55.

8 Address from the House of Representatives to Governor Francis Bernard, 11 January 1765, *Massachusetts House Journal* (1764), p. 148; Letter from Thomas Whately to John Temple, 12 June 1765, *Bowdoin Papers*, p. 61.

9 Salem Instructions, 21 October 1765, Phillips, *Salem*, p. 287 (see also Moore, *Taxing Colonies*, p. 47; *Connecticut Gazette*, 30 August 1765, reprinted in *South-Carolina Gazette*, 12 October 1765, p. 1, col. 1; article of costs from a Newport newspaper reprinted in *Boston Evening-Post*, 4 September 1765, p. 2, col. 2); trade: Adams, *Braintree Instructions*, p. 2, col. 3; Letter from John Hancock to Barnards and Harrison, April 1765, Brown, *John Hancock*, p. 69; Letter from John Dickinson to William Pitt, 21 December 1765, Morgan, *Prologue*, p. 121; Dickinson, *Late Regulations*, pp. 217–38. Future loyalists generally opposed the stamp tax on grounds of cost, not principle. Letter from William Smith to General Robert Monckton, 30 May 1765, *Memoirs of William Smith* 1:29: Morgan, "Thomas Hutchinson," p. 477; press: *Boston Evening-Post*, 4 September 1765, p. 2, col. 1, and 30 September 1765, p. 1, col. 3; specie: Petition from the Stamp Act Congress to the House of Commons, Morgan, *Prologue*, pp. 67–68.

10 Dickinson, *Late Regulations*, reprinted in Bailyn, *Pamphlets* 1:680; Examination of Franklin, *Prior Documents*, p. 74; Will. ALFRED to a London newspaper, reprinted in *Gazette & News-Letter* (Supplement), 23 January 1766, p. 1, col. 2. See also *Boston Post-Boy*, 21 January 1765, p. 1, col. 1; Anon., *Short and Friendly Caution*, p. 14.

11 [Whately,] *Regulations*, quoted in *Boston News-Letter* (Supplement), 11 April 1765, p. 1, col. 1; Anti-Sejanus, in *London Chronicle*, 28–30 November 1765, reprinted in Morgan, *Prologue*, p. 100; Protest of Dissentient Lords, *Prior Documents*, p. 82; "A Summary of the Arguments against repealing the Stamp-Act," *Gentleman's Magazine* 36 (1766): 107; Dickerson, *Acts*, p. 54; Letter from Thomas Whately to John Temple, February 1765, *Bowdoin Papers*, p. 51; "Pacificus," reprinted in Morgan, *Prologue*, p. 101; Anon., *Plain and Seasonable Address*, pp. 7–8.

12 *Monthly Review* 33 (1765): 398–99; Letter from Thomas Whately to John Temple, 11 October 1765, *Bowdoin Papers*, p. 72; Letter from Governor Francis Bernard to Richard Jackson, 17 April 1766, quoted in Brennan, "James Otis," p. 720; Letter of 28 February 1766, Bernard, *Select Letters*, p. 42 (see also Letter of 23 November 1765, id., pp. 31–32); Letter from General Thomas Gage to General Henry Seymour Conway, 12 October 1765, Gage, *Correspondence* 1:69–70. See also Letter from General Thomas Gage to General Robert Monckton, 28 September 1765, Gage, *Correspondence* 2:304.

13 Extract of a Letter from London, 14 December 1765, *Boston Post-Boy*, 3 March 1766, p. 1, col. 1. For a typical letter outlining the constitutional arguments in the Commons, see Extract of a letter from a gentleman in London to

his friend in Charles-Town, 8 February 1765, *South-Carolina Gazette*, 20 April 1765, p. 3, col. 2.

14 Barré even said he had opposed passage of the Stamp Act "because he thought it would teach the people of America to reason too closely upon the relative rights of this country and that." Speech of Isaac Barré, Commons Debates, 24 February 1766, Ryder, "Parliamentary Diaries," p. 310.

15 *Boston Post-Boy*, 6 May 1765, p. 3, col. 3; [Macpherson,] *Retrospective View*, p. 21; [Bacon,] *Short Address*, pp. 7–8.

16 Understood: *Critical Review* 19 (1765): 228–29; *Annual Register 1765*, p. [33]; Privy Council: Thomas, *British Politics*, p. 134; Minutes of the Privy Council, 12 December 1765, *Acts of the Privy Council* 4:692; law officers: Speech of Fletcher Norton, Commons Debates, 24 February 1766, and Speech of Charles Yorke, Commons Debates, 21 February 1766, Ryder, "Parliamentary Diaries," pp. 314, 306.

17 Difference: *Critical Review* 20 (1765): 473; Blackstone: Thomas, *British Politics*, p. 238; *Examination of Franklin*, pp. 15–16.

18 *Boston Post-Boy*, 12 May 1766, p. 2, col. 1; *Gazette and News-Letter*, 8 May 1766, p. 2, col. 1; *Prior Documents*, p. 57. A peppercorn was the item common lawyers used as "consideration" making promises legally enforceable in contract law.

19 *Examination of Franklin*, p. 4. Other colonists residing in London were giving the same answer: "[A]sk'd my opinion, as an American, whether, if such concessions were made, the colonies would be content? I said no, for that I apprehended the people were not so much distress'd by the heavy burthen intended to be laid on them by this act, as they are dissatisfied at the manner of their being taxed, without their consent, having no representation in parliament." "Extract of a Letter from London to a Gentleman in this Town, dated Feb. 11," *Gazette and News-Letter*, 25 April 1766, p. 1, col. 2.

20 Anon., *Reflections on the Contest*, p. 1; Pennsylvania Resolves, 21 September 1765, *Prior Documents*, p. 21.

21 Ruggles, "Reasons," col. 1.

22 Diary entry for 9 June 1776, *Memoirs of William Smith* 1:272–73.

CHAPTER NINETEEN: ISSUE OF THE TOWNSHEND DUTIES

1 Virginia Association, 18 May 1769, *Journal of Burgesses* 11:xl.

2 Marblehead Resolves, 8 December 1772, *Boston Evening-Post*, 14 December 1772, p. 2, col. 1; Testimony of Benjamin Franklin, House of Commons, 13 February 1766, Ryder, "Parliamentary Diaries," p. 301.

3 Petition of the Council and Burgesses to the House of Lords, 14 April 1768, *Journal of Burgesses* 11:168; Letter from the Massachusetts House of Representatives to Agent Dennys De Berdt, 12 January 1768, *Speeches*, p. 125; Instructions of Portsmouth, New Hampshire, 5 August 1768, *Boston Chronicle*, 8 August 1768, p. 315, col. 2; Dickinson, *Letters*, p. 355.

4 John Mackenzie, "Second Letter to the People," *Freeman Letters*, p. 25.

5 North: Letter from Charles Garth to the South Carolina Commons House Committee, 6 March 1770, "Garth Correspondence" 13:228 (see also Dickerson, *Acts*, p. 196; Christie, *Crisis*, p. 71); harm colonies: South Carolina Nonimportation Proposal, 28 June 1768, *Freeman Letters*, p. 5; harm Britain: petition of London merchants to the Commons quoted in Letter from Edward Montague to the Virginia Committee, 8 February 1770, "Proceedings Committee of Correspondence" 12:166; prohibition: Petition of the New York General Assembly to the King, 25 March 1775, *Journal of New York Assembly* (1766–76), p. 110.

6 7 George III, cap. 46 (1766); for Townshend's speech, see Horace Walpole's account quoted in Barrow, *Trade*, p. 217. For other reports, see Speech of Charles Townshend, Commons Debates, 13 May 1767, Ryder, "Parliamentary Diaries," p. 344; Namier & Brooke, *Charles Townshend*, pp. 178–79.

7 Representation from the Board of Trade, 27 September 1765, *Acts of the Privy Council* 4:739; *South-Carolina Gazette*, 21 September 1767, p. 2, col. 2; John Dickinson, "Address" to Merchants Meeting, 25 April 1768, *Scots Magazine* 30 (1768): 525.

8 Call of the Convention, 14 September 1768, *Boston Chronicle*, 19 September 1768, p. 362, col. 3. Besides being an innovation, the statute introduced new administrative practices that departed from traditional British constitutional ways. Dickerson, "Use of Revenue," p. 233.

9 Resolves of Providence and New Shoreham, 19 January and 2 March 1774, *Rhode Island Colony Records* 7:273, 277; Address of John Dickinson, 25 April 1769, *American Gazette*, p. 42. This complaint was not applicable to every colony, for in some, salaries already were paid by the imperial treasury. Greene, *Quest*, p. 147; Thomas, *British Politics*, p. 362.

10 Instructions of 22 December 1767, *Boston Town Records* 16:229; "Remarks" on Letter to De Berdt, p. 20; Dickinson, *Letters*, p. 371; Protest signed at New York, *Boston Evening-Post*, 3 September 1770, p. 1, col. 1; Minutes of 3 March 1775, *Journal of New York Assembly* (1766–76), p. 54.

11 Speech of Edmund Burke, Commons Debates, 9 May 1770, *Burke on American Revolution*, p. 11; Dickinson, *Letters*, p. 360.

12 Letter from the Massachusetts House of Representatives to the Agent, 29 June 1771, *Boston Evening-Post*, 29 July 1771, p. 2, col. 2.

13 "Proceedings in Parliament, 1766–67," *Scots Magazine* 30 (1768): 178–79.

14 Articles of Agreement, Salem, Massachusetts, 1 May 1770, *Boston Evening-Post*, 14 May 1770, p. 3, col. 1; Resolutions of "many respectable Gentlemen," Charles Town, South Carolina, 28 June 1769, *Political Register* 5 (1769): 139.

15 Kenyon, *Stuarts*, p. 81; *"Remarks" on Letter to De Berdt*, pp. 20–21.

16 James Iredell, Untitled Paper, June 1776, *Papers of Iredell* 1:374, 376. Similarly, see the Farmer's second letter, Dickinson, *Letters*, p. 316, and *Boston Evening-Post*, 28 December 1767, p. 1, col. 1; Dickinson, *Letter to Merchants*, p. 442.

17 Petition of the Virginia Council and Burgesses to the House of Commons,

14 April 1768, *Journal of Burgesses* 11:170. Similarly, see Letter from the Massachusetts House of Representatives to Lord Hillsborough, 30 June 1768, *Boston Chronicle*, 25 July 1768, p. 294, col. 1.

18 Letter from Governor Josias Lyndon to Lord Hillsborough, 17 September 1768, *Rhode Island Colony Records*, 6:561.

19 Petition of the General Assembly to the King, 7 May 1768, *New Jersey Votes and Proceedings* (1768), p. 38; *Boston Chronicle*, 25 July 1768, p. 293, col. 2. Similarly, see Address of the Commons House of Assembly to the King, 24 December 1768, *Georgia Commons House Journal* 14:644; Letter from the Massachusetts House of Representatives to the Lords of the Treasury, 17 February 1768, Adams, *Writings* 1:195; Instruction of Philadelphia, 30 July 1768, *Boston Chronicle*, 22 August 1768, p. 330, col. 3; Resolutions of Charlestown, 15 February 1770, *Boston Gazette*, 19 February 1770, p. 1, col. 3.

20 Petition of the New York General Assembly to the King, 31 December 1768 (entered on the journal 7 April 1769), *Journal of New York Assembly* (1766–76), p. 12. Similarly, see Petition of the Pennsylvania Assembly to the House of Commons, 22 September 1768, *Boston Post-Boy*, 20 February 1769, p. 2, col. 1; Address from the House of Assembly of the Counties upon Delaware to the King, 27 October 1768, *Delaware House Minutes* (1765–70), pp. 167–68; Letter from the Massachusetts House of Representatives to Agent Dennis De Berdt, 12 January 1768, *Speeches*, p. 125; Instructions of 22 December 1767, *Boston Town Records*, 16:229 and *Boston Evening-Post* (Supplement), 28 December 1767, p. 1, col. 2. In contrast to northern colonies where the plan to pay governors and judges from the royal treasury was a major grievance, southern colonies, where officials more commonly received Crown salaries, objected to the Townshend duties on the grounds that they raised revenue. Greene, *Quest*, pp. 373–75.

21 Petition of the New Hampshire House of Representatives to the King, 29 October 1768, *Documents of New Hampshire*, p. 249.

22 Letter from Thomas Cushing to Dennys De Berdt, 17 January 1767, *Collections of the Massachusetts Historical Society* 4 (1858): 349.

CHAPTER TWENTY: ISSUE OF THE TEA ACT

1 Anon., *Characters*, p. 2; Letter from Earl Camden to the duke of Grafton, 4 October 1768, Campbell, *Lives of Chancellors* 5:279.

2 Letter from William Dowdeswell to the marquis of Rockingham, 14 August 1768, quoted in Thomas, *British Politics*, pp. 367–68; Dickinson, *Letters*, p. 355; Speech of Edmund Burke, Commons Debates, 9 May 1770, *Burke on American Revolution*, p. 11. "The preamble of it was framed upon two principles. The ostensible part was to find a support independent of the people there. In the next place, it was to serve as a test, whereby the recognition of our right to tax them was to be ascertained. The firmness of the country, its dignity, and all its power were to be exerted." Ibid., p. 10.

3 Speech of Edmund Burke, Commons Debates, 22 January 1770, *Boston Eve-*

ning-Post, 23 April 1770, p. 4, col. 2 (for another nontaxation purpose of the Townshend legislation, see Thomas, *British Politics*, pp. 348, 357); Dickinson, *Letters*, pp. 395, 396; Letter from William Dowdeswell to the marquis of Rockingham, 14 August 1768, quoted in Thomas, *British Politics*, p. 368.

4 Letter from William Knox to George Grenville, 15 December 1768, and Letter from Dennys De Berdt to Richard Cary, 26 August 1768, quoted in Kammen, *Rope*, pp. 171–72; Letter from Benjamin Franklin to Noble Wimberly Jones, 7 June 1769, *Georgia Commons House Journal* 15:30; Christie & Labaree, *Empire*, p. 127.

5 Letter from Joseph Sherwood to Governor Joseph Wanton, 5 July 1769, *Rhode Island Colony Records* 6:593; Letter to Thomas Cushing, 1 November 1769, "Letters of Dennys De Berdt," p. 382; Anon., *Characters*, pp. 50–51.

6 Letter from Charles Garth to South Carolina Commons House Committee, 6 March 1770, "Garth Correspondence" 13:228; Christie & Labaree, *Empire*, p. 144. North Carolina's agent was to report that the duties "are to be repealed as anticommercial (what could be more so, as Lord North said in the House, than to tax the articles of our exportation? they did not know this last Session,—To find it out this must be the work of Inspiration—Absurd!)." Letter from Henry E. McCulloh to John Harvey, 26 January 1770. *North Carolina Colonial Records* 8:172.

7 George III: Schlesinger, "Uprising Against Company," p. 60; Pamphleteer: Anon., *Experience preferable to Theory*, pp. 58–59; "continued:" [Shebbeare,] *Answer to Edmund Burke*, p. 37.

8 Hartley, *Letters on the War*, p. 83; Report of 13 December 1769, *Boston Town Records* 16:324.

9 10 George III, cap. 17; 13 George III, cap. 44.

10 [Macpherson,] *Rights of Great Britain*, pp. 48–49; [Dalrymple,] *Address of the People*, p. 33.

11 Leonard, "Massachusettensis," p. 10 (see also [Randolph,] *Present State of Virginia*, p. 213); Dickinson, "Tea Tax," p. 460: Speech of Lord North, Commons Debates, 19 January 1775, *Scots Magazine* 37 (1775): 75; Letter from Benjamin Franklin to Thomas Cushing, 4 June 1773, quoted in Brown, *Middle-Class Democracy*, p. 311.

12 Anon., *Licentiousness Unmask'd*, p. 29; Address of the Merchants and Inhabitants of New York, 25 October 1773, *Scots Magazine* 35 (1773): 664; Letter from "Scaevola" to the Consignees of the Tea, *Gazette & Post-Boy*, 25 October 1773, p. 2, col. 1.

13 Letter from Major General Frederick Haldimand to the earl of Dartmouth, 28 December 1773, *Revolution Documents* 4:431; "Scaevola" in *Gazette & Post-Boy*, 25 October 1773, p. 2, col. 2; Dickinson, "Tea Tax," p. 459; Dickinson quoted in Bailyn, *Pamphlets*, p. 665; Hacker, "First American Revolution," p. 140.

14 *Gazette & Post-Boy*, 20 December 1773, p. 2, col. 3. For details of the argument, see Schlesinger, "Uprising Against Company," pp. 68–77.

15 John Hancock's Oration (1774), *Massacre Orations*, p. 53; Letter from Gov-

ernor William Tryon to the earl of Dartmouth, 3 November 1773, *Revolution Documents* 4:403.

16 Letter from the Massachusetts Committee of Correspondence to the Virginia Committee of Correspondence, 21 October 1773, *Journal of Burgesses* 13:56. Similarly, see Portsmouth Resolves, 16 December 1773, *Documents of New Hampshire*, p. 333; "Queries put to Dr. Franklin," *Scots Magazine* 36 (1774): 248.

17 Minutes of the Massachusetts Council, 29 November 1773, Gage, *Papers;* Adams, "Novanglus," p. 180.

18 "A Revolution Whig," 5 December 1775, *Scots Magazine* 37 (1775): 647–48; Letter from Governor Josiah Martin to the earl of Dartmouth, 4 November 1774, *Revolution Documents* 8:227; Speech of Constantine John Phipps, Commons Debates, 19 April 1774, *London Magazine* 44 (1775): 61; Speech of George Johnstone, Commons Debates, 25 March 1774, *American Archives* 1:55–56.

19 Speeches of Edmund Burke, Commons Debates, 19 April 1774, *Gentleman's Magazine* 44 (1774): 608, 25 March 1774, *London Magazine* 43 (1774): 178, and 19 April 1774, *Burke on American Revolution*, p. 32.

20 Address from the Commons House of Assembly to Governor James Wright, 2 November 1769, *Georgia Commons House Journal* 15:17; Petition from the House of Burgesses to the King, 27 June 1770, *Journal of Burgesses* 12:102.

21 *Boston Evening-Post*, 3 September 1770, p. 1, col. 2; Letter from the House of Representatives to the Agent, 29 June 1771, *Boston Evening-Post*, 29 July 1771, p. 2, col. 1.

22 Plymouth Resolves, 7 December 1773, *Gazette & Post-Boy*, 20 December 1773, p. 1, col. 2; "Scaevola," *Gazette & Post-Boy*, 25 October 1773, p. 2, col. 1.

23 Resolution of 5 November 1773, *Boston Town Records* 18:143; Resolves of Cambridge, *Gazette & Post-Boy*, 29 November 1773, p. 3, col. 1; Resolves of Providence, 19 January 1774, *Rhode Island Colony Records* 7:273; Resolves of York (Maine), 21 January 1774, Banks, *York*, p. 384.

24 Philadelphia Resolves, 18 October 1773, *Gentleman's Magazine* 44 (1774): 32; *Hibernian Magazine* 4 (1774): 100; *Scots Magazine* 36 (1774): 49.

25 Letter from Pennsylvania Committee of Correspondence to Virginia Committee of Correspondence, 21 May 1774, *Journal of Burgesses* 13:147; Letter from the Committee of Philadelphia to the Boston Committee, 21 May 1774, *Scots Magazine* 36 (1774): 351.

CHAPTER TWENTY-ONE: PROPOSED CONSTITUTIONAL SOLUTIONS

1 Letter from Jared Ingersoll to William Livingston, 1 October 1765, "Ingersoll Correspondence," p. 350.

2 Letter from Lord Barrington to the earl of Dartmouth, 24 December 1774, reprinted in Barrington, *Viscount Barrington*, p. 151; Anon., *Americanus Examined*, p. 12, n. i; Anon., *Right of British Legislature*, pp. 23–24.

3 Letter from the duke of Richmond to the marquis of Rockingham, 12 March 1775, quoted in Donoughue, *British Politics*, p. 256; "Edmund Pendleton's

Proposed Resolutions," 24–26 (?) May 1775, *Letters of Delegates to Congress* 1:403–4; *Letters and Papers of Pendleton* 1:106.

4 [Seabury,] *View of the Controversy*, p. 21, reprinted in *Scots Magazine* 37 (1775): 97. See also for 1776: [Erskine,] *Reflections on the Rise*, pp. 11–13; for 1777: Anon., *Essays Commercial and Political*, p. i. A related flawed assumption was that the American objection to parliamentary taxation was based on the argument that members of the House of Commons "can never be competent judges of the propriety of any tax, which is laid *in* the colonies." But "with respect to a tax upon articles of luxury" and products of foreign countries "the case is widely different"; hence such taxes would be constitutional. [Bacon,] *Short Address*, pp. 12–13.

5 Pownall, *Administration Fifth Edition* 2:78, 96–97; Pownall, *Administration*, pp. 150–52; [Lind,] *Thirteenth Parliament*, pp. 494–95.

6 Shelburne quoted in Price, *Nature of Civil Liberty*, p. 106, reprinted in *Hibernian Magazine* 6 (1776): 305–6. Similarly, see Anon., "Second Appeal to Justice," quoted in *Monthly Review* 54 (1776): 152. A related proposal was to have the colonies tax themselves but at the direction of Parliament to provide naval stores. [Jenings,] *Plan for Settling the Dispute*, pp. 3, 15–16.

7 [Ferguson,] *Remarks on Dr. Price*, pp. 31, 53–54 (Ferguson would be secretary to the peace commission to America, 1778); third suggestion: [Jenings,] *Plan for Settling the Dispute*, pp. 3, 15–16.

8 [Maseres,] *To Obtain an Assembly*, pp. 77–78; [Maseres,] *Canadian Freeholder* 1:287–88. Maseres mistakenly thought that his proposal was the same as the official proposal of Lord North, discussed below. Rather, it was closer to one suggested by Edmund Burke, who would have had Parliament raise duties only for purposes of trade regulation, not taxation, with all money raised to be held "for the disposal of the general assemblies, as if the same had been levied by [their authority]." Hartley, *Letters on War*, p. 30.

9 Amor Patriae, 7 May 1774, [Crowley,] *Letters*, p. 88.

10 [Stewart,] *Letter to Price*, pp. 30–31.

11 [Knox,] *Extra Official Papers*, Appendix, p. 30.

12 Anon., "Plan of Reconciliation," quoted in *Monthly Review* 54 (1776): 236; [Crowley,] *Dissertations*, pp. 5, 8; [Knox,] *Extra Official Papers*, Appendix, pp. 30–31.

13 [Shebbeare,] *Answer to Edmund Burke*, p. 206.

14 [Ramsay,] *Historical Essay*, p. 199. For a contemporary appraisal of this scheme, see *Critical Review* 31 (1771): 26–27.

15 [Ramsay,] *Historical Essay*, pp. 199–200; Dickinson, *Letters*, p. 369.

16 Fletcher, *American Patriotism*, p. 51; Address of the Representatives of Nova Scotia to the King, Lords, and Commons, 24 June 1775, *Scots Magazine* 38 (1776): 9–10; *Gentleman's Magazine* 46 (1776): 5–6.

17 Another importation plan would have been more absolute, taxing products of British manufacture, the fair proportion set by the rule that "no other duty should be laid on goods of this class, than on the same goods consumed in Great Britain." [Lind,] *Thirteenth Parliament*, pp. 494–95. The most elaborate and thoughtful of the proportionate plans also was limited

to customs duties. See [Knox,] *Extra Official Papers*, Appendix, pp. 32–37.

18 "A Plan for American Taxation," *Scots Magazine* 36 (1774): 120; [Lind,] *Thirteenth Parliament*, pp. 497–98.

19 Anon., *Plan for Conciliating*, pp. xii; [Ramsay,] *Historical Essay*, p. 205; Anon., *True Constitutional Means*, p. 14. For contemporary summary and criticism, see *Gentleman's Magazine* 39 (1769): 260; *Critical Review* 27 (1769): 314–15; *Political Register*, 6:326.

20 Speech of 6 February 1775, *Speeches of John Wilkes in Parliament* 1:22–24; *Hibernian Magazine* 5 (1775): 164–65; *Monthly Review* 55 (1776): 75.

21 *Political Register* 4 (1769): 326. Similarly, see Anon., "Plan of Reconciliation," quoted in *Monthly Review* 54 (1776): 237.

22 South Carolina Resolves, 29 November 1765, Morgan, *Prologue*, p. 59; Hartley, *Letters on War*, p. 17; New Jersey Resolves, 30 November 1765, Morgan, *Prologue*, p. 59.

23 Pennsylvania Resolves, 21 September 1765, Morgan, *Prologue*, p. 51. Following the Stamp Act's repeal the pledge was made directly to the king. "[A]ccept the strongest Assurances, that . . . We will at all times most chearfully contribute to your Majesty's Service to the utmost of our Abilities, when your Royal Requisitions, as heretofore, shall be made known." Address of the House of Assembly of the Counties upon Delaware to the King, 5 June 1766, *Delaware House Minutes* (1765–70), p. 60.

24 *Examination of Franklin*, p. 14. The speaker of the Pennsylvania House, who acknowledged Parliament's sovereign authority to tax, also endorsed the requisition method but thought it an indulgence. [Galloway,] *Americanus*, pp. 12–13.

25 Address and Petition of the Lord Mayor, Aldermen, and Commons of London to the King, 14 July 1775, *Gentlemen's Magazine* 45 (1775): 360. See also Letter from the New York Committee of Correspondence to the Mayor, Aldermen, and Commons of London, 5 May 1775, *Scots Magazine* 37 (1775): 400; Message from Deputy Governor John Penn to the Pennsylvania General Assembly, 2 May 1775, *Gentleman's Magazine* 45 (1775): 297; [Williamson,] *Plea of the Colonies*, pp. 24–25; Letter from William Smith to Lewis Morris, 5 June 1775, *Memoirs of William Smith* 1:228b.

26 Speech of Richard Pennant, Commons Debates, 19 April 1774, *London Magazine* 44 (1775): 61; Burke, "Speech on American Taxation," p. 149. Elaborate plans for obtaining requisitions were formulated. Hartley, *Letters on War*, pp. 13–17; *Gentleman's Magazine* 44 (1774): 310. The opposition claimed it was constitutionally impossible to have both supremacy and requisitions. It "supposes dominion without authority, and subjects without subordination." [Johnson,] *Political Tracts*, p. 186. Similarly, Anon., *Inquiry into the Nature*, p. 32; Anon., *Licentiousness Unmask'd*, p. 43.

27 Resolutions offered by Edmund Pendleton in the Continental Congress, May 1775, *Letters and Papers of Pendleton* 1:106. One writer even wanted the colonies to be free to question requisitions for imperial defense and to be able to refuse grants. Anon., *Middle Line*, pp. 14–15.

28 Message of the Continental Congress quoted in Hartley, *Letters on War*, pp.

97–98, and in Van Alstyne, "Bursts," p. 67; *Boston News-Letter* (Postscript), 8 September 1768, p. 2, col. 2; *Monthly Review* 54 (1776): 237; Pennsylvania whigs: "Benjamin Franklin's Vindication" [June–July 1775], *Letters of Delegates to Congress* 1:564–65; Instructions of the Pennsylvania Provincial Congress to Continental Congress Deputies, 15 July 1774, *London Magazine* 43 (1774): 586.

29 Bernard quoted in Morgan, "Postponement of Stamp Act," p. 368.

30 "A plan . . . ," *Gentleman's Magazine* 45 (1775): 342–43; Anon., *America Vindicated;* William Henry Drayton, "A Letter from "Freeman," 10 August 1774, Gibbes, *Documentary History*, pp. 18–19; *Memoirs of William Smith* 1:246. A variation of the plan was a congress made up of delegates from both houses of Parliament as well as from American assemblies. Anon., *Some Candid Suggestions*, pp. 13–14.

31 "Lord Chatham's proposed Bill . . . ," *London Magazine* 44 (1776): 72; *Parliamentary History* 18:198–203.

32 One plan proposed that half the congress be elected and the other half come from the appointed colonial councils.

> [T]his, with the reserved power of appointing governors and officers, civil and military, would keep such a superiority on the side of the mother-country as I apprehend would keep America in a state of perfect subjection; and *that* subordination would . . . be a sufficient security against future fears of their INDEPENDENCY, as they would have no *local* power but that of taxation. . . . This plan would be an apparent indulgence, though, in fact, no concession at all in their favor; as the SHARE of representation from the mother-country in the persons of the King's council, and other persons employed by this government, would throw such a weight of influence in the scale of representation, as to leave the colonists the name without the power of representation and taxation.

Anon., *Plan to Reconcile*, pp. 23–24.

33 Letter from George Grenville to William Knox, 15 September 1768, [Knox,] *Extra Official Papers* Appendix, pp. 20–21; Letter from George Grenville to William Knox, 15 July 1768, *Grenville Letterbooks;* Allen, *American Crisis*, p. 52. "If they are to . . . be the sole judges of the *mode, quantum, means*, and *abilities*, &c. of raising and appropriating aids, what security can we have for the performance of what is to be done on their part." Anon., *Experience preferable to Theory*, p. 94. John Lind formulated a plan of assessors to collect colonial taxes if local assemblies failed to act. His proposal would have had *American members elected to the House of Commons*, Parliament then making requisitions, and a Continental Congress assigning proportions to each colony. [Lind,] *Englishman's Answer*, p. 14.

CHAPTER TWENTY-TWO: THE ADMINISTRATION'S SOLUTION

1 De Lolme, *Constitution: New Edition*, pp. 511–12; "The right of G. Britain asserted," *Scots Magazine* 38 (1776): 125.

2 It was possible to make the same argument about American liberty, to say that royal requisitions set by the Crown would give too much power to a few men. If Americans paid such sums, "they must evidently in this case be wholly subject to ministerial government, and of course to ministerial tyranny." Anon., *Inquiry into the Nature*, pp. 31–32. This argument, however, posed much greater danger to the British than to the Americans.

3 Speech of Lord North, Commons Debates, 27 March 1775, *Gentleman's Magazine* 45 (1775): 625–26; Speech of David Hartley, Commons Debates, 27 March 1775, *Gentleman's Magazine* 45 (1775): 624; Hartley, *Speech and Motions*, p. 5.

4 Speech of George Johnstone, Commons Debates, 16 December 1774, *American Archives* 1:1482.

5 "Minute of a Cabinet meeting," 21 January 1775, *Dartmouth Manuscripts* 1:372–73; Cabinet minute quoted in Donoughue, *British Politics*, p. 224.

6 Speech of Lord North, Commons Debates, 27 February 1775, *London Magazine* 44 (1775): 561; *Parliamentary History* 18:352; Debate of 20 February 1775, *Parliamentary History* 18:320; *Gentleman's Magazine* 45 (1775): 310–11; Speech of Lord North, Commons Debates, 20 February 1775, *Scots Magazine* 37 (1775): 123.

7 [Chalmers,] *Answer from Bristol to Burke*, p. 34; Anon., *Conciliatory Bills Considered*, p. 5; Letter from Lord North to George III, 19 February 1775, quoted in Donoughue, *British Politics*, p. 249.

8 Speech of Lord North, Commons Debates, 20 February 1775, *Parliamentary History* 18:320; *London Magazine* 44 (1775): 501.

9 *Parliamentary History* 18:352–53; Message of Governor Lord Dunmore to the House of Burgesses, 1 June 1775, *Journal of Burgesses* 13:175.

10 Message from Governor William Franklin to the Council and Assembly, 16 May 1775, *New Jersey Votes and Proceedings* (May 1775), p. 10; Speech of Lord North, Commons Debates, 27 February 1775, *Gentleman's Magazine* 45 (1775): 611.

11 Message from Governor William Franklin to the Council and Assembly, 16 May 1775, *New Jersey Votes and Proceedings* (May 1775), p. 5; Message from Governor John Penn to the Assembly, 2 May 1775, *Pennsylvania Council* 10:251–52; *Remembrancer for 1775*, p. 221; Message from Governor Lord Dunmore to the House of Burgesses, 10 June 1775, *Journal of Burgesses* 13:215.

12 Circular Letter from the earl of Dartmouth to the Governors of Nova Scotia, New Hampshire et al., 3 March 1775, *Revolution Documents* 9:61–62; Message from Governor John Penn to the Assembly, 2 May 1775, *Pennsylvania Council* 10:252.

13 Address from Governor Lord Dunmore to the House of Burgesses, 1 June 1775, *Journal of Burgesses* 13:175; Answer from Lieutenant Governor Cadwallader Colden to the General Committee for New York, May 1775, *Remembrancer for 1775*, p. 216.

14 For the appearance of not obeying, see *Scots Magazine* 30 (1768): 74.

15 Message from Governor John Wentworth to the House of Representatives, 13 June 1775, *Documents of New Hampshire*, p. 380.

16 Hutchinson, *Diary* 1:380, quoted in Morgan, "Postponement of Stamp Act," p. 385; "Notes for Mr. Hamilton," *Memoirs of William Smith* 1:249. See also diary entry for 14 February 1776, p. 267.

17 Hartley, *Letters on War*, p. 18; Speech of Isaac Barré, Commons Debates, 20 February 1775, *London Magazine* 44 (1775): 504–6; Speech of General Henry Seymour Conway, Commons Debates, 29 February 1776, *Hibernian Magazine* 6 (1775): 563; Speech of Edmund Burke, Commons Debates, 20 February 1775, *London Magazine* 44 (1775): 505; Speech of Edmund Burke, Commons Debates, 22 March 1775, *Hibernian Magazine* 5 (1775): 402. On the last page cited, Burke is quoted as telling the House of Commons: "For, suppose the Colonies were to lay the duties which furnished their Contingent, upon the importation of your manufactures; you know you would never suffer such a tax to be laid. You know too, that you would not suffer many other modes of taxation. So that, when you come to explain yourself, it will be found, that you will neither leave to themselves the quantum nor the mode; nor indeed any thing."

18 Hartley, *Speech and Motions*, pp. 4, 6; *Burke on American Revolution*, p. 115; Price, *Nature of Civil Liberty*, p. 66.

19 *Burke on American Revolution*, p. 115.

20 Hartley, *Speech and Motions*, p. 6.

21 Speech of Ackland [John Dyke-Acland ?] Commons Debates, 27 February 1775, *London Magazine* 44 (1775): 558; Answer of Congress to North's Plan, 31 July 1775, *Gentleman's Magazine* 45 (1775): 427, 426; Message from the House of Burgesses to Governor Lord Dunmore, 12 June 1775, *Journal of Burgesses* 13:219.

22 *Papers of Jefferson* 1:171; Message from the House of Representatives to Governor William Franklin, 19 May 1775, *New Jersey Votes and Proceedings* (May 1775), p. 26; *Remembrancer for 1775*, p. 219; Petition and Remonstrance from the House of Assembly to the King, 5 December 1768, *North Carolina Colonial Records* 7:981.

23 Letter from Charles Carroll of Carrollton to Henry Graves, 15 September 1765, *Letters of Charles Carroll*, p. 89; Resolves of the Continental Congress, 31 July 1775, *Gentleman's Magazine* 45 (1775): 426.

24 "Edmund Pendleton's Proposed Resolutions," May 1775, *Letters of Delegates to Congress*, 1:404.

25 Message from the House of Representatives to Governor William Franklin, 20 May 1775, *New Jersey Votes and Proceedings* (May 1775), pp. 25–26; *Remembrancer for 1775*, pp. 218–19.

26 Resolves of the Continental Congress, 31 July 1775, *Papers of Jefferson* 1:231–32; *Gentleman's Magazine* 45 (1775): 426–27; *London Magazine* 44 (1775): 510.

27 "Sketch of propositions" from Lord Drummond to Lord Howe, 12 August 1776, *Scots Magazine* 38 (1776): 586 (all revenue collected incidentally to the regulation of trade was to be paid into the treasury of the colony where raised); "Draft of Resolutions on Lord Drummond's Peace Proposals," [22 ? August 1776,] *Papers of Jefferson* 1:501.

28 Speeches of Henry Seymour Conway and Lord North, Commons Debates, 22 May 1776, *Parliamentary History* 18:1357, 1362.

29 Speech of Lord George Germain, Commons Debates, 22 May 1776, *London Magazine* 45 (1776): 678.

30 Address from Commons House to Governor James Wright, 10 May 1780, and Resolutions of 9 May 1780, *Georgia Commons House Journal* 15: 556–57, 552–53; Protest of 9 March 1778, *Protests of the Lords* 2:174. An aspect of the statute, 18 George III, cap. 2 (1778), is discussed above, p. 52.

CHAPTER TWENTY-THREE: THE BRITISH PERSPECTIVE

1 Speech of Lord North, Commons Debates, 20 November 1775, *Gentleman's Magazine* 46 (1776): 99. For evidence that revenue was no longer expected, see the testimony of Governor William Tryon, *Memoirs of William Smith* 1:230; Tucker, *Letter to Burke*, p. 54; Anon., *Reflections on Contest*, p. 46.

2 [Williamson,] *Plea of the Colonies*, p. 25 (quoting *Rights of Great Britain asserted*, p. 54).

3 Speech of Lord North, Commons Debates, 20 February 1775, *London Magazine* 44 (1775): 501. "[W]hen his Majesty's ministers had said that taxation was only a secondary consideration, they did not mean it was ultimately without their view. They were not averse to the Americans chusing the mode, and that the tax should originate with themselves; not that they thought it would ever swell to any great amount, but that it is necessary to ensure obedience." Speech of Lord North, Commons Debates, 13 November 1775, *Gentleman's Magazine* 46 (1776): 4. But see same speech, *Parliamentary History* 18:940.

4 Speech of Lord North, Commons Debates, 27 February 1775, *Gentleman's Magazine* 45 (1775): 611; Speech of Charles Yorke, Commons Debates, 3 February 1766, Ryder, "Parliamentary Diaries," p. 267.

5 Speech of the earl of Suffolk, Lords Debates, 20 February 1775, *Parliamentary History* 18:162; *American Archives* 1:1499. See also the earl of Sandwich, Anon., *Characters*, p. 118. It was said of Ireland: "But if Parliament is not to use its right [to tax] over Ireland, what signifies a right when it is never used?" Anon., *Experience preferable to Theory*, pp. 95–96.

6 Speech of Lord Clare, Commons Debates, 19 April 1774, *Gentleman's Magazine* 44 (1774): 551; Speech of Charles Cornwall, Commons Debates, 19 April 1774, *Parliamentary History* 17:1213; Speech of John Burgoyne, Commons Debates, 19 April 1774, *Gentleman's Magazine* 44 (1774): 551; Speech of Lord Beauchamp, Commons Debates, 19 April 1774, *London Magazine* 44 (1775): 62. See also Speech of George Grenville, Commons Debates, 29 February 1776, *Hibernian Magazine* 6 (1776): 562; Speeches of Alexander Wedderburn and Charles Cornwall, Commons Debates, 19 April 1774, *Gentleman's Magazine* 44 (1774): 550, 549.

7 Speech of Lord Halifax, Lords Debates, 11 March 1766, "Stamp Act Debates,"

p. 581; Speech of Lord North, Commons Debates, 19 April 1774, *London Magazine* 44 (1775): 63.

8 Anon., *History of Lord North*, p. 7; Speech of Lord George Germain, Commons Debates, 4 March 1774, *Hibernian Magazine* 4 (1774): 290.

9 21 October 1774, *Journal of First Congress*, p. 96; Speech of Lord Mansfield, Lords Debates, 6 February 1775, *Gentleman's Magazine* 45 (1775): 108. See also [Chalmers,] *Answer from Bristol to Burke*, p. 75.

10 Stamp Act: *Boston Post-Boy*, 20 May 1765, p. 3, col. 3; Speech of William Blackstone, Commons Debates, 3 February 1766, Ryder, "Parliamentary Diaries," p. 314; Townshend: Letter to Thomas Cushing, 2 January 1769, "Letters of Dennys De Berdt," p. 351. Similarly, Letter from Benjamin Franklin to Noble Wimberley Jones, 3 April 1769, *Georgia Commons House Journal* 15:27.

11 Letter from the earl of Dartmouth to Governor James Wright, 3 March 1775, Gibbes, *Documentary History*, p. 95. See above (p. 255). The Governor of New Jersey repeated this warning to the legislature. Message of Governor William Franklin to the Council and Assembly, 16 May 1775, *New Jersey Votes and Proceedings* (May 1775), p. 6.

12 Letter from Edward Sedgwick to Edward Weston, 24 December 1765, "Weston Papers," p. 399; Letter from Charles Garth to South Carolina Commons House Committee, 10 December 1768, "Garth Correspondence" 10: 234; Germain: "Parliament," *Scots Magazine* 38 (1776): 84–85.

13 Speech of William Dowdeswell, Commons Debates, 1766, "Stamp Act Debates," p. 572.

14 Letter from Charles Garth to South Carolina Commons House Committee, 10 November 1768, "Garth Correspondence," 10:231; Speech of Lord North, Commons Debates, 19 January 1775, *Scots Magazine* 37 (1775): 77; Speech of Lord George Germaine, Commons Debates, 26 January 1775, *London Magazine* 44 (1775): 337 (Governor George Johnstone said that North wanted the colonies to "petition first and acknowledge the right, and then we will grant relief." Johnstone, *Speech on Question*, p. 11); Nugent: *Political Debates*, pp. 1–2.

15 Letter from Charles Garth to South Carolina Commons House Committee, 12 March 1769, and Letter from the Committee of Correspondence to Charles Garth, 7 July 1769, "Garth Correspondence," 11:53, 60. For more details on these events by one of the "Northern agents" saying they had "laid it [the right] aside for the present, but are determined in some way or other to bring it before the House before the session is over," see Letter to Thomas Cushing, 10 March 1769, and Letter to the Committee of the Counties on Delaware, 9 March 1769, "Letters of Dennys De Berdt," p. 366.

16 Speech of Charles James Fox, Commons Debates, 19 April 1774, *Gentleman's Magazine* 44 (1774): 550.

17 Speech of Charles Yorke, Commons Debates, 21 February 1766, Ryder, "Parliamentary Diaries," p. 306. Another member, generally credited with being a strong supporter of administration, said during the tea-tax debate: "Let America alone . . . ; do not let us search for trifling taxes, by way of

experiment, to try our power: the moment they see that taxation is not for effectually collecting of money, but for experiment only, they will always oppose you." Speech of Constantine John Phipps, Commons Debates, 14 March 1774, *Gentleman's Magazine* 44 (1774): 502.

18 Letter from the New York Committee of Correspondence to the Mayor, Aldermen, and Common Council of London, 5 May 1775, *Scots Magazine* 37 (1775): 400; Hartley, *Speech and Motions*, p. 4; Speech of Edmund Burke, Commons Debates, 19 April 1774, *Gentleman's Magazine* 44 (1774): 602.

19 Speech of David Hartley, Commons Debates, 29 February 1776, *Hibernian Magazine* 6 (1776): 488; "punctilio": Anon., *Conciliatory Bills Considered*, p. 12; Letter XXXIX, 28 May 1770, Wade, *Junius* 1:299; Letter from *Junius* to John Wilkes, 7 September 1771, *Gentleman's Magazine* 41 (1771): 587; Speech of the duke of Richmond, Lords Debates, 31 October 1776, *Scots Magazine* 38 (1776): 571–72; *Hibernian Magazine* 6 (1776): 763 (calling it a "twopenny duty on teas"); Burke quoted in Edgar, *Colonial Governor*, p. 242; [Williamson,] *Plea of the Colonies*, p. 21.

20 Speech of Edmund Burke, Commons Debates, 22 March 1775, *Burke on American Revolution*, pp. 95–96. Burke, although rejecting lawyers, did not reject their methods and, remarkably, once even cited a precedent for *not* mentioning the right: "This pattern statute [34 Edward I, *Statutum de tallagio non concedendo*] was absolutely *silent about the right*, but confined itself to giving satisfaction in future, and it laid down no *general principles* which might tend to affect the royal prerogative in *other* particulars. In all human probability the preservation of the other branches of the prerogative was owing to the clear and absolute surrender of this." Speech of Edmund Burke, Commons Debates, 16 November 1775, *Burke on American Revolution*, p. 131.

CHAPTER TWENTY-FOUR: THE AMERICAN PERSPECTIVE

1 Lee, *Second Appeal*, p. 20.

2 Representatives and Remonstrance of the New York General Assembly to the House of Commons, 25 March 1775, *Scots Magazine* 37 (1775): 236; *Hibernian Magazine* 5 (1775): 350*.

3 Letter from Jared Ingersoll to the Connecticut General Assembly, 18 September 1765, "Ingersoll Correspondence," p. 335; Instructions to Richard Jackson from the General Assembly, October 1765, *Public Records of Connecticut*, 12:421.

4 Letter from the Pennsylvania Committee of Correspondence to Agents, 22 September 1768, *Pennsylvania Archives* 7:6278.

5 Address of the New York House of Representatives to Lieutenant Governor Cadwallader Colden, 11 September 1764, *New York Journal of Votes*, pp. 749–50; Instructions of 17 June 1768, *Boston Town Records* 16:257; Petition and Remonstrance from the House of Assembly to the King, 5 December 1768, *North Carolina Colonial Records* 7:981.

6 [Priestley,] *Address to Dissenters*, p. 18; Letter from William Samuel Johnson

to William Pitkin, 25 May 1769, Benton, *Whig-Loyalism*, p. 93. See also Letter from Jonathan Trumbull to the earl of Dartmouth, 10 March 1775, *Revolution Documents* 9:75; Letter from Governor William Tryon to the earl of Dartmouth, 5 September 1775, *Revolution Documents* 11:100–101.

7 Letter from Philadelphia to London, 24 September 1765, *Scots Magazine* 27 (1765): 610. See also Instructions of the Town of Boston, 23 May 1764, *Boston Evening-Post*, 28 May 1764, p. 2, col. 2; Resolution of 5 November 1773, *Boston Town Records* 18:143; Adams, "Novanglus," p. 142.

8 Statements of Newburyport, 20 December 1773, *Boston Evening-Post*, 10 January 1774, p. 2, col. 3; Resolves of Upper Freehold, Monmouth County, New Jersey, 4 May 1775, *Remembrancer for 1775*, p. 118.

CHAPTER TWENTY-FIVE: THE SHARED PERSPECTIVE

1 Speech of Lord Chatham, Lords Debates, 20 January 1775, *Hibernian Magazine* 5 (1775): 89; Speech of Lord Chatham, Lords Debates, 20 January 1775, *Parliamentary History* 18:156, 159; Anon., *Prospect of Consequences*, p. 8; Anon., *Constitutional Advocate*, p. 27.

2 [Ruffhead,] *Considerations*, p. 15.

3 *North Briton* No. 43, p. 249; Damnoniensis, 10 May 1763, *Select Collection of Letters* 2:15; Letter from William Beckford to Joseph Brutton, 9 June 1763, *London Magazine* 32 (1763): 290; Representation of the Lord Mayor, Aldermen, and Commons of London to their Representatives, 23 March 1763, *Select Collection of Letters* 1:70; "To the Electors of Aylesbury," 22 October 1764, Wilkes, *English Liberty*, p. 127; Address to the Knights of the Shire for the County of Hereford to John Morgan, 6 June 1763, *Gentleman's Magazine* 33 (1763): 303; Address to William Beckford, Lord Mayor of London, from Gentlemen and Freeholders of Cullompton, Devon, 21 May 1763, *London Magazine* 32 (1763): 289.

4 "A Freeholder," *Gentleman's Magazine* 34 (1764): 116; Society: Sainsbury, "Pro-Americans," p. 431.

5 *Scots Magazine* 35 (1773): 442; Argument of Archibald Macdonald, *Campbell v. Hall*, 20 *State Trials* 239, 290 (King's Bench, 1774).

6 Speech of David Hartley, Commons Debates, 29 February 1776, *Hibernian Magazine* 6 (1776): 487; Speech of Richard Pennant, Commons Debates, 19 April 1774, *London Magazine* 44 (1775): 61; Speech of John Wilkes, Commons Debates, 26 October 1775, *London Magazine* 44 (1775): 565; *Scots Magazine* 37 (1775): 612; *Hibernian Magazine* 5 (1775): 682; *Parliamentary History* 18:734; Chatham, "Speech in Lords, 20 January 1775," p. 192. See also McIlwain, *Revolution*, pp. 187–89.

CHAPTER TWENTY-SIX: CONCLUSION

1 [Tucker,] *Series of Answers*, p. 26; [Stewart,] *Letter to Price*, pp. 46–47; Smith, *The Wealth of Nations*, pp. 896–97; Speech of Lord North, Commons Debates, 20 February 1775, *Scots Magazine* 37 (1775): 123. Remarkably, at

that late date there were people in Britain still interpreting the imperial contract as imposing a binding obligation on the colonies. Anon., *Arguments in Support of Supremacy*, p. 33.

2 Day, *Present State of England*, p. 5 (see also Anon., *Political Mirror or Summary Review*, pp. 36–37; Johnstone, "Speech of November, 1775," p. 85); Anon., *Characters*, p. 2 (see also True Briton, *American Independency*, p. 3; [Maseres,] *Canadian Freeholder* 1:87–93; R.H., "On the guilt of the present civil war," *Scots Magazine* 38 (1776): 201–2; S., "To the Editor," *London Magazine* 45 (1776): 306; Macaulay, *Address to the People*, pp. 20–24; Anon., *Supremacy of Legislature*, pp. 10–15); [Williamson,] *Plea of the Colonies*, p. 21 (see also Speech of Edmund Burke, Commons Debates, 16 November 1775, *Burke on American Revolution*, p. 133; Book Review, *Monthly Review* 55 (1776): 353).

3 Backus, *Government and Liberty*, p. 10. "For the End of the American War was to establish the *arbitrary* Power in Parliament of *Taxation without Representation*." Abingdon, *Thoughts on Burke's Letter*, p. lxxxiv n. See, similarly, Speech of Henry Seymour Conway, Commons Debates, 4 March 1774, *Hibernian Magazine* 4 (1774): 290–91.

4 Anon., *Appeal to Reason and Justice*, p. 23; [Rokeby,] *Further Examination*, p. 60.

5 Speech of Henry Cruger, Commons Debates, 27 February 1776, *Hibernian Magazine* 6 (1776): 484; Speech of Lord Granby, Commons Debates, 5 April 1775, *London Magazine* 44 (1775): 672.

6 Letter from Governor William Tryon to the earl of Dartmouth, 4 July 1775, and Letter from Governor William Franklin to the earl of Dartmouth, 2 August 1775, *Revolution Documents* 11:35, 66.

7 Speeches of Joseph Marryat and Edward Protheroe, Commons Debates, 13 June 1815, *The Parliamentary Debates from the Year 1803 to the Present Time* (London, 1815) 31:781, 779.

INDEX

405

DESIGNED BY IRVING PERKINS ASSOCIATES
COMPOSED BY METRICOMP, GRUNDY CENTER, IOWA
MANUFACTURED BY EDWARDS BROTHERS, INC., ANN ARBOR, MICHIGAN
TEXT AND DISPLAY LINES ARE SET IN CALEDONIA

Library of Congress Cataloging-in-Publication Data
Reid, John Phillip.
Constitutional history of the American Revolution.
Part of a three vol. work on U.S.
constitutional history.
Bibliography: pp. 289–342.
Includes index.
1. Taxing power—United States—History.
2. United States—Constitutional history.
3. United States—History—Revolution, 1775–1783.
I. Title.   II. Title: Authority to tax.
KF6289.R45   1987   343.7304'09   87-8256
ISBN 0-299-11290-X   347.303409

The question of taxation's role in the American Revolution is one that every American historian has confronted, going back to the time of the Revolution itself. Every American school-child has had, indelibly inscribed in memory, the concept that "taxation without representation" had some-thing very important to do with the American Revolution. And anyone who has studied the American Revo-lution, however lightly, realizes that those events cannot be understood without also gaining some under-standing of eighteenth-century at-titudes about taxation and govern-ment's authority to tax. In this book, the second in a trilogy devoted to the constitutional history of the Amer-ican Revolution John Phillip Reid presents the most complete, detailed, and closely argued discussion of the taxation question ever to appear in print. Scholars in a wide variety of fields, but especially those in Amer-ican legal history, will welcome Reid's erudition, comprehension, and clarity of presentation.

Reid outlines the distinctions that must be observed if we are to gain a full understanding of the controversy between Great Britain and the North American colonies. He draws a care-ful distinction between legal and con-stitutional rights and policies and ex-amines the distinctions among the English, the British, the British-American, and the various colonial constitutions. No other work so pre-cisely examines the taxation issue from this perspective. In so doing,